THE POLITICAL CULTURE OF THE
RUSSIAN 'DEMOCRATS'

The Political Culture of the Russian 'Democrats'

ALEXANDER LUKIN

OXFORD

UNIVERSITY PRESS

OXFORD

UNIVERSITY PRESS

Great Clarendon Street, Oxford OX2 6DP

Oxford University Press is a department of the University of Oxford.
It furthers the University's objective of excellence in research, scholarship,
and education by publishing worldwide in

Oxford New York

Athens Auckland Bangkok Bogotá Buenos Aires Calcutta
Cape Town Chennai Dar es Salaam Delhi Florence Hong Kong Istanbul
Karachi Kuala Lumpur Madrid Melbourne Mexico City Mumbai
Nairobi Paris São Paulo Singapore Taipei Tokyo Toronto Warsaw

with associated companies in Berlin Ibadan

Oxford is a registered trade mark of Oxford University Press
in the UK and in certain other countries

Published in the United States
by Oxford University Press Inc., New York

© Alexander Lukin 2000

British Library Cataloguing in Publication Data

Data available

Library of Congress Cataloging in Publication Data

Data available

ISBN 0–19–829558–8

1 3 5 7 9 10 8 6 4 2

Typeset in Times by
Cambrian Typesetters, Frimley, Surrey

Printed in Great Britain
on acid-free paper by
Biddles Ltd, Guildford and King's Lynn

For Vera

The alternative approach which I have adopted in the present case is to assume that the only ethnography about which a novice social anthropologist is likely to have any intimate knowledge is that which derives from his or her own life experience.

(Edmund Leach, anthropologist, 1976)
[Edmund Leach, *Culture and Communication: The Logic by which Symbols are Connected* (Cambridge: Cambridge University Press, 1976), 2]

Let us ask a question: how can we *out-democratize* the West? In the sense of surpassing them in the field of genuine democracy? Only after having adopted such a maximalist goal, which is not sabotaged by a hypocritical postulate of the priority of the state interests over private interests, and on the way to this goal having surpassed the rich capitalist world, having eradicated crime and lies and having got the economy going, is it possible to call ourselves the inhabitants of a genuinely socialist, but not a social-feudal, not a *nomenklatura*-bureaucratic world.

(Yevgeniy Kryskin, Russian 'democrat', 1989)
[(Yevgeniy Kryskin), 'Slovo o pol`ze demokratii', *Listok 'Grazhdanskoy initsiativy'*, 4, (24 Mar. 1989), 1.]

PREFACE

I have always wanted to become a researcher, and for some time I worked at the Institute of Oriental Studies of the Soviet Academy of Sciences before I was drawn into politics by the maelstrom of *perestroyka*. As did many in the late 1980s, I decided that Communist rule in my country should be put to an end, and that it was my job to assist in the process. At first, I began to help candidates who called themselves 'democratic' in their election campaigns, and I joined my district's democratic voters' club. Then in 1990 I myself was elected to Moscow City Soviet. I became a 'democrat' and I thought I knew perfectly well what that meant: to fight together with other 'democrats' against the dictatorship of the CPSU. But while working for this cause, I tried to observe myself and my new colleagues objectively, as a researcher should do. I talked to people, asked questions, and collected documents. Even in besieged Moscow's White House during the days of the putsch of August 1991, while trying to keep away from the windows in case the troops decided to storm the building, I was curious. I talked to the people, asking why they were there and what it was they were ready to give their lives for. I knew that we lived at an exciting time, a time of great changes. Our society, which for decades had been as unchanging as stone and looked static for decades to come, suddenly exploded. In front of my eyes classes and social groups inter-mingled, old alliances and connections were being severed and new ones born, and people who had little chance to meet in the old days were becoming colleagues and friends united by a common cause.

One of the newly emerging unions and brotherhoods was these 'democrats'. Members of numerous clubs and groupings, they always unmistakably recognized each other and distinguished themselves from their political opponents—whom they called 'partocrats', 'patriots', 'the Red and the Brown', etc. I was struck by the peculiarity of this brotherhood to which I belonged for several years. I believed that my duty was to explain how it came into being, how it was motivated, what it saw as its goals, why it gained such sudden and overwhelming popularity and, equally unexpectedly, lost this popularity, damned by those very people who only a few years ago had enthu-siastically joined democratic rallies and shouted 'Down with the CPSU!'

Many books and articles have already been written about the democratic movement in Soviet Russia in the last years of the Soviet Union. I hope that my study might show the phenomena in a new light. I have done my best to use my unique position as both a participant and a researcher, and to combine the knowledge of an insider (which increased significantly after my study trips to Russian provinces and interviews with democratic activists there) and the detached analysis of a scholar. It is for the reader to decide if this approach is successful.

I employ a particular interpretation of the concept of political culture, not as a means of explanation, but more as a methodology of analysis of the beliefs of a large social group with no distinct boundaries. One of the objections which has already been expressed to me by some political scientists is that in this book I do not clearly endorse or oppose any of the current theories of the collapse of the USSR and of Russia's transition, do not enter into the current polemics on this problem, and fail to draw clear conclusions on the basis of a rich fund of material. To this I must say that I did not see my goal as providing a simple explanation of the fundamental, exciting, and rapid changes experienced by my country, which came as a surprise to most people both inside and outside Russia. I do not even think that such explanations are possible and should be attempted by a social scientist. We can only record as accurately as possible the newly emerging phenomena, compare them with the old and familiar phenomena, with those of other countries and continents, and then speculate about the likely tendencies of future development. If in the process we manage to hear the music of history and to give our descendants a clear picture of our time, this in itself will be a significant achievement.

The main part of the book is devoted to the study of the emergence of the belief system of Russian 'democrats', and the analysis of its contents. The analysis is conducted along three major lines: attitudes towards the Soviet state and society; beliefs about the ideal future democracy; and beliefs about Russia's place in the world. Chapter 8 places the belief system of Russian democrats into the context of Russian and world intellectual history. I hope that the book will be useful not only to experts on Russia but also to anyone interested in the history of ideas and social movements, as well as the problems of a transition to democracy.

The major part of the book was written as my doctoral thesis at Oxford University. I was very lucky to spend several years of my life in this remarkable city, where every stone speaks of history at one of the oldest and most respected universities in the world, in an atmosphere of great respect for academic research. At the same time the modern, informal style of St Antony's College and the opportunity to be a part of its international community helped me keep in touch with the crucial problems of the world outside the ancient university walls. I was encouraged in my work by the profound interest in Russian affairs shown by the staff of the College's Russian and East European Centre, while the rich collection of Russian books and materials in the Centre's Russian library was highly instrumental to my research.

I am grateful to many people for providing comments, resources, and valuable materials during the completion of this book. This book could not have been written without the kind cooperation of many former members of Russian democratic groups, and the contribution of those who agreed to be interviewed and to share their thoughts and experiences was of special value.

I am especially grateful to my supervisor at Oxford, Professor Archie Brown, for his interest in and support of my project of studying the democratic movement in Soviet Russia and his careful consideration of earlier drafts of this book. Professor Brown, Dr Michael McFaul, Dr Warren Hatch, Dr Nikolas Gvosdev, Dr Jeffrey Kahn, Tiffany Troxel, and William Flemming read specific chapters, made useful suggestions, and helped improve the English. Professors Geoffrey Hosking, Paul Dukes, James R. Millar, and Timothy Colton, Dr Stephen Welch, and Dr Alex Pravda read the manuscript or parts of it at various stages, suggested important improvements, and encouraged me with their thoughtful comments.

I received invaluable assistance from the librarians of Narodnyy Arkhiv (People's Archive) in Moscow, the museums of Stavropol` *kray* and Penza *oblast`*, and Aleksandr Ginzburg of *Russkaya mysl`* in Paris, who guided me through their impressive collections of documents of various democratic groups and their individual members. I have benefited greatly from documents from the personal archives provided by Valeriy Fadeev, Oleg Rumyantsev, Aleksandr Eliovich, Aleksandr Shubin, Mariya Sublina, Yevgeniy Kryskin, Anatoliy Zamyatin, Vladimir Yelistratov, Nikolay Klepachev, Pavel Poluyan, Teodey Fel`dman, Sergey Shokolenko, Vasiliy Krasulya, Aleksandr Pavlov, Andrey Shcherkin, and Petr Popov. I also wish to thank the librarians of the Bodleian Library, the Social Studies Faculty Library, St Antony's College Library, and St Antony's College Russian and East Centre Library in Oxford. Finally, I wish to thank the Helen Dwight Reid Educational Foundation for allowing me to use an article from *Demokratizatsiya*, 3:4 (1995) for Chapter 5 of this volume.

Financial support for my research in Britain that resulted in this book was provided by the Foreign and Commonwealth Office Fellowship (administered by the British Council), the Joint Japan/World Bank Graduate Scholarship Program, and the Overseas Research Studentship scheme. Research in Russia was funded by the British Association for Slavonic and East European Studies, the Norman Chester Fund, the Stahl Fund, the Elliott Travel Fund of St Antony's College, and the Oxford University Committee for Graduate Studies.

Finally, I would like to thank my wife, Vera, for doing the enormous job of transcribing the interviews from tapes and making my life in a foreign land happy in the way that only she could do.

A.V.L.
Oxford and Moscow

CONTENTS

LIST OF ABBREVIATIONS

ASPC	All-union Socio-Political Club
CAS	Confederation of Anarcho-Syndicalists
CDP–PPF	Constitutional Democratic Party–Party of People's Freedom
CPSU	Communist Party of the Soviet Union
DP	Democratic Party
DPCR	Democratic Party of Communists of Russia
DPR	Democratic Party of Russia
DRM	Democratic Russia Movement
DU	Democratic Union
DUV	District Union of Voters
FDP	Free Democratic Party of Russia
FSPC	Federation of Socialist Political Clubs
LDP	Liberal Democratic Party of the Soviet Union
M-BIO	Moscow Bureau of Information Exchange
MPF	Moscow Popular Front
PPFR	People's Party of Free Russia
PPR	People's Party of Russia
RCDM	Russian Christian Democratic Movement
RPR	Republican Party of Russia
RSFSR	Russian Soviet Federative Socialist Republic
SDPR	Social Democratic Party of the Russian Federation
SPR	Socialist Party of Russia
UCD	Union of Constitutional Democrats

1

Introduction

1.1. GENERAL FRAMEWORK

This book is a study of the origins and development of the world-view of those who called themselves 'democrats' in Russia in the last years of the USSR. Political changes which began in the USSR after Mikhail Gorbachev came to power in 1985 led to a significant rise in unofficial political activities in the country. As the authorities greatly softened and then ceased repression of the organization of unofficial political groups, many such groups emerged, first in Moscow and Leningrad, and subsequently all over the country. For the first time since 1922, without being subject to severe repressions, the Bolshevik government banned the last independent parties, and since the first part of Brezhnev's rule, when 'dissident' groups were active (most of them crushed by 1985), the country saw organizations which openly questioned the views of the authorities. It is hardly possible to calculate the exact number of such groups (at least before the KGB archives are opened), but according to some estimates there were about 30,000 of them by 1988 and twice as many in 1989.[1]

Many books and articles have been written about the history of 'democratic' groups, groupings, and parties in Soviet Russia. They usually describe meetings and rallies, quote programmes and appeals, discuss the leaders, recount the sequence of events. However, in few of them are the critical questions raised: Who were the participants in all these events and the authors of these documents? What made these people, including both old and young, men and women, members and non-members of the Communist Party, the unprivileged and those who were doing very well under the existing system, those living in the capital and those in remote towns and villages, stand up and criticize the authorities, type up at home or copy by hand hundreds of leaflets, newspapers, and magazines, organize rallies and demonstrations, call for strikes and civil disobedience, and do many other things which were potentially dangerous for them? To provide answers one needs to understand what the Russian 'democrats' believed in, how they saw the world, and what they wanted to achieve.

---

[1] Oleg Shenin, 'Za steklyannoy stenoy chasto ostayutsya "neformaly" v pylu spora', *Pravda*, 5 Feb. 1988, 3; 'Demokratiya ne terpit demagogii', *Pravda*, 10 Feb. 1989, 1.

The approach of this book is based on the idea that people's beliefs influence and direct their actions. Elaborate thought is a property of human beings, and most probably exclusively of human beings, making them, as R. G. Collingwood put it, 'the only animal whose conduct is to any great extent determined by thought instead of by mere impulse and appetite'. Thus, a social scientist 'may begin by discovering the outside of an event, but it can never end there; he must always remember that the event was an action, and that his main task is to think himself into this action, to discern the thought of its agent'.[2]

It is not abstract and anonymous economic, social, or political structures or institutions, which are themselves creations of human imagination, that make people act like puppets, but people themselves who determine the situation in which they live, and any social abstraction can in the last analysis be reduced to the specific individuals who constitute it with their beliefs, hopes, and actions. This, however, does not mean that people are absolutely free to create their beliefs or determine the scope of their actions. In most cases they accept ideas and ways of doing things which already exist in their society. As Ronald Inglehart put it:

Few people invent concepts. It is vastly easier to take prefabricated ones from the available stock, based on experiences interpreted earlier by members of one's society. Having built an interpretation of reality around given concepts as one grows up, to reconstruct it anew would be a daunting task. Only the most traumatic experiences ever drive people to it. Thus, one orients one's life by following old road maps. They may be crude and they may be out of date, but even a crude map gives more guidance in reaching one's goals than does striking out on a random walk.[3]

But changes do occur. A time comes when more and more people begin to express doubts about dominant beliefs and norms, reject them, and put forward new ones. Those who share such new beliefs and who at first perhaps find themselves in a minority do not have to belong to the same social class, wear the same uniform, or otherwise differ from other people in order to recognize each other. An exchange of a few words is usually enough. Those who are sceptical of the status quo share the same symbols and meanings, and a simple check of what your counterpart thinks of the rulers, of the present political situation, or of the future can show if he is on your side. Though uniforms or other non-verbal symbols may follow, very often the sharing of verbal symbols or beliefs is the only indicator of such a group. The acceptance of the system of these beliefs unites individuals, who may be very different in many other ways, into a close community.

---

[2] R. G. Collingwood, *The Idea of History* (Oxford: Oxford University Press, 1989; 1st publ. 1946), 216, 213. Collingwood wrote about history but these ideas can be applied to social science in general.

[3] Ronald Inglehart, *Culture Shift in Advanced Industrial Society* (Princeton, NJ: Princeton University Press, 1990), 422.

One such group was the Russian 'democrats'. They agreed and disagreed with each other, sometimes criticized each other so sharply that one might have thought they had nothing in common. However, such a conclusion would be hasty. Of especial importance among groupings in Russia were the 'intelligentsia', *shestidesyatniki* ('the generation of the sixties'), and 'democrats'. Different definitions of such groupings can be given but the very fact that they were widely used for identification and self-identification shows that real groupings were behind them. It seems that the only way to understand what these groupings were is to study them as close communities, that is, to study the most important, and probably the only, property they share: their belief systems.

The Russian 'democrats' did form a close community which shared common beliefs and values. That does not mean that they shared all beliefs; such a harmony can hardly be expected even of people who are very close to each other. But there existed a particular set of beliefs which were united into an integrated system by both logical and non-logical connections, all or at least many of which were shared by every Russian 'democrat'. This belief system, which constituted a political culture or, to be more precise, a political subculture (if the dominant beliefs of the country's population as a whole is taken for the 'total' political culture) is the subject of this book. The study is not a simple one since the belief system was not worded in any one document or set of documents, and is derived from numerous sources which include both interviews conducted by the author and written materials. It is further complicated by the fact that the 'democratic' political subculture was a result of the interaction of different cultural traditions: 'official' Soviet political culture or official ideology, which, though formally rejected by 'democrats', could not be absolutely set aside since it constituted the very basis of the theoretical knowledge of the world for the majority of educated Soviet citizens; the 'dominant' Soviet political culture, or the most widely shared real political beliefs of the population, which in turn were an amalgam of the new and the old, of traditional beliefs which were transferred from generation to generation and contemporary Soviet norms and values;[4] and Western 'democratic' political culture, which came to the USSR in the form of theoretical texts only for a very few, but for the vast majority in the idealized form of propaganda and mass culture such as foreign radio broadcasts, films, and popular music.

The concept of political culture which is employed by this study provides the political scientist with a broad arsenal of methods to analyse belief systems. However, not all of these methods can be used to study the political

---

[4] On definitions of 'official' and 'dominant' political cultures, see Archie Brown, 'Introduction', in A. Brown and J. Gray (eds.), *Political Culture and Political Change in Communist States* (London: Macmillan Press, 1977), 7–8, and Ch. 2 of this book.

subculture of Russian 'democrats'. While accepting the most common definition of political culture as a set of a group's beliefs, attitudes, and values
which relate to politics,[5] this book agrees with those authors who understand
these beliefs, attitudes, and values not just as a casually compiled aggregate
but as an integrated system of interrelated elements which is subject to
constant evolution and change. Theoretically, I agree with Clifford Geertz's
approach, whereby the concept of culture 'is essentially a semiotic one'.
Geertz writes: 'Believing with Max Weber that man is an animal suspended
in webs of significance he himself has spun, I take culture to be those webs,
and the analysis of it to be therefore not an experimental science in search of
law, but an interpretive one in search of meaning.'[6]

This approach was developed by Stephen Welch, who proposed moving
from the study of political culture as a static 'given' to 'detailed investigation
of the process of construction of meaning' on the basis of phenomenological
sociology.[7] According to Welch, 'Culture is not a set of givens of which political culture is a subset; it is a process, and "political culture" refers to that
process in its political aspects'.[8] It could be added that this process should be
studied as proceeding from the individual consciousness of the members of a
society or a group, who by interacting among themselves continually create
and change their common understandings.

The use of the term 'semiotic' is important for this study since many
'democratic' beliefs were symbolic ones which were understood within the
'democratic' subculture differently from outside it. Beliefs which were
borrowed by 'democrats' from various sources were reinterpreted or
connected to each other in a different way, making their political subculture
distinctive. The very terms 'democrat' and 'democracy' as central symbols
had very special meanings and produced a whole array of associations which
were very different from those that come with this notion in other cultures. To
stress this fact and to avoid possible confusion with any other understanding
of democracy it should be made clear from the outset that whenever this study
speaks of the terms 'democracy' or 'democrats' as they were subjectively
understood by the 'democrats' themselves, the terms are used in quotation
marks.

For the 'semiotics of culture', as in phenomenology, beliefs are not a
'given' but an ever-changing phenomenon. Boris Uspenskiy, for example,

[5] For classic definitions, see Gabriel Almond, 'Comparative Political Systems', *Journal of
Politics*, 18 (1956), 391–409; Lucian W. Pye, 'Political Culture', in David Sills (ed.),
International Encyclopedia of Social Sciences (New York: Macmillan and Free Press, 1968), xii.
218–25; Archie Brown, 'Political Culture', in Adam Kuper and Jessica Kuper (eds.), *The Social
Science Encyclopedia*, 2nd edn. (London and New York: Routledge, 1996), 625–6.

[6] Clifford Geertz, *The Interpretations of Cultures* (London: Fontana Press, 1993; 1st publ.
1973), 5.

[7] Stephen Welch, *The Concept of Political Culture* (London: Macmillan, 1993), 117.

[8] Ibid. 164.

agrees with the idea that society's language changes over time. However, according to him, 'this alteration does not preclude the possibility of distinguishing synchronic cross sections that allow us to describe it as a working mechanism'.[9] In the same way, a language can be studied with no particular knowledge of its history. At the same time, just as the knowledge of the history of language significantly improves one's understanding and the knowledge of the etymology of a word widens one's ability to understand its use, so the knowledge of the history of single beliefs and belief systems deepens the understanding of contemporary political culture. Therefore, the study of one-time political culture 'cross-sections' and the comparison of such cross-sections as they existed at different times in history must both be undertaken in political culture research. In practice any study of a contemporary political culture would ideally include an element of the 'etymology' of beliefs. Such an approach is employed in this book. Its different parts investigate the political subculture of Russian 'democrats', analyse the process of its development, and reconstruct it as a synchronic cross-section.

This approach determines the methodology of the analysis. While not rejecting quantitative methods, which can provide important material for research, this study considers them to be supplementary both for practical and theoretical reasons. Practically speaking, a broad use of surveys was not possible: a representative sample could not be compiled as the exact membership of the group under study was unknown. In such cases, for the study of 'new phenomena and processes which are not yet widespread in society, especially during times of abrupt social changes', qualitative methods have proven to be effective.[10]

Since political culture is an integrated system of beliefs, the study of the political subculture of Russian 'democrats' should not isolate particular beliefs or attitudes and compare them with an abstract, theoretical democratic ideal, but should look at the way new beliefs came into existence and became connected to other beliefs to form a belief system. For the purpose of such an analysis this system is divided into four major parts:

1. beliefs about the existing social and political reality of the USSR which determined the opposition of the 'democrats' to the authorities and therefore constituted the core of the system;
2. those beliefs about the future of the USSR and of that part of the world which was understood as democratic which determined the specific strategy of the 'democrats';

---

[9] B. A. Uspenskij, 'Historia sub specie semioticae', in D. P. Lucid (ed.), *Soviet Semiotics: An Anthology* (Baltimore, Md.: Johns Hopkins University Press, 1977), 108.

[10] V. A. Yadov (with the cooperation of V. V. Semenova), *Strategiya sotsialogicheskogo issledovaniya. Opisanie, ob`yasnenie, ponimanie sotsial`noy real`nosti* (Moscow: Dobrosvet, 1998), 392–3.

3. beliefs about the outside world, about other countries and societies, including the Western world, a world which generally was thought to represent Russia's democratic future; and
4. beliefs about the history of Russia and its relationship to the rest of the world, about the nature and direction of history, which were connected to evaluation by the 'democrats' of the practicability of the aims of their movement.

I understand political culture as a permanent process of creation and change of meanings by individual members of collectives. This means that to understand how Russian 'democrats' arrived at a particular understanding and to create an analytical model of their subculture as it existed at a particular time, a study of the process of formation of these understandings, of their sources, and of the mechanism of their creation by the individual is needed. To conduct such a study all sources and materials should be seen not as reflecting a presupposed general opinion of the 'democrats' but as a manifestation of the beliefs of their authors. Only on the basis of an analysis of these individual beliefs that establishes which of them are shared by the majority and are representative of the subculture as a whole can the model of this subculture be reconstructed.

To achieve this aim the book has been structured as follows. This chapter provides a general introduction to the book and describes the practical methodology of research, including interview techniques and the methods of analysing written materials.

Chapter 2 analyses the literature on Russian 'democrats' and discusses its significance for the present study. It finds several problems within the Russian 'democratic' political culture that were not addressed in this literature and accordingly puts forward the main objectives for the present study. Chapter 3 gives a brief historical account of the development of the Russian 'democratic' movement in the Gorbachev period and of the specific groups and parties which constituted this movement. It analyses the pattern of recruitment to 'democratic' groups and their social composition. It shows that the acceptance of 'democratic' beliefs was a fundamental reason for joining a 'democratic' group and discusses the relation of this conclusion to general theories of social movements and of political conflict.

Chapter 4 reconstructs the process of emergence and development of the 'democratic' political belief system, shows its sources and their relative importance to the process of transformation of the dogmas of official Soviet ideology and the beliefs of the dominant Soviet political culture into 'democratic' beliefs in the minds of members of opposition groups, and investigates the mechanism of this transformation. Chapters 5, 6, and 7 reconstruct the model of the political culture of Russian 'democrats', giving its cross-section at the most developed stage. These chapters examine the contents of the main elements of the 'democratic' political subculture discussed above: their perceptions of Russia's past, present, and future and its place in the world. They analyse the beliefs of Russian 'democrats' about the Soviet state and social structure, and about democracy and democratic society, which they saw as a social ideal for the Soviet Union; their views on the methods and goals of economic reform, and on Russian and world history; and their understanding of the outside world and Russia's place and role in it. Conclusions in every chapter summarize the possible sources of these beliefs, arguing that the main source was official Soviet ideology, while there were also influences from Western 'democratic' theories and views and from life experience in the Soviet Union.

Chapter 8 is devoted to broader questions and theorizing about the political subculture of the Russian 'democrats'. It addresses the following questions:

1. How do Western theories and concepts of Soviet society and of democracy correlate with the corresponding beliefs of Russian 'democrats'? Why did particular Western theories or approaches become popular among Russian 'democrats' while others remained unknown or unused? The chapter argues that while Russian 'democratic' political culture used many Western terms, it was a unique system of beliefs since these terms were usually reinterpreted within it under various influences.

2. What were the sources and patterns of this reinterpretation? This chapter maintains that the main source of this reinterpretation was in most cases official Soviet ideology, in which Russian 'democrats' had been socialized from their childhood. The pattern of interpretation generally repeated the pattern of cultural change which was described by Yuriy Lotman and Boris Uspenskiy for pre-eighteenth-century Russia. To support this argument a broad comparison of the beliefs of Russian 'democrats' with those of previous Russian opposition and culturally innovative movements is undertaken. The resulting conclusion makes it possible to suggest that continuity in Russian history manifests itself not in the transmission of eternal, unchangeable beliefs, but in the pattern of perceiving new ideas and creating new cultures.

3. How did the analysis of the correlation between Russian 'democratic' subculture and the dominant Soviet political culture make it possible to understand the profound influence of the latter on the beliefs of Russian 'democrats'? This influence, together with that of official ideology, was one of the sources of reinterpretation of Western concepts. It also played a determinant role in the later period, when the will of the population began to manifest itself in election results.

4. The last part of the chapter discusses the role of 'democratic' beliefs in Russian politics before and immediately after the collapse of the USSR. It

asks why, before 1991, the political culture of Russian 'democrats' existed as a unified system, later split into various trends? It describes the consequent role of 'democratic' beliefs in post-Soviet Russian politics.

1.2. SOURCES AND METHODOLOGY

The first task with which any analysis should begin is to determine a distinct framework for the subject of study. The very course of late Soviet history provides this book with natural temporal boundaries, 1985 being the year of the beginning of the reforms which gave birth to most of the groups (although a very small number of them were formed earlier) and 1991 the year of the collapse of the USSR, which created a totally new situation in Russia and significantly changed the ideology, focus, and direction of many of the groups. These seven years are, therefore, the main, but not exclusive, concern of this study.

The present study deals only with groups which were formed in the ethnically 'Russian' regions of the Russian Federation. Groups in the republics of the Russian Federation should be studied separately, as the problems there are deeply related to ethnic questions. This study also does not deal with special interest groups, such as independent trade unions and ecological and religious organizations. However, the members of such groups are included in interviews to the extent that they took part in the activities of 'democratic' groups.

Defining which groups were 'democratic' and who was a 'democrat' became the main problem for selecting the subject matter for this study. To avoid possible distortion from one's own preconceptions, one should not proceed from an abstract definition of a term, but instead give its practical meaning as it is understood in a given society. For example, if a source speaks of 'democrats' and 'patriots' in Russia, it means that there are certain phenomena in this society which are associated with these terms. Thus, the task of a researcher is not to determine who was a 'democrat' in Russia on the basis of his abstract understanding of this term, which is derived from an analysis of totally different societies, but to try to understand what the term 'democrat' meant in the social context of Russia at that time. To do this one should initially accept the common use of this term in Russia at the time and should call 'democrats' people who described themselves as 'democrats' or who would have agreed to be called 'democrats' in Russia in the years 1985–91.

The same applies to groups and parties. This approach implies that there could have been and surely were 'democrats' outside 'democratic' groups: those who shared 'democratic' beliefs, but were not formally members. Moreover, in as much as membership in most cases was very loose, it would be difficult to be very formal in this matter. However, those who actively took part in the activities of 'democratic' groups, compiled policy documents, or wrote articles for the publications of these groups, were always considered to be active 'democrats' both by themselves and by the public. Thus, the purpose of this book is not to define who was a 'genuine' democrat in Russia, but to try to understand those who were known in Russia under the name of 'democrats' and what constituted their ideas. The analysis of the correlation between this inner point of view and more theoretical or foreign definitions of democracy can be conducted only when the first meaning is understood.

The sources

A broad range of sources has been used to make this study as rigorous and exhaustive as possible. The main groups are: literature of a descriptive character; interviews with the members of independent 'democratic' political groups and parties; articles and statements of the members of the groups (including newspaper articles and other publications, TV and radio presentations, etc.); results of quantitative survey research; memoirs of members of the groups; and official documents of the groups (programmes, statements, decisions of meetings and conferences, etc.).

The general methods of analysis of the sources

An analysis of a belief system of a group implies looking for typical beliefs. However, in a situation of loose membership, where the extent of membership is unknown and consequently no representative sample can be taken, what methods can be used to determine what is typical? This question was addressed by Nathan Leites in his study of the 'spirit of the Bolshevik elite'.[11] For Leites,

A typical statement to be made has—to put it very precisely—the following form: 'The belief B is a belief of the Bolshevik elite.' This means, spelled out: 'The belief B has been strongly held during much of the history of the Bolshevik elite by many of its members. . . .' Such a characteristic statement thus admits exceptions; it affirms the dominance, but not exclusiveness, of a certain belief in Bolshevism.[12]

This approach is close to the 'discourse analysis' of, for example, Gilbert and Mulkay in their study of the beliefs of scientists. Its central distinguishing feature is that 'it treats participants' discourse as a topic instead of a resource'.[13] Gilbert and Mulkay write: 'Previous approaches have been

[11] Nathan Leites, *A Study of Bolshevism* (Glencoe, Ill.: Free Press, 1953), 15.
[12] Ibid. 20.
[13] G. Nigel Gilbert and Michael Mulkay, *Opening Pandora's Box: A Sociological Analysis of Scientists' Discourse* (Cambridge: Cambridge University Press, 1984), 13.

designed to use scientists' symbolic products as resources which can be assembled in various ways to tell analysts' stories about "the way that science is". Discourse analysts, in contrast, begin from the assumption that participants' discourse is too variable and too dependent on the context of its production to be amenable to this kind of treatment.'[14]

One of the main features of discourse analysis is the stress on the multiplicity of the beliefs of different individuals and the importance of taking into consideration every variant of these beliefs, not only those which support or disprove existing theories. Such multiplicity does not mean, however, that no attempt at systematization is possible. Gilbert and Mulkay show that 'participants' discourse, although varied, displays certain observable patterns'.[15] These patterns, or typical beliefs, can therefore be depicted and analysed.

To use this method for this book it was necessary to collect first all the available material and only then to start the analysis. The result of this analysis was to establish all the existing patterns of discourse of the members of the political groups according to the issues of the question plan, namely the reasons for joining the 'democratic' groups, the sources of ideas, and the contents of these ideas. Only by doing so is it possible to classify the patterns and depict them meaningfully. To achieve this aim it is very important that every single case of distinctive belief be registered, as it may represent a pattern, other representatives of which are not discovered because of the limitations of the sample. That is why a great effort was made to look for any other manifestations of any single representation in order to find out whether it constituted a pattern.

This suggests treating all documents of 'democratic' groups at the first stage of analysis as representing individual beliefs—both individual documents, like articles, speeches, letters, and diaries, and collective 'sacred' documents: declarations, party programmes, and charters, which at this stage are taken to represent the beliefs of their authors or their group (if, for example, they were adopted by voting).

Further analysis of these materials showed that despite all the differences among numerous 'democratic' groups it was possible to identify patterns of belief which were shared by all or most of their members. Within this system different attitudes toward particular problems and situations were tolerated, but at the same time there were basic elements shared by all or at least by the dominant majority. It should be clear that there cannot be 'proof' that these patterns are typical in a quantitative sense, since this study is by no means quantitatively representative. This means that it cannot be demonstrated how many people supported this or that type of ideas. This problem has been discussed by Leites, who even suggests that to make this proposition testable it would have to be defined by an indication of critical

---

[14] Gilbert and Mulkay, *Opening Pandora's Box*, 13.   [15] Ibid. 39.

degrees and frequencies. According to Leites, unless such quantitative verification is conducted, the study of an operational code will remain a hypothesis.[16] However, taking into consideration the limitations of quantitative analysis discussed in Chapter 2, it can be said that such a hypothesis can be at least as reliable as those made on the basis of survey methods. This makes typological interpretation an equally important tool of political analysis and the only possible one when studying the beliefs of loose groups with no formal membership. The recognition of the equality of both methods and of the fact that there are advantages and shortcomings in both of them suggests the need for mutual verification. Accordingly, available quantitative data were used in the present book to support and verify its conclusions.

It thus became possible to determine the whole range of ideas which were characteristic of the Russian 'democrats', together with the contents and the limits of their belief system. In some cases, as happened with attitudes toward Communist power which still existed then, only one type of opinion was registered. This can be interpreted as a manifestation of the unity of opinion on this issue which united the 'democrats', making it possible to speak of all the different 'democratic' groups as one movement. In other cases several different beliefs were registered on one question. This means that all these variants were acceptable at that time and could be parts of one belief system, but at a certain moment in the future the contradictions between them could have led to conflicts within the movement and even within the groups.

The multiplicity of variants possible in the 'democratic' belief system raises another question, which is also addressed by Leites in his study of the Bolshevik code: whether this code 'does anything more than provide a language in which all conceivable calculations can be couched'. Leites argues that this would be an exaggeration since 'there are many important calculations which the code excludes'.[17] The analysis of the belief system of Russian 'democrats' supports this conclusion. It is right that a great variety of different and sometimes even logically contradictory beliefs were possible within it, but at the same time many beliefs, which existed at the same time in a broader Russian society, were for 'democrats' unacceptable and even unimaginable. Embracing a 'democratic' faith meant not only accepting some beliefs but also rejecting other beliefs. The rejection of certain beliefs made the 'democratic' belief system distinctive. The fact that the 'democratic' belief system created an intellectual framework for 'democrats' makes it possible to reconstruct it and to compare it to other belief systems.

There is another approach which this book shares with Leites's works: the frequent use of lengthy quotations, which sometimes seem obscure and deal

---

[16] Leites, *A Study of Bolshevism*, 20.   [17] Ibid. 18.

with something quite different to the belief being discussed. Some scholars have criticized this approach, even arguing that Leites's writings can only be used 'as a classified directory of quotations'.[18] This criticism is rooted in a different approach to discourse. While Leites's critics look at the surface and take words at face value—more precisely, at their face value in their own culture (which leads to shortcomings in their analyses)—Leites analyses their subjective meaning in the culture under study.

These meanings must be extracted from 'a special language in which a limited number of terms and statements is required, a few are just possible and very many excluded. Intellectually and politically it is necessary to learn this language; for this purpose the large-scale use of paraphrases would not do'. Paraphrases are also insufficient since 'an important point may not be consciously stressed; it may be incidentally conveyed with little awareness of its presence.'[19] Another reason for preserving the broader context of discourse is the necessity, in Leites's words, 'to evoke the spirit' of the movement, learn its emotions, and attain 'empathy with its strange feelings and thoughts',[20] or, to put it in the terminology of political culture theory, to show not only its cognitive, but also its affective, element, not only its metalinguistic, but also its connotative, property.

Descriptive literature as a source

The limitations of providing descriptions and chronologies of the activities of independent 'democratic' groups, without attempting an analysis, have been discussed above. This literature is nevertheless an important source for this book. Historical accounts of some of the 'democratic' activities in several regions where the interviews were conducted are used in this study to reconstruct the background for the interview. Such accounts were impossible to find in Moscow publications, so they were obtained from the local press, or even from local activists in the form of manuscripts.[21] It has also been possible to use a great deal of information from interviews with the members of the groups and their separate statements, as well as quantitative data from such sources. It is well understood that such information and data are subject to the same types of bias as interviews and data from other sources (see below).

---

[18] Stephen White, *Political Culture and Soviet Politics* (London: Macmillan, 1979), 7.
[19] Leites, *A Study of Bolshevism*, 20–2.   [20] Ibid. 22.
[21] For example: Andrey Shcherkin, 'Protsessy zarozhdeniya, razvitiya i stanovleniya politicheskikh partiy i massovykh obshchestvennykh dvizheniy v Pskovskoy oblasti v 1988–1994', unpubl. MS [Pskov, 1994]. A thorough account of the history of the independent political groups in Krasnoyarsk *kray* can be found in Pavel Vinogradov, 'Pokhozhdeniya atomarnykh lichnostey na zakate', *Krasnoyarskiy komsomolets*, 6 and 8 Apr. 1993.

Methods of conducting and analysing interviews

The sample

Within the framework of this book sixty-seven interviews were conducted with the members of 'democratic' political groups and parties. From the very beginning it was clear that the subject of the study would not allow the construction of a quantitatively representative sample for a structured survey. The main obstacle here is the absence of clear membership of the groups. The majority of them did not have a list of members and clear criteria according to which one could divide members from one-off participants in any specific action of the group. In most cases one could find three levels of membership in such groups: (1) a limited number of leaders or chief organizers (a list of whom was available or could be easily reconstructed); (2) a wider circle of activists (usually several dozen people, a list of whom existed only in a small number of well-organized groups); (3) an unfixed number of supporters and sympathizers, who took part in group activities of the of different kinds (meetings, rallies, demonstrations, etc.) on a more or less regular basis (their exact number was never known even at the time of the active work of the groups).

As it is not possible to have a representative sample group to determine the social, sex, or age composition of the groups, and taking into consideration that one of the main objectives of this study is a reconstruction of the belief system of 'democratic' groups, an unstructured form of interviewing (which is also called non-standardized, focused, or depth interviewing) was used.[22]

The sampling methods suitable for this kind of interview were used. First, the question of geographical representativeness was addressed. Seven regions of Russia were selected, each representing a major historical economic-geographic area: Moscow (the capital and the political centre); Pskov *oblast`* (the North and North-West); Penza *oblast`* (the Volga region); Stavropol` *kray* (the South); Orenburg *oblast`* (the Urals); Krasnoyarsk *kray* (Siberia); and Maritime *kray* (the Far East).

Most of the interviews were conducted in the regional capitals, as it was there that the main 'democratic' groups were concentrated. However, in some cases, if such groups were active in district centres (*rayonnyy tsentr*), at least one such centre in an *oblast`* or *kray* was visited. Thus, several interviews were conducted with the members of a political discussion club in Belinskiy (Penza *oblast`*) and of a voters' union in Nevinnomyssk (Stavropol` *kray*).

One of the important features of this study is that the most significant part

---

[22] Nigel Fielding, 'Qualitative Interviewing', in Nigel Gilbert (ed.), *Researching Social Life* (London: SAGE, 1993).

of the data came from provincial areas, which previously had been little studied. These data were combined with the Moscow materials and compared to
them. Thus, an important and very common source of bias, caused by using
only material from big cities, and usually just Moscow and Leningrad (St
Petersburg), was kept in check.

The desire to avoid such a common mistake resulted in the selection of
cities for conducting interviews. An effort was made to choose cities with a
middle level of 'democratic' activity, not the most famous 'democratic'
centres or any other kind of special case (like Leningrad, the 'second capital';
Sverdlovsk, Yel'tsin's power base and 'democratic' centre; or Kaliningrad
oblast`, with its special problems related to its peculiar geographic position).
Rather, an attempt was made to accumulate the most typical, mid-level data
(apart from Moscow, which serves as a focus of comparison).

The same aim was pursued with the selection of the interviewees. Before
arrival in a specific region only general information about 'democratic'
groups there was available: usually this was nothing more than the names of
the groups and one or two names of leaders, which were mentioned in reference books. That is why 'snowball' sampling was used.[23] The first interviewee in a given place provided information on other activists and members of
other independent groups and this worked as a chain to locate other group
members.

The main shortcoming of this method is the possibility of having interviewees from only one network. Moreover one might deliberately not be given
information about people whose views are different from those of the first
informant or of the network as a whole, as well as about those former
colleagues who now have a bad personal relationship with others (this
happens very often with members of independent political groups).
Accordingly, an effort was, made to diversify the original sources of information, using people currently holding different opinions and positions for
'pilot interviews'.

Attention was paid to conducting at least one interview with a representative of every pattern which was registered in a given area. Taking into consideration the total number of the regions where interviews were conducted,
such an approach permitted at least five interviews in each of the areas representing a specific pattern of beliefs, and sixty-seven interviews in all, which
meets the recommendations of specialists.[24] This made the sample representative from the qualitative, if not the quantitative, point of view. In other

---

[23] On 'snowball' sampling, see Sara Arber, 'Designing Samples', in Gilbert (ed.),
Researching Social Life, 73; Yadov, V. A., *Strategiya sotsialogicheskogo issledovaniya*, 412–13.

[24] Sergey Belanovskiy recommends that the total number of focused interviews in one
study should not exceed 100 and that the number of interviews conducted with representatives
of one 'mass role position' should be in the range of 5–20: S. A. Belanovskiy, *Metodika i
tekhnika fokusirovannogo interv`yu* (Moscow: Nauka, 1993), 111, 117.

words, all typical political notions of the group members were included, defined, and analysed.

The interviewing techniques

Many different opinions exist among practical sociologists about the techniques of unstructured interviews. Recommended approaches vary from a free and totally unlimited discussion to a question-and-answer session performed according to a strict plan.[25] In one recent handbook Nigel Fielding, for example, gives the following definition: 'Here interviewers simply have a list of topics which they want the respondent to talk about, but are free to phrase the questions as they wish, ask them in any order that seems sensible at the time, and even to join in the conversation by discussing what they think of the topics themselves.'[26]

Such a description (apart from joining in the conversation, as it was thought that this could influence the answers) fits well the interview pattern used in this study. However, this does not mean that interviews were unrestricted. Most specialists recommend that the interviewer have a written interview guide with the main themes of the discussion.[27] In this case the study plan itself was used as such a guide. Accordingly, during the interview the questions were aimed at getting information on the following main topics: (1) data on the history of the independent 'democratic' political groups in the given region, their membership, forms of activities, etc.; (2) the main aspects of the interviewee's life story, with particular attention on the sources of the interviewee's ideas and the reasons for his turning to politics; (3) the interviewee's attitudes toward the main realities of the period under study, Russia's past and future, and the West—in other words, the interviewee's political views.

The third part of the interview was naturally the most difficult and the least amenable to structuring. However, in the process of the work it became possible to isolate several typical opinions as well as to formulate key questions, attitudes toward which could facilitate the classification of an interviewee's point of view. The method of defining such patterns of beliefs has already been described above.

The methods of questioning used in focused interviews which are recommended by many manuals in order to achieve the most effective results are not discussed here in detail.[28] It should be noted that the method of retrospection,

---

[25] See e.g. Tim May, *Social Research* (Buckingham: Open University Press, 1993).

[26] Fielding, 'Qualitative Interviewing', 136.

[27] See Jean Morton-Williams, 'Making Qualitative Research Work: Aspects of Administration', in Robert Walker (ed.), *Applied Qualitative Research* (Aldershot: Gower, 1985), 31; Belanovskiy, *Metodika i tekhnika fokusirovannogo interv'yu*, 120.

[28] See particularly the classic work: Robert K. Merton, Marjorie Fiske, and Patricia L. Kendal, *The Focused Interview* (London: Collier Macmillan, 1990).

as well as the criteria of range, specificity, and depth recommended by Merton, Fiske, and Kendall for evaluating the results of the interview, were used during the process of interviewing.

All the interviews were tape-recorded. The interviewing experience of this study showed that the vast majority of the former members of the 'democratic' groups did not express any reservations about the recording and did not show any fear of the possible consequences. On the contrary, especially in the provinces, many seemed eager to be recorded, as they were happy to know that a scholar regarded their experience as important. Only two persons from the entire sample objected to being recorded.

Opinions of specialists differ on the need to transcribe the recorded interviews in order to analyse the written text. Belanovskiy, for example, insists that this is necessary.[29] Sue Jones, however, writes that 'it is important that reading of transcripts does not become a substitute for listening to the non-linguistic data on the tape: emphasis, mood, intonation and so on that crucially elaborate meaning'.[30]

In any case the majority of the interviews were transcribed, but in the process of analysis considerable attention was paid to the factors mentioned by Jones. Abstracts were made of the interviews, both to illustrate patterns and for purposes of quotation; the transcript was as close as possible to speech in order to present the ideas of the participant as precisely as possible, and only obvious mistakes in the spoken language were corrected.

The problem of bias

The problem of bias is one of the main obstacles in social research. In this study, as in most others, the source of bias could be both the interviewer and the interviewee. To avoid bias resulting from interviewer pressure, which can emerge in the very form of questions (the question itself can contain an implied answer or show what kind of answer would be preferable to the interviewer), specialists usually recommend the use of 'open-ended' questions.[31] Most of the questions in this study which concerned the views of the participant were formulated in the following way: 'What is your attitude towards a certain phenomenon?' or 'How do you understand this or that term?' The experience of much empirical research suggests that questions in this form minimize interviewer pressure on the respondent.

Sources of bias caused by the interviewee can be divided into several types. The first is connected to the problem of timing. The events discussed

---

[29]   Belanovskiy, *Metodika i tekhnika fokusirovannogo interv`yu*, 201.

[30]   Sue Jones, 'The Analysis of Depth Interviews', in Walker (ed.), *Applied Qualitative Research*, 58.

[31]   See Sue Jones, 'Depth Interviewing', in Walker (ed.), *Applied Qualitative Research*, 48.

in the interviews occurred from two to eight years earlier than the time the interviews actually took place. Over these years the situation in the Russian Federation changed drastically, including the disappearance of the larger state (the USSR) of which it was a part. It is hardly surprising that the participants' views in most cases were very different from those they held at the time and that their attitudes toward the past were often coloured by their present experiences. During the interview a participant could unintentionally mix up his former and current views and even substitute new ones for old.

To obviate this difficulty two methods were used. First, the questions were put in such a way as to make the interviewee understand this contradiction and to analyse the difference himself. Usually the interviewees expressed understanding of the problem and were eager to cooperate, analysing with interest the evolution of their views and its causes. Second, other sources were used to check the authenticity of the interviewees' data.

Another type of possible bias was a result of an intentional attempt of an interviewee to present his or her former views in a false light because the interviewee now thinks those views to be wrong and is not prepared to admit to having held them. This type of behaviour is particularly characteristic of those who are still active in politics and of those activists who are now disillusioned with 'democracy' and have come to sympathize with a rival camp. For example, a former activist who has become disillusioned with President Yel`tsin could have said that he or she saw Yel`tsin's shortcomings from the very beginning, yet in fact may have firmly supported him at the time. An active politician who is now concerned with the question of Russia's unity and statehood could have said that he or she has always stood for this, though in practice he or she did not even consider these questions at that time.

It should be mentioned that in practice there were very few attempts on the part of interviewees intentionally to confuse the interviewer. On the contrary, even those activists who have changed their views were unexpectedly prepared to cooperate in admitting their former 'mistakes' and analysing them. The comparison of the interviewees' data with other sources (which are described below) tends to confirm this, while also helping to solve the problem and to minimize the risk of bias.

Another method which helped in this case was that in constructing the sample, a deliberate decision was taken to include only a minimal number of active politicians and to make an effort to interview a significant number of people who have left political life. Their stories tended to be less influenced by their current position.

Further bias was caused by changes in personal relations between former colleagues. Over the past few years former friends and comrades have often become rivals and even personal enemies. Their views about each other were often to a large extent determined by their present relations. In this case it was only possible to note such a contradiction and not to use the data, which were seriously biased by personal feelings.

Written/recorded articles and the discourse of group members

The general principle of the treatment of written documents in this book is discussed in Chapter 2. They were first analysed as representing the views of their individual authors in the same way as interviews represent the views of the interviewee. Only at the next stage were they compared so as to depict typical views.

The detailed description of the interviewing methods presented above does not mean that interviews provided the largest part of the information or even the most important data for this study. Even more important were written sources, of which the most extensive were the written materials of the members of 'democratic' groups and parties. It was possible to find such information in different publications of these groups, some printed by official printing houses, others circulated as unofficial manuscripts which were typed or even handwritten. The most common forms of exchange were articles, published speeches, commentaries, and other written texts by individual activists of the groups.

Compared to interviews, such materials have both advantages and short-comings. While a researcher has an opportunity in an interview to get the necessary information, with written sources he or she has to select the necessary data from a larger text, the whole of which may not be necessary at the time. However, an obvious advantage of written discourses is that they belong to the time which is being studied. This makes them a unique, fixed reflection of the original beliefs of the group members, at least in a form which was intended for the public. This removes the possibility of bias caused by the changes in the beliefs of a member over time, and it creates an opportunity to check if the beliefs of a participant presented in an interview differ from his or her beliefs as expressed during that time.

It is necessary to note that the written sources, particularly political articles and speeches, can also be subject to another kind of bias—most of them were written in order to achieve a political aim, in the light of the political situation at the time, and have been changed or adjusted their representation of reality and individual ideas could therefore according to such an aim. For example, a Russian 'democrat' could have regarded General Augusto Pinochet as a fine example of a 'strong leader', but not be prepared to admit it in public at the time, because public opinion, which was used to seeing Pinochet's example as negative, would not have got the message. So Lenin or, perhaps later, General de Gaulle would be used as positive examples of a 'strong leader'.

Written sources came from several libraries and archives. In Moscow extensive collections of materials used for this book are concentrated in the People's Archive (Narodnyy arkhiv) and the Institute for Humanist Political Research (Institut gumanitarno-politicheskikh issledovaniy). The People's Archive, originally a part of the Moscow State Institute of History and Archives (later the Moscow Humanitarian University), has become an independent information centre. Since its establishment in June 1988 it has been collecting 'non-official' materials, from examples of the independent press to personal letters and documents from different periods in the history of Russia. It holds an extensive, though geographically not very systematic, collection of independent publications of the late-USSR period, including newspapers, magazines, official documents, and propaganda materials (such as leaflets and posters used for canvassing during elections and referenda), as well as several personal archives of the activists of 'democratic' groups.

The Institute for Humanist Political Research, created out of the Moscow Bureau of Information Exchange (M-BIO), was organized by Vyacheslav Igrunov (a former political prisoner who later became a deputy of the State Duma). Its main aim was to organize an alternative library and information centre to promote contacts and mutual exchange between different independent groups. The Institute possesses what is probably the largest collection of publications and documents of independent political groups in the former USSR.

Outside Moscow the documents and publications of independent political groups could in some cases be found in local libraries and museums. For example, a thorough archive of such materials about the Stavropol` independent political movement was passed by activists to the Stavropol` *kray* museum; an important archive of the same type is being kind in the Penza museum. An extensive collection of publications of independent groups in the USSR held by the Paris-based Russian-language newspaper *Russkaya mysl`* was also used in this study. The existence of this collection became possible thanks to the efforts of Aleksandr Ginzburg, a former long-time political prisoner, who from the very beginning of the Gorbachev reforms established epistolary contacts with many such groups all over the country.

Finally, during study visits to Russian provincial cities, as well as while working in Moscow, the author himself collected a unique archive of documents of independent political groups. Valuable materials were provided by many former members of the groups from their personal archives. Apart from publications these include such important documents as draft speeches and publications, diaries, personal notes, and video recordings of internal meetings and of discussions on local TV. The use of such documents brought this study closer to understanding the real ideas and plans of group members, compensating for the bias of the official group publications.

The author has analysed not only documents from the regions where the interviews were conducted, but also materials from the whole of Russia. This was intended to make the study more geographically representative and the final conclusions more general and more applicable to the whole of Russia.

The results of quantitative research

The fact that most of the materials for this study had to be analysed by qualitative methods does not mean that the author deems such methods to be superior. This was determined by the subject of the research itself. In fact, all kinds of sources are important, and qualitative and quantitative data should complement each other. In spite of the fact that the use of quantitative methods in this study is, of necessity, limited, both the author's own calculations and the figures from existing studies are used whenever it is both possible and appropriate. In every case when a list of members of a group or a list of its supporters was acquired, calculations were made of the representation by profession, age, sex, and educational level. These data were used to illustrate and check the conclusions of the qualitative analysis. Some statistical observations were made on the basis of interviews. All this does not, to be sure, present a comprehensively representative picture. However, such statistical data are important as supplementary material.

The same could be said about the quantitative data taken from existing literature on the subject. Some data on professional, sex, and age representation of 'democratic groups', as supplied by the groups themselves, can be found in reference books, especially in the most thorough of these, *Rossiya: partii, assotsiatsii, soyuzy, kluby.*[32] Some larger groups, movements, and parties had their own sociological groups or at least collected statistical data about their members from time to time. In this book the data collected by the Democratic Russia Sociological Service, the sociological groups of the Moscow People's Front and the Social-Democratic Party of Russia, and the Executive Committee of the Democratic Party of Russia were used. In some cases similar research was conducted by independent institutions, such as the Institute for Humanist Political Research, the results of which were published.[33]

---

[32] Rossiysko-amerikanskiy universitet, Institut massovykh politicheskikh dvizheniy, *Rossiya: partii, assotsiatsii, soyuzy, kluby. Spravochnik*, 10 vols. (Moscow: RAU-Press, 1991–2).

[33] See Sergei Mitrokhin and Michael Urban, 'Social Groups, Party Elites and Russia's New Democrats', in David Lane (ed.), *Russia in Flux: The Political and Social Consequences of Reform* (Aldershot: Edward Elgar, 1992).

Participants' memoirs

Memoirs written by the members of 'democratic' groups and parties are among the more important sources used in this book.[34] Though still not as numerous as other kinds of sources, they are very important because of their thorough accounts of events and their expression of activists' personal views. However, it is clear that such publications are liable to bias, in common with most political memoirs, which are generally written with the aim of justifying the authors' earlier positions and actions.

Official documents of 'democratic' groups and parties

The official documents of 'democratic' political groups and parties, such as programmes, charters, resolutions, and declarations, are an important source for research into the formation and evolution of the ideas of the Russian 'democrats'. Many such documents have been collected in special reference books, published both in Russia and abroad. It was also possible to find such documents in the publications of these groups and sometimes in official Soviet publications. During his work in Moscow as well as his study trips to 'the seven regions of Russia', the author collected valuable material of this type, including some unpublished drafts. These documents were used to study the evolution of the general goals of a group, the principles of its organizational structure, and its characteristic general ideological orientation.

---

[34] Some examples are: Valeriy Fadeev, *Pokhozhdeniya neformala: Ocherk 1988*, 2 vols. (Moscow: Russkoe slovo, 1992); Vasiliy Krasulya, *Dissident iz nomenklatury* (Stavropol`: Severo-kavkazskoye informatsionno-reklamnoye agenstvo, 1992); Valeriya Novodvorskaya, *Po tu storonu otchayaniya* (Moscow: Novosti, 1993); Gavriil Popov, *Snova v oppozitsii* (Moscow: Galaktika, 1994); Mikhail Chelnokov, *Rossiya bez Soyuza, Rossiya bez Rossii. . . . Zapiski deputata Rasstrelyannogo parlamenta* (Moscow: Novaya sloboda, 1994).

2

'Democratic' Groups in Soviet Russia:
An Assessment of the Literature

A great deal has been written already on 'democratic' political groups in Soviet Russia. While some of these studies are based on valuable material and contain interesting conclusions, most of them are characterized by two major shortcomings: they either totally disregard the influence of beliefs and political culture on 'democratic' politics or approach these beliefs only formally, analysing the surface level of the belief system and interpreting 'democratic' language from the perspective of its common meaning in their own culture or in Western democratic theory, but not as it was understood by Russian 'democrats' themselves. This often prevents them from giving accurate answers to the questions they raise. The reason for these shortcomings cannot be clearly understood without analysing the general problems of studying Russian political culture.

2.1. RUSSIAN AND SOVIET POLITICAL CULTURE: PROBLEMS OF ANALYSIS

Russian political culture and Soviet reality

There were two main problems addressed by the students of Soviet political culture before the Gorbachev reforms opened up Soviet society to surveys and field research: (1) the level of influence of the traditional Russian political culture on the formation of the Soviet political system; (2) the nature of Soviet political culture and its possible influence on the future of the USSR. One widely accepted view of Russian (and Soviet) political culture stresses its 'authoritarian' character. According to Archie Brown, 'there is no getting away from the predominantly authoritarian nature of Soviet and Russian political experience'. Although Brown points to the existence in Russia of 'non-authoritarian' tendencies, he sees them as less significant subcultures.[1]

---

[1] Archie Brown, 'Ideology and Political Culture', in Seweryn Bialer (ed.), *Politics, Society, and Nationality inside Gorbachev's Russia* (Boulder, Colo. and London: Westview, 1989), 18–19.

The essence of the alleged traditional Russian authoritarianism is described in a distilled form by Zbigniew Brzezinski:

The central and significant reality of Russian politics has been its predominantly autocratic character. Unlike its western European neighbors, Russia had not experienced a prolonged feudal phase. The overthrow of the Tartar yoke gave rise to an increasingly assertive and dominant autocracy. Property and people were the possessions of the state, personalized by the Autocrat (designed as such explicitly and proudly). The obligation of well-nigh complete subordination of any individual to the personalized symbol of the state was expressly asserted. Control over society—including the church by the state—among other means, through a census mechanism adopted centuries ahead of any corresponding European device, was reminiscent of Oriental despotisms and, in fact, was derived directly from that historical experience. The result has been to establish a relationship of state supremacy over society, of politics over social affairs, of the functionary over the citizen (or subject), to a degree not matched in Europe; and differences of degree do become differences of kind.[2]

According to this view Bolshevik policy was a mere continuation of the pre-revolutionary tsarist course which only strengthened existing tendencies. As Stephen White put it, the predominantly 'centralised, collectivist political culture which the Bolsheviks inherited in 1917 . . . has in many ways persisted up to the present day'.[3]

However, other views have existed. Marc Raeff, for example, adheres to the view that by the beginning of the twentieth century there existed two political cultures in Russia: that of the liberal intelligentsia and that of the backward peasantry. Since both classes were destroyed by the Bolsheviks it is impossible to speak of the influence of either of these political cultures on Soviet or post-Soviet societies. Rejecting the idea of continuity with pre-revolutionary political culture, Raeff argues that '1917 and the experiences of the civil war radically changed Russia's historical evolution'.[4]

Nicolai Petro agrees that there were two political cultures in tsarist Russia, but extends the struggle between the two into the Soviet period, thus supporting the idea of continuity. According to Petro, in Russia the official 'authoritarian' political culture was challenged over the centuries by the 'alternative' one, which 'is reflected in the struggle to define the proper scope of the autocracy, the proper nature of church-state relations, and Russia's proper national identity'. According to Petro,

These three issues formed the political and cultural battleground between the official statist and Slavophile political traditions during the late nineteenth century. In 1905,

---

[2] Zbigniew Brzezinski, 'Soviet Politics: From the Future to the Past', in Paul Cocks, Robert V. Daniels, and Nancy Whittier Heer (eds.), *The Dynamics of Soviet Politics* (Cambridge, Mass.: Harvard University Press, 1976), 69–70.

[3] Stephen White, *Political Culture and Soviet Politics* (London: Macmillan, 1979), 168.

[4] Marc Raeff, 'The People, the Intelligentsia and Political Culture', *Political Studies*, 41 (1993), 106 and 100.

civil society, inspired by the alternative political culture, succeeded in forcing Tsar Nicholas II to recognize the principles of popular government and civil rights. Then, in February 1917, civil society replaced the monarchy with a republic committed to duly elected popular representation.[5]

Unlike Raeff, Petro believes that although this victory 'was snatched away just nine months later, the battle to restore it continued throughout the entire Soviet period'.[6]

A similar approach can be found in some Russian studies of political culture. Thus, Yu. V. Lepeshkin finds everywhere in Russian history a struggle between 'democratic' and 'authoritarian-patriarchal' political cultures. He points out that 'Stalin's dictatorship grew . . . on a well fertilized soil which bears fruit even now. The regime was based on the centuries-long repression of independent activity, and on the alienation of the masses from politics'. However, Lepeshkin argues, another, democratic tradition was present in Russian history:

It has deep roots and bears a strong imprint of patriarchal relations. A classic example is the *veche* republics of Novgorod, Pskov and Vyatka which existed until they were annexed by the Muscovite state in the fifteenth century. The free communities of Cossacks formed in distant places which were free from serfdom and despotism. The Russian state was ruled not only by a centralized bureaucracy. *Zemskie Sobory* were convened when there was a need to gauge national opinion. Rural communities, in which five-sixths of the population lived, remained to a great extent outside the influence of the bureaucracy.[7]

Lepeshkin acknowledges, however, that democratic traditions in Russia 'have not properly developed' and that reforms which could provide an opportunity for the development of democratic political culture 'with literally fatal inevitability were followed by counter-reforms'.[8]

There is nothing new in these arguments. The issue of the relationship between pre-Soviet and Soviet political ideas was at the centre of academic and political discussions in post-revolutionary Russia. Then, after freedom of discussion was suppressed, they continued in emigrants' writings and later re-emerged in *samizdat*. The two main positions were formulated not later than 1918. Nikolay Berdyaev and other authors of the famous collection of essays, *Vekhi* (published in 1909), argued in favour of the continuity and rebirth in Russia of pre-revolutionary traditions. At the same time the Bolsheviks themselves and their extreme right-wing enemies (for different reasons) supported the view that the old Russia had been completely destroyed and a totally new culture (or non-culture) had been created. From the point of view of extreme

---

[5] Nicolai N. Petro, *The Rebirth of Russian Democracy: An Interpretation of Political Culture* (Cambridge, Mass.: Harvard University Press, 1995), 3.   [6] Ibid.

[7] Yu. V. Lepeshkin, 'Chto glavnoe v politicheskoy kul'ture?', in P. I. Simush (ed.), *Politologiya na rossiyskom fone* (Moscow: Luch, 1993), 260–1.   [8] Ibid. 261.

opponents of the continuity thesis the Communist authorities, 'neither according to their own views, nor objectively, are a national government of Russia; they are international in their essence'.[9]

This discussion was transferred to the writings of non-Russian authors. Before World War II there was a general consensus in the West that Soviet ideology was a new phenomenon, Marxist but not 'Russian' in its essence. However, after Stalin restored certain national symbols in the 1940s, the opposite view began to gain ground. In both cases, before the difference between official ideology and dominant popular beliefs was established by several important studies conducted in the 1950s and 1960s, little doubt was expressed concerning the congruence of the two. Thus, in accordance with the concept of 'totalitarianism', official Soviet ideology and consequently the beliefs of the population were found to be closer to that of Nazi Germany and Fascist Italy than to that of old Russia.

The concept of political culture, specifically the continuity and the strength of tradition, was used to explain the gap between ideology and dominant beliefs in the Soviet Union and other Communist countries. However, traditions themselves can be seen in different ways. Russian history is rich in facts and events and as Petro rightly points out 'the "insightful" researcher should have little difficulty finding corroborative views from different sources that "prove" his or her opinions about Russian political culture'.[10] In the extreme case political culture is even seen as a mystical substance which cannot be explained by logical analysis since it is allegedly not contained in any documents or physical objects, but can only be comprehended through the researcher's intuition. Such an approach can be found, for example, in Edward Keenan's essay 'Muscovite Political Folkways', in which Russian political culture is discussed without a single quotation from a source and practically without reference to specific epochs, events, or actors, since, according to the author, the main goal of the Russians was deliberately to conceal the 'deep structures' from outsiders.[11] Keenan's conclusion about the absolute uniqueness of virtually every trait of Russian political culture is highly disputable.

The problem is that in their study of so-called 'Russian political tradition' students of political culture have tended to select facts arbitrarily regardless

---

[9] See Nikolay Berdyaev, 'Dukhi russkoi revolyutsii', in Nikolay Berdyaer, *Vekhi. Iz Glubiny* (Moscow: Pravda, 1991; 1st publ. 1918), 251; 'An Open Letter to the Editor of *The New York Times*', in *Sotsialisticheskiy Vestnik*, 6–7 (1951), as quoted in Nikolay Ul'yanov, 'Kompleks Filofeya', *Voprosy istorii*, 4 (1994), 152.

[10] Petro, *The Rebirth of Russian Democracy*, 15. Several other authors have supported this view. See Mary McAuley, 'Political Culture and Communist Politics: One Step Forward, Two Steps Back', in Archie Brown (ed.), *Political Culture and Communist Studies* (London: Macmillan, 1984), 17; Alexander Dallin, 'Uses and Abuses of Russian History', in Frederic J. Fleron, and Eric P. Hoffman (eds.), *Post-Communist Studies and Political Science: Methodology and Empirical Theory in Sovietology* (Boulder, Colo.: Westview, 1993).

[11] Edward Keenan, 'Muscovite Political Folkways', *Russian Review*, 45:2 (1986), 115–81.

of historical period. Though this method was long ago rejected by serious historians it has survived in traditional essays by Russian authors on 'Russia's destiny' and in half-historical, half-political writings by non-Russian writers such as Tibor Szamuely or Richard Pipes.[12] Their arguments have been uncritically repeated in many accounts of Russian political culture.[13] Political considerations play a major role in such an approach. Thus, as Alexander Dallin observes,

> The stress on distinctive and unchanging (and presumably unchangeable) characteristics of Russian history has appealed to, and has been particularly compatible with the views of, those who see the Soviet regime as beyond the pale and perhaps beyond redemption. Some of the most vociferous affirmations of historical determinism, which sees the Soviet system as an extrapolation of the Russian past (at times accompanied by the view that 'every nation gets the government it deserves'), have come from the most militant and anti-Soviet positions.[14]

The argument that Russia's political culture could never change and would always be 'autocratic' or 'totalitarian', in sharp opposition to the 'West' (which often was meant to include some parts of the USSR like the Baltic republics and Ukraine), well suited those politicians who argued for a tough line towards Moscow and predicted that the regime would collapse and the country split apart under the strain. Since Russia itself was written off as 'un-Westernizable' this view was agreeable to those interested in detaching the parts of the USSR (and its empire) that could be assimilated by the West. Likewise, the assumption that the Russians were basically Europeans, who had experienced a similar, though perhaps slower, historical development towards 'modernity' and had 'democratic' traditions of their own, supported the view of those who argued for dialogue and cooperation in order to promote the gradual evolution of the country towards democracy.[15] However politically important, neither view had very much to do with Russia's real history, and the method of arbitrarily invoking historical facts, which perhaps is understandable in, or at least common to, tendentious writings, can hardly be used in the study of political culture if it is to be a part of political *science* as the study of politics but not a part of politics itself.

[12]   See Tibor Szamuely, *The Russian Tradition* (London: Secker & Warburg, 1974); Richard Pipes, *Russia under the Old Regime* (New York: Scribner, 1974).

[13]   See e.g. Brzezinski, 'Soviet Politics: From the Future to the Past'; Frederick C. Barghoorn and Thomas F. Remington, *Politics in the USSR* (Boston: Little, Brown and Co., 1986), esp. chs. 1 and 2; Gerhard Simon, 'Political Culture in Russia', *Aussenpolitik*, 3 (1995), 242–53.

[14]   Dallin gives as examples Richard Pipes, Edward Rowney, and William Odom, who all worked in the Reagan administration (Dallin, 'Uses and Abuses of Russian History', 132 and 140). Zbigniew Brzezinski is another example, although he served in the Carter administration.

[15]   On the influence of politics on Soviet studies see, for example, Alfred G. Meyer, 'Politics and Methodology in Soviet Studies', in Fleron and Hoffman (eds.), *Post-Communist Studies and Political Science*.

There are two major shortcomings in the approach used by the majority of Sovietologists who employ the concept of political culture to study the problem of continuity between pre-revolutionary Russia and the USSR: (1) it attempts to place Russian traditional culture on a one-dimensional scale where everything is measured against an idealized view of Western democracy; (2) facts and events of Russian history, as well as beliefs and concepts, are analysed outside their historical context and 'modernized' under the influence of contemporary beliefs. A good example of both tendencies is Robert Tucker's article 'Sovietology and Russian History'.[16] According to Tucker, for every event or personality in Soviet history one can find an analogy in the Russian past: Stalin resembles Ivan the Terrible, Gorbachev resembles Alexander II, the collapse of Communism has led to a new Time of Troubles, etc. For some reason Tucker calls this approach 'historical' while in fact it is obviously non-historical, since it disregards historical context and gives excessive importance to surface similarity. Criticizing this 'historical' approach to culture, which is also employed in the writings on Russia by Brzezinski, Pipes, White, and others, Bertrand Badie points out that its main flaw is the separation of the actor from culture by insisting on the passivity of the former and the permanence of the latter. According to Badie, 'it thus leads to a double dead-end: explaining nothing about the conditions of the creation of culture it presents culture as an exclusively static phenomenon which reproduces itself from one epoch to another. Socialisation and reproduction by no means can be superimposed on the concept of culture if this only leads us toward seeing the present as a mere continuation of the past and culture as only a force of conservation.'[17]

From the totality of facts, events, or phenomena of a country's history it is always possible to choose some which would (or would not) look similar at first glance. The question is: Do we have enough evidence to speak of a tendency beyond the fact that certain events happened in the same country (or to put it more precisely, on the same soil, since countries change over time)? Tucker, who simply postulates similarity, does not even consider this question. His critics, who, like Aleksandr Solzhenitsyn, merely postulate the opposite, are no closer to reality.[18] An analysis of the evolution of Russian and Soviet political culture should not consist of a construction of empty analogies or a mere assertion that the continuity thesis is false. One should analyse specific belief systems of a specific period, how they transfer to later generations, and how they change during the transfer process. Only by treating political culture not as a certain 'substance' which 'lives and resounds

---

[16] Robert C. Tucker, 'Sovietology and Russian History', *Post-Soviet Affairs*, 8:3 (1992), 175–96.

[17] Bertrand Badie, *Culture et politique*, 3rd edn. (Paris: Economica, 1993), 12.

[18] See Aleksandr I. Solzhenitsyn, 'The Mortal Danger', in Erik P. Hoffman and Robbin F. Laird (eds.), *The Soviet Polity in the Modern Era* (New York: Aldine, 1984).

throughout the centuries' in the soul of Russians,[19] but as a belief system which as one particular form exists only in one particular time, can one obtain a better understanding of continuity in Russian (and not only Russian) history.

The study of political culture within an historical context leads to the rejection of its 'modernization', which defines it using contemporary terms, imputes present-day meanings to past situations, and uses a contemporary social ideal as an absolute reference point and the final stage of historical development. According to Tucker, for example, traditional Russian political culture was 'authoritarian' or 'étatiste' and periodic liberal reforms, themselves a part of that tradition, were usually followed by counter-reforms. Thus, in his view, the problem of contemporary political development in Russia is the following: 'Has Russia matured and progressed to the point of being able to break out of the past pattern and semi-isolation from the external world that has been a part of it, while developing an authentically Russian form of civilization? Or will it emerge from the present Time of Troubles into another circle?'[20]

Tucker's use of such terms as 'matured' and 'progressed' clearly shows his vision of history as a progressive movement toward the 'modern' (or 'Western') world, a vision which is actually a version of political modernization or political development theories. The main problem of such theories is not the fact that in their most radical forms they may come close to acknowledging a 'political-cultural supremacy', though this is dangerous in its own way. The methodological fallacy here is that history is being reinterpreted from the point of view of contemporary aims and ideals and in this respect it does not really matter whether this ideal is 'democracy', 'Communism', 'the three principles of Sun Yat-sen', or something else. From a historical point of view, to say that 'traditional Russian political culture' was 'authoritarian', 'democratic', 'Communist', 'humane' or 'inhumane', 'imperialist' or 'non-imperialist' is not simply right or wrong. To say these things is, in fact, to say very little about that culture since these notions either did not exist in pre-revolutionary Russia at all or had very different meanings. Rather than stretching terminology to describe very different realities, a student of the history of political culture should try properly to 'translate' into the modern language of social science what the concepts of the time meant for the people of the time.

Soviet political culture: problems of methodology

Some studies of Soviet political culture itself were more fruitful. The most convincing generalizations about it were based on the results of the Harvard

---

[19] Ul'yanov, 'Kompleks Filofeya', 161.
[20] Tucker, 'Sovietology and Russian History', 193.

Project on the Soviet Social System, which itself did not formally employ the concept of political culture but methodologically was part of a broad trend of 'psycho-cultural research' and was influenced above all by the concept of 'modal personality'.[21] The major publication emerging from the project was Alex Inkeles' and Raymond Bauer's *The Soviet Citizen*. On the basis of different kinds of interviews with several hundred emigrants from the USSR who one way or another found themselves in the West before, during, or just after World War II, and also on the basis of written questionnaires which were answered by about two thousand such emigrants, who were randomly selected to reflect as accurately as possible the social configuration of Soviet society, the authors drew quite a convincing picture of various aspects of life in Stalin's USSR, including people's 'values and beliefs, their desires and frustrations'.[22] The Harvard Project was later followed by other studies, based on interviews with emigrants.[23]

Most students of political culture use interviews and surveys in their analyses. In fact interview data were the main source for the originators of the concept, Gabriel Almond and Sydney Verba, and many of their followers.[24] However, the majority of the students of Soviet political culture had to turn to other sources as a supplement when the possibilities of directly interviewing Soviet citizens were very limited and conducting direct surveys in the USSR was not possible at all. Understanding these limitations, Archie Brown suggested a whole list of sources which could be used in such a study to substitute for the results of direct surveys. This list, apart from interviews with emigrants, included: creative literature, memoirs, historiography, and official literature on creating the *new man* and a *Communist consciousness* (containing not only official Communist values but also criticism of existing 'shortcomings' which may reflect the actually existing values and attitudes).[25]

Petro criticizes Brown's approach, arguing that this kind of 'subjective' source itself leads to biased conclusions since 'unlike the modicum of objectivity which accurate surveys of public opinion can offer', it 'serves mainly to confirm the researcher's *a priori* assumptions regarding Russian political

[21] See Alex Inkeles and Daniel J. Levinson, 'National Character: The Study of Modal Personality and Sociocultural Systems', in Gardner Lindzey and Elliot Aronson (eds.), *The Handbook of Social Psychology*, 2nd edn., iv (Reading, Mass.: Addison-Wesley, 1969).

[22] Alex Inkeles and Raymond A. Bauer, *The Soviet Citizen: Daily Life in a Totalitarian Society* (Cambridge, Mass.: Harvard University Press, 1959), 4.

[23] See e.g. James R. Millar (ed.), *Politics, Work and Daily Life in the USSR: A Survey of Former Soviet Citizens* (Cambridge: Cambridge University Press, 1987); Wayne DiFranceisco and Zvi Gitelman, 'Soviet Political Culture and "Covert Participation" ' in Policy Implementation', *American Political Science Review*, 78 (1984), 603–21.

[24] Gabriel A. Almond and Sidney Verba, *The Civic Culture: Political Attitudes and Democracy in Five Nations* (Princeton, NJ: Princeton University Press, 1963).

[25] Brown, 'Introduction', 11. See also Archie Brown, *Soviet Politics and Political Science* (London: Macmillan, 1974), 96–100.

culture and too easily overlooks evidence that might lead to different interpretations'.[26] This criticism is misplaced: the cause of bias is not the sources
themselves but the way they are interpreted. For a researcher all sources are
valuable and in a way all are 'subjective' since all products of human activity
are 'biased' by the imprint of the beliefs of those who created them. But this
very fact makes it possible to study these beliefs. If only interviews provided
accurate information, then neither archaeology nor even history could exist as
disciplines. At the same time the 'accuracy' of respondents' answers are also
disputable at best, since they can be influenced by many different factors. The
bald figures of a survey need to be interpreted anyway and a recorded in-
depth interview differs very little from an article or memoirs by the same
author. In any case one can speak only of the level of 'accuracy' and much
depends on the methodology used to analyse the source.

Petro is right to criticize the subjectivism in studies of Soviet political
culture, but for the wrong reasons. The subjectivism is to be found not in the
character of the sources, but in the way they have been treated by many scholars—including Petro himself.[27] Many students of Soviet political culture
seem to accept Brown's list of sources, but rarely do they discuss methods for
their use. As a result they just pick from these sources those views which
seem to them to reflect the most popular belief.

The following example can illustrate how such treatment of sources can
lead to highly disputable conclusions. In one of his articles on Soviet political culture Brown argues that one of the 'central values of the dominant
Soviet political culture is the emphasis placed upon order (*poryadok*)'. He
illustrates this argument by quoting one article by a foreign correspondent in
Moscow and the opinions of two Soviet intellectuals. Brown writes:

> Nadezhda Mandelshtam, commenting on the intelligentsia's fear of what would
> happen if ever 'the mob' got out of hand ('We should be the first to be hanged from
> the lamppost'), observed, 'Whenever I hear this constantly repeated phrase, I remem-
> ber Herzen's words about the intelligentsia which so much fears its own people that
> it prefers to go in chains itself, provided the people, too, remain fettered'. Andrey
> Amalrik recalled the response of one Russian worker to the political turmoil, as he
> saw it, of Czechoslovakia in 1968: 'What sort of government is it,' the worker asked,
> 'that tolerates so much disorder? Power must be such that I live in fear of it—not that
> *it* lives in fear of me!'[28]

On this basis Brown comes to the far-reaching conclusion that the mood of
intellectuals and workers as a whole 'may be regarded as unpromising soil for
the growth of democracy'.[29] He further supports this view with the anecdotal

---

[26] Petro, *The Rebirth of Russian Democracy*, 15.

[27] As noted by Archie Brown in his review of Petro's book. See *American Political Science
Review*, 90 (1996), 680–1.   [28] Brown, 'Ideology and Political Culture', 20.

[29] Ibid.

evidence of a British journalist, Mary Dejevsky, who while standing in Red Square had heard some people argue in favour of breaking up a demonstration of Crimean Tatars. From the point of view of Brown himself, who issued the call for the use of as many sources as possible and for the comparison of sources with one another, the conclusions are well grounded: several sources were used and the opinions expressed in them were similar. However, do these opinions represent a dominant belief? Surely, in the whole totality of sources one can easily find just as many different or even totally opposite opinions. So there is no indication that either point of view should be taken as part of the dominant political culture. Moreover, Brown uses all three of his sources as though they accurately represent the opinions under study. However, from the commentaries of the authors it is very clear that all three of them disagree with the opinions which they supposedly heard. Therefore there are good reasons to believe that their accounts were biased by their own views and positions. Thus, there is no way of telling if they provide accurate accounts of other people's beliefs, especially of the most widely held beliefs.

This is not to say that these sources have no value for a researcher. They provide accurate information not about those who are spoken of, but about the speakers themselves. What can be said about them with absolute precision is that they accurately reflect the beliefs of Mandel`shtam and Amal`rik themselves (since the political perception of British journalists is not studied in the article, the case of Dejevsky will not be discussed). What conclusions, then, can be made with relative reliability on the basis of the sources discussed in Brown's article? It would be fair to say that at least in a section of the Soviet intelligentsia and more precisely in dissident circles (to which both Mandel`shtam and Amal`rik belonged) there existed the belief that one should not be afraid of 'the people', that the government should not be feared, that the Soviet invasion of Czechoslovakia should be condemned, and that the political liberalization in that country should be supported. Of course these conclusions are more modest but they are also better corroborated. They may conceivably be representative of the dominant political culture, but because of the limited number of sources they might only represent a part of a political subculture of Soviet dissidents. In the latter case they may not contradict Brown's characterization of the dominant political culture if it proves to be accurate. However, if a study of many more sources, preferably using a representative sample, shows that they are actually characteristic of the majority of the population, then Brown's conclusion about Soviet society before the Gorbachev reforms got under way would be inaccurate.

Another example of the customary treatment of sources can be found in White's *Political Culture and Soviet Politics*. The book evaluates the level of political participation in the USSR on the basis of official Soviet statistics which show the growth of such activities as participation in elections, membership of the Komsomol and official trade unions, and attendance at

official lectures and 'political informations'. White acknowledges that all
these kinds of activities are not fully voluntary and therefore do not necessarily confirm ideological support for the regime. However, in his view,
these data make it possible to conclude that the 'overall levels of socio-
political activism have increased very considerably over the total period of
Soviet rule'.[30] White sees in the USSR a game which he thinks is similar to
that of his political culture and by analogy ascribes to it a similar meaning:
voting, attending political meetings and lectures, and membership of a
political group all translate into political activism. However, it is very
doubtful that in the Soviet context all these compulsory acts were connected
to political activism at all. Most of these figures were probably manipulated
for propaganda purposes. But even if they were not, they do not establish
much, except possibly the 'mobilizational abilities' of the regime. Even for
those pursuing an official political career these activities were simply a
show of 'good behaviour', but to take part in politics—to influence political decisions—was something else entirely. For most of the others, especially those who did not believe in official propaganda, participation in
official 'political' events and groups actually showed either passivity and
reluctance to make trouble or fear of the consequences of not participating.
In fact political activism, which surely existed in the USSR as it does in any
society, manifested itself in totally different activities: by participation in
the unseen struggle for power in Communist party committees, by influencing authorities through a network of connections, by Aesopian discussions of very real problems in the press, by attending unofficial concerts,
lectures, and plays, by the reading of *samizdat*, etc. This phenomenon was
described by Wayne DiFranceisco and Zvi Gitelman, who concluded that
there were 'meaningful forms of participation in the system, but they take
place either outside the nominally participatory institutions, or within those
institutions but in nonprescribed ways'. According to these authors 'the way
Soviet people relate to the political administrative system is to go through
the motions of participation in the nominally democratic process of making
decisions, but to put far more serious effort into trying to influence the way
decisions are implemented'. On the basis of these conclusions DiFranceisco
and Gitelman challenge Almond and Verba's classification of types of political culture and argue that 'Soviet political culture is neither a democratic
nor a subject one, but an amalgam of traditional, pre-revolutionary modes
of citizen-state relations and a superstructure of participatory institutions
that superficially resemble those of Western democracies in many
respects'.[31]

[30] White, *Political Culture and Soviet Politics*, 87–9.
[31] DiFranceisco and Gitelman, 'Soviet Political Culture and "Covert Participation" in
Policy Implementation', 603 and 605.

The occidocentrism of research on Soviet and Russian political culture

The reforms started by Mikhail Gorbachev created an atmosphere of open-ness which provided both Soviet and foreign scholars with the opportunity to establish direct contacts with the population without having to conceal the real purposes of these contacts. This led to a rapid growth of various surveys and opinion polls, some of which were designed to test earlier theoretical conclusions, including those on Soviet political culture.

The first researchers who conducted such surveys and analysed their results were usually impressed by the finding that the values and beliefs of the Soviet population were generally close to those of the population of Western democracies. Most researchers at that stage concluded that though the popu-lation under study 'lagged behind' Western democracies on some specific 'democratic' attitudes, their general 'democratic' level differed only slightly from that found in most stable democracies and was close to that of the popu-lation of some Western countries with younger and less stable democratic regimes. Moreover they found that democratic values were more popular among the young and came to the conclusion that the USSR (and later Russia) had good prospects for democratization.[32] These findings led some authors to criticize the theory of the eternal authoritarianism of the Russian tradition and its direct impact on contemporary politics. Thus, in a book published in 1993 based on these first survey results, William Reisinger concluded that the arguments in support of the importance of a 'Russian' political culture in contemporary Russian and Soviet politics were 'faring poorly'.[33]

However, as the regime in the USSR and then in Russia appeared less and less democratic, and especially after the bloody conflict between President Yel'tsin and the Supreme Soviet in 1993, the prognoses became more cautious. Already in 1993 James Gibson and Raymond Duch, after testing the results of their first Moscow survey with a larger one representative of the population of the European part of Russia, while still arguing that 'there is a

---

[32] Jeffrey W. Hahn, 'Continuity and Change in Russian Political Culture', *British Journal of Political Science*, 21 (1991), 393–421; James L. Gibson, Raymond M. Duch, and Kent L. Tedin, 'Democratic Values and the Transformation of the Soviet Union', *Journal of Politics*, 54 (1992), 329–71; William M. Reisinger, Arthur H. Miller, Vicki L. Hesli, and Kristen Hill Maher, 'Political Values in Russia, Ukraine and Lithuania: Sources and Implications for Democracy', *British Journal of Political Science*, 24 (1994), 183–223; Arthur H. Miller, Vicki L. Hesli, and William M. Reisinger, 'Reassessing Mass Support for Political and Economic Change in the Former USSR', *American Political Science Review*, 88 (1994), 399.

[33] William M. Reisinger, 'Conclusions: Mass Public Opinion and the Study of Post-Soviet Societies', in Arthur H. Miller, William M. Reisinger, and Vicki L. Hesli (eds.), *Public Opinion and Regime Change: The New Politics of Post-Soviet Societies* (Boulder, Colo.: Westview, 1993), 274.

reason to believe that a democratic political culture is currently emerging in the states of the former USSR and that the beliefs, values, and attitudes of ordinary citizens will give sustenance to the drive for further democratiza-tion', nevertheless concluded that 'the values that are currently supported are the easier "majority rule" sorts of values, while the more difficult "minority rights" values have not been widely assimilated'.[34] In 1995 Arthur Miller, Vicki Hesli, and William Reisinger, after finding significant differences between the political elite's and the mass public's understanding of democ-racy in both Russia and Ukraine, concluded that 'the evolution toward a democratic, market-oriented society will follow a haltingly difficult path'.[35] The unexpected electoral success of the nationalist Vladimir Zhirinovskiy in December 1993 cast further doubt on the earlier conclusions about the depth of democratic feeling among Russians. As 'democrats' and 'democratic' reforms are becoming more and more discredited in Russia, theories of the return of Russia's immanent 'authoritarianism' and 'imperial consciousness' are regaining their popularity among both academics and journalists, and the old proponents of such theories have themselves reawakened.[36]

The question arises: why did researchers, instead of establishing possible future trends, in fact follow the events, trying to explain them *post factum*? Is it right, as Alexander Dallin put it, that the first wave of Western-type surveys 'were only skindeep and were articulated when it was "politically correct" to do so, and that by the end of 1993 at least a substantial part of the Russian popu-lation—and one might specify particular demographic groups—either had shed such ideas or at least were confused about their validity'?[37] Or perhaps, because of disillusionment with Western-style survey research in Russia, one has to concur with the argument of those authors who, like Frederic Fleron and Michael McFaul, deny any role to political culture in general.[38]

---

[34] James L. Gibson and Raymond M. Duch, 'Emerging Democratic Values in Soviet Political Culture', in Miller, Reisinger, and Hesli (eds.), *Public Opinion and Regime Change*, 89–90.

[35] Arthur H. Miller, Vicki L. Hesli, and William M. Reisinger, 'Comparing Citizen and Elite Belief Systems in Post-Soviet Russia and Ukraine', *Public Opinion Quarterly*, 59 (1995), 33.

[36] Examples of this trend include a recent article by Gerhard Simon which treats Russian political culture as absolutely isolated from all 'Western' influences and immanently 'authori-tarian' and repeats most of the arguments of Ukrainian nationalists at the beginning of the century, and a book by a former *Times* Moscow correspondent, Bruce Clark, which interprets practically every political event in the Yel`tsin period as a sign of the revival of 'imperial spirit'. See Gerhard Simon, 'Political Culture in Russia'; Bruce Clark, *An Empire's New Clothes: The End of Russia's Liberal Dream* (London: Vintage, 1995).

[37] Alexander Dallin, 'Where Have All the Flowers Gone?', in Gail W. Lapidus (ed.), *The New Russia: Troubled Transformation* (Boulder, Colo.: Westview, 1995), 259.

[38] Frederic J. Fleron, Jr., 'Political Culture in Russia', *Europe-Asia Studies*, 48 (1996), 251; Michael McFaul, 'The Perils of a Protracted Transition', *Journal of Democracy*, 10:2 (1999), 16.

Rejection of the cultural determinism and even 'mysticism' of the traditional approach towards Russian political culture, which holds that Russian political beliefs and practices have changed little since the days of Ivan the Terrible, and that the Russian political system is thus for ever doomed to be autocratic, does not necessarily imply that political culture plays no role whatsoever. The main problem with the approach of most political scientists to Russia (both Western and Russian, since Russian political science has uncritically borrowed Western, above all Anglo-American, theories and methods) is its Euro- (or occido-)centrism. The Russian researcher, Yu. S. Pivovarov, is surely correct in saying that this Eurocentric approach prevents students from seeing 'the originality of the Russian political and legal culture, its national traditions and distinctive features. Anything in Russia's political experience which is different from the corresponding West European experience is generally explained by its "underdevelopment", "Asiatic nature", etc.' In his book on Russian political culture after the reforms of Tsar Alexander II, Pivovarov points out another weakness of Western studies: disproportionate attention to one or a few particular lines of national development which are most familiar to Western scholars. As a result entire layers of material are ignored and the analysis is one-sided,[39] or, to quote Dallin again, 'too simplistic, one dimensional, or "American" '.[40] For a qualitative analysis this means attributing every Russian political problem of any period of the country's history to the opposition between pro-Westerners and anti-Westerners, reformers and conservatives, and later, democrats and Communists. For a Western-style study based on surveys it means studying only those beliefs which (according to 'democratic theory') are believed to determine the stability of democratic regimes anywhere in the world. The alternative is to study political culture as a system in the process of development and change without overstressing or disregarding any of its elements.

2.2. STUDIES OF THE RUSSIAN 'DEMOCRATS'

Reference literature

The first reaction of scholars to the emergence of a large number of new political groups was to record them. Thus, in the USSR many different reference

---

[39] Yu. S. Pivovarov, *Politicheskaya kul`tura poreformennoy Rossii* (Moscow: Rossiyskaya Akademiya Nauk, Institut nauchnoy informatsii po obshchestvennym naukam, 1994), 97–8. Pivovarov himself uses the traditional methodology of arbitrary selection of sources; besides, his book, like Tucker's, focuses more on the analysis of political and legal doctrines than the beliefs of social groups or the population as a whole.

[40] Dallin, 'Where Have All the Flowers Gone?', 259.

books were published which contained general information about different groups and their brief history, and the names of the leaders and interviews with them, the programmes of the groups, and other documents.[41] Some of these reference books were translated from Russian; later other reference books were published abroad.[42]

Sometimes analytical introductions were included in such reference books. Such articles are discussed below. The reference materials provide valuable source material to a greater or lesser degree, but do not themselves contain serious analysis. Besides, these reference books differ greatly in their thoroughness and representativeness. Some of them deal mainly with certain regions, others do not differentiate large from insignificant groups. Thus, reference books can be an important source for this kind of study, but cannot, of course, provide a theoretical basis for it.

Descriptive literature

The initial works on the Russian 'democratic' movement were aimed at describing groups which were part of it, either in the whole of Russia or in one of its regions, often in chronological sequence. The first studies of this kind were mainly published outside Russia, but later Russian 'democratic' groups, especially in the provinces, found their own chroniclers.[43] The principal aim

---

[41] See *Spravochnik po 'neformal`nym' obshchestvennym organizatsiyam i presse*, Informatsionnyy byulleten` SMOT, 5 (Moscow, 1988) and 16 (Moscow, 1989); V. N. Berezovskiy and N. I. Krotov (eds.), *Neformalnaya Rossiya. O neformal`nykh politizirivannykh dvizheniyakh i gruppakh v RSFSR (opyt spravochnika)* (Moscow: Molodaya gvardiya, 1990); *Neformaly: kto oni? Kuda zovut?* (Moscow: Politicheskaya literatura, 1990); B. I. Koval` (ed.), *Rossiya segodnya. Politicheskiy portret, 1985–1990* (Moscow: Mezhdunarodnye otnosheniya, 1991); Rossiysko-amerikanskiy universitet, Institut massovykh politicheskikh dvizheniy, *Rossiya: partii, assotsiatsii, soyuzy, kluby. Spravochnik*, 10 vols. (Moscow: RAU-Press, 1991–2); V. Savel`ev (ed.), *Malaya entsiklopediya rossiyskoy politiki. Osnovnye partii i dvizheniya, zaregistrirovannye ministerstvom yustitsii* (Moscow: Verkhovnyy Sovet Rossiyskoy Federatsii, Parlamentskiy Tsentr, 1992); and Vladimir Pribylovskiy, *Slovar` oppositsii: novye politicheskie partii i organizatsii Rossii*, PostFactum Analytical Review, No. 4–5 (Moscow: PostFactum, 1991).

[42] See Vladimir Pribylovskii, *Dictionary of Political Parties and Organizations in Russia* (Moscow: PostFactum/Integral; Washington, DC: Center for Strategic and International Studies, 1992); M. A. Babkina, *New Parties and Movements in the Soviet Union* (Commack, NY: Nova Science Publishers, 1991); and Michael McFaul and Sergei Markov, *The Troubled Birth of Russian Democracy: Parties, Personalities, Programs* (Stanford, Calif.: Hoover Institution Press, 1993).

[43] See the articles by Geoffrey Hosking, Jonathan Aves, and Peter Duncan in G. Hosking, J. Aves, and P. Duncan (eds.), *The Road to Post-Communism: Independent Political Movements in the Soviet Union, 1985–1991* (London: Pinter, 1992); Andrey Shcherkin, 'Protsessy zarozhdeniya, razvitiya i stanovleniya politicheskikh partiy i massovykh obshchestvennykh dvizheniy v Pskovskoy oblasti v 1988–1994', unpubl. MS [Pskov, 1994]; Pavel Vinogradov, 'Pokhozhdeniya atomarnykh lichnostey na zakate', *Krasnoyarskiy komsomolets*, 6 and 8 Apr. 1993, p. 2.

of the authors was usually to bring immediately to the reader the formal features of a new social phenomenon. The majority of these authors relied upon the mass media for information, though some conducted interviews with the leaders of various groups.[44] The relevance of this literature is less in the analysis provided, which is scant, than the data included, which in some cases cannot be found elsewhere.

There were of course some general questions which the authors of such works attempted to answer. The most common and obvious of these is why the independent political groups in Russia did not evolve into 'proper' political parties which would have been able to achieve the support of a stable and significant part of the electorate, or at least to develop into united and stable movements such as those in the Baltic states. Answering this question, Geoffrey Hosking wrote: 'In most of the non-Russian republics Popular Fronts had already taken up the challenge . . . In Russia, however, no single movement had shown itself equal to the task, for the enemy could not be identified as a simple ethnic target: the oppressors and murderers of Russians had usually been Russians, which much complicated the emotional equation.'[45]

This argument obviously oversimplifies the situation since more or less stable and influential movements were formed, apart from the Baltic states, only in Moldavia, Armenia, Azerbaijan, and to a certain extent in Ukraine, which by no means constituted the majority of the non-Russian republics. The existence of a common ethnic enemy probably played a role, but it was not the only factor. In the republics of Central Asia, for example, united anti-regime movements did not form, although the Communist repressions could also have been interpreted in anti-Russian terms. Though Hosking rightly looks for the answer in the sphere of beliefs of group members, a single attitude toward a common enemy is hardly enough: the whole system of beliefs should be analysed.

Agreeing with Hosking's argument, Peter Duncan adds several other reasons for the failure to create a Popular Front as a national movement: the role of established cultural organizations, such as the Writers' Union, which in Russia allegedly were 'neutralised or in the conservative camp'; the hostility to democratization of much of the party-state apparatus; the fact that 'many reformers in Russia were in the CPSU (as in the non-Russian republics) and were unwilling to break with Gorbachev'; and 'the sheer vastness of Russia', which 'made it harder to hold a nation-wide movement together under adverse conditions'. According to Duncan, the main reasons for this included the widespread expectation of a split within the CPSU and the emergence of a democratic party on this basis; the general discrediting of

---

[44] For example, Geoffrey Hosking, 'The Beginnings of Independent Political Activity', in Hosking, Aves, and Duncan (eds.), *The Road to Post-Communism*, 1–28.

[45] Ibid. 18.

the idea of a 'party' among the population; and the absence of differences between the democratic parties in the eyes of the voters.[46] Some of these points are highly arguable or inaccurate. For example, most of the established cultural organizations in Russia, like the Unions of Journalists, Film-makers, and Theatre Workers of the USSR, supported democratic reforms and were by no means in the conservative camp, and even the Writers' Union of the USSR was split on the issue. Though their unions were formally of an all-union nature, since they were based in Moscow, their greatest influence was in the Russian Federation, which, unlike the other republics, did not have its own unions in these professions. Hostility to the reforms by the party-state apparatus and CPSU membership of many reformers obtained in other republics, including some of those where nationwide movements were formed. As for some of the other factors, such as the similarity of the 'democratic' parties' programmes, the unpopularity of the very idea of a 'party', and the expectation of the split in the CPSU, their relevance in turn needs to be explained as parts of a 'democratic' political subculture.

More analysis of new independent political groups in Russia can be found in Richard Sakwa's *Russian Politics and Society*. Sakwa, who defines the post-coup (post-August 1991) Russian party system as 'embryonic rather than full-blown multi-party', suggests that 'this was partially a reflection of the society in which the new parties were born'.[47] Among the nine factors that according to Sakwa influenced the evolution of new Russian parties, most of which appeared before 1991, were: (1) the similarities between their programmes, which appealed to no distinct or specific constituencies; (2) the dominance of individual leaders within the parties; (3) the hostility of the public to the idea of party politics; (4) the outflow of the most active and able people to the new administrative structures; (5) the absence of a recognizable social base in the new parties; and (6) the increasingly regional character of Russian politics.[48] The formulation of these factors, several of which are similar to some of Duncan's, is based on close observation of the activities of the new Russian political groups. However, Sakwa does not explain why the factors themselves emerged during the late Soviet period; for example, why the public was hostile to the idea of party politics, or why the most talented people preferred to work in the executive branch of the Russian government and thought that this type of activity was more important and prestigious than becoming involved in party work. In addition, Sakwa does not discuss precisely why the new parties were often 'one-man parties' and thus were associated more with the personality of the individual leader than any ideological programme. This can only

[46] Peter J. S. Duncan, 'The Rebirth of Politics in Russia', in Hosking, Aves, and Duncan, (eds.), *The Road to Post-Communism*, 108–9.
[47] Richard Sakwa, *Russian Politics and Society* (London: Routledge, 1993), 165.
[48] Ibid. 166–8.

be explained by analysing the attitudes of the members of these groups and parties toward authority, and toward the political process in Russia and their role in it. But Sakwa does not attempt this task.

Most of the early Western works on Russian 'democrats' (and some later ones) were characterized by the lack of systematic selection of sources. In most such studies there is not even an attempt to discuss the validity of sources, problems of representativeness, bias, and methodology in general. This often leads to one-sided interpretations. For example, all the interviews with the members of Soviet independent groups used in the article 'The Beginnings of Independent Political Activity' by Geoffrey Hosking were conducted in Moscow, but nine of the thirty-six references to articles by, or interviews with, members of Russian independent groups are to works by, or interviews with, Boris Kagarlitskiy, who represents only a very small and peculiar trend in the 'democratic' movement.[49] Kagarlitskiy's works are disproportionately cited in many English-language studies.[50] Ready availability may partly account for this: Kagarlitskiy was the first and until recently the only member of a new independent political group who managed to publish his writings abroad.

Another trait of this early Western literature was that it often failed to determine objectively the role that was played by particular parties or groups, sometimes taking their own declarations of goals, membership, and influence at face value. One such article is Richard Sakwa's 'Christian Democracy in Russia'.[51] In its descriptive part the article is a very full and valuable case study of the birth and development of Christian Democratic organizations in late Soviet Russia, which is followed by English translations of the main documents of the largest of them, the Russian Christian Democratic Movement (RCDM). But in the theoretical part it obviously exaggerates the role of the Movement, treating it as comparable, indeed almost equal, to Christian Democratic parties in Germany and some East European countries. In fact Christian Democrats did not play an important role in the Russian 'democratic' movement and disappeared soon after the publication of Sakwa's article. (Some of its leaders ended up in the Nationalist-Communist opposition.) Moreover, Sakwa's characterization of the leaders of the RCDM as belonging to the Russian Orthodox Christian tradition turned out to be wishful thinking. It is true that Christian ideas have played an important role in the history of Russian political thought in the twentieth

---

[49] Hosking, 'The Beginnings of Independent Political Activity', 24–8.

[50] See: Jonathan Aves, 'The Evolution of Independent Political Movements after 1988', in Hosking, Aves, and Duncan (eds.), *The Road to Post-Communism*; Peter Duncan, 'The Rebirth of Politics in Russia' and Graeme Gill, 'The Emergence of Competitive Politics', in Stephen White, Graeme Gill, and Darrell Slider (eds.), *The Politics of Transition: Shaping a Post-Soviet Future* (Cambridge: Cambridge University Press, 1993).

[51] Richard Sakwa, 'Christian Democracy in Russia', *Religion, State and Society*, 20:2 (1992), 135–200; abridged Russian translation: Richard Sakwa, 'Khristianskaya demokratiya v Rossii', *Sotsiologicheskie issledivaniya*, 4 (1993), 126–34 and 7 (1993), 122–31.

century, but the Church never supported openly political activities, especially in Westernized form, and a serious Christian Democratic party has never been formed in Russia, either before 1917 or after 1991.

Politically motivated literature

The influence of politics is particularly obvious in the Soviet analyses. This influence was usually manifested by authors who were either members of the groups they were discussing, or close to them. They can be seen to be attempting to influence the attitude of the authorities towards the groups described in their writings. In this way it is possible to explain the numerous quotations from Karl Marx and Vladimir Lenin in the first work of this type, 'On the Independent Movement of Public Initiatives' by Oleg Rumyantsev, the leader of the Perestroyka Club in Moscow, whose obvious aim was to explain the usefulness of the independent groups to the authorities.[52] The same tendency can be seen in the article 'The Informals: Who Are They?' by V. Berezovskiy and N. Krotov.[53] Independent groups were seen in such works as a force which advanced Gorbachev's *perestroyka*, which was understood as a process of developing 'socialist democracy'.[54] At the same time there were authors who argued, obviously in line with the official strategy, for Communist control over the new independent groups.[55]

However, these works already contained some interesting generalizations which this study will test. Rumyantsev, for example, was the first to point to 'a certain unity of the movement of public clubs . . . based on a similar value orientation'.[56] A. Shershnev developed a model of common social ideals of Soviet 'democrats'.[57] Several such works offered classifications of independent groups.[58]

---

[52] O. G. Rumyantsev, *O samodeyatel`nom dvizhenii obshchestvennykh initsiativ (neformal`nye ob`edineniya i ikh rol` v perestroyke obshchestvennoy zhizni v SSSR)* (Moscow: Academiya nauk SSSR, Institut economiki mirovoy sotsialisticheskoy sistemy, 1988).

[53] V. Berezovskiy and N. Krotov, ' "Neformaly"—kto oni?', in Berezovskiy and Krotov (eds.), *Neformal`naya Rossiya*.

[54] Rumyantsev, *O samodeyatel`nom dvizhenii obshchestvennykh initsiativ*, 45–6.

[55] See, for example, A. V. Gromov and O. S. Kuzin, *Neformaly: kto est` kto?* (Moscow: Mysl`, 1990).

[56] Rumyantsev, *O samodeyatel`nom dvizhenii obshchestvennykh initsiativ*, 8.

[57] As quoted in V. N. Berezovskiy, N. I. Krotov, and V. V. Chervyakov, 'Novye obshchestvenno-politicheskie organizatsii i dvizheniya RSFSR (opyt analiza i classifikatsii)', in *Rossiya: partii, assotsiatsii, soyuzy, kluby,* i/1, 10–11.

[58] See Rumyantsev, *O samodeyatel`nom dvizhenii obshchestvennykh initsiativ*; Berezovskiy and Krotov (ed.), ' "Neformaly"—kto oni?'; B. I. Koval`, 'Ot redaktora', in Koval` (ed.), *Rossiya segodnya*, 13–15; Berezovskiy, Krotov, and Chervyakov, 'Novye obshchestvenno-politicheskie organizatsii i dvizheniya RSFSR'; and McFaul and Markov, *The Troubled Birth of Russian Democracy*.

Most of these classifications include not only political, but also ecological, labour, student, and local self-governing groups. Some writers, like Koval`, use differences in political programmes for their classifications. In Russia this principle is quite misleading, as the official programme, to say nothing of a group's name, often does not reflect the real positions of the group. Evidence of this is the fact that Koval` puts such different groups as the Liberal Democratic Party of Vladimir Zhirinovskiy and three constitutional-democratic parties in one group.[59] Berezovskiy and Krotov use both programmes and organizational principles, which makes the whole classification inconsistent. For example, they put all 'fronts' and 'unions' together, and such different groups as Popular Fronts ('democratic') and United Working People's Fronts ('pro-Communist') in one group, but put 'Pamyat`-type movements' and 'groups close to Pamyat`' in two separate categories.[60]

Russian 'democrats' and general theories

At a later stage students of Russian 'democratic' groups turned to analysing them by applying general theories in political science. Sometimes this application led to a mere search for validation of a particular theory in Russian material. To achieve this aim only those sources and opinions were used which supported the pre-determined views of the researcher. Many social scientists have warned of the dangers of such an approach, which nevertheless is quite common, and not only in Soviet and Russian studies. As students of scientists' beliefs G. Nigel Gilbert and Michael Mulkay wrote in their important work: 'Most sociological analyses are dominated by the authorial voice of the sociologist. Participants are allowed to speak through the author's text only when they appear to endorse his story. Most sociological research reports are, in this sense, univocal. We believe that this form of presentation grossly misrepresents the participants' discourse.'[61]

It is, of course, true that every author begins with an implicit conceptual framework which, in any case, influences the selection of material. However, a researcher should at least be aware of this problem and consciously try to avoid it by using methods which are likely to minimize bias, and submit the results for criticism.

Despite these warnings, many studies of Russian 'democrats' simply applied to the USSR methods and theories which were derived from the practices of very different societies. Terry Cox, for example, tries to understand

---

[59] Koval`, 'Ot redaktora', 25.

[60] Berezovskiy and Krotov, ' "Neformaly"—kto oni?', 60–2.

[61] G. Nigel Gilbert and Michael Mulkay, *Opening Pandora's Box: A Sociological Analysis of Scientists' Discourse* (Cambridge: Cambridge University Press, 1984), 2.

the 'democrats' in terms of the theory of pressure groups. Cox's article merely records the emergence of new independent political groups, some of which he defines as pressure groups. He argues that the 'absence of any detailed research on the political influence of the new groups' makes it difficult 'to judge how great their political impact has been'. Despite this, he assumes that the influence of some of them was significant.[62] Cox offers two possible explanations of the role of the new groups. According to him their growth can be understood either as part of the growth of civil society based on pluralism of interests, or in the context of the deeper structure of political power. He finds shortcomings in both explanations and calls for further research.[63] Cox, however, completely sets aside the specific beliefs and subjective goals of the movement and his arguments are too general and abstract.

Several authors employed the concept of 'social movement' in their analysis of the new Russian 'democrats'. However, 'social movement' theory contains two very different approaches. One of them sees the development of new social movements in Russia as the result of the interaction of state and society and totally disregards the importance of the beliefs of their members, seeing them as fully conditioned by the institutions of these two sides and the correlation of forces between them. The other, on the contrary, is particularly interested in the role of what is called the 'ideology of the movement'.[64]

The first approach can be found in one of the first studies of Soviet 'informals', by Jim Butterfield and Marcia Weigle.[65] Only part of this relatively short article is relevant to this book, since it attempts to deal with new social groups throughout the Soviet Union. Butterfield and Weigle approach the process of unofficial group formation through the concept of state–group relations and construct five types of these relations for the USSR; of these only two are based on examples drawn from Russian 'democratic' groups (the Memorial Society and the Democratic Perestroyka Club). The typology itself can be disputed since every type is based on just one or two examples. But the main problem of Butterfield and Weigle's analysis is that, while they provide examples of the actions of unofficial groups and of the reactions of central government and local authorities, they do not show the reasons for these actions, since the motives of the sides are not discussed.

Another example of disregard for subjective motives and points of view is

----

[62] Terry Cox, 'Democratization and the Growth of Pressure Groups in Soviet and Post-Soviet Politics', in Jeremy J. Richardson (ed.), *Pressure Groups* (Oxford: Oxford University Press, 1993), 83.

[63] Ibid. 84–5.

[64] On the importance of the study of the ideology of 'political movements', see e.g. Anthony Obershall, *Social Movements: Ideologies, Interests, and Identities* (New Brunswick, NJ: Transaction, 1993).

[65] Jim Butterfield and Marcia Weigle, 'Unofficial Social Groups and Regime Response in the Soviet Union', in Judith B. Sedaitis and Jim Butterfield (eds.), *Perestroyka from Below: Social Movements in the Soviet Union* (Boulder, Colo.: Westview, 1991), 175–95.

Steven Fish's *Democracy from Scratch*.[66] It studies 'democratic' groups in Soviet Russia from 1985 to 1991. Fish employs the concept of 'political movement', and, like Butterfield and Weigle, sees their activities as a reflection of the opposition between state and society.

Fish begins with a detailed criticism of the methods of Sovietology. He argues that most of the dominant approaches in Soviet studies substituted the investigation of the real Soviet society and the real ideas of the Soviet people with an easier analysis of official Soviet theories and documents. In Fish's view, this led to the failure of Sovietologists to foresee the collapse of the Soviet Union. Such criticism, which is very easy *post factum* and is becoming more and more popular, is only partially true. Students of Soviet political culture, for example, distinguished from the very beginning between official and dominant political cultures and produced a number of studies of the latter, though not all of equal quality. In some of these studies, though perhaps not in the majority of them, the possibility of the collapse of the Soviet regime was discussed as one of the possible options.

Unlike other critics of traditional approaches to the analysis of the beliefs of the Soviet and Russian populations, Fish appears to be disillusioned with the study of the whole sphere of beliefs, since in his view it is totally conditioned by abstract processes which take place within the society. He writes: 'Just as ideology and belief systems will be deemphasized in treatment of the state, notions of popular political culture and psychology will play no part in explanations of the organization and behavior of societal actors.'[67] Instead Fish suggests his own scheme of Soviet social development, which is based on the idea of a confrontation between state and society. He defines 'state' as 'the party apparat, including the agencies of state security and the system of economic administration lying within the framework of the nomenklatura system' and 'society' as 'organizations, groups, and individuals standing outside state institutions'.[68] In the Soviet case, writes Fish, 'the central dynamic of the construction of a new political society lay in the struggle between emergent autonomous organizations and the institutions of state power'.[69]

From this point of view Fish looks at the reform process in the USSR and Russia. According to him, 'liberalization in associational rights did not engender the formation of "civil society" of the Western type. Rather, the persistence of structural barriers such as the system of dependency in the workplace and state control over property, including the means of production and communication, strongly influenced the development of the new independent political institutions and their relationship with the state.'[70] Summing up his approach, Fish concludes:

---

[66] M. Steven Fish, *Democracy from Scratch: Opposition and Regime in the New Russian Revolution* (Princeton, NJ: Princeton University Press, 1995).　　[67] Ibid. 27.
[68] Ibid. 25, 27.　　　　　　　　　[69] Ibid. 26.　　　　　　　　[70] Ibid.

A central argument put in this study is that the character of state power furnishes the key to understanding the independent political society that emerged in Russia during the Gorbachev period. It has been argued that the conditions under which elections were held, state repression and control of popular political participation, and the fusion of polity and economy—all of which were shaped by *vlast`*—determined the scope of popular mobilization, the content of social movement demands and the organizational forms through which they were expressed, and the behavior and strategies of independent political associations. The causal argument has accorded primacy to the structure and character of state power rather than the beliefs, ideas, and policy orientations of particular power holders; domination, resistance, and struggle rather than modernization and development; fortuitous breakthroughs and 'path-dependence' rather than evolution; and political opportunity structures and political entrepreneurship rather than ideology and culture.[71]

This approach totally excludes the element of conscious action and the role of beliefs from the work of a social mechanism. But a question can be asked: even if the role of the state in the USSR was really so great, how was its influence over the lives of people being realized practically? How in practice did the 'structural barriers' menioned by Fish—the system of dependency in the workplace, state control over property, including the means of production and communication, methods of conducting elections—shape the new society, including new independent political groups? State, society, and all political groups consist of people, and in that at least they do not differ. State and society do not communicate directly, as two transcendental entities: it is people who communicate with each other. A closer look at the process of interaction between state and individual shows that the individual is not tempered by the strokes of the state like metal by the strokes of a hammer. The 'strokes', for example, of official state ideology shape the individual from childhood and are perceived in the form of language, broadly understood as the language of signs, the language of culture. Since official ideology is not the only source of individuals' beliefs, this is just one part of the process of socialization. Events or influences do not make individuals act automatically, like a tool, or instinctively, like an animal (save perhaps in a very limited range of situations), but affect their belief systems, within the framework of which they make decisions. To exclude beliefs from the process of interaction between state and society, between state and individual, is to construct a pure abstraction, an abstract interaction between the fetish of the state and the fetish of society, with no people in them, since there are no people without beliefs. This is exactly what is done by Fish, whose 'new' approach is in no sense better than all of the old ones, which he criticizes so vigorously, since in his book there is also no place for real people with their real thoughts and wishes, but only for abstract models.

---

[71] Fish, *Democracy from Scratch*, 200.

The beliefs of those individuals, whom Fish would divide into two distinct categories, would on closer study show that some people in 'state' positions and some members of the most 'anti-state' groups in fact held similar views and moved in the same direction, regardless of their position. For example, they could have been 'friends of reform' (like Oleg Rumyantsev, a junior researcher at the Academy of Sciences Socialist System Institute and an organizer of a number of 'democratic' groups and parties, and Oleg Bogomolov, an academician, director of the same institute and a consultant to the CPSU Central Committee), or their 'enemies' (like the very 'anti-state' Nina Andreeva and one of the 'state' leaders, Yegor Ligachev). Thus, the struggle was not between abstract 'state' and abstract 'society', but between real people and, of course, between social groups, which consisted of these people, with their ideas, motives, and wishes. Moreover, because of the total 'statization' of the USSR it is very difficult to draw a line between the state and society since, strictly speaking, everybody, with small exceptions (such as tramps, hippies, and underground artists), in one way or another belonged to the state system. Of course, the position of individuals in the state system influences their views, but this influence is far from being direct, and varies greatly, making it impossible to guess where a person stands just from knowing his or her official status. Such an approach unavoidably leads to mistakes.

Fish makes such errors when he analyses the 'democratic' movement in Russia and obviously tries to fit the beliefs of its members into his scheme. One can only wonder how Fish, who collected materials not only in Moscow but in four regions of Russia and conducted sixty interviews with various 'democrats', failed to observe at least some of the views which did not fit his analysis. According to Fish, a 'democrat' should stand for 'liberalism' or 'social democracy' as 'these terms are commonly understood in the West'.[72] There is no precise explanation in Fish's book of what this understanding is, but in various parts the author suggests that 'democracy' is connected with 'elections', 'compromise', 'parties', to which most of the population is sympathetic, or even which most of the people join. However, it seems that for Fish it is self-evident what democracy is, since he sees it as a 'normal', 'progressive' state of the majority of nations, from which Russia moved away. The language and notions of the contemporary Western (and, more precisely, US) political system he considers to be 'normal', and their absence in, for example, Soviet Russia is naturally abnormal. The situation in Soviet Russia, in Fish's view, was characterized by a 'near total loss . . . of "normal" forms of political communication, and the disappearance from political life of philosophical and organizational categories taken for granted in much of the world—social democracy, trade unionism, liberalism, nationalism, Christian democracy, and so on'.[73]

---

[72] Ibid. 28.   [73] Ibid. 86.

Such an understanding of the world shows the absolutization by the author of the type of culture in which he was educated and with which he is familiar, and this makes his views obviously biased. In fact in much of the world today (regardless of how one counts: by population or territory)—China, India, most of Africa—the notions mentioned by Fish are alien to at least the same extent as in Russia. Besides, to speak of widespread social or Christian democracy, for example, in the USA, or to say that most American citizens necessarily support a political party, is a clear exaggeration.

Even if one accepts that there is an ideal 'Western' pattern of a political system, Fish's attempt to impute a programme of striving for a 'genuine transition' to democracy[74] to the Russian 'democratic' movement inevitably leads him to ungrounded generalizations. By claiming that all Russian 'democrats' supported 'the democratization of society'[75] or a 'market economy',[76] the author is ascribing to Russian 'democrats' a level of unity in understanding their aims (unity among themselves and with an abstract 'Western' democracy) which in fact was not characteristic of them. As for 'democracy', the author does not notice that the conceptions of it held by Russian 'democrats' were very different from those 'common in the West'. There were also significant differences in conceptions of 'democracy' between such parts of the movement, as, for example, the Anarchists, who were a very active part of the movement in its early stages and whom Fish does not mention at all, and the members of the Democratic Party of Russia. As for a market economy, a significant part of the movement (including left Socialists and Anarchists) rejected it, while some others (like Social Democrats) stood for a 'soft' transition very different from what was later chosen by Yegor Gaydar. Fish presents all 'democratic' groups as characterized by a very, or even excessively, democratic organizational structure, but the examples he cites are not convincing, such as the Moscow Voters' Union, which in practice was ruled by a narrow circle. In fact his description of meetings of Russian 'democrats' as hyperdemocratic and almost chaotic hardly shows them to be similar to party meetings in established democracies. All these misjudgements are caused by neglecting the inner logic of the beliefs of 'democrats', a neglect predetermined by Fish's theoretical position.

There is another methodological reason behind the shortcomings of Fish's analysis of the 'democratic' movement in Soviet Russia. His own perceptions of the social system and the essence of political process in the USSR are that: there is a fundamental dichotomy between society and the all-absorbing state; the state exerts an absolute influence on all social processes, on the 'face' of the opposition, and even on personality; the abstract 'Western world' is the centre of the normal development of civilization; it is in Russia's natural interests to

---

[74] Fish, *Democracy from Scratch*, 77.   [75] Ibid. 94.
[76] Ibid. 215.

join this civilization; and finally, the Russian 'democratic' movement is the main vehicle for gaining access to this civilization. Fish's sympathy towards Russian 'democrats' is very clear. His book displays many patterns of the common 'Western' understanding of democracy, especially its 'occido-centrism', which also, moreover, echoes the rhetoric of Russian 'democrats'.

Fish himself would probably not agree with such a conclusion. He bases his 'state–society' scheme on various little-known studies of 'Communist' societies published in the West. However, a closer look at those studies positively shows that the majority, if not all, of their authors are former citizens of those 'Communist' countries. This is absolutely natural, since the beliefs of Russian (and Eastern European) 'democrats' did not emerge 'from scratch'. For a long time these beliefs, which are the main subject of this book, had been spreading in opposition-minded circles and were exported to the West by those who emigrated to Western Europe and the USA and published their works there. It is not by chance that Fish, influenced by the ideas of Russian 'democrats', chose this approach to Soviet society among all the other available approaches in Western studies of the Soviet Union and Eastern Europe.

Fish's well-grounded criticism of some Western political scientists' disregard of beliefs and ideas of common people in the USSR, and of their attempts to attribute to these common people the stereotypes of official ideology, could have brought him to different conclusions by leading him to acknowledge the necessity of studying the real content of the beliefs which constituted a 'democratic' political subculture, without postulating their congruence with the understanding of democracy in Western democratic theory.

Another example of a superficial approach to 'democratic' beliefs is Graeme Gill's chapter in the book by Stephen White, Graeme Gill, and Darrell Slider, *The Politics of Transition*. Analysing Russian 'democratic' programmes from the point of view not of their internal logic, but of their correspondence to 'real democracy', Gill concludes that few 'democratic' parties 'developed the sort of highly-detailed specific legislative programmes that would provide a real guide to their intentions were they to gain control of government' and that 'ideological and policy differences have shaded into one another, and that the basis of partisan affiliation has often been more personalistic than ideological'.[77] Though the role of personalities in partisan affiliation in Russia, as in many countries, was important, Gill overlooks beliefs different from those to which he is accustomed, and on this basis rejects the importance of beliefs in general.

Studies of the beliefs of Russian 'democrats'

The existing literature on the beliefs of members of Russian 'democratic' groups can be divided into three main types. The first sees these beliefs as

---

[77] Gill, 'The Emergence of Competitive Politics', 159.

totally democratic, that is to say as similar to those usually found in Western democratic theories and political groups. The authors belonging to this group see the main source of these beliefs in Western democratic theory and Western political literature and discourse. The authors of the second group, on the contrary, see the beliefs of Russian 'democrats' as autocratic, or even totalitarian, being different from the Soviet ideology only in form, but not in essence; in words, but not in meaning. They see them as the reverse of Soviet ideology and therefore its continuation in a different form. The third group of authors, while finding these 'democratic' beliefs derived to a considerable extent from official Soviet ideology, see them as gradually deviating from that ideology under the influence of outside sources and the struggle against the regime. They see the 'democratic' belief system as being in a process of change and as a mixture of elements which came from a variety of sources.

Beliefs of Russian 'democrats' as democratic

Several authors who have used different theoretical approaches acknowledge the importance of the study of the beliefs of Russian 'democrats' as an independent phenomenon and devote their works or parts of them to such a study. A more superficial approach to such a study manifests itself in taking 'democratic' declarations for granted and accepting their democratic character, seeing no difference between the beliefs of Russian 'democrats' and those approved of in Western democratic theory. The limitations of this approach have already been discussed with reference to Fish's book. In *The Rise of Russia and the Fall of the Soviet Union* John Dunlop has similarly postulated the democratic character of Russian 'democrats' and 'informals'. Dunlop argues that 'the society that *neformaly* were demanding was unmistakably a Western-style pluralist one' and that emerging 'democrats' 'wanted the USSR to become a Western-style democracy'. Describing the Inter-regional Group of Deputies, Dunlop argues that it explicitly advocated 'Western-style multi-party democracy and market economy'.[78]

In a study by Michael McFaul and Sergey Markov the political process in the USSR was seen in the same way as a struggle between 'democrats' and 'conservatives', whose groups they sometimes also label 'right-wing' or 'reactionary' without explaining what is meant by these terms in the Russian political context.[79] Such simplistic schemes were easily accepted by Russian authors when it was no longer necessary to express one's loyalty to Communist theory.

---

[78] John B. Dunlop, *The Rise and the Fall of the Soviet Empire* (Princeton, NJ: Princeton University Press, 1993), 75, 77, 83.

[79] McFaul and Markov, *The Troubled Birth of Russian Democracy*.

Soviet roots of 'democratic' beliefs

Unlike Dunlop, Michael Urban and John McClure, in a study of the Inter-regional Group, attempt to 'abstract from individuals, organisations, party programmes and so on in order to focus on something a bit "deeper" and by that measure, more important to the party formation in the longer term'. Following Frederic Jameson they call this deeper level 'the unconscious value or system of representation which orders social life'. To analyse this 'non-empirically present layer of political reality' the authors study the political speeches of six leading members of the Inter-regional Group at the USSR Congress of People's Deputies. Urban and McClure find important patterns in the approaches of 'democrats', observing that on a wide range of issues their discourse 'reverses the set of expectations that stand behind the authority of a government claiming to promote *perestroyka*'. However, the authors themselves do not address the question of the sources of these patterns or their relation to Western 'democratic' theory. The representativeness of the study can also be questioned since only a very limited group of personalities and discourse is studied.[80]

Judith Devlin in *The Rise of the Russian Democrats* attempts 'to analyse the democratic movement, its strengths, weaknesses and ultimate impact'. According to Devlin, her book is concerned 'with the emergence of new democratically-inclined political formations and their contribution to the political culture of contemporary Russia'.[81] Unlike those who postulate a common understanding of democracy by Russian 'democrats' and 'normal' Western theorists, Devlin argues that the democratic coalition was more complex. For Devlin, 'its intellectual origins lay in the anti-Stalinism and reform socialism of the Thaw rather than in classical liberal theory of the eighteenth and nineteenth centuries' and the democrats 'objected less to the socialism the regime proclaimed than to the specific form of rule Soviet socialism had engendered'.[82] These conclusions are very important, since for the first time in the Western literature Devlin points to the need to look for the roots of Russian 'democratic' ideas not in Western liberal theories but in the dominant Soviet political culture and oppositional subcultures. However, to term the Russian 'democratic' social ideal 'socialist', as Devlin does, may be just as misleading as calling it liberal or democratic, since it projects onto it another theoretical concept prior to the analysis of the ideas themselves. This book concentrates on the analysis of the content of the ideas and only then compares it to different theoretical concepts.

---

[80] Michael E. Urban and John McClure, 'Discourse, Ideology and Party Formation on the Democratic Left in the USSR', in Michael E. Urban (ed.), *Ideology and System Change in the USSR and East Europe* (New York: St. Martin's Press, 1992), 93, 100.

[81] Judith Devlin, *The Rise of the Russian Democrats: The Causes and Consequences of the Elite Revolution* (Aldershot: Edward Elgar, 1995), 9.

[82] Ibid. 255, 227.

Another shortcoming of Devlin's analysis is that unlike Fish, who saw all 'democrats' united by Western democratic ideas, she goes to an opposite extreme. While rightly noting that the democratic movement was not united by liberal political ideals and theories, she argues that it was not united by any ideals at all but rather 'was a coalition of divergent interest groups and outlooks, welded together by opposition to the remnants of Stalinism'.[83] This conclusion is an exaggeration. The fact that the Russian 'democratic' movement was not united by liberalism, socialism, or any other theoretical 'ism' does not mean that it was not united by any belief system at all. In fact a dominant belief system of a political group, especially at times of great social changes, is very often a mixture of different influences and not just derived from one current theoretical concept.[84]

In her study Devlin also exaggerates the elitism of the Russian 'democratic' movement, restricting it largely to Moscow, Leningrad, and several other big cities, and only to the intelligentsia. The reason for this could be that most of the groups she studied, most of her sources and interviewees, came from these areas and social groups. In this respect Fish's book has an obvious advantage. Fish's analysis of provincial 'democratic' groups, which will be supported by the conclusions of this study, shows that at their peak (1990–1) such groups were working in almost every district centre, and not only intellectuals but also industrial workers and sometimes new private farmers played active roles. It was elitism and the lack of a united positive agenda, according to Devlin, that led to the weakness of the 'democratic' movement, which split after its victory in August 1991, while only the pragmatic part of the coalition, with no really democratic ideals, remained in power.

Devlin's view is not shared by Sergey Cheshko, who in his study of what he calls the 'ideology' of Russian 'democrats' argues that it was the victory of this very ideology and the coming to power of the leading 'democrats' which led to a new totalitarianism in Russia, since their ideology in fact was 'a kind of radical revolutionary romanticism'.[85] Pointing out that the concept of democracy itself has changed over time, Cheshko argues that in the second half of the twentieth century democracy is understood as 'a particular type of political organization of society, which is based on the legislative and controlling activities of representative organs that are formed according to the principle of individual

---

[83] Devlin, *The Rise of the Russian Democrats*, 255.

[84] See Ju. M. Lotman and B. A. Uspenskij, 'Echoes of the Notion of "Moscow as the Third Rome" in Peter the Great's Ideology', in Ju. M. Lotman and B. A. Uspenskij, *The Semiotics of Russian Culture*, ed. A. Shukman (Ann Arbor, Mich.: Michigan Slavic Publications, 1984: 1st publ. 1982 in Russian), 53; V. I. Semenovskiy, *Politicheskie i obshchestvennye idei dekabristov* (St Petersburg: Tipogrphiya Pervoy spt. trudovoy arteli, 1909); V. Bogucharskiy, *Aktivnoe narodnichestvo semidesyatykh godov* (Moscow: Izdatel`stvo M. i S. Sabashnikovykh, 1912).

[85] S. V. Cheshko, *Ideologiya raspada* (Moscow: Koordinatsionno-metodologicheskiy tsentr prikladnoy etnografii Instituta etnologii i antropologii RAN, 1993), 89.

civic rights of the members of the society'.[86] According to Cheshko, this organization is based on four main principles: (1) the supremacy of law over the will of any bureaucrat or decisions of the executive; (2) decisions by the executive are secondary relative to decisions of representative organs and are accountable to them; (3) the competences of legislative, executive, and judicial powers are separated; (4) a complex system of balances works in order to prevent the excessive strengthening of any structures of power.[87]

Comparing this concept with the ideal of Russian 'democrats', Cheshko argues that neither the political, nor the economic, nor the social components of the latter show any features of 'genuine democracy' and that fundamental principles of democracy are absolutely alien to them.[88] According to Cheshko, 'by democracy they understand not so much a corresponding political system as the implementation of a certain social ideal. But it is quite difficult to express this ideal in any specific socio-political categories: it is often wrapped in highly abstract, intangible forms and resembles an equally abstract aim to that of the construction of Communist society, which constituted the core of the ideology of the CPSU'.[89] Cheshko concludes that 'our democracy appeared to be a movement of revolutionary radicalism and its ideas were incidentally much closer to Bolshevism than to those of the orthodox *nomenklatura* with its conservative, protective ideology' and that the essence of the political programme of the 'democrats' 'is mainly a change of ideological symbols of totalitarianism, but not the elimination of it as such', not a destruction of the Communist totalitarian system, but a mere substitution of another totalitarianism.[90] According to Cheshko, several main features of the ideology of Russian 'democrats' support this conclusion. First, their 'model of "democracy" is the power of a political elite headed by a "popularly elected" dictator, which thrusts its own doctrine of "progressive reforms" on society. The idea of progress is placed higher than those political and legal institutions which hinder its implementation. On this basis representative organs of power and constitutional norms, for example, are declared undemocratic.'[91]

Among other indications of the alleged radicalism and totalitarianism of 'democratic' ideology, Cheshko identifies an excessive enthusiasm for a particular social doctrine and a desire for its immediate implementation in a pure form, by breaking any obstacle which hinders this process, such as traditions, inertia of consciousness, and political rivals; political intolerance of rival ideas and personalities, which manifested itself in plans to ban the Communist party and to organize a new 'Nuremberg trial' of Communists; and an understanding of democratic procedures as a means of attaining ideological goals, but not as a genuine polity.

---

[86] Ibid. 71.   [87] Ibid. 72.   [88] Ibid. 89.
[89] Ibid. 74.   [90] Ibid. 80, 81, 89.   [91] Ibid. 73.

In his book Cheshko develops several important ideas. Like Devlin, he looks for the origins of the beliefs of the Russian 'democrats' in contemporary Soviet ideology and political culture, and not in Western theories of democracy, and he maintains that these beliefs are basically similar not to democratic socialist opposition to Stalinist totalitarianism, but to this totalitarianism itself. While such similarities surely existed, and Cheshko rightly points to official ideology as the main source of 'democratic' beliefs, his claim that these beliefs remained basically totalitarian and are structurally identical to classical Bolshevism is excessive. In his emotive analysis Cheshko obviously overlooks the fact that the emergence of a 'democratic' political subculture changed not only the symbols of official ideology, but also many of its structural components, while retaining a number of others. Besides, unlike Devlin, who saw no common positive ideal which united Russian 'democrats', Cheshko goes to another extreme and speaks of this ideal as a commonly known set of ideas and values, shared by all, and overlooks the divisions between different trends of 'democratic' thought.

The 'democratic' belief system as a mixture of different influences

Soltan Dzarasov also finds the roots of the belief system of Russian 'democrats' in Soviet 'totalitarianism'. However, he sees it not just as a new form of totalitarian ideology, but as a mixture of Russian traditionalism—which in his view was responsible for Russian 'totalitarianism'—and Western liberalism of the first half of the nineteenth century—which was the only form of liberalism 'democrats' were aware of. This mixture led to the creation of a peculiar ideology of the Russian 'democratic' movement which Dzarasov calls Russian Anarcho-liberalism. According to Dzarasov this mixture of different ideological trends resulted in such logical inconsistencies as a belief in the necessity of a 'socially oriented market economy' simultaneous with the rejection of the role of the state in the economy. Dzarasov argues that the idea of the negation of the state, one of the central ideas of reformers, was formed 'under the shocking influence of our totalitarianism'.[92]

In Dzarasov's view, the beliefs of Russian 'democrats' about the methods of transition to democracy are also contradictory:

They are reduced mainly to the declaration of two of its indisputably important pillars: human rights and separation of powers. But this is done without transferring the centre of gravity to the real conditions of their implementation. Freedom is seen more as a rejection of the regulative functions of the state than as their democratization. This understanding must be seen as the reverse (the opposite extreme) of our *étatiste* consciousness.[93]

---

[92] S. S. Dzarasov, *Rossiyskiy put`: liberalizm ili sotsial-demokratism* (Moscow: Rossiyskiy gosudarstvennyy gumanitarnyy universitet, 1994), 114.   [93] Ibid. 113–14.

According to Dzarasov, many developments in Russian politics after the 'democrats' came to power in Russia, especially the policy of Yel'tsin's leadership aimed at the dissolution of the USSR, can be explained by these anti-state sentiments. Like Cheshko, Dzarasov points to differences between the contemporary Western understanding of democracy and the beliefs of Russian 'democrats'. But while Cheshko speaks of a direct transfer of 'totalitarian' beliefs into 'democratic' ideology under different names, Dzarasov finds a second pattern of continuity between the two: the rejection of a 'totalitarian' norm leads to an adoption of a radically opposite belief, which is still not necessarily liberal or democratic in a theoretical sense. While from the point of view of Russian 'democrats' everything radically opposite to the existing Soviet order was inherently democratic, in fact it was not always so.

In his unpublished article 'Opposition and Totalitarianism in the USSR' Il'ya Kudryavtsev takes a similar view of the relationship between what he calls 'totalitarian society' and the anti-totalitarian opposition. In his opinion 'the opposition built some of its structural features on the basis of the totalitarian structure' but these features got mixed in with others, borrowed from the 'pluralist political structure' which was coming to take its place.[94] Thus, according to Kudryavtsev, 'Both on the level of organizational structure and of programme ideology, the totalitarian system of Soviet socialism in the unity of its manifestations formed the framework and foundation of the opposition ("democratic") movement in the USSR, establishing its unity and architecture.'[95]

Like Cheshko and Dzarasov, Kudryavtsev posits that the influence of 'totalitarian' ideology on oppositional beliefs manifested itself in the latter's acceptance of the former in reverse form. The result was that the opposition became a 'mirror image' of the totalitarian system. Kudryavtsev writes that 'the opposition became a peculiar "democratic antipode" of the totalitarian system, but not at all independent from that system, an organic element of a new democratic system. The emergence of the opposition marked an entrance to a new political space. But the opposition itself remained set into a post-totalitarian structure.'[96]

In Kudryavtsev's view, this was predetermined by the opposition maintaining the 'totalitarian' political culture. As a result the real political culture of the opposition was characterized by the coexistence of a desire to destroy the specific totalitarian system on the macrolevel and the preservation and reproduction of totalitarian relations in the newly created structures on the level of cultural and traditional patterns of behaviour. Kudryavtsev stresses that a study of this real political culture of the opposition is important since

---

[94] I. Kudryavtsev, 'Oppositsiya i totalitarizm v SSSR', unpubl. MS [Moscow, 1992], courtesy of Mary McAuley, 24.   [95] Ibid. 34.
[96] Ibid. 37.

this culture contains, in an implicit form, the traits of the structure which is being built to replace totalitarianism.[97]

According to Kudryavtsev, the dual character of oppositional political culture resulted in changes in society after its unexpected coming to power. As he put it:

The political blitzkrieg of the opposition did not change the majority of relations within the society (in particular, it hardly influenced economic relations), but it brought in a multiplicity of political subjects, political pluralism, and competition (often in uncivilized forms which are alien to democratic Western political culture). However, it was with this blitzkrieg that a new area of mass public politics, structures of *political society*, was formed in the USSR and that at least some lines of transmission of the activities of society to the actions of power structures began to appear.[98]

Kudryavtsev's suggestion about the total dependency of the political culture of the opposition on totalitarianism leads him to the conclusion that when the political culture of totalitarianism disappears, so too will that of the opposition. But his own analysis of the influence of 'democratic' thinking on the policies of 'democratic' authorities after the collapse of the USSR contradicts this prediction. Another shortcoming of Kudryavtsev's analysis is his unwillingness to see any substance in democratic beliefs other than their anti-totalitarianism. According to Kudryavtsev, a 'democrat' could be anybody who rejected the existing Soviet system. It is true that the term 'democrat' had a meaning broader than such terms as 'liberal', 'social democrat', 'anarchist', etc., and included all of them, but there existed many groups which were simultaneously anti-system and anti-'democratic'. Therefore a narrower, more precise definition of 'democracy' in the Russian context should be developed.

Sergey Mitrokhin suggests a way of understanding the process of change in 'democratic' belief systems. His analysis is based on the idea of a determinative role for value orientations in politics. According to Mitrokhin, value orientations form a system of coordinates within which political action gains institutional significance and positiveness. These coordinates are themselves formed by specific individuals or social groups only to a very limited extent, being created instead over many years in a process of deeper historical changes alongside the evolution of religion, ethics, and metaphysics. Specific dominant combinations of value orientations Mitrokhin calls value paradigms, a concept very close to that of the concept of value or belief system more common in political science. There are two levels of values in a value paradigm: deeper absolute values and superficial subordinate values with behavioural norms. Since all components of a value paradigm are interrelated and form a hierarchical structure, behind the norms there is a general or

---

[97] Kudryavtsev, 'Oppositsiya i totalitarizm v SSSR', 46–7.   [98] Ibid. 58.

metanorm which regulates individual interaction with the level of absolute values and which determines the system of concrete norms, methods, and means of achieving these ideal constructions. Mitrokhin writes: 'in studying a value paradigm one should not, as is usually done, limit the examination to the contents and correlations of values as such; it is necessary to understand *how* these values come to conform to reality in accordance with the general norm of the given paradigm.'[99]

Mitrokhin terms this an 'axiological project' and describes its main function as determining and prescribing to individuals the norms and specific actions and behaviour which they should see as means of achieving their absolute values. From this point of view, according to Mitrokhin, the structure of an axiological paradigm consists of the level of values and the level of the means of their realization. Mitrokhin suggests two historical types of axiological paradigms: traditional, based on religious morality, which later, after the inclusion of the idea of freedom of the will, evolved into an autonomous paradigm; and instrumental, which came as a result of unprecedented concretization and operationalization of the level of means and found its classical manifestation in Marxism.

In Mitrokhin's scheme Soviet consciousness is an instrumental paradigm in its purest form. It is characterized by: (1) collectivism, which operates as a universal regulator of human behaviour; (2) the presence in the consciousness of a Soviet individual of deep 'proletariat' ('working class') values, and less distinct values for the 'working people' and the 'Soviet people'; (3) the idea of social justice, which obliterated previous values of economic independence and private property; (4) a high position for the state in the hierarchy of values; (5) the idea of the Demiurge, or leader, which manifested itself in either individual or collective personalities such as Lenin, Stalin, Marx–Engels, and the Communist Party. For Mitrokhin, all these components of the Soviet instrumental axiological paradigm existed, 'on the one hand, as real means of implementation of absolute good, and on the other, as ideal-value formations in people's consciousness'.[100] As real instruments they had a tendency to unlimited intensification and absolutization, since they were meant to serve absolute aims. The Soviet reality showed clear examples of this tendency: total collectivism, the unlimited arbitrariness of the state, the unlimited cult of the leader, absurd extolment of the Soviet working people as opposed to ludicrous denunciation of imperialism, boundless ideologization and propaganda. However, the very popularity of the instrumental paradigm was due to the fact that it promoted the realization of traditional-autonomous

[99] S. S. Mitrokhin, 'Aksiologicheskie korni obshchestvennykh dvizheniy v SSSR', in A. N. Alekseev, E. A. Zdravomyslova and V. V. Kostyushev (eds.), *Sotsiologiya obshchestvennykh dvizheniy: kontseptual'nye modeli issledovaniya 1989–1990* (Moscow: Institut sotsiologii RAN, 1992), 73.   [100] Ibid. 91.

values. This meant that its supremacy did not totally eliminate earlier values and that they remained in some 'oases', mainly in the sphere of personal relations. This coexistence of opposite values created tensions which could lead to a crisis in the instrumental paradigm, especially as even the fullest use of its means does not bring its own ideal aim any closer.[101]

In Mitrokhin's view, new political movements in the Soviet Union were manifestations of these processes. He divides them into particularist movements with limited economic and political objectives, and universal movements which aim to change (or preserve) the existing social system as a whole and set out an alternative to it (and which therefore are more dependent on the upper levels of value hierarchy). According to this classification the Russian 'democratic' movement can be called universal.

Mitrokhin argues that the rejection of the whole system of instrumental values cannot happen at once. At the first stage, traditional evaluation evolves and comes to define the level of means of the instrumental axiological project as evil. This, however, does not mean complete elimination of the instrumental project from the consciousness of 'the enlightened':

Consciousness as a rule cannot reconsider its axiological basis 'at one stroke'. A partial limitation of the level of means, which it dares to undertake, does not go further than discrediting a single element of this level: one of the hypostases of the Demiurge (the person of Stalin). In other words a relatively easy re-accentuation of the instrumental axiological project occurs, but not its total re-evaluation. Nevertheless, this re-accentuation is a first step toward destruction of the whole instrumental paradigm, since it draws it into an incorrigible contradiction by attempting to limit what in its purport resists any limitation.[102]

Mitrokhin calls this stage 'first-order destructive re-accentuation' and finds its manifestation in the ideology of 'genuine Marxism-Leninism', which was 'perverted' by Stalin, and its historical realization in the reforms of Khrushchev's thaw.

'Second-order destructive re-accentuation', according to Mitrokhin, is characterized by a more intensive revision of instrumental values and a more mature stage of the reanimation of autonomous values: the character of the Demiurge is reconsidered, to the point of discrediting the personality of Lenin and the Communist party; the concepts of the ruling class and of the social justice of the universality of state power are rejected or significantly rethought. At the same time second-order destructive re-accentuation is characterized by a broad expansion of autonomous values, such as 'personal inviolability' and 'human rights'. This makes the world-view, which still retains its instrumental basis, extremely mixed and eclectic. However, Mitrokhin points out, ideologies of different movements which

---

[101] Mitrokhin, *Sotsiologiya obshchestvennykh dvizheniy*, 92–3.
[102] Ibid. 94.

belong to this stage, and range from 'genuine Marxism' to anarchism, can be recognized by their adherence to the idea of 'genuine socialism' purged of any distortions. Historically this stage manifested itself in the ideology of *perestroyka*.[103]

According to Mitrokhin the second stage is the last in the re-accentuation of the instrumental paradigm. The next stage is its total re-evaluation. The second stage was manifested historically in the dissident movement of the Brezhnev period and the liberal democratic ideology of the *perestroyka* era. However, this leap to the second stage could sometimes be deceptive:

> The supremacy throughout many decades of the instrumental axiological paradigm in Soviet consciousness gave birth to reflexes, habits, and stereotypes in Soviet man, which are not easy to overcome in one leap. Some of these rudiments of the instrumental axiological paradigm move to the new system of coordinates with the 'jumper'. As a result we sometimes can witness a situation in which a consistent autonomous (liberal) system of values becomes a pretext for a partial reanimation of the instrumental axiological paradigm with its revolutionary means. This is the source of *radicalism* in the contemporary democratic movement.[104]

Mitrokhin also perceives the source of the liberal populism of the Democratic Party of Russia and the social populism of the New Socialists, as well as the neo-Bolshevism and national populism of some anti-reform groups, in the continuing influence of the core-value orientations which Soviet consciousness has inherited from the instrumental paradigm. According to Mitrokhin, the strongest influence is the discriminatory complex with its pathos of social justice, which manifested itself in opposition movements as the emergence of new subjects for condemnation: 'the party apparatus', 'the Mafia', 'the CPSU', etc. Contemporary populism also included the Demiurge stereotype and the spirit of collectivism. In Mitrokhin's view,

> Instrumental relics of Soviet consciousness, which give birth to the element of populism, are irrational and cannot give birth to any ideology. Only a clearly articulated ideology, brought from outside, can 'pull' an individual out from this element. At first it inculcates its separate tenets. Later a full structuralization of value consciousness and the transfer of an individual from the populist camp into one of ideologically 'stable' detachments, i.e. the continuation and deepening of the value split in Soviet society, is possible.[105]

Mitrokhin's scheme, while too general and highly disputable in its global historical aspects, becomes very useful for analysis of the correlation between and continuity in specific contemporary Soviet belief systems. Like Devlin and Cheshko, Mitrokhin points to official Soviet ideology as the source of the contemporary 'democratic' subculture, but unlike Cheshko, he does not understand the latter as a mere revival of the former in different

---

[103] Ibid. 95.   [104] Ibid. 96.   [105] Ibid. 99.

symbolic forms, arguing instead for elements of both continuity and change. It is quite natural that official ideology, which was the main basis for the theoretical beliefs of most educated people in the USSR, cannot disappear at once and leaves a deep imprint on any subsequent belief systems. It is also natural that the rejection of this ideology is a process which starts from the abolition of its more obvious and superficial levels; underneath formally very anti-Soviet symbols and slogans, belief structures which were characteristic of Soviet ideology can be found. It is important that Mitrokhin identifies two major sources of this rejection: unofficial beliefs that survived under Communism and outside influences. It is not, however, obvious that this process of rejection must necessarily proceed to its logical end and that all belief systems of the former Soviet Union will at one stage become either 'autonomous' or instrumental. In fact there may not be such a logical end at all, and postulating the existence of it, based on a simplistic division of all historical world belief systems and ideologies into two types, may itself be a relic of the Soviet way of thinking. The same concerns apply to Mitrokhin's idea that the final stable belief system should come from outside, but will not be a mixture of different external and Soviet or earlier Russian influences.

A further shortcoming of Mitrokhin's approach is that he does not analyse the 'democratic' movement as a whole, but divides it into liberal democratic, radical, populist, and other groups. All these as well as many other different trends surely existed in the movement. This was partially a result of the fact that Mitrokhin's stages in the rejection of official ideology are logical and not historical. In fact, some of those who, according to the scheme, were at different stages could themselves be in one and the same movement and even group. This means that, apart from beliefs that divided Russian 'democrats', there were also beliefs that united them. A study of the latter is perhaps even more important if one analyses the Russian 'democratic' subculture as a unified belief system which influenced political developments in the USSR and Russia.

In fact this last point is endorsed in another work of which Mitrokhin is co-author, along with Michael Urban. Mitrokhin and Urban compare the programmes of two major 'democratic' parties: the Democratic Party of Russia (DPR) and the Social Democratic Party of Russia (SDPR). While finding some minor differences in the two parties' programmes, membership, and political style, they observe that,

Judging from the formal orientations of these two parties, expressed in programmes and in the speeches of their leaders, there would appear to be very little that distinguishes them one from another. They both regard themselves as 'normal', 'parliamentary' parties oriented towards the creation of a market economy, a legal-rational state and a democratic political order. What is more, they both seek to organize and to represent the same constituency, namely, what they regard as an emerging 'middle class' composed primarily of professionals, businessmen (managers in the state sector, entrepreneurs in the co-operative and private sectors) and skilled workers.[106]

On the basis of the results of a survey conducted in April 1991 among the activists of the DPR and the SDPR, Mitrokhin and Urban point out that 'with allowance for programmatic manoeuvre, it would not seem mistaken to regard the orientations of the DPR and the SDPR as indistinguishable in the areas of social and economic policy'.[107] According to Mitrokhin and Urban this simi-larity in programmes, which was characteristic of all democratically oriented parties in Russia, was the result of the fact that their agendas were dominated 'by the desideratum of extirpating the Communist order', since as long as this order remained intact, their common projects for becoming 'normal', 'parlia-mentary' parties could not be realized. Mitrokhin and Urban argue that

On the level of political organization, this unity of purpose among the parties has been embodied in Democratic Russia, an alliance of, effectively, all democratic parties, groups and forces that had been formed in October 1990 with the express aim of destroying the communist system and replacing it with a democratic one. On the level of political discourse, something similar seems to have been going on both within the democratic movement and, judging from our survey results, within at least some of the democratic parties a discourse of democracy that pointed outwards towards things to come, either has occluded the expression of distinct social interests or has wrapped them all in the same indistinguishable packing.[108]

Though the level of unity of democratic party groups is exaggerated here, since far from all of them were members of Democratic Russia, and the reason for the similarity of their programmes is oversimplified, Mitrokhin and Urban rightly draw attention to this unity and to the fact that there was a direct connection between this and social interests. This makes it necessary to study these programmes from the point of view of the inner logic of the develop-ment of the beliefs they reflected and not as a simple projection of the social position of the 'democratic' parties' members.[109]

---

[106] Sergei Mitrokhin and Michael Urban, 'Social Groups, Party Elites and Russia's New Democrats', in David Lane (ed.), *Russia in Flux: The Political and Social Consequences of Reform* (Aldershot: Edward Elgar, 1992), 63.   [107] Ibid. 64.

[108] Ibid. 72.

[109] Unfortunately, Mitrokhin and Urban's article contains some factual mistakes. For exam-ple, describing the difference in the programmes of the DPR and the SDPR, they write that the DPR 'has taken a position calling for . . . the de facto reinstitution of the pre-revolutionary administrative system of guberniyas, with the Russian president appointing local prefects as the Tsar had done in a previous era' and that the SDPR 'does place more emphasis on providing social security for those economically dislocated during the transition to a market economy than does the DPR' (63–4). In reality the DPR sharply criticized the presidential decree on appoint-ing governors and called for their election, and its emphasis on social security was stronger than that of the SDPR. This can be seen from the programmes and documents of both parties and from the political position of the DPR, which is closer to that of the Communist opposition. (See, for example, Koval` (ed.), *Rossiya segodnya*, 122–7, 191–204.)

The studies of Devlin, Cheshko, and Mitrokhin provide valuable insights into the character of the process of creation of the new 'democratic' belief system and its relation to both Soviet and foreign theories and concepts. However, their conclusions are often too abstract, based on general principles, and do not provide much room for the discourse of 'democrats' themselves. In contrast, another study of Russian 'democrats', conducted in Moscow in 1991–2 by Russian and French sociologists, did allow them to speak for themselves. This project is based on the methodology of Alaine Touraine, who studies social movements by what he calls 'sociological intervention'.[110] Touraine's approach, unlike that of Fish, pays much attention to what is called the 'ideology' of social movements and is based on a series of group interviews, the aim of which is 'an intensive study of a group of militants who carry out self-analysis of their movement and are confronted as often as possible by the researchers with the entire body of their statements and with their behaviour during the intervention'.[111] The group, consisting of twelve to fourteen people, conducts discussions with specially invited 'interlocutors', who can be either sympathetic or hostile, and who represent different opinions and different social positions. Usually several sessions are organized in different regions and at least two sessions with the same group, within a certain time interval, to secure geographical representativeness and to understand their ideas as they evolve. This methodology had been field-tested: Touraine had already studied a number of social movements, including the Polish Solidarity movement.[112] One part of the research by Touraine's group into new social movements in Russia, in cooperation with a group of Russian sociologists headed by Leonid Gordon and Eduard Klopov and devoted to the Russian 'democratic' movement, is particularly important for this book, as it is practically the only analysis of the beliefs of Russian 'democrats' based completely on their own words.

The results of the work of the Franco-Russian group, who, apart from 'democrats', also studied 'new entrepreneurs' and ecological and workers' movements, was published in Russian in 1993 under the title *Novye social'hye dvizheniya v Rossii* (New Social Movements in Russia). The 'democratic part' of the book consists of articles by Eduard Klopov, Veronika Kabalina, Alexis Berelowitch, and Galina Monusova.[113] They were written

---

[110] Alain Touraine, *The Voice and the Eye: An Analysis of Social Movements* (Cambridge: Cambridge University Press, 1981); Alain Touraine, *La Méthode de l'Intervention Sociologique* (Paris: Textes, 1993).

[111] Touraine, *The Voice and the Eye*, 159.

[112] Alain Touraine, *Solidarity. The Analysis of a Social Movement: Poland 1980–1981* (Cambridge: Cambridge University Press, 1983).

[113] Eduard Klopov, 'Sila i slabosti dvizheniya—vzglyad cherez prizmu samoanaliza ego uchastnikov'; Veronika Kabalina, 'Ot imeni kogo, protiv kogo, vo imya kakikh tsennostey. Politicheskaya sostavlyayushchaya demokraticheskogo dvizheniya'; Alexis Berelovich, 'Politicheskie aktivisty demokraticheskogo dvizheniya: trudnosti samoopredeleniya'; Galina

on the basis of transcripts of a series of discussions held in December 1991 and January 1992 in which fourteen Democratic Russia activists from Moscow and Moscow *oblast*` and interlocutors from different organizations took part. An expanded and revised version of Berelowitch's chapter (which included data from some interviews conducted with the same respondents in 1993 and later) was published in 1996.[114]

The Franco-Russian study showed several important characteristics of the political beliefs of the Russian 'democratic' movement. It confirmed the idea that the 'democratic' movement was united not by purely political goals, but by fundamental social and moral beliefs, first of all by 'the single belief' of hostility toward totalitarian society, and by the 'supra-task' of its demolition, in pursuit of which purely political organizational tasks were seen as secondary. Klopov argues that an understanding of the Russian 'democratic' movement as purely political and an underestimation of its social and moral aims led to a concentration in most previous studies on the participation of different groups in the formation of new political structures, with a particular focus on developments in their political leadership. Therefore the authors of such studies, ruminating on the past, present, and future of the 'democratic' movement in Russia, concentrated primarily on its failures and weaknesses, and on the mistakes and miscalculations of its leaders, but not on its strong social and moral potential and its ability to influence the general character of reforms in post-totalitarian Russia. Such an approach was misleading, since 'the political component of the democratic movement was—and perhaps still remains—secondary relative to its "supra-task", which determines the priorities of the aims and tasks in the social reorganization of society'.[115]

All authors of the articles based on the Franco-Russian study stressed that one of the main ideas which united the 'democratic' movement was the absolute rejection of the existing system based on the understanding of it not just as politically faulty but as unnatural and immoral. According to Klopov, the members of the 'democratic' movement shared 'one burning passion': 'They all felt a pressing necessity to remove in a radical fashion the political and ideological diktat of the CPSU, of the immoral and irresponsible apparat of power and government. It was exactly this organic and sincere unity of thousands of activists and the multi-million-strong "basis" of the movement that made it possible to concentrate and direct its energy to achieving the main aim, the destruction of the totalitarian regime.'[116]

Monusova, 'Motivy i tsennosty uchastiya v demokraticheskom dvizhenii', in Leonid Gordon and Eduard Klopov (eds.), *Novye social`nye dvizheniya v Rossii. Po materialam rossiysko-frantsuzskogo issledovaniya* (Moscow: Progress-Kompleks, 1993).

[114] See Alexis Berelowitch and Michel Wieviorka, *Les Russes d'en bas*: *Énquête sur la Russie post-communiste* (Paris: Éditions du seuil, 1996), ch. 1.

[115] Klopov, 'Sila i slabosti dvizheniya', 24.   [116] Ibid. 25–6.

Kabalina concluded that 'democrats' understood themselves to be representatives of the interests of the entire unstructured society, welded together
by the idea of destroying the totalitarian state embodied in the CPSU.[117]
Berelowitch believed that 'democrats' were united by the desire to finish with
the 'monster' since they felt that 'it was impossible to go on like this'.[118]
Berelowitch and Michel Wieviorka called the 'democratic' attitude toward the
CPSU 'hatred'.[119]

The authors of the study found that 'democrats' saw their aim as replacing
the abnormal, unnatural, and immoral totalitarian society with democracy,
which they saw as normal, natural, and moral. The specific programme of
bringing about democratic society was not carefully thought out by them,
since they believed that the mere destruction of unnatural totalitarianism
would allow natural democracy to develop by itself.[120] The authors also
noticed the moral and idealistic understanding by 'democrats' of their own
mission and of 'democratic' society, which they often defined as a society
where everyone would simply live 'well' and 'with a clear conscience'.[121]
According to Klopov, 'the idea of the moral purification of society, its spiritual revival, constituted one of the elements of the sum of ideas which, with
some reservations, can be called the programme of the democratic movement'.[122]

Finally, on the basis of the words of the 'democrats' themselves, the
authors reached a conclusion which confirmed some results of more abstract
works. They discovered a tendency to approve authoritarian methods, which,
according to some respondents, were more effective in rapidly toppling totalitarianism and promoting reforms and democracy. General Augusto Pinochet,
whose name was positively cited several times by some respondents, was the
hero of this kind of activist, some of whom even called him 'the best democrat in the world'.[123] At the same time other 'democrats' strongly protested
against authoritarian methods, considering them harmful, conducive to dictatorship, and morally unjustified.[124] This conclusion was particularly important for a better understanding of the consequent splits in the 'democratic'
movement and in some of the policies of the new 'democratic' Russian leadership.

At the same time the authors of the Franco-Russian study failed to present
thoroughly and deeply 'democratic' beliefs as a system. According to them,

---

[117] Kabalina, 'Ot imeni kogo, protiv kogo, vo imya kakikh tsennostey', 42.
[118] Berelowitch, 'Politicheskie aktivisty demokraticheskogo dvizheniya', 56.
[119] Berelowitch and Wieviorka, *Les Russes d'en bas*, 61–4.
[120] Ibid. 68–70.   [121] Klopov, 'Sila i slabosti dvizheniya', 26.
[122] Ibid. 27; see also Berelowitch and Wieviorka, *Les Russes d'en bas*, 65–6.
[123] Klopov, 'Sila i slabosti dvizheniya', 32; Berelowitch, 'Politicheskie aktivisty
demokraticheskogo dvizheniya', 63.
[124] Kabalina, 'Ot imeni kogo, protiv kogo, vo imya kakikh tsennostey', 46–9.

apart from hatred toward the existing state they were 'united by an unclear and sketchy outline of Western liberal democratic society in which ideas of the national and cultural revival of Russia as an independent state were not thought of at all',[125] and did not realize how to achieve their own ideals of human rights, civil society, the law-based state, and the market economy.[126]

If one approaches the positive aims of the 'democratic' movement as do the authors of the Franco-Russian study, that is by comparing them only with programmes typical of Western political parties, such conclusions are surely right. In fact, compared to the elaborated programmes of contemporary parties of established democracies, the beliefs of Russian 'democrats' about how to achieve democracy, secure individual rights and the rule of law, and develop a multi-party system and a market economy were unclear and inconsistent. Moreover, there were different approaches towards these problems among Russian 'democrats' themselves. The authors were right in arguing that a broad movement in general cannot be united by an elaborate programme and is more likely to share symbolic slogans.[127] According to Kabalina, who stresses the symbolic character of these newly emerging concepts, the term 'democracy' itself became a symbol of struggle with the totalitarian system, of the break with the totalitarian past. Kabalina argues that the symbolic understanding of democracy by 'democrats' made it possible to unite in one 'democratic' movement people with different theoretical views of democracy as a goal. In Kabalina's view, a symbolic consciousness is generally characteristic of actors during the period of transition. She notes that the past was perceived and rejected by 'democratic' activists through symbols, and that on many occasions during the group sessions of the study they showed a particular reaction to the terms which symbolized that past: 'socialism', 'Communism', 'party', etc. Thus, the future is at first also established in idea-symbols: 'In this symbolic-slogan form new ideas reach broad masses and gain mobilizing force'.[128]

This does not mean, however, that 'democratic' symbols both negative and positive, even those different from symbols common to Western supporters of democracy, could not be part of a relatively consistent system of meanings and interpretation which permitted individual 'democrats' to feel part of one movement striving to achieve common aims. The present study analyses this particular system of beliefs in detail.

Another shortcoming of the Franco-Russian study, which is connected to the previous one, is that 'democratic' beliefs are not examined within a broader historical and intellectual context. It does not analyse the connection of this system with official Soviet ideology, Western 'democratic' theories,

---

[125] Ibid. 49. [126] Klopov, 'Sila i slabosti dvizheniya', 27.
[127] Ibid.
[128] Kabalina, 'Ot imeni kogo, protiv kogo, vo imya kakikh tsennostey', 41.

earlier Russian belief systems, or Soviet dominant political culture as a whole. Therefore, the question of cultural continuity and innovation in 'democratic' political subculture is not addressed. Berelowitch only once notes a distinctive pattern in the emergence of 'democratic' symbols:

> After the collapse of the system of 'Marxist-Leninist' terminology, Soviet ideology will have to re-invent all its notions and even its vocabulary. Therefore, formulas, concepts, and ideas which appear in the press can be imposed on society surprisingly fast and become expressions obligatory for all journalists, sociologists, political scientists, etc. Thus, we were present at the emergence of the Chilean (positive connotation) model, of Weber's Protestant ethics (the absence of which in Russia is the basis of all its contemporary difficulties), civil society, the law-based state, etc. 'Lumpen' is one such formula which became highly popular. What is remarkable in this case is that the origin of the formula lies in rejected Marxism. But one of the characteristic features of the contemporary ideological situation in Russia is that Russian intellectuals, while rejecting Marxism-Leninism on the conscious level, unwillingly preserve its fragments.[129]

With the example of the term 'lumpen' Berelowitch shows the specific pattern of the creation of new meaning for a term in the 'democratic' belief system. The term itself may be borrowed from an external social theory or from official Marxism, but the meaning changes and gains the meaning of another notion, itself common in official Marxism. While the name remains, the concept changes its meaning. Thus 'lumpen' becomes a name for all 'dangerous' or regressive classes.[130]

However, an analysis of a single example is surely not sufficient to substantiate the interesting conclusion of a direct connection between the 'democratic' belief system and official Soviet ideology. The present study fills this gap, conducting a detailed analysis of this connection as well as the correlation between 'democratic' beliefs and other ideologies and belief systems. It also examines another topic which is not addressed in the Franco-Russian study: the impact of the 'democratic' subculture on the entire Russian political culture and on further political developments in the country.

2.3. CONCLUSIONS

Speaking in general about the existing literature on the beliefs of Russian 'democrats', it can be said that the first two groups of authors, namely those who see these beliefs as an adequate copy of either Western democratic or Soviet totalitarian ideologies, are oversimplifying the situation. The first

---

[129] Berelovich, 'Politicheskie aktivisty demokraticheskogo dvizheniya', 60.
[130] Ibid.

group looks only at the surface and takes the language of Russian 'democrats' at face value, overlooking the considerable differences between the understanding of democracy by Russian 'democrats' and that of most mainstream Western democratic theorists and political groups. At the same time the second group, rightly pointing to some structural similarities between the official Soviet ideology and the 'democratic' belief system and the significant influence of the former on the latter, tends to absolutize this influence and overlooks no less significant differences caused by the borrowing of beliefs from other sources and their interaction with those that existed earlier.

The argument of the third group of authors, who see the new belief system of Russian 'democrats' as a mixture of influences in the process of formation and development, is the one from which this study proceeds. However, none of the authors in this group have presented a systematic book-length study of the subject. Virtually all of them have formulated their conclusions in brief and unsystematic form, failing to present the political culture of Russian 'democrats' as a relatively consistent system of beliefs, while providing often valuable, but mostly fragmentary, comments on it. No systematic attempt has been made to analyse the correlation between different sources of 'democratic' political culture and different influences on it, to conclude which source was the most fundamental, to discover the precise contents of different influences, to determine the pattern of borrowing and rethinking of borrowed beliefs within the framework of the structure of the existing belief system, to compare the belief system of Russian 'democrats' as a whole with existing theories of democracy and Soviet society, earlier Soviet and Russian beliefs, and the total Soviet political culture, or to examine the influence of the Russian 'democratic' political subculture on Russian politics. All these matters are addressed in this study.

3

The Emergence and Development of 'Democratic' Groups and Embryonic Political Parties

The aim of this chapter is to present an objective picture of the activities and types of independent 'democratic' political groups in the years 1985–91 in Russia as a whole and with particular attention to the regions where the interviews were conducted. This is helpful for a better understanding of the context of the activities of the interviewees and the authors of the documents which form the sources of this study. An effort has been made to avoid value judgements or generalizations, and to provide only information. However, in cases where this was not possible the reader is welcome to check the generalizations of this chapter by using the same sources.

All of the groups are divided into three main categories: (1) clubs and groups of activists; (2) associations and unions; and (3) election movements and parties. These categories generally coincide with the evolution of the forms of the groups over time, though it is difficult to draw a strict line between the periods. One should also take into consideration the fact that the provinces usually lay behind the main cities, the provinces, which means that processes which had ended in Moscow or Leningrad by 1988 started two years later in a provincial city.

3.1. INDEPENDENT GROUPS BEFORE *PERESTROYKA*

The softening of political control under Gorbachev led to the rapid emergence of different independent political groups, which were at first called 'informal' (as opposed to the 'formal', or official, 'social organizations' such as trade unions, the Komsomol, and writers' or journalists' unions, which were in practice controlled by the authorities). However, these groups did not appear out of the blue. There is evidence that a limited number of independent groups, including political groups, had always existed in the USSR, even after Stalin had crushed all open opposition.[1] One type of independent group was

---

[1] See S. R. Rozhdestvenskiy, *Materialy k istoriy samodeyatel`nykh politicheskikh ob`yedineniy v SSSR posle 1945 goda* (Moscow and Paris: Pamyat`, 1981–2).

student or youth discussion clubs, often inspired by studying original Marxist texts and impressed by the gap between official theory and Soviet practice. On several occasions such groups were even engaged in underground agitation, such as distributing leaflets or declarations. Such groups are known to have existed in Voronezh (the 'Zhigulin group', late 1940s),[2] Leningrad University (the 'Pimenov group', arrested in 1956), and Moscow University (the 'Krasnopevtsev group', arrested in 1957).[3] Later examples which preceded the Gorbachev period included the 'Kagarlitskiy group' in the Moscow Institute of World Economy and International Relations (arrested in 1982), political clubs in Krasnoyarsk University (closed under the pressure of the KGB in 1979 and 1984), and unofficial Marxist clubs in Vladivostok University and the Vladivostok House of Scientists (late 1970s–early 1980s).[4]

In academic institutions in general a critical and even oppositional spirit was often maintained throughout Communist rule and by Brezhnev's time many of them had become centres of liberal ideas. Many researchers from such research centres of the Academy of Sciences of the USSR as the Institute of Economics of the World Socialist System (whose director, Oleg Bogomolov, was elected People's Deputy of the USSR in 1989 and became an active member of the Inter-regional Group), the Institute of World Economy and International Relations, the Central Economic-Mathematical Institute in Moscow, the Academy of Sciences branches in Novosibirsk and the Far East, and many others became activists of various 'democratic' groups.

Another type of independent political group which existed before Gorbachev was the human rights dissident movement.[5] Almost all such groups had been effectively crushed by 1985, although the idea of human rights activities and the networks of contacts were still there. (Individual dissidents outside Moscow who were in contact with their colleagues in the capital were found in at least two of the seven cities visited during field research: Krasnoyarsk and Vladivostok.)

Non-political 'informal' youth groups and movements, such as hippies, the

---

[2] Anatoliy Zhigulin, 'Chernye kamni', *Znamya*, 7 (1988), 10–75 and 8 (1988), 48–119.

[3] ' "Delo" molodykh istorikov', *Voprosy istorii*, 4 (1994), 106–35.

[4] Lyudmila Alekseeva, *Istoriya inakomysliya v SSSR* (Vilnius and Moscow: Vest`, 1992), 307–9; (English edn.: Lyudmila Alexeyeva, *Soviet Dissent: Contemporary Movements for National, Religious and Human Rights* [Middletown, Conn.: Wesleyan University Press, 1987]); Pavel Vinogradov, 'Pokhozhdeniya atomarnykh lichnostey na zakate', *Krasnoyarskiy komsomolets*, 6 and 8 Apr. 1993; P. V. Poluyan, 'Ob`yasnenie P. V. Poluyana prokuroru Tsentral`nogo rayona goroda Krasnoyarska A. I. Grishinu', unpubl. MS [Krasnoyarsk, 13 Mar. 1989], courtesy of Pavel Poluyan; interview with Vladimir Makhora (Vladivostok, 23 Apr. 1994).

[5] See Alekseeva, *Istoriya inakomysliya v SSSR*, 191–299; Peter Reddaway (ed.), *Uncensored Russia: The Human Rights Movement in the Soviet Union* (London: Jonathan Cape, 1972); Rudolf L. Tokes (ed.), *Dissent in the USSR: Politics, Ideology, and People* (Baltimore, Md.: Johns Hopkins University Press, 1975).

rock movement, and the movement of amateur singing clubs (*Klub samod-eyateli`noy pesni*), became widespread and highly influential in the Brezhnev period. Though such movements did not pursue openly political aims, oppositional ideas were dominant and they played an important role in creating the basis for future political groups. Some such movements had thousands of supporters. For example, underground rock concerts attracted hundreds of people, and unofficial rock magazines which discussed some social issues were distributed there. Festivals of amateur singers (later called 'composer-singing', a kind of singing in which the composer sings his own songs, and normally accompanies himself or herself on a guitar), which were often organized in the USSR, sometimes attracted tens of thousands of listeners. The political orientation of such festivals was determined by the songs of the leading composers, who were close to or sympathetic with the dissident movement, including Aleksandr Galich, Bulat Okudzhava, Vladimir Vysotskiy, and Yuliy Kim. In different periods the authorities attempted either to ban such movements or to put them under official control, usually using the Komsomol for this purpose. However, such attempts generally failed and, on the contrary, a number of Komsomol liber-als became sympathetic to them. Some examples given below show the close link between independent groups of the pre-Gorbachev and Gorbachev eras in terms of both membership and ideas.

3.2. CLUBS AND GROUPS OF ACTIVISTS

Discussion clubs

Discussion clubs became one of the first and one of the most widespread type of early independent political group in the Gorbachev period. They were typi-cally organized by young researchers, university lecturers, and students educated in the humanities. The main aim of such clubs was to discuss profes-sional issues, often questions on the development of Soviet society from a Marxist perspective, but in a free and informal atmosphere which could not have been created in their official institutions, where all discussions were controlled by Party officials and the KGB.

In Moscow the most important group of this kind was the Perestroyka Club, organized in February 1987 by several young researchers of the institutes of the USSR Academy of Sciences, who met in the Central Economic-Mathematical Institute in Moscow. The club was joined by activists from other groups, including most of the members of the former 'Kagarlitskiy group' and the future Democratic Russia organizer Mikhail Schneyder from a socio-polit-ical association called Lingva. For at least a year the Perestroyka Club was the main centre for 'informal' debate in Moscow, the main organizer of other clubs and coalitions, and the birthplace of different political 'parties'.

In 1988, after a split, the club changed its name to Demokraticheskaya perestroyka (Democratic Perestroyka) and worked until 1989. In January 1989 it had about sixty members, most of whom were young social scientists or were representatives of the technical intelligentsia. Their activities included discussions with specially invited prominent *perestroyka* personalities, especially economists and journalists, the preparation of alternative draft laws and programmes, and the publication and distribution of the unofficial magazine *Otkrytaya zona* (circulation 200–600). Many future well-known politicians began their political careers in Democratic Perestroyka. The leader of the club, Oleg Rumyantsev, a young specialist on Hungary from the Institute of Economics of the World Socialist System, later became the leader of the Social Democratic Party of the Russian Federation, a Russian Federation People's Deputy, and the secretary of the Supreme Soviet Constitutional Committee. Many other members were elected to the Moscow City Council and became founders and leading members of various 'democratic' parties and groups: the Democratic Union, Memorial, the Social Democratic and Socialist Parties, the Moscow People's Front, the Democratic Russia Movement, etc.

Another similar discussion club in Moscow, Obshchina, evolved from a student discussion circle at the History Faculty of the Moscow State Pedagogical Institute, which had existed since 1982. The members of Obshchina later formed different groups and associations of anarchists, which never became either numerous or influential in the 'democratic' movement.

Clubs similar to Perestroyka existed in most of the cities in Russia. Penza Politklub is a typical example. The club was organized in Penza in autumn 1987 by several young lecturers in social studies from different institutes in the city. The most active members were two lecturers in philosophy from Penza Polytechnic Institute, Mikhail Pogodin and Igor' Nagdimunov; a lecturer in history and social sciences at Penza art school, Yevgeniy Govorukhin; and a lecturer in philosophy at Peuza Pedagogical Institute, Valentin Manuylov. The only member of Penza Politklub with a natural sciences background was a professor of physics at the Penza Institute of Engineering and Construction. The members of the club discussed new articles on the problems of society published in the central press and interpreted them in Marxist terms.[6] In Orenburg the Politklub was organized by the *oblast'* Komsomol Committee instructor Sergey Golovin and rapidly evolved into an action group, supporting the activities of the Green Committee (see below).

---

[6] Interview with Valentin Manuylov (Penza, 4 Apr. 1994); V. N. Berezovskiy and N. I. Krotov (eds.), *Neformalnaya Rossiya. O neformal'nykh politizirivannykh dvizheniyakh i gruppakh v RSFSR (opyt spravochnika)* (Moscow: Molodaya gvardiya, 1990), 178.

A similar club, Dialog, was organized in 1989 in the town of Belinskiy, a district centre of Penza *oblast*`. The members of Dialog met in the Museum of Vissarion Belinskiy, a radical literary critic of the nineteenth century, and discussed new articles and the latest political developments. Apart from the organizer Vladimir Yelistratov, who was an instructor in the district CPSU committee, most of the members belonged to the local humanities intelligentsia: some worked at the Belinskiy museum, others were lecturers in local institutes and colleges.[7] By 1988–9 there were dozens of such clubs in every big city and thousands in the whole of Russia.

Action groups

In the process of their evolution, many of the discussion clubs came to a point where the possibility of more active participation in politics arose. Eventually the professional discussions were joined by representatives of wider circles of the population, for whom the 'scholarly discussions' seemed useless and ineffective. At the same time the continuing democratization in the Soviet Union made political activity increasingly less dangerous for those who for tactical reasons would not have turned to it earlier. As a result a new type of political group emerged, often following a split in the original discussion clubs between moderates and radicals. In action groups the leading role was often played not by academics but by representatives of the technical intelligentsia, students, and workers.

In Moscow, for example, in 1988 the Perestroyka Club split into two parts: a moderate Democraticheskaya perestroyka and a radical Perestroyka 88. Perestroyka 88 was organized by a journalist and future Moscow City Soviet deputy, Valeriy Fadeev, a lawyer, Viktor Kuzin, and a specialist on Africa, Yuriy Skubko. The activists of Perestroyka 88 organized pro-democracy rallies, began a campaign for renaming the streets of Moscow to get rid of the names of Communist leaders, and circulated leaflets and declarations. Later Kuzin and Skubko joined the founding group of the Democratic Union.[8]

Similar processes took place in many cities of Russia. In Penza, for example, several Politklub activists, headed by a worker, Anatoliy Zamyatin, and an engineer, Yevgeniy Kryskin, formed the group Civic Initiative (Grazhdanskaya initsiativa) in October 1988, which published and circulated a bulletin that contained information about the 'democratic' movement in Moscow and other parts of the country, took part in official demonstrations

---

[7] Interview with Vladimir Yelistratov (Belinskiy, 5 Apr. 1994); V. I. Yelistratov, diary and notes, unpubl. MS [Belinskiy: 1989–90], courtesy of the author.

[8] Interview with Valeriy Fadeev (Moscow, 13 Aug. 1993).

carrying its own opposition banners, recruited supporters, and organized rallies.[9]

Similar methods used by the activists of the Democrat Club in Vladivostok, which was founded in autumn 1988 by a group of radical members of the Vladivostok Popular Front (which in Vladivostok was an umbrella discussion club, under whose shelter many different groups and clubs were formed: 'democratic', 'patriotic', ecologist, and even photolaboratories) headed by a Vladivostok Shipping Company telegraphist named Il`ya Grinchenko. Apart from discussions, the Democrat Club, from the very beginning, engaged in street actions such as circulating petitions and organizing rallies against the admission of atomic ships to Vladivostok port. They also circulated leaflets and 'democratic' literature. Around 400 people took part in such rallies. By 1989 the club had about fifty members, most of whom were between 30 and 40 years of age, and the club obtained official registration and a two-room office.[10] In Orenburg the main action group was originally formed as an ecological *zelenyy komitet* (Green Committee). It organized active petition campaigns and demonstrations and became involved in political activities. One of its leaders, Vladislav Shapovalenko, was elected a People's Deputy of the USSR and became an active member of the Inter-regional Group. At the Congress of People's Deputies Shapovalenko used his speaking time to read the declaration of the Inter-regional Group and as a result engaged in open conflict with Gorbachev. After the failure of the August 1991 putsch Shapovalenko was appointed presidential representative in Orenburg *oblast`*.

Human rights groups

Unlike the two types of independent groups described above, which mainly consisted of people who were just beginning their political activities, human rights groups continued the dissident tradition of the Brezhnev era. The earliest of these was probably the Committee for Trust between the East and the West (originally the Committee for Trust between the USSR and the USA). The group was founded in 1982 and was one of the few which had not been crushed by 1985. One of the reasons for its survival was that its announced goal did not at all contradict official Soviet propaganda. It claimed to be an independent peace group which created contacts with various Western pacifist

---

[9] Rossiysko-amerikanskiy universitet, Institut massovykh politicheskikh dvizheniy, *Rossiya: partii, assotsiatsii, soyuzy, kluby. Spravochnik*, 10 vols. (Moscow: RAU-Press, 1991–2), i/2. 207; interviews with Anatoliy Zamyatin (Penza, 15 Aug. 1994) and Yevgeniy Kryskin (Penza, 3 Apr. 1994).

[10] Berezovskiy and Krotov (eds.), *Neformalnaya Rossiya*, 94–5; interview with Il`ya Grinchenko (Vladivostok, 24 Apr. 1994).

movements. However, having been founded by a group of refuseniks, the Committee in practice demanded freedom of emigration, alternative military service, and Soviet withdrawal from Afghanistan. The members of the group were under constant pressure from the KGB, being frequently arrested or forced to emigrate.[11] Nevertheless, the group itself managed to survive. By 1987 it had a membership of about twenty people in Moscow as well as smaller branches in Leningrad, L`vov, Kuybyshev, Rovno, and Riga. It organized weekly seminars in a private flat, published and circulated an unofficial magazine. In 1987 a standing seminar, 'Democracy and Humanism', was organized by the Committee member Valeriya Novodvorskaya, who was formally involved in the dissident movement. The seminar later became the nucleus of the Democratic Union organizing committee.[12]

Other well-known human rights groups were the activists led by a former political prisoner, Sergey Grigoryants, who since 1987 had published the unofficial magazine *Glasnost`*, and a group headed by another former political prisoner, Aleksandr Podrabinek, which published an information weekly, *Express-khronika*. Grigoryants's supporters formed a group in June 1989 called the Movement for Freedom and Democracy, one member of which, Valeriy Fadeev (who at the same time was one of the leaders of Perestroyka 88), was elected to Moscow City Soviet.[13]

The idea of the defence of human rights became popular in the provinces. However, there they were usually organized not by former dissidents, but by activists of a new type. These were often former local officials who had lost their jobs because of a conflict with the system. In Krasnoyarsk, for example, the main independent 'democratic' group was the Committee for the Rehabilitation of N. A. Klepachev, which was formed in 1984 to support a former head of the *kray* architectural/construction inspectorate who had lost his job because of his refusal to sanction the building of houses without the observance of construction rules. Nikolay Klepachev became famous after the story was widely circulated in the central press and after a local author, Roman Solntsev, wrote a play sympathetic to Klepachev, which was staged in Moscow. Later the group, headed by Klepachev, was renamed the Committee for Assistance to Perestroyka. It helped anybody whose rights were violated by the authorities, organized rallies and demonstrations against the *kray* Communist leaders, and took an active part in the elections of 1989. Two of the three candidates supported by the Committee became People's Deputies of the USSR: Solntsev and worker I. Misun. The Committee consisted of

---

[11]   This information is based on the interview with one of the leaders of the group, Andrey Krivov, who now lives in Paris (Paris, 22 July 1994).

[12]   *Rossiya: partii, assotsiatsii, soyuzy, kluby*, i/2. 187.

[13]   Vladimir Pribylovskii, *Dictionary of Political Parties and Organizations in Russia* (Moscow: PostFactum/Integral; Washington, DC: Center for Strategic and International Studies, 1992), 51.

about twenty activists and published and circulated an unofficial information bulletin, *Sotsial`naya spravedlivost`* (Social Justice).[14]

A similar group was formed in Penza by a former deputy head of the *oblast`* Department of Internal Affairs, Georgiy Didichenko, who in 1978 had lost his job as a result of his investigation of a corruption case. After he was discharged, Didichenko did not engage in public activities for several years. However, from 1982 he began giving lectures for different organizations on legal themes, including the Znanie (Knowledge) Society (an official society which organized public lectures of specialists to popularize knowledge in their fields). Though the topics of his lectures were always on official themes, such as 'the preservation of socialist property', in practice they consisted of accusations of corruption and nepotism against the local authorities and were based on numerous facts that Didichenko knew from his previous job. These lectures became very popular in Penza. The authorities tried to influence Didichenko; several times he was 'invited' by the KGB for discussions with them, but they did not use tougher measures, probably in view of his work record and because of a change in the political atmosphere. During all of this time Didichenko worked as a lawyer for different organizations.

Gradually, he became famous as a crusader for justice, and many people who suffered from the actions of the authorities sought his support in different ways. As a lawyer Didichenko tried to help these plaintiffs, though it was not his official job. By 1988 an unofficial human rights group emerged around him, which had activists in many Penza factories and in other towns and villages of the *oblast`*. In the same year the group managed to secure the dismissal of a *sovkhoz* (state farm) director under the threat of a strike. A telegram with the threat was sent to the CPSU Central Committee and the whole affair made Didichenko's group popular in the entire *oblast`*.

The group, not surprisingly, was not officially registered and did not have fixed membership. Its activists usually called it a human rights group or a group for the support of citizens. By 1989 other, more 'theoretical' independent groups appeared in Penza and the Didichenko group established contact with them. In 1990 Didichenko became a People's Deputy of the Russian Federation and later the presidential representative in Penza *oblast`*.[15]

3.3. UNIONS AND ASSOCIATIONS

The further softening of the Soviet regime and the logic of the development of independent political groups led to the emergence of larger 'democratic'

[14] Interview with Nikolay Klepachev (Krasnoyarsk, 19 Apr. 1994); *Rossiya: partii, assotsiatsii, soyuzy, kluby*, i/2. 168.
[15] Interview with Geogriy Didichenko (Penza, 4 Apr. 1994).

unions and associations. The first result of this process was the creation of loose federations and associations of clubs, and later the creation of better-organized unions, with fixed memberships and branches all over the country. The associations and unions began to emerge in 1987–8, when the main aim was not yet participation in elections, but the creation of stronger groups to obtain more support and influence.

Associations of clubs and groups

One of the first spontaneous initiatives to unite groups and supporters of change in different parts of the country was the All-union Socio-Political Club (ASPC). Its roots date to 1986, when a young researcher from Orenburg, Aleksandr Sukharev, wrote a letter to *Komsomol`skaya pravda* and proposed to start an exchange of opinions on social issues. The newspaper passed hundreds of answers from all over the country to Sukharev, who started an active correspondence with their authors. On this basis the Correspondence Socio-Political Club was formed, which at a conference in Taganrog in 1987 became the ASPC. About a hundred people took part in the Taganrog conference, which represented fifty cities. In 1987–8 the club organized several conferences and the member groups published dozens of unofficial bulletins and magazines. In 1988 the Novodvorskaya seminar 'Democracy and Humanism' became a collective member of the ASPC. In 1989 some members of the ASPC became deputies of local soviets. After 1989, however, as a result of constant splits, most ASPC members drifted off to other movements or associations.

Another initiative of this kind was the creation of the Federation of Socialist Public Clubs (FSPC), which was formed by the groups which signed the 'Declaration of the Socialist Social Clubs' at the meeting-dialogue 'Social Initiatives in *Perestroyka*' in Moscow in August 1987. By 1988 the FSPC included about fifteen groups from different regions of Russia and some USSR republics, which for various reasons at that time maintained a socialist orientation. However, the most active in the federation were the members of the Perestroyka Club. The federation organized seminars and information exchange, published newspapers and magazines. Though formally not disbanded, the FSPC, for the same reason as the ASPC, virtually ceased to exist by 1990, and its Moscow members became the nucleus for the Moscow Popular Front.[16]

The Confederation of Anarcho-Syndicalists (CAS) was a union of different clubs of anarchist orientation. At a joint conference of the FSPC and the ASPC in August 1988, clubs and groups supporting anarchist Obshchina

---

[16] *Rossiya: partii, assotsiatsii, soyuzy, kluby,* i/1, 40–1, 87.

declared the creation of an Alliance of Socialist Federalists. In September 1988 it was renamed the Union of Independent Socialists and in January 1989 reorganized into the Confederation of Anarcho-Syndicalists. The CAS founding congress in May 1989 was attended by delegates of twelve cities, mainly from Russia and Ukraine. In 1991 the CAS was still active and its third congress was held in May in Samara. The anarchist movement, however, was never numerous, and its activists were mainly students. But its influence was quite significant before the Democratic Russia Movement was formed, which anarchists did not join. This influence was based on their active role in the 'informal' movement and 'democratic' rallies in Moscow, where their striking black flag attracted much attention (according to newspaper reports, some bystanders thought they were pirates). CAS members also published many *samizdat* newspapers and magazines (sixteen in 1990), and their Moscow magazine, *Obshchina*, became one of the first 'informal' publications to find a proper printer and was on sale in official *Soyuzpechat'* kiosks.[17]

The Democratic Union

The Democratic Union (DU), which was founded at a conference in May 1988 and from the very beginning claimed to be an 'opposition party', was in fact a union of groups, clubs, and individuals, but differed from other unions by its radicalism. Such radicalism was manifested not in theoretical positions (among the members and factions of the Democratic Union there were not only supporters of 'Western democracy', but also 'social democrats' and even 'Marxists'), but in the methods of political activism. From the very beginning the DU called for radical street actions: demonstrations without applying for permission from the 'illegal' Communist authorities, pickets, public hunger strikes, etc.

The Democratic Union was formed by the members of the 'Democracy and Humanism' seminar, Kuzin and Skubko from Perestroyka 88, the Society of Young Marxists, and several other groups. Prominent 'informal' individuals were also present, including the former political prisoner Lev Ubozhko, the future leader of the so-called Liberal Democratic Party (LDP) Vladimir Zhirinovskiy, and representatives of some provincial groups (during the first day of the first congress delegates actually met in the flat of Zhirinovskiy's future deputy Vladimir Bogachev; the LDP was founded in the same place two years later). Sergey Grigoryants also supported the organization of the DU, though did not join the organization formally.

During a certain period the radicalism of the Democratic Union was quite

---

[17] Pribylovskii, *Dictionary of Political Parties and Organizations in Russia*, 14–15, *Rossiya: partii, assotsiatsii, soyuzy, kluby*, i/1. 54–6.

popular. Its activities reached a peak in the second half of 1989 and early 1990, when the Union regularly organized small but noisy rallies in Pushkin Square, in the centre of Moscow, which usually ended in clashes with special forces of the Interior Ministry and administrative arrests. Such rallies or 'information meetings' were also held in several other cities in Russia. By that time the Democratic Union had organized small but very active local branches (usually of ten to twenty members) in more than thirty cities of the USSR (mainly in Russia and Ukraine), with individual members in 160 cities. The central and local organizations of the Union had more than thirty publications, which in most cases were typed or photocopied, though the newspaper of the Moscow organization Svobodnoye slovo was printed in Latvia from 1990 on. The number of officially registered members in the peak period was about one thousand, and, together with individual supporters, about two thousand.[18]

The Democratic Union had active organizations in at least two of the seven regional centres studied for this book: Vladivostok and Krasnoyarsk. In each of the seven cities there were individual supporters who circulated the literature of the group, distributed its ideas, and took part in united 'democratic' actions as the representatives of the Democratic Union. In both cities the organizations had about twenty members and published their own magazines and both groups became the main organizers of street actions. Both organizations held regular rallies in the centres of Vladivostok and Krasnoyarsk. In Vladivostok the group was headed by a former political prisoner who had contacts with dissidents, Pavel Borovik,[19] and in Krasnoyarsk by a young physicist, Yevgeniy Goncharov.[20] In Stavropol` a smaller group of the Democratic Union was headed by Sergey Karpenko, and in Pskov a Memorial member, Yriy Ivlev, was its local representative.[21]

From the second half of 1990 the popularity of the Democratic Union began to decline. One of the probable reasons was that by that time the radicalism of the mainstream 'democratic' groups had almost reached the level

[18] *Rossiya: partii, assotsiatsii, soyuzy, kluby*, i/1. 45.

[19] The case of an accountant, Pavel Borovik, who was put into a psychiatric hospital in Khrushchev's time for complaining about the financial wrongdoing of his superiors, is mentioned in several Soviet dissident and Western reports. See: Reddaway (ed.), *Uncensored Russia*, 229; Sidney Bloch and Peter Reddaway, *Russia's Political Hospitals: The Abuse of Psychiatry in the Soviet Union* (London: Victor Gollancz, 1977), 348 f.; and Sidney Bloch and Peter Reddaway, *Soviet Psychiatric Abuse: The Shadow over World Psychiatry* (Boulder, Colo: Westview, 1984), 254.

[20] Vinogradov, 'Pokhozhdeniya atomarnykh lichnostey na zakate', *Krasnoyarskiy komsomolets*, 6 and 8 Apr. 1993, p. 2.

[21] Vasiliy Krasulya, *Dissident iz nomenklatury* (Stavropol`: Severo-kavkazskoye informatsionno-reklamnoye agenstvo, 1992), 293–4; Andrey Shcherkin, 'Protsessy zarozhdeniya, razvitiya i stanovleniya politicheskikh partiy i massovykh obshchestvennykh dvizheniy v Pskovskoy oblasti v 1988–1994', unpubl. MS [Pskov, 1994].

of the Democratic Union, which undermined its unique image. Trying to maintain the group's radical reputation, its leadership decided in 1990 to boycott the elections to the 'illegal' representative bodies and not to join the 'Democratic Russia' electoral bloc. This decision actually led to a catastrophic result: the majority of new ambitious activists preferred to join more constructive groups like voters' unions, which did join Democratic Russia. Though some individual Democratic Union members who disagreed with the boycott decision were elected to representative bodies, after the 1990 elections the organization as a whole lost its appeal and most of the local branches disintegrated.[22]

Memorial

The all-union voluntary historical-educational society Memorial was the first independent group organized by young activists which was taken seriously and joined by many well-known reformers of the older generation. The importance of Memorial is that it became a meeting place of all the main reformist currents: activists of 'informal' youth clubs, liberal journalists and academics of the *glasnost*` period, most of whom belonged to the *shestidesyatniki* (the generation of those whose youth coincided with the Khrushchev years), reformist officials, dissidents of the Brezhnev period, and victims of Stalin's repressions.

The idea uniting all these different people was the construction of a monument or memorial to the victims of Stalin's repressions. The decision to construct such a monument was actually taken by the Twenty-second Congress of the CPSU in 1961 but was never implemented either by Khrushchev or by later Communist leaderships. Thus, the idea was on the one hand reformist enough to attract the oppositional and independent groups, and on the other hand, it was not openly anti-Communist or anti-government, which made possible the active participation of less radical reformists. At first Memorial was able to unite people with very different views, from radical anti-Communists to supporters of 'genuine Leninist ideals'.

The first move to create the Memorial Society was made by a group of participants of the Memorial section of a meeting-dialogue, held in Moscow in August 1987, most of whom were members of the Perestroyka Club: Yuriy Samodurov, Viktor Kuzin, and others. They started a petition campaign which called for the construction of the memorial. The signature campaign went on until the next summer in several cities and the activists were occasionally detained by the militia. However, the organizers managed to pass about thirty thousand signatures to the Nineteenth Conference of the CPSU

---

[22] *Rossiya: partii, assotsiatsii, soyuzy, kluby*, i/1. 44–7.

in 1988. The idea was supported by the reformist party leaders and the Conference reaffirmed the decision to construct the monument. This made Memorial well known throughout the country.

At the same time the organizers conducted a survey in the streets of Moscow on who should be included in the Public Council of the new group. On the basis of the survey's results, a sixteen-member Council was formed from the most popular *perestroyka* activists of the time, including the historian Yuriy Afanas`ev, the writers Ales` Adamovich and Vasil` Bykov, the poet Yevgeniy Yevtushenko, the former Moscow Communist leader Boris Yel`tsin, the literary critic Yuriy Karyakin, the Academician Andrey Sakharov, and others. Some of the Council members never took an active part in the work of Memorial, others became busy with other activities after they were elected Peoples' Deputies of the USSR. Though Memorial failed to become a political party and form a faction in either the Soviet or Russian parliaments, for a period of time it was the most influential 'democratic' organization, and united the greatest proportion of supporters of reforms. According to Geoffrey Hosking, 'at this stage the significance of Memorial as a formative influence on public attitudes and as a nursery for future political movements can scarcely be overstated'.[23] At its preparatory conference in Moscow in October 1988, 338 delegates from 59 cities of the USSR were present, and by mid-1990 it had about 170 local branches, many of which collected impressive archives on repressions, and published newspapers, magazines, memoirs, and research materials.[24] Prior to the 1990 elections Memorial became one of the founding members of the Democratic Russia bloc. After the elections the political activities of the society diminished, as most of its members with political ambitions joined other, more politically orientated groups. Memorial itself concentrated on human rights activities, support for the victims of Communist repressions, collecting historical documents, and publishing memoirs.

Because of its initially moderate programme, in many provincial cities the first independent political group was a Memorial branch. This was the case, for example, in Pskov, where, according to a local 'democratic' activist, Andrey Shcherkin, it was 'the first mass proto-party'. The founding conference of the Pskov Memorial Society was held in autumn 1988. The representatives of the city Communist authorities took part in the conference, trying to put the new group under the control of the CPSU. However, they failed to get elected to the leadership of the society, and instead a local priest and former political prisoner, Father Pavel Adel`geym, became one of the leaders. During the election campaign of 1989 Pskov Memorial activists organized a

---

[23]   Geoffrey Hosking, 'The Beginnings of Independent Political Activity', in G. Hosking, J. Aves, and P. Duncan (eds.), *The Road to Post-Communism: Independent Political Movements in the Soviet Union, 1985–1991* (London: Pinter, 1992), 17.

[24]   *Rossiya: partii, assotsiatsii, soyuzy, kluby*, i/1. 62.

meeting of four thousand voters which nominated Father Pavel, but he was voted down at the so-called 'constituency election meeting'. After the 1990 elections, Pskov Memorial formally continued to exist, but no real activities took place and most of its activists became leaders of other groups, and its co-chairman Andrey Shcherkin became a member of the Council of Representatives of the Democratic Russia Movement.[25]

In Krasnoyarsk the local Memorial branch was headed by Vladimir Sirotinin, who had good relations with several dissident groups, circulated dissident literature, and was once under KGB investigation. His opinions greatly influenced many younger local activists. After a short period of political activism Krasnoyarsk Memorial, like most other surviving branches, though generally supporting Democratic Russia, turned to non-political activities: searching for places of executions, organizing exhibitions on political repressions, and publishing archive materials.[26]

Attempts to create a local Memorial branch also took place in the other five regions of field research. However, in some cases, as in Penza, the local activists did not go further than writing declarations, and very quickly moved to other political groups. In Vladivostok and Stavropol` they moved to a variety of groups after Memorial ceased political activities.[27]

3.4. POPULAR FRONTS

The creation of popular fronts, which initially were often called Popular Fronts of Assistance to Perestroyka, was a result of a willingness to create larger, more active, and influential political movements in a particular region which would be able to influence the authorities by both pressure and constructive dialogue with reformist leaders. This idea of dialogue with at least a section of the establishment was manifested in the very idea of a 'popular front', which came from the history of Communist calls to create united fronts against the rightist threat in the 1930s. However, in practice the idea of the creation of popular fronts in Russia came from the Baltic republics, where popular fronts very soon became powerful movements which dominated the political scene.

Organizations which called themselves 'popular fronts' appeared after 1988 in many cities in Russia. The 'popular' name was given to groups of

[25] Shcherkin, 'Protsessy zarozhdeniya, razvitiya i stanovleniya politicheskikh partiy i massovykh obshchestvennykh dvizheniy v Pskovskoy oblasti v 1988–1994', pp. 1–4.

[26] Interview with Vladimir Sirotinin (Krasnoyarsk, 20 Apr. 1994). On *Memorial*, see Hosking, 'The Beginnings of Independent Political Activity', 16–19; Anne White, 'The Memorial Society in the Russian Provinces', *Europe-Asia Studies*, 47 (1995), 1343–66.

[27] Interview with Grinchenko; Krasulya, *Dissident iz nomenklatury*, 293–4.

very different kinds: sometimes it was a discussion group or a group of activists which just renamed itself to sound more important; sometimes authorities attempted to create their own popular front in order to put the independent political movement under official control. However, a typical popular front was an attempt to unite all the 'democratic' groups of a particular region in one organization.

The Moscow Popular Front (MPF), for example, was created in the summer of 1988 at a conference of forty of the most important independent political groups and clubs in the city. The Front published several newspapers and magazines, organized rallies, and attempted to create 'support groups' at factories, research institutes, and other institutions (such groups were organized at the Institute of Slavonic and Balkan Studies of the USSR Academy of Sciences and at the large state enterprise Salut, among others). In 1990 many of the activists in the Moscow Popular Front were elected to the Moscow City Soviet and two of the Front's leaders, Sergey Stankevich and Anatoliy Medvedev, became a People's Deputy of the USSR and of the Russian Federation respectively. Before the elections of 1990 the Moscow Popular Front became one of the main founding members of both the Moscow Voters' Union and the Democratic Russia Movement and were gradually absorbed within them.[28]

In all seven regions of field research popular fronts (or popular front organizing committees) existed in some form. In Penza, a popular front was organized just before the 1990 elections but was absorbed very quickly within local Democratic Russia.[29] In Vladivostok the Popular Front of Assistance to Perestroyka was created as early as autumn 1988; however, it cannot be regarded as purely 'democratic', as it was more of a discussion club which consisted of representatives of every political trend as well as members of non-political groups.[30] In Pskov the Popular Front Initiative Group was founded by the former activists of a local rock club who were at the same time the radical group within Pskov Memorial (Valeriy Nikol`skiy, Yuriy Ivlev, and Andrey Shcherkin). The initiative group published an information bulletin and a newspaper, *Veche*, and had about fifteen members.[31]

The most active and influential popular fronts were in Krasnoyarsk and Stavropol`. The Krasnoyarsk Popular Front was created on the foundations of the Committee for Assistance to Perestroyka in October 1989, though several other local groups took part as well. The Front in fact continued the activities of the Committee. It supported several candidates during the 1990 elections

[28] *Rossiya: partii, assotsiatsii, soyuzy, kluby*, i/2. 191–3.
[29] Interview with Aleksandr Yerasov (Penza, 3 Apr. 1994).
[30] Berezovskiy and Krotov (eds.), *Neformalnaya Rossiya*, 95; interview with Grinchenko.
[31] Shcherkin, 'Protsessy zarozhdeniya, razvitiya i stanovleniya politicheskikh partiy i massovykh obshchestvennykh dvizheniy v Pskovskoy oblasti v 1988–1994', p. 3.

and its leader, Nikolay Klepachev, and several other members were elected to the *kray* soviet.[32]

The Popular Front of Stavropol` Region was organized in October 1988 (until February 1989 it was called the Initiative Group 'Popular Front for Assistance to Perestroyka'). The Front united the supporters of Vasiliy Krasulya, the former deputy editor of the local CPSU newspaper, *Stavropol`skaya pravda*, who had been fired after writing and publishing a reformist article, as well as the members of a local ecological group, a fan club of a popular reformist magazine, *Ogonek*, and a club of amateur singers. The members of the Front organized a hunger strike and demonstrations against violations of election law by the Stavropol` city authorities in January 1989, and in March of the same year organized a large rally and petition campaign against the construction of the Volga–Chogray canal. The front published a theoretical magazine, *Grazhdanin* (Citizen), and an information bulletin, *Khronika bor`by za demokratiyu* (The Chronicle of the Struggle for Democracy). About a thousand copies of every issue were typed up and then distributed among the population. The Front had groups of supporters in many cities of Stavropol` *kray*. Its own coordinating committee consisted of eleven members, and rallies typically attracted two to three hundred people. Front members often suffered from administrative arrests and many of them lost their jobs because of political activities. During the elections of 1990 several activists, including Krasulya, were elected deputies of the *kray* soviet. Later in 1990 the Front collectively joined the Democratic Party of Russia.[33]

3.5. ELECTION UNIONS AND PARTIES

Voters' clubs and unions

Elections of the People's Deputies of the USSR in 1989 and to the Russian Federation federal and local soviets in 1990 completely changed the character of Russian independent political groups. Before this, despite various impressive names, the 'democratic' movement actually consisted of many small clubs. All so-called 'associations' and 'federations' in reality consisted of more or less the same people, amounting to several dozen in Moscow and Leningrad and about a dozen in the big provincial cities, who knew each other very well. However, the prospect of sending to the state or local legislature somebody that one supported, or even getting elected oneself, aroused interest in political activities among considerably wider circles of the population,

---

[32] *Rossiya: partii, assotsiatsii, soyuzy, kluby*, i/2. 168; interview with Klepachev.
[33] Krasulya, *Dissident iz nomenklatury*, 136.

including those who earlier had considered that taking part in 'democratic' groups was not a serious undertaking.

The elections prompted the emergence of a mass movement of clubs and unions of voters. A typical example of grassroots voters' clubs, which grew up all over the country before or immediately after the 1989 elections, was the District Union of Voters (DUV) of Oktyabr`skiy district (*rayon*) in Moscow. The Union was founded by several groups of supporters of the 'democratic' candidates. These local groups had been organized in each neighbourhood of the district by the activists of the Moscow Popular Front, Memorial, and other 'democratic' groups, by activists from several institutes of the Academy of Sciences which were situated in the district, and by the local population. In every neighbourhood a coordinator was appointed, around whom local 'democratic' activists gathered. In several cases the leaders of the independent local self-governing committees, which united local residents who wanted a bigger say in local affairs, became the coordinators.

Il`ya Zaslavskiy, the candidate who was supported by the district 'democrats', was elected a USSR People's Deputy in spring 1989. On 10 August 1989 a founding conference adopted the charter of the District Union of Voters, and on 13 December the District Soviet Executive Committee officially registered the group, obviously trying to avoid conflict with an influential force in the run-up to the elections. Official registration of an independent group was rare before 1990, and on this occasion it was achieved with the help of the secretary of the District Soviet Executive Committee, who chose to assist the Union and later was re-elected to the district soviet with the Union's support.

At the time of registration the coordinating Council of the Union consisted of nine people, among whom were district residents and activists of the USSR Academy of Sciences Voters' Club, the Voters' Club of the Academy of Sciences Institute of Physics (Andrey Sakharov's institute, which is located in the district), the Moscow Popular Front, and Memorial. Later the co-ordinating committee was joined by representatives of each neighbourhood, who usually were neighbourhood coordinators during the elections. Four chairmen were elected, one of whom was Zaslavskiy. Between the elections of 1989 and 1990 the *Oktyabr`skiy* District Voters' Union was mainly engaged in supporting the USSR People's Deputies from Moscow, who joined the oppositional Inter-regional Parliamentary Group, in particular Zaslavskiy himself, and participated in the organization of various 'democratic' rallies and other actions, initiated by the Inter-regional Group and the Moscow Union of Voters (of which the Oktyabr`skiy District Union, which was named Obnovleniye, became a part).

The real work, however, began in the run-up to the 1990 elections. As an officially registered 'social organization', the District Union of Voters had the right to nominate candidates to the District City Soviet as well as observers to the precinct and district election committees. It nominated candidates in more than 130 out of 150 district Soviet constituencies. Having no right to nominate candidates to the upper-level soviets, the Union declared its support for those whose views seemed to be acceptable. The Union also tried to nominate its own candidates through some of the district's 'labour collectives', which were sympathetic to its goals, mainly the institutes of the Academy of Sciences.

The main problem during the elections was the lack of suitable candidates for the district soviet. Despite considerable popularity among the population of the district for being a part of the 'democratic movement', the Union was not a big group. Its coordinating council at the time of the elections consisted of about thirty people. Its meetings during the peak time of interest in the elections were attended by about fifty people, which was approximately the total number of activists. So the Union had to support people whom it did not know very well. In fact there were too many 'democratic' candidates to the city and republican soviets, and the Union, in coordination with the Democratic Russia Movement, had to support several candidates in each constituency in order 'not to violate democracy' (the Union, like all groups of its kind, became a member of the Democratic Russia bloc and the bloc's campaign organizers operated from the Union's office during the elections). Most of the activists in the Union became deputies of the Oktyabr`skiy district or Moscow city soviets and two co-chairmen (physicists Anatoliy Shabad and Anatoliy Medvedev) were elected People's Deputies of the Russian Federation. In the Oktyabr`skiy District Soviet the Union gained the majority of seats and won all the Moscow city and Russian Federation soviet constituencies in the Oktyabr`skiy district. The Union's leader, Zaslavskiy, was elected the Oktyabr`skiy District Soviet chairman. After the elections the Union, as a part of the Moscow Union of Voters, joined the Democratic Russia Movement and became its grassroots organization in the Oktyabr`skiy district of Moscow.[34]

Similar unions of voters emerged between the two elections in most of Russia's regions. In Pskov, for example, the union of voters, Veche, was joined not only by the 'informals' from Memorial and the Popular Front, but also by the administrators and the CPSU committee members of a large state machine-building factory, Pskovmash, the manager of which, Sergey Gorbunov, who had tried in vain to become a USSR People's Deputy in 1989, decided to court the 'democrats' at the next elections. The USSR People's Deputy from Pskov, air pilot Nikolay Panov, also became a member. However, radical activists very soon began to play the leading role in the Pskov Union of Voters and it began organizing opposition rallies, like the one

---

[34] Records of meetings of the Oktyabrskiy District Union of Voters; unpubl. MS [Moscow, 1990–1], courtesy of Mariya Sublina.

on 25 February 1990, which was part of the All-Union Action of the Inter-regional Group and in which about five thousand people took part. The Union was supported by the *oblast`* committee of the employees of cooperatives and its newspaper, *Golos* (Voice). During the elections of 1990 two of the leaders of the Union became deputies of the Pskov City Soviet and Sergey Shatalov, whose candidacy was supported by it, was elected the People's Deputy of the Russian Federation from Pskov *oblast`*. After the elections the Union joined the Democratic Russia Movement.[35] In Orenburg the public club of voters Vlast` Sovetam (Power to the People) was formed in November 1989. In the 1990 elections the club managed to win for the 'democrats' 40% of the seats in the Orenburg City Soviet and about 10% in the *oblast`* soviet, two of its leaders, I. Holda and E. F. Pol`shchikov, becoming a deputy of the *oblast`* soviet and deputy chairman of the city soviet respectively.

Unlike Moscow's Oktyabr`skiy district, in most places the voters' unions failed to obtain official registration and their election results were less impressive. However, the activities they engaged in were similar everywhere: endorsement of 'democratic' candidates and active campaigning for them. Voters' clubs and unions, which emerged all over Russia, attempted to form larger associations. In July 1989 at a conference in Moscow, the Moscow Union of Voters was established; it united 35 voters' clubs from 30 districts of the city (Moscow had 33 districts at the time), as well as gaining the support of about twenty People's Deputies of the USSR and several dozen People's Deputies of the Russian Federation, representatives of the 'Committee of the Nineteen' (a union of nineteen voters' clubs of the industrial factories, which nominated Boris Yel`tsin as a candidate in the 1989 elections), the Committee of Support for Tel`man Gdlyan and Nikolay Ivanov, the Voters' Club of the Academy of Sciences, Memorial, the Moscow Popular Front, and a number of others. In December of the same year the Inter-regional Union of Voters was founded on the initiative of the Moscow Voters' Union. About 300 people from 50 cities in eight USSR republics were present at the founding conference. Both the Moscow and Inter-regional Unions

played a decisive role in securing the successful functioning of the Democratic Russia election bloc, and became one of its founding members . . . In practice all the organization and agitation work during the election campaign was done in Moscow by the Inter-regional Union of Voters and in the regions of the republic—by the corresponding structures. The Inter-regional Union of Voters was the main organizer of the mass actions in Moscow on 4 February 1990 and in 50 major cities on 25 February 1990 in support of the democrats and the candidates of the Democratic Russia bloc (200–300,000 people took part).[36]

---

[35] Shcherkin, 'Protsessy zarozhdeniya, razvitiya i stanovleniya politicheskikh partiy i massovykh obshchestvennykh dvizheniy v Pskovskoy oblasti v 1988–1994', pp. 3–4.

[36] *Rossiya: partii, assotsiatsii, soyuzy, kluby*, i/1. 95.

The union published a newspaper, *Golos izberatelya* (The Voter's Voice), and numerous leaflets and other propaganda materials. Many of its activists were elected to the soviets at various levels. After the elections of 1990 the union, with its local branches, joined the Democratic Russia Movement.

Another, less successful attempt to unite the voters' clubs was made by Viktor Mironov, the publisher of an independent 'democratic' newspaper, *Khronika*. Mironov's All-Union Voters' Association merged with the Inter-regional Union of Voters and they were both absorbed within the Democratic Russia Movement, Mironov himself becoming the People's Deputy of both the Moscow City Soviet and the Russian Federation.

The Democratic Russia Movement

The Democratic Russia Movement (DRM) was organized on the basis of a bloc of 'democratic' groups which had been created on the eve of the 1990 elections (it had earlier been called 'Elections 1990' and 'Democratic Bloc'). The bloc's programme was officially adopted at the founding conference on 20–1 January 1990. The programme appeared in the most popular *glasnost*` publications, the weekly *Moscow News* and the weekly *Ogonek*. To join the new movement it was enough to express support for the programme. As a result Democratic Russia was joined by other Russian 'democratic' groups (except anarchists and the Democratic Union, though some Democratic Union candidates cooperated with Democratic Russia). Several 'parties' won the status of collective members. According to Beresovskiy, Krotov, and Chrvyakov,

In practice the activities of Democratic Russia during the election campaign were guided by the members of the Inter-regional Group, who used their prestige, their connections, and the mass media. On their initiative, all 'democratic election blocs and committees' in seventy cities and towns of the RSFSR declared themselves local branches of Democratic Russia or announced that they shared its programme. In Moscow the entire campaign was practically organized by the Moscow Voters' Union and in Leningrad by the Leningrad Popular Front.[37]

During the election campaign Democratic Russia groups circulated lists of candidates whom they supported. There could be several DR-supported candidates in one constituency. Candidates supported by DR won about 30 per cent of the constituencies at the Russian federal level, but because of the election of the Inter-regional Group member Boris Yel`tsin to the position of RSFSR Supreme Soviet Chairman its faction became the most influential group. The DR candidates also won a majority in Moscow and Leningrad City Soviets and a significant amount of seats in many local soviets.

[37] Ibid. 93.

During the second half of 1990 and the first half of 1991, despite the emerging conflicts between Democratic Russia members working in executive and representative bodies and increasing questions about the future of the Soviet Union and Russia, Democratic Russia in general managed to maintain its unity until the August 1991 coup. This made it possible for the movement to mobilize its supporters for the defence of the Russian parliament. The serious splits which Democratic Russia suffered after the collapse of the USSR in late December 1991 are beyond the scope of this book.

'Democratic' parties

Like other self-identifications used by the members of 'democratic groups', the word 'party' in the Russian context could signify very different realities. A discussion club which only met a few times and consisted of five or ten members and a relatively big organization with thousands of members and branches in dozens of cities could both call themselves 'parties'. It is impossible to enumerate all these 'parties', the total number of which was at least several hundred, and most of them fit into the categories discussed above. This section discusses only those groups which at least for a certain period of time enjoyed a considerable following and played an important role in election campaigns, in line with the accepted view in political science that the key criterion of a party is that it put forward candidates for office.[38] (This is one of the reasons why the Democratic Union, which called itself a party and was a relatively large and influential group, but which from the very beginning rejected electoral activities, has been discussed in a separate section.)

Most parties were collective members of the Democratic Russia Movement. Among them were the Democratic Party of Russia (DPR), the Social Democratic Party of the Russian Federation (SDPR), the Russian Christian Democratic Movement (RCDM), the Republican Party of Russia (RPR), the Free Democratic Party of Russia (FDP), the Constitutional Democratic Party-Party of People's Freedom (CDP–PPF), the Union of Constitutional Democrats (UCD), and the Peasants' Party of Russia. Among non-members of the Democratic Russia Movement the most significant were the People's Party of Free Russia (PPFR), the People's Party of Russia (PPR), and the Socialist Party.

The *Democratic Party of Russia* was by far the largest collective member of the Democratic Russia Movement. The formation of the DPR was planned by

---

[38] According to Giovanni Sartori, for example, 'A party is any political group that presents at elections, and is capable of placing through elections, candidates for public office': Giovanni Sartori, *Parties and Party Systems: A Framework for Analysis* (Cambridge: Cambridge University Press, 1976), i., 64.

those leading Russian 'democrats' who wanted to create a well-organized and united party of 'democrats' to oppose the ruling CPSU. The party was to be based on different local 'democratic' groups and voters' associations and to organize them into a more disciplined party. After the 1990 elections the idea gained the support of some of the most active members of the Inter-regional Group and 'democratic' deputies of the Russian Federation Supreme Soviet, many of whom were at the same time leaders of different 'democratic' groups: Nikolay Travkin and Gennadiy Burbulis (the CPSU Democratic Platform), Lev Ponomarev (the Moscow Association of Voters), Arkadiy Murashev (secretary of the coordinating council of the Inter-regional Group), Marina Sal`e and Il`ya Konstantinov (the Leningrad People's Front), and others. The plan was also supported by the world chess champion Garri Kasparov.

The project failed because of disagreements among the leaders and their personal ambitions. At the founding conference at the end of May 1990, Travkin insisted on a single chairmanship of the party, arguing that it should be more disciplined than Democratic Russia. Sal`e and Ponomarev, who insisted on co-chairmanship, walked out, taking with them almost all the activists from Leningrad and many from the Moscow voters' clubs. Kasparov and Murashev stayed but formed a Free Democratic Faction, which controlled the DPR's Moscow organization. However, some important provincial 'democratic' groups joined the DPR. Among them were the Kazan` Initiative Centre of the Tatar People's Front, the organizing committee for the Stavropol` People's Front, and a section of the Yaroslavl` People's Front.[39]

There was a more fundamental reason for the DPR's failure to unite all of the 'democrats': the idea of party discipline and everything that comes with it was unpopular among a significant section of 'democratic' activists, who saw the creation of any party as an attempt to reintroduce Communist 'democratic centralism'. The looser Democratic Russia Movement enjoyed broader support, and the process of its organization occurred alongside the formation of the DPR. In Democratic Russia the most active organizers were those who had left the DPR and the leaders of the DPR's Free Democratic Faction. Travkin reluctantly agreed to join the Democratic Russia Movement under the pressure of the DPR's grassroots organizations, which supported the idea of the unity of the 'democratic' movement. At the party's Second Congress in April 1991, Murashev and Kasparov finally withdrew from it, and subsequently the DPR suffered several more splits. Though it obviously failed to unite all the 'democratic' groups and became only one of many 'democratic' parties, by the end of 1991 it remained one of the largest and most influential. In 1991 it claimed to have 50,000 members. Because of an elaborate system of party cards and party dues this figure is more reliable than those given by

---

[39] Pribylovskii, *Dictionary of Political Parties and Organizations in Russia*, 20.

most other 'democratic' parties, though perhaps it is slightly exaggerated since former members did not usually surrender their cards on leaving the party and continued to be counted.

The Second Congress ratified a declaration establishing the People's Accord bloc, which included the DPR, the RCDM, and the CDP–PPF. The parties in the bloc disapproved of the support given by the majority of Democratic Russia's membership to what they viewed as a strategy to split up the USSR, and argued fervently in favour of the unity of the Russian Federation. The DPR Tatar organization became the main anti-separatist force in the Republic of Tatarstan. At the Second Congress of Democratic Russia in November 1991, the three parties withdrew from the movement because of its opposition to the Union Treaty. In December of the same year the DPR organized a rally in Moscow against the dissolution of the USSR and later found itself in open opposition to the rest of the 'democrats' and to Yel`tsin's government. The party issued an official newspaper, *Demokraticheskaya Rossiya*, and several local publications. After *Demokraticheskaya Rossiya* became independent in November 1990 as a result of conflict between its editor Georgiy Khatsenkov and Travkin, the party started another official newspaper, *Demokraticheskaya gazeta*.

The DPR had organizations in most of Russia's regions, and some of them were relatively strong. In Stavropol` the party was collectively joined by the Stavropol` Popular Front with all its developed regional structure. Even in the industrial town of Nevinnomyssk a local DPR group was quite active in election campaigns and published a typewritten magazine, *Demokrat*. After the failure of the August 1991 coup many members of the Stavropol` organization of the DPR obtained jobs at the *kray* administration, and its leader, Vasiliy Krasulya, was appointed deputy governor. In Pskov the local DPR branch was set up in February 1991 by a USSR People's Deputy, Nikolay Panov, who organized a visit to the *oblast`* by Travkin, the DPR leader. In August 1991 Panov was the main organizer of anti-coup activities in Pskov *oblast`*. Though Panov failed to become *oblast`* governor himself after the failure of the coup, the governor, Anatoliy Dobryakov, had the support of the DPR. The branch was joined by the editor of a local newspaper, *Spektr* (later *Rossiyskie vedomosty*), Vladimir Filatov, who published the newspaper's telephone number as a contact number for the DPR. One of the leaders of the DPR in Pskov, Aleksandr Solov'ev, was appointed chairman of the *oblast`* Anti-monopoly Committee. Another DPR activist, Vladimir Tolkachev, formerly the editor of the newspaper *Profsoyuznaya gazeta* (which, despite being the organ of Pskov's official trade unions, supported 'democrats'), became the head of Pskov television.[40] In Penza, the DPR had a strong organization with an office in the centre of the city,

---

[40] Shcherkin, 'Protsessy zarozhdeniya, razvitiya i stanovleniya politicheskikh partiy i massovykh obshchestvennykh dvizheniy v Pskovskoy oblasti v 1988–1994', pp. 12–13.

published one of the popular local newspapers, *Vybor*, and had organizations in every district of the *oblast*`, though party members were not appointed to the local government. In Vladivostok the DPR organization was less strong, consisting of perhaps about twenty members. In Krasnoyarsk and Orenburg, DPR organizations either did not exist or were not active.

The *Russian Christian Democratic Movement* was founded in April 1990 by non-conformist Christian intellectuals and clerics, most of whom wrote for *samizdat*, took part in human rights groups, and even served prison sentences before *perestroyka*.[41] The co-chairmen of the movement, Viktor Aksyuchits and Gleb Anishchenko, and Father Vyacheslav Polosin became editors of an unofficial magazine, *Vybor*. Among other leaders were former political prisoner Father Gleb Yakunin and human rights activist Valeriy Borshchev. Within the movement a narrower party was formed to achieve purely political aims, while the movement was supposed to work for the broad Christian education of the population. However, in practice the party and the movement were led by the same people and were virtually indistinguishable.

At the First Congress of Democratic Russia, members of the RCDM were the largest group, forming 30 per cent of the delegates.[42] But by the second half of 1991 the most influential group within the RCDM leadership, headed by Aksyuchits, became more and more critical of what they saw as the anti-unionist position of the majority of 'democrats' and of their support of separatism in the USSR and in the Russian Federation republics. This led to the RCDM joining the People's Accord bloc and later withdrawing from Democratic Russia. This course of action caused several splits in the RCDM. Father Gleb Yakunin and many other members preferred to stay in Democratic Russia; others, like Borshchev, formed or joined other parties. In July 1991 the RCDM claimed to have 62,000 members,[43] but this figure seems to be highly unrealistic: no local organization was found in any of the regions selected for study in this book.

Another Christian Democratic party, the Christian Democratic Union of Russia, was formed even earlier than the RCDM in August 1989 by former political prisoner Aleksandr Ogorodnikov. Because of constant splits it failed to achieve significant influence and was better known abroad than in Russia.

The *Constitutional Democratic Party-Party of People's Freedom*, formed as a small splinter group from the Union of Constitutional Democrats, attempted to revive a major political party of late tsarist Russia and adopted its name.

---

[41] See Richard Sakwa, 'Christian Democracy in Russia', *Religion, State and Society*, 20:2 (1992), 135–200.

[42] B. I. Koval` (ed.), *Rossiya segodnya. Politicheskiy portret, 1985–1990* (Moscow: Mezhdunarodnye otnosheniya, 1991), 305.

[43] Pribylovskii, *Dictionary of Political Parties and Organizations in Russia*, 77.

The project failed, but the party gained some influence within the 'democratic' movement after Mikhail Astaf'ev, an RSFSR People's Deputy and an active member of the 'democratic' faction at the Congress of People's Deputies of the Russian Federation, was elected its leader. Astaf'ev was among the founding members of Democratic Russia and is even said to have invented its name. The CDP–PPF was a collective member of the movement until its withdrawal in November 1991 with other members of People's Accord. The membership of the party probably never exceeded several dozen.

The *Social Democratic Party of the Russian Federation* was among the first officially formed and most influential parties in Russia. Its regional membership was based on numerous early social democratic clubs and discussion groups and in Moscow its leadership and core membership came directly from the Perestroyka Club and its regional counterparts. The direct connection between the party and earlier 'informal' groups and clubs is shown in an April 1991 survey of the SDPR activists, functionaries, and officers, which showed that 60 per cent of the party's elite had become active in the 'democratic' movement before 1990.[44]

Social democratic groups began to emerge from 1987 as a logical and less dangerous step in the rejection of official Communist doctrine. At the second conference of the All-Union Socio-political Club, held in Taganrog in August 1987, a social democratic faction was formed. Almost simultaneously, some members of the Moscow Democratic Perestroyka Club (Pavel Kudyukin, Andrey Fadin, and Oleg Rumyantsev) declared their social democratic orientation in one of the first 'informal' magazines, *Otkrytaya zona* (Open Zone). In March 1988 a group of Leningrad 'informals' set up the Social Democratic Union and declared plans to form a social democratic party. Later that year social democratic groups were formed within Moscow Democratic Perestroyka club (Kudyukin, Rumyantsev, Leonid Volkov, and others)—and within the Leningrad Perestroyka group (Petr Filippov, Anatoliy Golov). In May 1989 Moscow Democratic Perestroyka organized an inter-city working session for clubs with a social orientation. An agreement was reached on creating the Social Democratic Association, which was finally set up at a congress at Tallinn in January 1990. The Association united seventy groups from almost every Soviet republic, published about sixty *samizdat* newspapers and magazines, and started an information bulletin. The bulletin was published in censorship-free Tallinn and was in fact one of the first independent newspapers circulated in Russia.[45]

[44] Sergei Mitrokhin and Michael Urban, 'Social Groups, Party Elites and Russia's New Democrats', in David Lane (ed.), *Russia in Flux: The Political and Social Consequences of Reform* (Aldershot: Edward Elgar, 1992), 75.

[45] Pribylovskii, *Dictionary of Political Parties and Organizations in Russia*, 92; *Rossiya: partii, assotsiatsii, soyuzy, kluby*, i/1. 113.

At a congress in Moscow in May 1990 Russian members of the Social Democratic Association created the SDPR. The new party was quite impressive: the 238 delegates of the congress represented 104 local organizations with a total membership of 4,245. Several USSR and RSFSR People's Deputies were elected to its leading bodies, among them Aleksandr Obolenskiy (Appatity, Murmansk *oblast*), Nikolay Tutov (Orenburg), Oleg Rumyantsev (Moscow), and others. The SDPR became a collective member of Democratic Russia and though it remained one of the most influential and organized parties, with a considerable local following, like many other 'democratic' groups it tended to melt into the broader movement. The Third Congress in May 1991 was attended by only 162 delegates who represented 2,500 members from 62 organizations. At the end of 1991 the party was continuing to split as it lost most of its popular leaders, many of whom were too busy with their duties as parliamentary deputies or their activities in Democratic Russia.

The SDPR had local organizations in many regions, but they were usually small and did not participate in local administration. In Primorskiy *kray* the party was joined by a very active Vladivostok Democrat Club whose leader, Il`ya Grinchenko, was elected to the SDPR central board, and by the Social Democratic Association in Nakhodka. In Orenburg the local Social Democratic Committee, headed by the leader of the Orenburg 'informals' and the All-Union Socio-political Club, Aleksandr Sukharev, joined the Social Democratic Association and took part in the organizing work of the SDPR, but in the end Sukharev refused to join the more organized party. However, a USSR People's Deputy from Orenburg, Nikolay Tutov, became another member of the central board. In Penza the local organization of the SDPR was headed by Anatoliy Zamyatin, one of the founders of the Civic Initiative group, and a leader of the unofficial labour movement.

The *Republican Party of Russia* was formed from the Democratic Platform, which split from the CPSU. Its origins go back to the Inter-club Party Group, which was organized in May 1988 by activists of different 'informal' clubs who were members of the CPSU. Among them were Vladimir Lysenko, Igor` Chubays, Sergey Stankevich, and Mikhail Malyutin. A year later more radical members of the Inter-club Party Group formed the Moscow Party Club. In January 1990 at a conference organized by Moscow Party Club, at which 102 representatives of similar CPSU reformist clubs from 13 Soviet republics were present, the Democratic Platform within the CPSU was established. Well-known 'democratic' leaders joined the new organization, including Yuriy Afanas`ev, Nikolay Travkin, Tel`man Gdlyan, and some liberal Communist party officials, such as the rector of the Moscow Higher Party School, Vyacheslav Shostakovskiy. After the Democratic Platform's proposals for the democratization of the CPSU were rejected by the Russian

Communist conference and later by the Twenty-eighth Congress of the CPSU in the summer of 1990, the Platform collectively left the CPSU and formed a new party at a conference in October that year. The RPR claimed 4,000 followers in Moscow and 30,000 in Russia. If this was indeed the case in 1990, after that the RPR gradually lost membership and influence. While the Democratic Platform within the CPSU was seen by many Communists as a legal form of fighting for 'democratic' reform without leaving the strongest party, the Republican Party became just one of many 'democratic' parties with almost no distinct goals and programmes. Understanding this, the Republican Party leaders joined Democratic Russia and tried to merge with the Social Democrats, but because of the personal ambitions of the leaders the alliance was never formed. However, by the end of 1991 the RPR was still one of the largest 'democratic' parties.

The RPR had local organizations in some regions of Russia. Among the regions selected for this book, an active republican organization existed only in Primorskiy *kray*. It evolved from a group of lecturers at Vladivostok State University, who united around a well-known specialist in archaeology, Professor David Brodyanskiy. In January 1989 at a meeting to nominate the candidates to the USSR People's Deputies, Brodyanskiy supported an unofficial candidate and fellow-university professor, and became his adviser (*doverennoye litso*). In January 1990, Brodyanskiy with several supporters, who were all CPSU members, formed an Initiative Group of Communists, which was in the forefront of the campaign to collect signatures for convening an extraordinary conference of the *kray* Communist Party organization in connection with charges of corruption levied against several local leaders. The group members were elected to the conference, which was held in May 1990, and managed to circulate there an alternative report. Later the group announced its support for the Democratic Platform within the CPSU and finally formed the core of the local organization of the RPR, Brodyanskiy becoming its co-chairman. A smaller RPR group existed in Stavropol`, where it was headed by a former deputy editor of the official *kray* Communist newspaper, Nikolay Baladzhants.[46]

The *Free Democratic Party of Russia* was formed during the founding congress of the DPR in May 1990, when part of the preparatory group walked out after Travkin's election as chairman. The party had its strongest support in Leningrad, where its organization was headed by the city's voter's movement leader, People's Deputy of the USSR Marina Sal'e. In Moscow it was joined by Lev Ponomarev's supporters from the Moscow Voters' Union. The party was never very active since its leaders were at the same time among the chief organizers of the Democratic Russia Movement and did not have much

---

[46] Krasulya, *Dissident iz nomenklatury*, 131–4.

time for party work. Party membership was 400–500 and most of the members were former Leningrad 'democratic' activists.

The *Union of Constitutional Democrats* was a minor 'democratic' party of several dozen members which evolved out of the Moscow informal human rights group Grazhdanskoye dostoinstvo 'Civic Dignity'. Its influence was a result of the fact that the bulletin of Civic Dignity was one of the best-known informal publications. This made it possible for the UCD to become a collective member of the Democratic Russia Movement.

The *Peasants' Party of Russia*, another collective member of the Democratic Russia Movement, was only influential because of its leader, a well-known agrarian journalist and writer, Yuriy Chernichenko. The party was formed at a conference in March 1991. Among its 286 delegates, 200 were independent farmers and sharecroppers, whose interests the party was to represent. Its total membership was estimated at 500–600.

The *People's Party of Russia* was quite a late attempt by some of the most radical anti-Gorbachev 'democrats' to unite the whole of the 'democratic' movement. Its formation was announced in March 1991 at a rally in support of Boris Yel`tsin by the former special investigator Tel`man Gdlyan and was joined by the RSFSR People's Deputies Aleksey Surkov, Bella Denisenko, Oleg Kalugin, and Vladimir Rebrikov. Its real leader was Gdlyan and its main base was his support groups, which were formed in several cities during his sharp confrontation with CPSU Politburo members over alleged corruption. The strongest organization of this kind, the Committee in Defence of Gdlyan and Ivanov, was formed in Gdlyan's USSR Congress of People's Deputies constituency in the town of Zelenograd, which administratively is a part of Moscow. The party failed to unite all 'democrats' and, like its leader, who failed to prove most of his allegations, gradually lost popularity.

The *Socialist Party of Russia* united left-wing elements of the informal movement. It evolved from an early informal group, Socialist Initiative, which later joined the Moscow Popular Front. Its leader, Boris Kagarlitskiy, became one of the most influential members of the Front's coordinating council. After a split with the MPF's 'democratic' wing, Kagarlitskiy's socialist group formed the Moscow Committee of New Socialists, which later became the base for the Socialist Party. In December 1989 socialist clubs from eight Russian cities united in the All-union Committee for a Socialist Party (ACSP). During the 1990 elections six Moscow New Socialists, including Kagarlitskiy, were elected to Moscow City Soviet and an ACSP member from Prokop`evsk, Vladimir Makhanov, became an RSFSR People's Deputy. In June 1990, at the founding congress in Moscow, the Socialist Party of the USSR was formed.

The congress was attended by approximately sixty representatives from fourteen cities in Russia, Ukraine, Byelorussia, and Kazakhstan. At its Second Congress in March 1991 the party ceased to be union-wide and became known as the Socialist Party of Russia.

While Kagarlitskiy's group played a very active role within the early informal movement, after 1989 the influence of socialists among 'democrats' faded. There were both ideological and personal reasons for this. While in 1989 the socialists' agenda seemed reformist, later, with the rapid development in the position of the authorities, the mainstream 'democratic' movement failed to see much difference between the authorities and the socialists. After the Socialist Party rejected the Shatalin–Yavlinskiy Plan for the transition to a market economy, which was also eventually rejected by Gorbachev but supported by Yel'tsin and other 'democrats', they were denied membership in the Democratic Russia Movement and later started to look for an alliance with official trade unions. Also, some of the 'democratic' activists, especially those with connections to former dissidents, were very cautious about Kagarlitskiy, who, after his arrest in 1982 for organizing a socialist group, fully cooperated with the authorities and was released, while some other, less cooperative members of the group served prison sentences.[47] It is unlikely that the Socialist Party of Russia ever had more than a hundred members and its influence was never great.

The *People's Party of Free Russia*, which once enjoyed the biggest membership among the oppositional parties in Russia, emerged from another attempt to split the CPSU. It was formed in October 1991 from the Democratic Party of Communists of Russia (DPCR), a peculiar attempt to create a party within the existing Communist Party. The idea of forming the DPCR came from Aleksandr Rutskoy, then a member of the presidium of the RSFSR Supreme Soviet, and was undoubtedly supported by the Supreme Soviet chairman, Boris Yel'tsin, who wanted to split the CPSU and gain the support of reformist Communists for the Russian presidential elections. The process was accelerated when Rutskoy's influence grew after he was elected Yel'tsin's vice-president. But after August 1991, Yel'tsin lost his interest in the plan, since the CPSU was gone anyway and the creation of a new party could only strengthen the position of Rutskoy, who began openly to disagree with the president. Rutskoy, however, went ahead, and the PPFR was founded in October 1991. The party claimed to have 100,000 members, but the figure is difficult to verify. Because the PPFR was formed relatively late and the whole project was more the result of the splits among the Russian leaders than a grassroots initiative, it can only be called partially 'democratic'. Its leaders rarely claimed to be a part of a broader

---

[47] Alekseeva, *Istoriya inakomysliya v SSSR*, 308–9.

'democratic' movement, though its local activists often did so and worked closely with other 'democratic' groups.

A typical example of this contradiction is the story of the PPFR's Pskov *oblast*' organization, which was created from above in order to strengthen support for the Russian leadership among members of the CPSU. In Pskov the party was headed by the party's Central Council member, Valentin Grylev, a manager of the building-industrial concern Pskovstroy, who in an interview on 15 November 1991 announced that the Pskov *oblast*' PPFR group had only thirty members. Grylev called on the intelligentsia to join the new party, spoke in favour of cooperation with Democratic Russia, and criticized the Congress of Civic and Patriotic Forces, a meeting of mainly nationalist groups held in Moscow which was addressed by the PPFR leader Rutskoy. Later the Pskov organization of PPFR worked together with the Democratic Russia Movement and even supported the creation of the People's Choice bloc.[48]

Another party whose programme documents are often mentioned in this book is the *Democratic Party*. The Democratic Party is one of the micro-parties, and was formed by a former political prisoner confined to psychiatric hospitals, Lev Ubozhko. Ubozhko was among the founding members of the Democratic Union but was expelled from it after a conflict with Valeriya Novodvorskaya. The Democratic Party was formed at a conference in November 1989. After a split in October 1990 Ubozhko left the party and formed the Conservative Party. After that the Democratic Party was headed by Nikolay Proselkov and Anatoliy Cherepanov. Despite its moderate membership of a few dozen activists, the Democratic Party had activists in several cities, including Orenburg. Although not an official member of the Democratic Russia Movement, the party took part in all major 'democratic' rallies and meetings.

3.6. PATTERNS OF JOINING 'DEMOCRATIC' GROUPS AND THEORIES OF RECRUITMENT

The question of the mechanism of recruitment to 'democratic' groups is important since as well as being interesting in itself it can also provide new information for the long-standing theoretical discussion on the emergence of new political movements. There is a widely accepted view in political science that political parties and movements are there to represent the interests of

---

[48] Shcherkin, 'Protsessy zarozhdeniya, razvitiya i stanovleniya politicheskikh partiy i massovykh obshchestvennykh dvizheniy v Pskovskoy oblasti v 1988–1994', pp. 13–14.

social groups and classes and fight for them. Theories of social conflict which are based on this idea maintain that when the development of society creates new deprived social groups or classes which are deeply dissatisfied with their low social status, the members lose their customary stable position in society. These groups and classes create new political groups which assert their interests against the ruling establishment, thus creating political conflict. The social composition of these new political groups should naturally represent this situation, i.e. most of their members should come from the deprived social groups. These concepts, which are often called breakdown or deprivation theories, have as their source Marxist ideas of class struggle and Durkheim's notion of anomie. They stress the role of ideology or shared beliefs in the process of recruitment of members to new political groups, since according to them the members of the deprived classes are more susceptible to the political propaganda of ideologies which aim at changing the existing situation.[49]

However, some later studies challenged the main tenets of deprivation theories. They showed that such processes as industrialization and urbanization, which were thought to create anomie by breaking customary social ties, in fact led to the creation of new ties in modern industrial cities which were no less strong and extensive than in traditional and rural societies.[50] Moreover, close studies of some new unorthodox social groups in the USA showed that these groups, far from consisting of poor, disturbed, and socially deprived personalities, often united absolutely normal and well-to-do citizens.[51] As a result those theories which explained membership in new social and political movements by the need to compensate for lost social bonds and stability came under criticism. For example, on the basis of a study of the mechanism of joining the first group of American members of the then very young but rapidly growing Korean-based cult of the Reverend Sun Myung Moon, John Lofland and Rodney Stark established

the essential role played by interpersonal bonds between cult members and the potential recruit. When such bonds did not exist and failed to develop, newcomers failed to join. When such bonds did exist or develop (and when they were stronger than the

---

[49] For a thorough outline of theories of social conflict, see Anthony Obershall, *Social Movements: Ideologies, Interests, and Identities* (New Brunswick, NJ: Transaction, 1993), 39–66.

[50] See e.g. William Foote Whyte, *Street Corner Society* (Chicago: University of Chicago Press, 1943); Michael Young and Peter Willmott, *Family and Kinship in East London* (Baltimore: Penguin, 1957); Oscar Lewis, 'Further Observations on the Folk-Urban Continuum and Urbanization', in P. H. Hauser and L. Schnore (eds.), *The Study of Urbanization* (New York: Wiley, 1965), 491–503.

[51] See Bert Useem, 'Solidarity Model, Breakdown Model and the Boston Anti-busing Movement', *American Sociological Review*, 45 (1980), 357–69; Rodney Stark and William Bainbridge, 'Networks of Faith: Interpersonal Bonds and Recruitment to Cults and Sects', *American Journal of Sociology*, 6 (1980), 1376–95.

bonds to others who opposed the individual's recruitment), people did join. Indeed, persons were sometimes drawn by their attachment to group members to move into the Moonie commune while still openly expressing rejection of the Moon ideology. Acceptance of the ideology, and the decision to become full-time cultists, often came only *after* a long period of day-to-day interaction with cult members. Rather than being drawn to the group because of the appeal of its ideology, people were drawn to the ideology because of their ties to the group—'final conversion was coming to accept the opinions of one's friends'.[52]

After similar results were obtained by several other researchers, the conclusion about the primary role of interpersonal bonds as opposed to ideological appeal began to be applied not just to religious cults but to new social movements in general. However, at the same time other studies continued to show an important role for deprivation and ideological attachment. This made the adherents of the 'interpersonal bonds' theory soften their approach. Thus, Rodney Stark and William Bainbridge argued: 'There is nothing contradictory between the deprivation and ideological appeal line of analysis and the analysis that stresses the importance of social networks. Both seem obvious requirements of any adequate theory. If deprivation alone explained recruitment to cults, then millions more people would become members than actually do.'[53] Combining both approaches, Stark and Bainbridge nevertheless still maintained that having a social relation with a member was a necessary condition for a new member to join: 'Recruits must not only suffer relevant deprivations and be open to a radical group's ideological appeal; they must also be placed in a situation where they will develop social bonds with existing members of the group.'[54]

However, this argument can easily be put the other way. If one can argue that among the ideologically attached it is only those who already have friends, relatives, or colleagues in a group who join it, one can also argue that among numerous friends, colleagues, and relatives it is only those who are ideologically attached who join a group. Neither approach explains such important phenomena as the creation of a new group by a founder who cannot have had previous personal connections with the group, or the joining of a group by complete strangers with no connections to its members (if one were to find such cases).

These phenomena could be explained by a different approach. This approach continues to stress the primary role of acceptance by a founder or a new member of the beliefs of a social movement or even an ideological trend which may precede the actual emergence of a movement or group. For

---

[52] Rodney Stark and William Sims Bainbridge, *The Future of Religion: Secularization, Revival and Cult Formation* (Berkeley, Calif.: University of California Press, 1985), 308–9; quotation from John Lofland and Rodney Stark, 'Becoming a World-Saver: A Theory of Conversion to a Deviant Perspective', *American Sociological Review*, 30 (1965), 871.

[53] Stark and Bainbridge, *The Future of Religion*, 312.   [54] Ibid.

example, Anthony Oberschall, while recognizing the role of interpersonal bonds which manifest themselves in the participants of mass actions and social movements bringing with them family members, colleagues, and neighbours, at the same time argues that most participants 'tend to be self-selected from those who are already in agreement with the goals of the leaders and sponsoring organizations'. According to Oberschall, 'the self-selection and assembly of similarly predisposed participants in collective action—religious minded crusaders and politically engaged demonstrators— is called convergence'.[55]

The author's study of recruitment patterns in Russian 'democratic' groups suggests that at least in this case self-selection based on sharing broad 'democratic' beliefs and a perception of the whole society played a much more important role than interpersonal bonds. It is true that in some cases new 'democratic' groups were joined by colleagues, friends, or relatives who followed the a more pioneering activist whom they trusted and whose opinions they shared. For example, Stavropol` Popular Front (later the local branch of the Democratic Party of Russia) was joined by a whole group of employees of the local anti-plague institute: at the first stage, two employees (Sergey Popov and Yuriy Nesis) were among the founding members; others, including the head of the institute himself, joined at later stages.[56] Another group of members (Sergey Popov, Valeriy Mitrofanenko, and Yelena Suslova) had become friends earlier when they were organizing the activities of an amateur singing club which was already engaging in political action, for example, in signing political letters to the authorities.[57] Both groups had a common informal leader—Sergey Popov—who became the chief organizer of the Front. Furthermore, some members joined the Front after their relatives or friends did. For example, Oleg Lushnikov found out about it from his wife, who worked at the anti-plague institute, and from Yelena Suslova, who happened to be her friend.[58] Alla Lipchanskaya acknowledged that she joined the Front because of her personal sympathy towards its leader, Vasiliy Krasulya, whom she later married.[59] Popov, Mitrofanenko, Nesis, and Lipchanskaya became members of the informal leadership core of the Front, which consisted at different times of about 10–15 members. These facts could support the theory of personal bonds if they were not just one part of the story. The other part is that the majority of the other members of the Front, like the leader of both circles, Sergey Popov, joined it without following anyone.

As shown above, the idea of creating an independent pro-*perestroyka* group emerged in Stavropol` after the deputy editor of the local Communist

[55] Obershall, *Social Movements: Ideologies, Interests, and Identities*, 13.
[56] Krasulya, *Dissident iz nomenklatury*, 162.
[57] Interview with Yelena Suslova (Stavropol`, 4 Sept. 1994).
[58] Interview with Oleg Lushnikov (Stavropol`, 4 Sept. 1994).
[59] Interview with Alla Lipchanskaya (Stavropol`, 2 Sept. 1994).

newspaper, Vasiliy Krasulya, was sacked for publishing an article titled 'We are Born to be Free', which supported and developed official ideas of universal values, rejected the class approach, and criticized bureaucracy.[60] The persecution of the author made the article very popular and many people read it or found out about its contents. Supporters, some of whom were total strangers to him, began to contact Krasulya and suggest different ways of reaction. Since at that stage Krasulya had not gone much further than the official proposals of Moscow's leaders, the whole thing was understood by the majority as sabotage by the Stavropol` authorities of Gorbachev's *perestroyka* (which in Stavropol` was seen as an even greater shame since the Soviet leader himself was a native of Stavropol` *kray* and its leader from 1970 to 1978). At that time the idea of creating a Popular Front for Perestroyka became popular because of the successes of popular fronts in Estonia and Latvia. A future Stavropol` Popular Front activist, Yelena Suslova, described the events which followed:

We had a club where authors sang their songs, we all went there. Somebody could bring a letter there and all the members would sign it. One time [Krasulya's] article was brought. The situation was explained. And it went on after that . . . At that time the name 'Popular Front' was fashionable, there was a popular front in Estonia. . . . Our members Popov and Mitrofanov had just come back from Estonia where they had attended a song festival, but at the same time Popov was thinking constantly about the First Congress of the Estonian Popular Front. They came back and were telling everyone about it. And then we organized a meeting in the House of Writers as if to discuss the article, its official purpose was to discuss the article 'We are Born to be Free'. And then it turned out to be . . . as if everybody who came already knew that it would be an organizing conference of the Popular Front.[61]

It is correct to say that some members of the Popular Front were previously members of the amateur singing club, some came from the Friends of *Ogonek*, some of Popov's colleagues at the anti-plague institute followed him, and some came with their relatives and friends. But since membership was open and the meeting was announced in leaflets distributed in the city, many admirers of Krasulya's article came without knowing anybody or later called the contact telephone number of the organizing committee. Most of the other members of the informal core of the Front joined it in this way. It is obvious that it was not interpersonal bonds which united Stavropol` activists in the Popular Front, but the ideas of *perestroyka*, which came from the central press, and the fact that their fellow Stavropolite for promoting these ideas was persecuted. On the one hand, members of the Front who followed those they knew and trusted (like Nesis, Mitrofanov, Suslova, Lipchanskaya, and Lushnikov) already shared the beliefs of these informal leaders. On the other,

---

[60] Vasiliy Krasulya, 'My rodilis`, chtoby byt` svobodnymi', in Krasulya, *Dissident iz Nomenklatury*, 90–102.   [61] Interview with Suslova.

these leaders themselves and many other future activists shared a broad milieu of ideas of *perestroyka* and democratization and the most active of them decided to organize and join a group to promote these ideas without having any personal links with their future comrades in arms.

This model of recruitment was typical of other Russian cities. In Pskov, for example, some of the activists of the first 'democratic' group, Memorial, were formerly members of the local rock club (Nikolskiy, Shcherkin, Ivlev, and others); however, other activists had no connections with them before joining. In Vladivostok, Penza, Krasnoyarsk, and the Oktyabr`skiy district of Moscow even fewer members of 'democratic' groups followed their colleagues, relatives, friends, or neighbours. The majority had no connections with each other before joining. Therefore, the interpersonal bonds theory cannot explain either the emergence of the 'democratic' movement in Russia, or its rapid growth.

Self-selection on the basis of shared beliefs was the dominant model of recruitment in all regions of Russia that were analysed for this study. As in Stavropol`, the initial organizers typically addressed their project of forming an independent group directly to the entire population. These organizers could be well-known personalities who had often been persecuted by the authorities (Vasiliy Krasulya in Stavropol`, Nikolay Klepachev in Krasnoyarsk, Vladimir Yelistratov in Belinskiy, Georgiy Didichenko in Penza), or ordinary citizens who called for a public discussion of general issues (discussion clubs, clubs of friends of *Ogonek*, etc.) or for action to promote a specific cause (for example, re-electing local Communist authorities at a party conference, like the Initiative Group of Communists in Vladivostok; preventing the building of an environmentally damaging factory, like the Green Committee in Orenburg, or supporting 'democratic' candidates at elections, like numerous unions of voters).

These initial organizers typically decided to form an independent group under the influence of new ideas which were spread by the central mass media, and at the beginning they aimed at promoting these ideas in their region. They openly propagated their ideas and plans, organized meetings and rallies and spread information about them by every possible means, usually by leaflets which were stuck in public places, but sometimes in the liberal local mass media. Membership in new groups was open and everybody who claimed to share their goals and wanted to help could join. New members joined by calling a contact telephone number which they saw in a leaflet or a newspaper, by coming straight to a group's meeting or its headquarters, which was usually an organizer's flat, or by signing up directly at a rally. The ideas of 'democrats' were supported by many, sometimes long before an actual 'democrat' began to operate in a particular area. Converts to 'democracy' looked for someone to support and therefore the authorities, criticism of somebody only pushed them in the direction of 'democratic' activities and actually helped create 'democratic' leaders. For example, the future activists of the 'democratic' club Aprel` and of the Green Committee in Orenburg, Vladislav Shapovalenko, Vitaliy Yeykin, and Tamara Zlotnikova, found out about these groups from critical articles in official local newspapers. Shapovalenko and Yeykin came to a meeting of Aprel` out of protest, since they both thought that a group which came under criticism from the authorities must stand for something good.[62] Zlotnikova, an ecologist became interested in the Green Committee for reasons.[63] Neither of them knew anybody from these groups before joining. A future 'democratic' activist, Petr Popov, found out about Aprel` in the same way: 'I saw some information and advertisements about the work of a voter's or political club Aprel` in the newspaper *Yuzhnyy Ural*, which we subscribed to at that time. I thought of going there but not very seriously, but once I was in the city centre, popped in by chance and took part in a meeting. I liked what people discussed there.'[64]

A closer study of all these and other recruitment stories shows that in each case the general acceptance of 'democratic' beliefs preceded the actual joining of a group (as discussed in Chapter 2, these beliefs themselves were subject to constant evolution both before and after joining). For example, before joining Aprel`, Shapovalenko spoke critically of the authorities during the elections of delegates to the Nineteenth Conference of the CPSU,[65] Yeykin lost his job for attempting to liberalize the Komsomol,[66] and Popov criticized the managers of his factory for lack of *glasnost`* and democratization in an open letter to a newspaper,[67] and before joining the Green Committee, Zlotnikova expressed dissatisfaction with the authorities' inability to tackle environmental issues.[68] Despite the fact that many of those they knew shared their dissatisfaction and concerns, future activists often failed to find people who were ready to act decisively enough in their immediate surroundings. So when they found out that people whom they did not know had already organized or planned to organize a group which intended to fight for values and aims they believed in, they did not hesitate to join.

This was the pattern for all the regions which were studied. The story told by an activist of the Oktyabr`skiy District Union of Voters, Il`ya Gezentsvey, was very typical. According to Gezentsvey, while he was walking in the street soon after he lost his job at a cooperative for trying to implement new ideas about workers' rights, he saw advertisements on a wall saying that Zaslavskiy was going to meet his voters. Though he had met Zaslavskiy on several previous occasions when the deputy was trying to help workers in their conflict

---

[62] Interviews with Vladislav Shapovalenko (Orenburg, 21 Dec. 1994) and Vitaliy Yeykin (Orenburg, 22 Dec. 1994).

[63] Interview with Tamara Zlotnikova (Orenburg, 21 Dec. 1994).

[64] Interview with Petr Popov (Orenburg, 22 Dec. 1994).

[65] Interview with Shapovalenko.   [66] Interview with Yeykin.

[67] Interview with Popov.   [68] Interview with Zlotnikova.

with the management at a factory where Gezentsvey previously worked, he did not know him well. At the meeting Gezentsvey felt sympathy for Zaslavskiy's ideas and his proposal to form a votes' union to support 'democratic' candidates at the coming elections, since Gezentsvey himself 'understood that the future belonged to a new movement, to enterprising independent people, and this constituted the meaning of my future life'.[69] He was later offered a job as an assistant to Zaslavskiy and became one of the organizers of the Union.

Another Union activist, Mariya Sublina, did not meet any of her future 'democratic' colleagues before joining. According to her,

as soon as Yel`tsin emerged and became the First Secretary of the City Committee, I already began to think that I would definitely join the progressives. . . . From the very beginning I thought of him positively. I did not know anybody. Absolutely nobody. How did I join? I was walking in a subway near my house from Dimitrova Street to Krymskiy Val and saw an advertisement about a meeting at FIAN.[70] It said that there was a democratic initiative to form a voters' group, an active voters' group in Oktyabr`skiy district. And I went. At FIAN, when I went, I listened. Medvedev and Kataev were there, Shabad was also present. I listened to the speeches and I liked them. And when enrolment in the group of activists began I also put down my name.[71]

The story of my joining the 'democratic' movement is very similar. I first joined a branch of Memorial at the Institute of Oriental Studies of the Soviet Academy of Sciences, where I worked, but the branch was not very active before the election campaign of 1989. At the beginning of the campaign I asked the head of the group what I could do to help the cause of 'democracy' and found out that various 'democratic' groups were nominating campaign coordinators in every district of the city. I got the telephone number of the coordinator of Oktyabr`skiy district, where I lived, and through him the name of the coordinator of my sub-district (*mikro-rayon* or REU).[72] I later found out that at that time, apart from the coordinator himself, I was the first to volunteer in the sub-district. The reason was not lack of support, but lack of information, so the task was to mobilize numerous potential supporters who did not know where to go and what to do to help 'democratic' candidates from our constituency, among whom were such famous 'democrats' as Andrey Sakharov and Yuriy Afanas`ev. During the campaign Afanas`ev and Sakharov, who had been nominated in dozens of constituencies, decided to stand in constituencies other than ours, and we supported a radical young university

---

[69] Interview with Il`ya Gezentsvey (Moscow; 27 Aug, 1993).

[70] The Institute of Physics of the Academy of Science, an institution with a liberal atmosphere where Andrey Sakharov worked.

[71] Interview with Maria Sublina (Moscow, 28 Aug. 1993).

[72] REU is an abbreviation of Rayonnoe Ekspluatatsionnoe Upravlenie (District Managing Department), which was in charge of managing accommodation in a sub-district. If a subdistrict did not have a name it was just called after its REU–REU–1, REU–2, etc.

lecturer, Il`ya Zaslavskiy, whom nobody knew but whose programme sounded very 'democratic'. After Zaslavskiy was elected, the sub-district coordinator, who was a young physicist, preferred to proceed with his professional career, and I became the sub-district's representative on the coordinating committee of the newly formed district union of voters. Mine was a perfect case of self-selection on the basis of shared beliefs: I did not know any 'democratic' activists in my district before joining the campaign and was ready to support Sakharov, Afanas`ev, or anybody else with a similar programme only because I generally shared the 'democratic' ideals they were advocating.

This pattern of joining Russian 'democratic' groups was the most typical. It shows the primary role of self-selection on the basis of shared beliefs and the secondary role of social bonds: a new member who joined a 'democratic' group without previously knowing any other members or who even decided to form a new group, and was guided purely by belief in the cause of 'democratization', could bring relatives, friends, or colleagues to the group, but could not do so if there were no active people around. The question why different recruitment patterns worked for religious movements in America and for a political movement in Russia needs further investigation. The cause is likely to be found in the considerable difference between a social movement with a highly politicized agenda, especially when it emerges in a non-pluralist environment, and religious groups which are being formed in a pluralist environment. When there exist numerous options for the realization of the same desire (in the case of religion, for example, to seek the truth and to investigate the transcendental meaning of life) a potential member choosing among different but similar sects tends to follow the example of a friend or colleague as a kind of recommendation and guarantee of the rightness of a particular choice. When a movement has a very sensitive and distinctly political agenda which makes a potential member sharply divide society into two ways of thinking, two political camps, there is only one option to take. In this case sides are usually taken according to what people believe in (in fact, in this situation friends and even relatives can often find themselves in opposite camps).

3.7. SOCIAL COMPOSITION AND RECRUITMENT

The theory that members of new social movements tend to be representatives of deprived groups, of people who have lost their customary social bonds as a result of the process of economic and social development, is also not supported by the example of the Russian 'democratic' movement. The majority of 'democratic' groups and organizations did not have a fixed membership: the meetings were open to anyone, and all who came to take part usually could be regarded as members if they wished to be. Typically the membership of an early 'democratic' group was small, mostly ranging from only a few to several dozen people, and rarely exceeding one hundred. Most groups did not require formal membership, though a few groups and some parties, for example, the Demokrat Club in Vladivostok, the Democratic Union, and the Democratic Party of Russia, introduced membership cards and dues. However, in most cases meetings of 'democratic' groups were open to the general public and sometimes all of those present at a meeting could take part, even in voting. In many cases even a group leader could not give a definite figure for the number of its members; besides, for propaganda purposes groups themselves tended to overestimate their support. Usually, instead of a fixed number of supporters, a group had several circles of followers: a narrow core of leaders (usually 5–10 people); a wider group of activists gathering at regular meetings (20–100 people); a circle of supporters who were ready to attend major actions such as rallies and demonstrations (several thousand for a group of the popular front type); and general sympathizers who voted for 'democratic' candidates.

Under these circumstances it is not an easy task to determine the social composition of 'democratic' groups. Some basic conclusions, however, can be made using the data from several surveys conducted between 1985 and 1991 and provided by 'democratic' groups themselves. As mentioned above, in 1988 *Pravda* estimated the number of different independent (including non-political) groups in the whole of the USSR to be 30,000. By February 1989 the estimate had grown to more than 60,000.[73] According to an opinion poll taken in Moscow in March 1987, 52% of young engineers, 65% of young workers, more than 70% of university and high school students, and about 90% of the students of professional-technical schools (PTUs) indicated that they were 'informals', but this probably gives an idea not of the membership of the groups, but of the level of broad support for ideas and goals (including non-democratic and even non-political ideas and goals).[74] The figure of 70% of all young people was quoted at a conference of Soviet and Bulgarian philosophers and sociologists in Minsk in autumn 1987.[75] However, according to surveys conducted by Ye. Levashov in 1985–7, only 9.7% of all 'informals' claimed the activities of their groups to be political, and not all political groups were 'democratic'.[76] The largest 'democratic' organization, the Democratic Russia Movement, which embraced most smaller 'democratic' groups, claimed 450–500,000 members in November 1991.[77] However, all these figures come from very rough estimates.

[73] See Ch. 1 above.

[74] Quoted in: Berezovskiy and Krotov (eds.), *Neformalnaya Rossiya*, 4.

[75] Berezovskiy and Krotov (eds.), *Neformalnaya Rossiya*, 4.   [76] Ibid.

[77] Koordinatsionnyy sovet Dvizheniya 'Dvizhenie "Demokraticheskaya Rossiya"': politicheskiy avtoportret', *Rossiyskaya gazeta*, 29 Nov. 1991, 2.

The great majority of members of 'democratic' groups came from the intelligentsia. Most had a university education. This conclusion can be illustrated by data from several surveys. The earliest of them, conducted by the activists of the Perestroyka Club among those who took part in the club's discussion of 25 April 1988 (totalling about 200 respondents), suggests that 20.5% of those present belonged to the *inzhenerno-tekhnicheskie rabotniki* or ITR ('engineering technical workers': managers and technical personnel in industry and agriculture); 19.5% were academics in technology; 16.4% humanities academics; 11% doctors and teachers; 8% students; 6.7% creative intelligentsia (writers, artists, etc.); 6.1% academics-scientists; 6.5% industry managers and state and party apparat workers of different levels; and only 4% workers. All age groups were present in almost equal proportions and there were twice as many men as women.[78] Since the Perestroyka Club was organized by young academics and met at one of the research institutes, the share of academics there was higher than in some other groups.

A survey of delegates of the Second Congress of Democratic Russia conducted in November 1991 gave much more balanced results. Among 728 respondents 19.7% were industrial ITR; 10.6% academics; 10.2% education workers; 7.9% entrepreneurs; 7.6% workers; 6.9% employees of state organizations; 6.2% People's Deputies working full time at soviets of different levels; 5.1% cultural workers (creative intelligentsia); 4.5% pensioners; 4.1% workers engaged in the non-state sector; 3.5% heads of state organizations; 2.9% students; 2.5% military or law enforcement officers; 1.6% health workers; 0.9% farmers or land-lease holders; and 3.9% others. There were no collective-farm workers.[79] According to a study of the social composition of the elites of two Russian parties, the DPR and the SDPR, carried out in April 1991, 65% of the parties' elite held a higher education diploma (10% for the total population of the USSR), and 72% were non-manual workers—10% *sluzhashchie* (state, CPSU, and official trade union functionaries, petty military officers, and other civil servants) 16% ITR, 30% intelligentsia (those engaged in intellectual work outside the production sector), 16% and businessmen (non-state). The study also gives the proportion of 6% of students as 6%, dependants (who could be pensioners, students, etc.) 5%, and peasants 0%.[80]

Despite some differences in the methodology and results of these surveys, some general conclusions can be drawn. It is quite clear that the first 'democratic' groups in Russia were almost entirely an urban phenomenon: only in a very few isolated cases was it possible to trace the participation of 'new

---

[78] 'Nekotorye resul'taty oprosa uchastnikov diskussii v klube "Perestroyka" 25 aprelya 1988 g.', unpubl. MS [Moscow, 1988], courtesy of Oleg Rumyantsev.

[79] Sotsiologicheskaya sluzhba fonda, 'Demokraticheskaya Rossiya', *DR-Socio*, 4 (9 Nov. 1991), 4.

[80] Mitrokhin and Urban, 'Social Groups, Party Elites and Russia's New Democrats', 66, 69.

farmers' (those former members of state or collective farms who chose to start private businesses) in the meetings of these groups. Despite some participation by workers, the movement was dominated by the intelligentsia, both technical and non-technical. Holders of higher education diplomas and non-manual workers constituted approximately two-thirds of the movement.

Studies of the social composition of Soviet society as a whole showed that the proportion of exactly those sections of the population which were most active in the 'democratic' movement was steadily growing in the USSR over the decades. This tendency was caused by growing urbanization and the rise of the educational level of the population. According to David Lane, 'a study of the urban and occupational composition of the population establishes that by the 1980s the USSR was an urban industrial society comparable in many respects to advanced Western states'.[81] Official Soviet data cited in Lane's book show that the increase in population in the whole of the USSR between 1917 and 1989 was 123.7 million (from 163 million to 286.7 million). The proportion of urban population during the same period rose from 17.9% in 1917 to 66% in 1989. Thus, the level of urbanization in the USSR came close to that of mid-1970s North America (72%) and northern Europe (83%).[82] The changes in the RSFSR were even more drastic as population growth here was significantly slower and the level of urbanization higher than in many other parts of the country. According to Lane, in 1989 the Russian Republic had an urban population of 74%, Latvia 71%, and the Ukraine 67%, whereas Tadzhikistan had only 33%, Kirghizia 38%, and Uzbekistan 41%.[83] This change is a recent phenomenon. Lane concludes: 'Only in the early 1960s did the USSR became mainly urban—a condition reached in Britain before the mid-nineteenth century'.[84] This was a result of the Khrushchev and Brezhnev administrations' softening of Stalin's policy of restricting migration to the cities. Another important factor in the social development of Soviet society was the growth in the proportion of non-manual workers and the rise in their educational level. The proportion of non-manual workers grew from 15.01% in 1940 to 28% in 1987 and by 1987 the largest economic sector was services and transport (43% of total employment).[85]

The rise in the educational level of the population was also significant. In 1939 there were only 1.2 million people in the USSR who had completed higher education (that is, 8 per 1,000 of the population over the age of 10). By 1987 the number had risen to 20.8 million (90 per 1,000) and, in addition, there were another 3.5 million with incomplete higher education and 30.9 million with a secondary specialist background. Even between 1980 and 1986

[81] David Lane, *Soviet Society under Perestroika* (Boston: Unwin Hyman, 1990), 126.

[82] *Narodnoe khozyaystvo SSSR v 1987 g.* (Moscow, 1988); *Pravda*, 29 Apr. 1989, quoted in *Narodnoe khozyaystvo SSSR v 1987 g.* 126.

[83] *Narodnoe khozyaystvo SSSR v 1987 g.* 128. [84] Ibid. 126.

[85] Ibid. 128, 129.

the number of specialists employed in the economy rose by 4.5 million—reaching a total of 34.6 million. The elite of the intelligentsia, those with higher degrees, rose from just over a third of a million in 1960 to 1.5 million in 1987.[86] Taking into consideration the significant rise in incomes and living standards of the urban population, it can be concluded that by the 1980s a specifically Soviet middle class, which consisted of state-employed specialists and educated workers, had emerged. In the Soviet capital and the large cities the proportion of this middle class was naturally higher than anywhere else and it was only a matter of time before it began to gain more political influence. This tendency was first noticed by independent Russian sociologists in the late 1960s. For example, Andrey Amal`rik, in his essay *Will the Soviet Union Survive until 1984?*, directly connected future change in the system with the interests of what he called the new Soviet 'class of specialists', which was beginning 'to become conscious of its unity and to make its presence felt'.[87] This conclusion was partly based on analysis of the social composition of the dissident movement of the 1960s. According to Amal`rik this class included 'people in liberal professions, such as writers and actors, those occupied in academic or academic-administrative work, the managerial group in the economic field and so on' and was created by the Soviet regime itself, since in order to exist and carry out its activities it 'was obliged throughout the post-war period to encourage the country's economy and scientific resources'.[88] Since, according to Amal`rik, the very existence of this class naturally requires 'a certain measure of pragmatic and intellectual freedom' and can only function under the rule of law, he claimed that the Soviet dictatorship was bound to change.

What strikes the reader in Amal`rik's and other similar definitions of the Soviet 'middle class' is that the emphasis was not so much on income or social status (these factors were described vaguely: 'respectable position', 'relatively high living standards') but on education and beliefs, level of culture, political awareness. Though Amal`rik's prediction was seven years off, he was obviously looking in the right direction. His educated class of specialists were exactly the people who dominated the 'democratic' movement. Of course, the growth of the oppositional 'democratic' movement was not the only manifestation of the growing role of professionals in Soviet society which played a significant port in the destruction of the Soviet regime. Before *perestroyka* and during its first years, arguably even more important was the process of 'intellectualization' and 'professionalization' of the CPSU and the existing elites, which made the initial changes in policy

[86] Ibid. 138.
[87] Andrei Amalrik, *Will the Soviet Union Survive until 1984?*, ed. Hillary Stemberg (New York: Penguin, 1970; originally written in 1969 and circulated in *samizdat*, 25.
[88] Ibid. 24.

possible.[89] However, when the spirit of change had already been let out and the process of reform got out of the control of the Soviet establishment, the formerly weak 'democratic' movement became a decisive force in destroying the Soviet Union and creating a new 'democratic' Russia.

The only kind of 'democrats' who may be defined as deprived can be better understood as a psychological type, not as a social group (since the social positions of those who constituted it were various). They could belong to different social groups but what they had in common was that they all represented a type of person which can be called a Soviet truth-seeker or a fighter for social justice. Of this study's interviewees, Klepachev, Didichenko, Loskutov, Rybalko, Yelistratov, Knyazeva, Borovik, and some others clearly belonged to this type. This kind of person is vividly described in a famous story by Boris Mozhaev, 'One and a Half Square Metres'.[90] Beginning with a complaint about a minor injustice or from an attempt to solve a personal problem (in Mozhaev's story, a conflict with a hard-drinking neighbour) and after failing to find support from the local authorities, such a person would pursue the truth through all kinds of high authorities, finally appealing to the Supreme Soviet, the Central Committee of the CPSU, or the Prosecutor General. These appeals were usually sent back to local authorities for action, but these authorities, trying to defend their position, became even more hostile toward the applicant. Such freedom-seekers might finally get what they wanted at a very high level. But they were more likely to lose their battle and then forget about the whole thing, or even to be put in jail or in a mental hospital on a fabricated charge or diagnosis (the latter happened to one of the respondents, Pavel Borovik, who complained about financial fraud by the authorities in the 1960s).[91]

A truth-seeker usually began the quest for justice from the official understanding of Soviet laws and morals and was merely a persistent and stubborn fighter for their realization, often a doctrinaire or even fanatic believer in Soviet ideology, especially its idea of social justice. But in reality the truth-seeker encountered lawlessness and a systematic closing of ranks by different local authorities who were supposed to control each other and who saw such a person first as a nuisance and then as a dangerous obstacle to their comfortable existence. This situation raised a simple applicant to the position of a combatant against the authorities and turned every minor problem into an issue of national significance. Truth-seekers existed in the Soviet Union well

---

[89] On the growing educational and professional level of the CPSU, see KPSS. Spravochnik, 5th edn. (Moscow: Izdatel`stvo politicheskoy literatury, 1983), 438–40; Bohdan Harasymiw, *Political Elite Recruitment in the Soviet Union* (London: Allen and Unwin, 1984).

[90] Boris Mozhaev, 'Poltora kvadratnykh metra', in Boris Mozhaev, *Sobranie sochineniy* (Moscow: Khudozhestvennaya literatura, 1990; written in 1970), iii. 204–86.

[91] Interview with Pavel Borovik (Vladivostok, 25 Apr. 1994).

before *perestroyka*, and usually were not characterized by anti-Communist or anti-government attitudes. Only a very few of them, like Borovik, developed such attitudes before the late 1980s. However, their experience made them susceptible to anti-Communist 'democratic' theories and the flow of information during *glasnost* particularly the anti-establishment 'democratic' ideas helped them make sense of their life.[92]

Clearly, however, 'democratic' activists consisted not only of such truth-seekers' but also of people from dissident circles who became anti-Communists well before *perestroyka*, professionals striving to create freer conditions for their work, those who were interested in free, non-supervised social activities, some formerly politically passive citizens, whose accumulated discontent surfaced as soon as conditions were safe enough, and, at a later stage, those who thought it was too late to make a career within the disintegrating official institutions and thought the growing prospects of the 'democratic' movement were better. But truth-seekers, especially in the early period (1986–8), constituted the most dynamic part of the membership of 'democratic' groups, and were respected for their past experience and often became leaders. This can be partly explained by their uncompromising position, which resulted from the fact that, having already lost their official standing, they usually had nothing more to lose. In contrast, for other members of the groups, such as people who worked in official research institutes, universities, social organizations, or various ministries and departments, it was much more dangerous to adhere to a tough anti-Communist line.[93]

Most truth-seekers originally were not particularly poor or deprived in any other sense, though their continuous fight with the authorities could turn them into persecuted outcasts, and sometimes even homeless wanderers. However, it was their beliefs and their uncompromising attitude that made them deprived, not the other way round. This again shows the primary role of beliefs in the conflict between 'democrats' and the authorities. It was beliefs, not social status, that united 'democrats', that stimulated them to look among absolute strangers for those who agreed with them.

The study of the social composition of the Russian 'democratic' movement therefore shows that deprivation theory in its traditional form does not work in this case. However, its more modern, modified version, which sees 'relative deprivation' as the main cause of social conflict, can be applied. Relative deprivation is defined as 'a negative discrepancy between legitimate

---

[92] For a detailed account of these beliefs see Ch. 5 below.

[93] This was recognized by some 'democrats'. For example, the organizer of the Popular Front in Penza, Aleksandr Yerasov, complained that at first he was surrounded by 'schizophrenics, failures and other people who were hurt in some way, while more serious people came only later'. Yerasov, who was not himself a Communist, had to accept that most of these serious people were Party members (interview with Yerasov).

expectations and actuality'[94] or as 'actors' perception of discrepancy between their value expectations and their value capabilities', where value expectations are 'the goods and conditions of life to which people believe they are rightfully entitled' and value capabilities 'the goods and conditions they think they are capable of getting and keeping'.[95] What is important for this study is that this point of view looks for the causes of social conflict and for the emergence of new social movements not in the 'objective' state of society and various social groups but in the sphere of beliefs, in the sphere of actors' perceptions of this state and of their own situation. A new political movement can thus emerge, not as a result of an absolute lowering of living standards of a particular group of the population but of the widening gap between rising expectations and growing dissatisfaction with life. The rise of expectations is usually seen as resulting from such factors as exposure to new modes of life or to new ideologies, growing demands for equal conditions with other, more privileged groups, etc. These factors are in turn normally caused by the growth of education and of access to outside information following the process of a regime's liberalization and its opening up to the outside world. At the same time the authorities' failure to keep pace with the rising expectations leads to growing dissatisfaction. In some cases this happened despite the fact that actual living conditions improved; since they did not improve fast enough the situation was perceived as deteriorating. At the same time the lessening of the danger of a strong reaction from the regime, of force and coercion, makes the opposition more active.[96] All these factors existed in the late Soviet Union. As shown above, the growth of education created a new educated class open to new ideological influences which caused greater expectations. At the same time, during Brezhnev's government economic development slowed down and gradually came to a halt. Gorbachev's reforms opened the doors for more new ideas, loosened political control, and almost lifted political persecution, but at the same time not only failed to improve the economic situation but worsened it. From the point of view of the theory of relative deprivation this was a perfect road to the creation of a growing opposition movement and to the collapse of the regime.

The fact that most of the members of this new political movement belonged to the educated strata supports the conclusion of the relative deprivation theory that more education makes people more receptive to new ideas and raises expectations. This conclusion is illustrated by the studies of the beliefs of Soviet emigrants in 1970 and 1980 which determined that the young and more educated showed less support for official values and goals.[97]

[94] David F. Aberle, 'A Note on Relative Deprivation Theory', in Sylvia L. Thrupp (ed.), *Millennian Dreams in Action: Essays in Comparative Studies* (The Hague: Mouton, 1962), 209.

[95] Ted Robert Gurr, *Why Men Rebel* (Princeton, NJ: Princeton University Press, 1971), 24.

[96] Ibid. 92–154, 232–73.

[97] Stephen White, *Political Culture and Soviet Politics* (London: Macmillan, 1979), 186–8.

Analysing the data of one of the most impressive studies, the Soviet Interview Project, Brian Silver concluded that support for the values of the regime was not directly dependent on the objective material conditions, but on the 'subjective material satisfaction' of the population. The latter in turn was positively related to 'objective material conditions', but negatively related to the level of education.[98] If one adds to Silver's 'subjective material satisfaction' subjective non-material satisfaction, i.e. expectations about the level of freedom, justice, and legality to which people are entitled, and thinks of a situation in which this satisfaction falls, one arrives at the concept of relative deprivation. From this point of view it is clear that the most 'relatively deprived' in the Soviet Union were the better-educated people who had greater expectations compared to their real status and living standards, and it is understandable that they were the most active in joining 'democratic' groups.

It is important to note that the terms 'relative deprivation' and 'subjective satisfaction' signify nothing more than beliefs, since they express not the 'objective' social position of a person but his evaluation of this status, not the real state of society but its members' perception of it. Therefore an analysis of the system of such beliefs of the members of the 'democratic' movement, which consistently pressed for change of the existing society, can lead to a better understanding of the reasons for social conflicts in the late Soviet Union and of the consequences of these conflicts.

3.8. CONCLUSIONS

This chapter has provided a historical background for the analysis of the 'democratic' political culture. In 1985–95, for the first time since the 1917 revolution, Russia experienced a boom of independent political activities. Thousands of new groups, large and small, entered the political arena. Many of them were quite unstable, with no clear membership and goals. Some, such as Memorial, the Democratic Union, Democratic Russia, and the Democratic Party of Russia, became quite influential and for a time enjoyed a nationwide following.

However, for the period under study it is too early to speak of the programmes, agendas, or beliefs of any one particular group or its role in Russian politics. The programmes of most 'democratic' groups were virtually indistinguishable, and no single party or group enjoyed sufficient influence to

---

[98] Brian D. Silver, 'Political Beliefs of the Soviet Citizen: Sources of Support for Regime Norms', in James R. Millar (ed.), *Politics, Work and Daily Life in the USSR: A Survey of Former Soviet Citizens* (Cambridge: Cambridge University Press, 1987), 126–33.

pressure the government to take decisions. But the 'democrats', or the 'democratic' movement as a whole, had such influence and frequently demonstrated its ability to exercise it by conducting mass rallies, organizing campaigns in the mass media, working through sympathetic presidential advisers, and other means. Though it is very difficult to determine precisely all the members of the movement, there existed a broad understanding that it included such components as various parties, groups, and clubs, which despite all their differences, acknowledged their 'democratic' orientation. The 'democratic' movement also included the 'democratic' press (newspapers, TV, and radio stations or particular programmes and individual journalists), 'democratically minded' officials (who, though working in the government or even the CPSU, in fact promoted 'democratic' reforms), 'democratic' 'creative unions' (such as the Unions of Cinematographists, Theatre Workers, and Journalists), and other groups and individuals.

After the 1989 elections the movement was reinforced by a large group of 'democratic' members of parliament, who formed the Inter-regional Group of Deputies, and after 1990 'democrats', by electing their representative to the post of the Chairman of the Supreme Soviet of the Russian Federation, achieved control over the governmental bodies of the Russian Republic. This book argues that, despite lack of organization, the 'democratic' movements existed as a relatively united political force, its main uniting factor being not organizational structures, but common beliefs. These common beliefs became the main factor in the emergence and formation of 'democratic' groups. The next four chapters of this book are devoted to the analysis of these beliefs, which constituted the 'democratic' political subculture.

4

From Marxism to Anti-Communism:
The Sources and Evolution of the Political
Beliefs of Russian 'Democrats'

This chapter studies the evolution of the political beliefs of Russian 'democrats' and the relative influence of various sources and influences on this process. The research for this study made it possible to identify the following kinds of sources:

1. official Soviet ideology;
2. family tradition and family education;
3. personal life experience;
4. literature and other sources officially available in the USSR but either non-Marxist (like classical literature and philosophy) or featuring non-Soviet ideas and experiences (usually criticizing them);
5. impressions of foreign travel;
6. banned literature, either published abroad (*tamizdat*) or typed or hand-written in the USSR (*samizdat*);
7. foreign radio broadcasts in Russian;
8. *glasnost`*-period literature and mass media.

An analysis of the genesis of the 'democratic' political culture is important for better understanding its analytical model, which is reconstructed in Chapters 5–7.

4.1. OFFICIAL IDEOLOGY

Official Soviet ideology formed the foundation for the political beliefs of all citizens, regardless of how their views subsequently evolved. This is not surprising since official dogmas were instilled into everyone from infancy with the goal of transforming the entire Soviet population into model Communist citizens. The literature on political socialization, especially the earlier contributions, used to place great importance on childhood experiences in the formation of political beliefs.[1] Even if early impressions and experiences are not this important (and later studies have found a greater role for adult experiences),[2] official Soviet ideology was almost always the first major influence shaping childhood development. This does not mean that the majority of Soviet parents were actively instilling Communist dogmas into their children. Many were politically passive and did not pay much attention to official ideology; some did not even believe in it. However, in as much as the official ideology was a part of the general culture, it automatically penetrated the process of family upbringing. Almost all fairy tales, children's verse, and stories which were written after 1917 (such as the very popular writings of Arkadiy Gaidar, Anatoliy Rybakov, Sergey Mikhalkov, and others) were imbued with official values, and the same can be said of school textbooks, radio and TV programmes, and films. Further, even if parents did not accept or remained passive toward official dogmas, for example, in the fields of history or politics, many of them, being a product of Soviet education, simply were not aware of approaches different from those they had been taught at school, and when it came to explaining things to children they had to rely on what they knew. Nursery school and primary education were designed to implant official ideology and began the process of political education which continued at universities and workplaces.

The world-view which was officially propagated in the USSR, despite the thousands of books and articles devoted to it, was not very complicated, especially at the level of secondary school or even of a university department not specializing in ideology. However, it was relatively cohesive and very comprehensive, designed to provide answers to any possible human question, from the most abstract philosophical issue to the very specific phenomena of day-to-day life. This world-view is succinctly formulated in a standard Soviet textbook on 'social knowledge', a course which was taught in every Soviet secondary school and which contained the concentrated wisdom of the Marxist philosophy of nature and history (dialectical and historical materialism), economics (the political economy of capitalism and socialism), politics (scientific Communism), and ethics.[3] In the institutes of higher education these subjects were taught separately and were compulsory for every student

---

[1] See e.g. Robert D. Hess and Judith V. Torney, *The Development of Political Attitudes in Children* (Chicago: Aldine Publishing Co., 1967).

[2] For a discussion of different approaches to political socialization, see Richard E. Dawson and Kenneth Prewitt, *Political Socialization* (Boston: Little, Brown and Co., 1969).

[3] G. Kh. Shakhnazarov, A. D. Boborykin, Yu. A. Krasin, V. V. Sukhodeev, and O. N. Pisarzhevskiy, *Obshchestvovedenie. Uchebnik dlya vypusknogo klassa sredney shkoly i srednikh spetsial'nykh uchebnykh zavedeniy* (Moscow: Politizdat, 1971). In the 1960s and 1970s this textbook ran into more than a dozen editions and was the basis of the secondary school course at the time when the beliefs of most of the 'democrats' were formed. Earlier textbooks of 'social knowledge' and other textbooks of the same period differed from one another only in details and in their evaluations of the roles of specific leaders.

regardless of department or specialization. The epigraph to the textbook, taken from the programme of the CPSU, clearly formulates the aim of the course:

The party puts forward the task of educating the entire population in the spirit of scientific communism so that working people deeply comprehend the process and perspectives of world development, correctly understand events inside the country and in the international arena, consciously build life along communist lines. Communist ideas should be organically combined with communist deeds in the behaviour of every person and in the activities of every collective.[4]

So what kind of understanding was supposed to be 'correct'? The general approach to the world accepted by dialectical materialism was based on the materialist dogma that everything in the world consists of 'matter' and that consciousness is a quality of highly organized matter. Marxism inherited the Hegelian idea of development and the main tenets of Hegel's dialectics, with the difference that matter was seen to be primary while consciousness was secondary. An important part of this teaching was understanding nature as subject to evolution from simpler to more complicated forms. Social development was interpreted in a similar fashion: every society was supposed to pass through five stages, or 'social and economic structures'—primitive communal, slave-holding, feudal, capitalist, and communist. Each structure was based on a specific level of development of productive forces on which a corresponding form of relations of production (and ideological superstructure) was based. The natural development of productive forces led to contradictions with the existing superstructure, which was always seen as a manifestation of the interests of the ruling class. This contradiction led to the strengthening of the struggle of the oppressed but progressive classes and their inevitable victory resulted in a change of social structure. Class struggle was considered to be natural in every stage except communism, where the most progressive class, the proletariat, after coming to power, eliminated the economic basis of the existence of the exploiter classes, namely, private property. According to this scheme, from approximately the beginning of the twentieth century the Western world has been living in the last stage of the capitalist social and economic structure, imperialism. The USSR after 1917 and the countries of Eastern Europe after the establishment of Communist regimes found themselves in socialism, which was the first stage of the communist structure. Socialism differed from the final stage of communism by virtue of the continued existence of the state, two non-antagonistic classes (workers and peasants, which were supposed to disappear in mature communism by merging together), commodity–money relations, differences between urban and rural areas, distribution according to labour, crime, and other

---

[4] Quoted in Shakhnazarov *et al.*, *Obshchestvovedenie*, 3.

'vestiges of capitalism'. Under mature communism all this would die out and communism would be a society of universal public property, of distribution according to needs, of creative labour for everybody, and of a new communist morality. This society was to appear after the victory of socialism all over the world. The Soviet Union, as the strongest socialist state, was seen as the natural guarantor of this process and its fight against imperialism in the world arena was at the same time a battle for the progress of humanity. Within the Soviet Union the Communist Party (CPSU) was the 'organizing and direct-ing' force of the people in its movement along the road of social progress. Being originally a working-class party, it represented the progressive interests of all Soviet people and secured the advance of Soviet society in the correct direction.

Most 'democrats' admit in their interviews or memoirs that they shared these dogmas of official ideology at some stage of their lives, while they deeply regret yielding to the influence of official propaganda. For example, the memoirs of the leader of the Stavropol` Popular Front, Vasily Krasulya, contains a passage highly moving in its sincerity:

Every evening I go to sleep with one question which, probably, has come to mean damnation, and not just for me: how could it happen that I sincerely believed in Communism and took part in Communist construction?

How could it happen that until I was thirty years old I had been living in comfort-able ignorance that the entire post-October history of my people was mixed with blood, crime, and lies? That the people whom I believed, whose portraits were encouragingly looking at me from the pages of school textbooks, whom I worshipped and whom I considered to be disinterested fighters for the radiant future, turned out to be either criminals or maniacs?

The system managed to turn me into an idiotic true believer. I was a frenzied Marxist-Leninist. Not only did I believe in communism, but I knew that it would come at the time set by the founders, though possibly with some delay caused by some unforeseen historic developments. Like any conscientious Soviet person, with the aid of a special organ implanted in me by our education I knew, perhaps, from birth that Marxism-Leninism was the only true teaching. Any other simply could not exist.[5]

Teodey Fel`dman, a 'democrat' from Vladivostok, echoes the same thoughts:

I am ashamed, I really am: when I was nineteen I cried in the corner of the barracks when Stalin died. I cried quietly, it was a personal feeling, and my example shows that millions of people experienced this. Perhaps some did earlier, some later, but as a man who finished ten years of school, who already by that time had read Heine, I am ashamed . . . I am ashamed, but this is a fact.[6]

---

[5] Vasiliy Krasulya, *Dissident iz nomenklatury* (Stavropol`: Severo-kavkazskoye informat-sionno-reklamnoye agenstvo, 1992), 4–5.

[6] Interview with Teodey Fel`dman (Vladivostok, 23 Apr. 1994).

A younger 'democrat', a worker from Vladivostok, Vladimir Krylov, acknowledges that in the 1970s he was educated in the spirit of Communism, believed in this idea, and conscientiously joined the Komsomol.[7]

The words of Petr Popov, an engineer and 'democratic' activist from Orenburg, show how significant was the impact of the system of political education on the formation of the first political beliefs of future 'democrats'. Describing his views at the time of joining the discussion club Aprel` in Orenburg, he said that they were generally pro-Communist:

> In the sense that I was not afraid but I did not see the advantages of capitalism, the freedom of property and so on. Moreover we knew nothing about the reality. We knew clichés about how bad everything was there. I, for instance, was cautious because in theory there was exploitation of men by men—this was a cliché. That if there is no property belonging to all people and there is private property, exploitation of men by men is inevitable. But when I realized that there was exploitation anyway, just in a concealed form, and that we just did not speak of it, that we were not shown the exploitation by the state, the exploitation by bureaucrats and so on, then I understood that the capitalist system had some advantages as well as some faults.[8]

Beliefs accepted in the process of education were not limited to abstract theoretical approaches to the world which were part of special Marxist courses. According to George Avis, writing before *glasnost*, the aim of creating a new man 'permeates the content and teaching of all subjects in academic curricula and is the underlying aim of many school and extra-mural activities. Furthermore it is reinforced by other agencies of socialization in Soviet society, in particular children's and youth organizations.'[9]

The new type of personality was meant to be based on a set of qualities and moral values which were taught in the official education institutions, beginning with the nurseries. On the basis of an analysis of Soviet articles and documents in the 1970s and 1980s on the methodology of education, James Muckle concluded that official ideology wanted a new Soviet man to be

> a patriot; an internationalist; sober; incorruptible; conscientious at work and study; respectful of the environment, of state property and resources; an atheist; able to find fulfilment working in a team; courageous and adventurous. He should have been supportive of Soviet industry; disinclined to seek material wealth; in favour of stable marriage and respectful of his elders; respectful of manual labour and the craft of the artisan; mindful of war dead; forward looking and technologically minded; understanding in treatment of the opposite sex; well-behaved in public and considerate of other people in general; conventional by Soviet norms.[10]

---

[7] Interview with Vladimir Krylov (Vladivostok, 24 Apr. 1994).

[8] Interview with Petr Popov (Orenburg, 22 Dec. 1994).

[9] George Avis, 'Preface', in George Avis (ed.), *The Making of the Soviet Citizen* (London: Croom Helm, 1987).

[10] James Muckle, 'The New Soviet Child: Moral Education in Soviet Schools', in Avis (ed.), *The Making of the Soviet Citizen*, 19.

It is obvious that not all of these qualities and values are exclusively Communist; many of them are quite traditional and are encouraged by many different moral systems. Moreover, some of the aspects of the Soviet education system cultivated values which were not alien to liberalism and other systems, such as hostility to aggression and despotism. However, these values should be seen within the framework of the Soviet ideological system as a whole. Typical are the words of Yevgeniy Kryskin: 'In my heart at that time I was, nevertheless, a patriot. I was strongly against American intervention in Vietnam ... I was a patriot of my Motherland, but I was an opponent of despotism: "Cuba—my love, island of crimson sunrise".'[11] It is clear that his feelings about despotism were part and parcel of the system of official beliefs, which attributed despotism and intervention only to America and the West. Only after a serious restructuring of the whole belief system could they potentially be directed against the Soviet system (as happened much later).

The selection and combination of beliefs and values for promulgation made the official belief system unique. Some of the problems of accepting official ideology as a consistent system arose from the fact that over time some of its specific components changed, sometimes even to their opposites (for example, the early Soviet stress on unreserved internationalism changed in the 1940s to almost open nationalism; the encouragement of free relationships between the sexes in the 1920s later shifted to a stress on family values). However, the main problem was that many officially promulgated beliefs and values clearly contradicted Soviet reality. The cultivation of internationalism, incorruptibility, respect for the environment, and disregard for material wealth were in striking contrast with the disregard for the rights of ethnic minorities and for the environment, the corruption, and the pursuit of material wealth which were widespread in the Soviet Union of the 1970s and 1980s. Thus, school education, if taken at its word, could lead to a serious contradiction with real life, and the officially cultivated 'active attitude toward life' could result in a desire to actively fight against what were seen as shortcomings. This combat would have been understood subjectively as a struggle for perfect communism against specific politically backward individuals and anti-social phenomena. But in practice the Soviet education system formed active fighters who were ready to struggle against many fundamental phenomena of Soviet life.

These conclusions are consistent with the answers of most of the 'democratic' interviewees. Many of them acknowledged that during some specific period of their life they accepted not only Communist theory but also official moral values and actively tried to implement them by decisively criticizing individuals and phenomena which, from their point of view, were inconsistent with them. They often joined the CPSU and Komsomol not for career reasons

---

[11] Interview with Yevgeniy Kryskin (Penza, 3 Apr. 1994).

(as many others did) but because of their sincere beliefs, since they regarded these organizations as natural leaders of the struggle for a better society. This pattern of behaviour was found among 'democrats' of every social group and generation in each of the regions investigated, the majority of whom claimed that at some time in their life they were active members of the Komsomol, the CPSU, Communist-dominated official trade unions, women's councils, etc., and fought decisively for their ideals in these organizations.

At the beginning of their adult lives these future 'democrats' were naturally hostile to everything that, within the framework of their views, was thought to be a dangerous deviation from the socialist ideal: corruption, hard drinking, cynicism, double morality, etc., especially if they characterized higher Komsomol or Communist officials, who were supposed to be examples of Communist morality. At first they usually did not apply their criticism to the system as a whole or to the top leadership of the CPSU; on the contrary, specific local leaders were criticized in the name of that system and that leadership. Aleksandr Kislov, for example, who before becoming a 'democrat' worked the Penza *oblast'* committee of the CPSU, remembered that while seeing many shortcomings in the Party's work, he thought that they were only present at the level of the *rayon* party leadership and that the highest party officials were 'some kind of celestial beings' and that 'everything they decided was absolutely right and even if there were some clear incongruities which were sometimes only too obvious, they were commented upon and interpreted for us as if . . . there were some concealed meaning behind them, which was none of our business and that as a result the whole matter was logical enough and would lead to flourishing and prosperity'.[12] Nikolay Klepachev recalls that in 1952, when Stalin was still alive, he 'already was a Komsomol organizer and demanded social justice. I spoke about that and did not understand that I could have been punished; my parents did not tell me the reason. The propaganda was very severe—for example, arguing that it was right to send people into exile'.[13] From these words one can clearly see how dissatisfaction and certain beliefs which, if taken separately, could be parts of very different world-views, possibly even hostile to the Soviet system, were built into the system of official Soviet beliefs and could even support it.

General theoretical beliefs consistent with official ideology determined attitudes toward political events. For example, speaking of his attitude toward Andrey Sakharov, Petr Popov remembered that during the Academician's persecution in the USSR he absolutely trusted the official media. However, later Sakharov became 'an idol' of Orenburg 'democrats'.[14] The typical

---

[12] Interview with Aleksandr Kislov (Penza, 29 Sept. 1994).
[13] Interview with Nikolay Klepachev (Krasnoyarsk, 19 Apr. 1994).
[14] Interview with Petr Popov.

general attitude toward the system was described by Il`ya Gezentsvey, who began his work in the Komsomol in the late 1970s: 'I was already a very active Komsomol member in the institute . . . Despite all the contradictions in the Komsomol it always seemed to me that [it was] not the system but bad people who ensconced themselves in top positions, who did not know the problems of ordinary people, who did not understand the issues and who somehow only resolve everything in their own favour [that was to blame]. And if only decent, normal people would come . . .'[15]

It was not only provincial or rank-and-file 'democrats' who at a certain stage shared this kind of attitude. Many 'democratic' leaders at the national level, such as Boris Yel`tsin, Yuriy Afanas`ev, Gennadiy Burbulis, Gavriil Popov, Vyacheslav Shostakovskiy, and Anatoliy Sobchak, were active and, as many of them admit, sincere supporters of the official ideology at some time in their careers. For example, Yel`tsin was a career Communist official and for a long time believed in what he was doing,[16] Afanas`ev worked as a secretary of a *kray* Komsomol committee and as a secretary of the Communist Party committee of the High Komsomol School, Burbulis taught Marxism for fifteen years in different institutes in Sverdlovsk, Shostakovskiy worked as the head of Moscow City Party High School, and Sobchak joined the CPSU in 1988 when already this could hardly have helped his career and can only be understood by genuine belief in *perestroyka*. Gavriil Popov recognizes in his autobiography, which was published in 1994 and the first chapter of which is characteristically entitled 'The Orthodox', that up to the early 1980s he 'sincerely believed that the socialist system was the best'. He went on: 'I knew that it had many defects. But I was convinced that it had a future'.[17]

While most future 'democrats' were socially active not all of them combined this activism with deep belief in the official ideals. Some joined the Komsomol, the CPSU, or other official organizations not so much because they had such belief as because they could not find an alternative outlet for their social activism. Gavriil Popov, who, like many 'democrats', began his social activities in the Komsomol during his student years and became a secretary of the Komsomol committee of the whole of Moscow University, wrote about this phenomenon:

Since apart from the Komsomol there were no other youth organizations in the Soviet Union and since all youth activities were within the competence of the Komsomol, be it innocent sport, tourism, or even a dance night, in fact any young person craving for any kind of activism could find it in the Komsomol. And the Komsomol simultaneously had two functions: ideological, which was demanded from the top, and to create an outlet for youthful energy.[18]

[15] Interview with Il`ya Gezentsvey (Moscow, 27 Aug. 1993).
[16] See Boris Yel`tsin, *Ispoved' na zadannuyu temu* (Leningrad: Sovetskiy pisatel', 1990).
[17] Gavriil Popov, *Snova v oppozitsii* (Moscow: Galaktika, 1994), 11.
[18] Ibid. 14.

Some examples of the life experience of the interviewees for this study confirm Popov's words. While many of them (like Popov himself) actively worked in the Komsomol or the CPSU sharing official Communist ideology, some explained that they merely wanted to work as organizers of social activities. For example, Yuriy Ivlev acknowledged that he was already an active Komsomol member at school but noted that he 'did not believe in the radiant future' and that at first, not thinking of politics at all, he worked in the Komsomol because he was interested in organizing discos and youth nights.[19] Andrey Shcherkin, who even maintained that he was an opponent of the official ideology at the time, nevertheless became a Komsomol secretary at Pskov airport. According to him, he did it not because of political considerations, but because his friends saw that he was a good and enthusiastic organizer of youth leisure activities and asked him to do so.[20]

At the same time Popov is only partly right. Already during Khrushchev's time and even more so in Brezhnev's USSR there existed some unofficial youth groups, such as hippies, football fans, rock enthusiasts, and lovers of amateur singing. However, most such unofficial groups were non-political or not large enough to attract people interested in serious social activities. Besides, the Komsomol always wanted to put even such 'innocent' activities under its control. Any unofficial political activities were stopped immediately by the authorities and young people had a choice of either accepting persecution (which could be chosen only by those very few who became disappointed with the official ideology very early in life) or working in the official structures. Only a very few in the sample joined a 'democratic' group directly from an unofficial youth group. Some others, like Ivlev, Shcherkin, Sergey Popov, and Yelena Suslova, worked both with Komsomol and unofficial groups.

Generally the example of Russian 'democrats' shows that Communist education in the USSR was in a way quite effective. Most 'democrats' at some period in their lives believed in official aims and wanted to achieve them. Only a handful of interviewees claimed that they had always been hostile toward the Soviet system (and one should take into consideration that some of them might have regretted their former pro-official views and might not have been willing to admit to them). A more significant part of the 'democrats' were passive about politics, did not care much about official or any other ideology, and worked in official organizations because they wanted to realize their potential as social organizers. But even these people, though not being over-enthusiastic about official ideological goals, took them for granted and did not dwell on any alternative.

There existed, however, a serious obstacle to the realization of both political and non-political social activity in the USSR even if it was absolutely in

---

[19] Interview with Yuriy Ivlev (Pskov, 25 Sept. 1994).
[20] Interview with Andrey Shcherkin (Pskov, 25 Sept. 1994).

line with official ideology. Though encouraged in theory, in practical life, especially if it became too intensive and creative, the authorities treated it with suspicion, fearing that it could get out of hand, and wanted to limit it. The fact that many officially propagated formulas clearly contradicted the daily experience of the Soviet population, especially in the spheres of economics and politics, created another problem. For example, in economics the postulate of communal (in practice, state) property, which wholly dominated the Soviet economy, and of the supposed efficiency of the state-owned enterprises, contrasted with the reality of serious shortages of the most necessary commodities, the daily experience of hours of queuing, the poor quality of Soviet-made goods, and the disorderly state of management. In politics the theory that 'in the USSR all power belonged to the working people in the person of their representative organs—the soviets of the deputies of the working people'[21] elected by direct, equal, and secret ballot openly contradicted the clear domination of the apparatus by the CPSU at every level. The assertion that the USSR had achieved the highest living standards on earth ran contrary to the experience of those Soviet citizens who went abroad and saw higher living standards in the West, and of everybody who saw the better quality of imported goods. Even in ethics the official appeals to be sincere, active, conscious, and disinterested builders of society did not match the atmosphere of suspicion, dogmatism, and self-interest in which even the very attempt to became an ideal member of society was often met with misunderstanding and even persecution.

Therefore the very attempt to realize the official ideals in practical Soviet life could lead to serious problems and disappointments; the personal life experience of the future 'democrats' who wanted to put these ideals into practice, or at least did not question them, became the source of their first doubts. Naturally, at the first stage these doubts only touched the surface of the official belief system, without affecting the deep level of abstract concepts, which survived much longer.

4.2. PERSONAL LIFE EXPERIENCE AS A SOURCE OF 'DEMOCRATIC' BELIEFS

Confronted with the reality of life in the Soviet Union, especially with the role of the Communist bureaucracy, future 'democrats' began to think over the theory they had been taught and found that not everything was to be taken literally. One of the oldest of the interviewees, Yefim Lyuboshits, recalled that he 'became a candidate member of the CPSU in 1939 when I had just turned

---

[21] Shakhnazarov *et al.*, *Obshchestvovedenie*, 195.

eighteen. And I generally was quite an active Komsomol member and Communist. But during the war I already began to realize that not everything was all right. During the war many had the feeling that after the war everything would be different, that, perhaps, even the collective farms would be dissolved.'[22]

An urbanite from Moscow, Lyuboshits formed an unfavourable attitude toward collective farms in the army after talking to many soldiers from villages. During his work at a research institute of the strategic missile forces after the war his negative attitude toward the authorities became stronger and in 1968 in private conversations he spoke against the Soviet invasion of Czechoslovakia.[23]

Many future 'democrats' became disillusioned with the official ideology precisely because of their previously excessive belief in it and their frustrated hopes of implementing its goals. This evolution was vividly described by Penza 'democrat' Evgeniy Kryskin:

> I think that the teachers unintentionally inclined us to dissent. They taught us to be idealists, they taught us to be starry-eyed dreamers, builders of communism. When I studied at school, before I was seventeen, if anybody had told me that communism would not be built I could have bitten through his throat. I was like a Chinese Red Guard. We were made Red Guards. Fanatics. And when life began, and when in this life there was only drunkenness, theft, cheating at work, eyewash, these fanaticized, exalted young boys and girls, all their exaltation turns against the deceivers and in this way by making good citizens of the country the teachers were already creating explosive material.[24]

Kryskin himself had become an ardent Communist believer under the instruction of his schoolteacher. However, immediately after finishing school life made him hesitate about what he had been taught. This happened when together with his former schoolmates he tried to get a passport to enter an institute. Kryskin recalled:

> This was 1964. The last year of the rule of Nikita Sergeevich Khrushchev . . . People in rural areas did not have passports. I come to the rural soviet and I am told: 'Well, you know, we don't issue passports.' I say: 'But I need one.' 'No, you know, go to the chairman of the collective farm, he'll tell you . . .' I say: 'What he's got to do with this?' I did not even work at the collective farm. Though my parents were collective farmers. 'Well, you know, this is the procedure. The Party committee meets there . . .' So I go there with my four classmates . . . One fellow wanted to train to be a doctor and the girls wanted to enter a pedagogical institute. And nobody could get a passport. So we could not make a proper application for an institute. It was practically serfdom.

Kryskin continues:

---

[22] Interview with Yefim Lyuboshits (Moscow, 18 Sept. 1993).   [23] Ibid.
[24] Interview with Kryskin.

We went to that Party committee and there was the committee meeting and an offi-cial from the *oblast`* committee was present. And our director of studies, Gorbyleva, who also taught literature and was a member of the committee, was also there, her husband was a people's judge. By the way, she taught us that all roads were open for us and that a radiant future was ahead of us after school, but as soon as we finished school we got slapped in the face and got black eyes. Life is a harsh thing. . . . We had a chairman, such a scoundrel, a certain Belyakov. He got a specialized secondary education, graduated from a technical school of machine-building and as a member of the *nomenklatura* he was appointed chairman of the collective farm in Bessonovka. And he says: 'But I want you to work at the farm.' At that time I already suffered from polyarthritis, I was not accepted by the army. Polyarthritis, then myasthenia, it's a rheumatism of the tendons, muscular rheumatism . . . So, imagine, I finished with just fours in biology (I did not like it) and in geography, and fives in all other subjects. I was the top pupil in the class and one of the best in the school. So they force me: there's nothing for you in the institute, go take the pitchfork and spread the dung in the field . . . And the teacher doesn't say anything. I am angry, I think 'Damn it.' I thought she would stand up for me, but far from it, she was saying one thing at the lessons and when life began—something completely different . . . They don't open the door for us, they fail us, they do not let us into higher education. Despite that it was written in my reference that I had good knowledge of maths and was inclined towards design engineering. And now, here we are, go and work with the pitchfork. Or be a milkmaid, or a herdsman . . . So these were the ways they opened to us . . .[25]

Kryskin and his friend appealed to the *oblast`* party committee but were told that they had to work at the farm. The shock of his first encounter with real life was so strong that speaking of it thirty years later Kryskin could not hide his deep frustration. To enter an institute Kryskin first had to become a worker:

What did I do? I could not take a full-time day course [at an institute]. I had to become a trainee turner at the compressor factory, and after working there for one and a half years I said that I needed a passport [the factory was in a rural area] I took a corre-spondence course . . . at the Penza Polytechnic . . . Speciality—technology of machine-building, metal-cutting machines, and instruments. So this is how my intro-duction to life happened.[26]

Kryskin, nevertheless, came to the factory as an active Komsomol member. Here he was faced with new problems and disappointments, which finally prompted him to leave the Komsomol:

When I had been working there as a turner for one and a half years—I was nine-teen—a foreman comes up to me: 'Zhenya, you are nineteen already, have you thought of joining the Communist Party?' I say: 'I don't deserve it.' I already knew what the Communist Party was, though: I was an active member of Komsomol, I was on the editorial board of *Komsomol`skiy prozhektor.*[27] Later I left the Komsomol, in

---

[25] Interview with Kryskin.   [26] Ibid.

[27] The *Komsomol Searchlight*, a common name for a Komsomol newspaper posted on the wall at a Soviet organization.

1968. 1968 came, the events in Czechoslovakia. I was a member of the Komsomol bureau. And there was such an incident. Once we came to the canteen at lunch-break, and there was a member of the factory Party committee, a *nomenklatura* kind of turner . . . I came and they were drinking, they had beer, I don't know what they were celebrating, and after that party they never showed up at their workplaces after the break. So I immediately drew up a report for *Komsomol`skiy prozhektor* . . . But we had an engineer . . . He looked it over and put it in his pocket. He says: 'Zhenya, you are, of course, a just fellow, but you are not politically literate.' I say: 'What then is *Komsomol`skiy prozhektor* for, if a committee member violates discipline? Workers are required to be disciplined, so, if a member of the bureau violates discipline and people see it . . . What is this, then? That's disintegration of discipline.' I say: 'Such a man should be asked to leave the committee' . . . 'No, Zhenya, this matter should be discussed with the bureau; *Komsomol`skiy prozhektor* can only criticize non-members of the Party, and with Party members one should go and ask the advice of the Party committee.' At that I shed my final illusions and I stopped paying membership fees. And in six months I left the factory, it was 1968. . . . In about two months I was asked: 'Are you a Komsomol member?' I said: 'No.'[28]

The main reason given by the future 'democratic' activists for doubting official ideology was a sudden realization of the fact that many ideas in which they had believed from childhood stood in striking contrast to real life and to the real practice of those who propagated these ideas, first and foremost the functionaries of the CPSU. For example, a worker from Pskov, Aleksandr Pavlov, acknowledged that he was active at school and in the army, but said that after finding out how the Komsomol and the Communist Party worked he 'just became convinced that these organizations, the CPSU and Komsomol, in fact they say one thing and do another'.[29] Pavlov came to this conclusion as a result of contacting the Communist Party organs while trying to solve his personal problems. In the process he drew the typical conclusions:

When you begin, say, solving your problem, going to various offices, start quoting the classics of Marxism, they say, 'Oh, they used to say this and that, but we have a different thing here', and when they tell you that they're in the right, that the classics said one thing but that really it's different, then you just see that these people are lying, that they have the official ideology for one purpose but that in life everything is very different. So after that you become convinced that this organization does nothing but harm.[30]

As a result Pavlov refused to join the Party in quite a revealing way. Answering a Party organizer's proposal he said: 'What would I do in your CPSU? I neither drink nor steal. So, what do I need your CPSU for?' According to Pavlov, he was warned that 'he could suffer because of his tongue', but no serious consequences followed.[31]

---

[28] Interview with Kryskin.
[29] Interview with Aleksandr Pavlov (Pskov, 25 Sept. 1994).   [30] Ibid.
[31] Ibid.

A docker at the port, Viktor Rybalko, also was an active Komsomol member. Rybalko recalled that during Komsomol and trade union meetings at the port he tried to defend both himself and other people: 'This was built into me, probably, from my childhood, at the time I read Dickens . . . After my active work in the Komsomol I was entrusted with keeping my Komsomol membership card for ever[32] and was approved for Party membership'.[33] However, Rybalko refused to join the Communist Party and to avoid the consequences he stated, just like Kryskin, that he did not deserve it. In fact he too was already becoming disappointed with the Party officials, who were trying to contain his social activism. Rybalko was attempting to defend dockers' rights by working through the official trade union channels and 'was seeking an opportunity to be helpful to the masses, that is to say to help people through official structures'.[34] But he had to admit that his first attempts to re-animate the official trade union system failed after meeting resistance from management and Party officials.

An engineer from Orenburg, Vitaliy Yeykin, also became disappointed with the Communist Party's when he worked as a Komsomol organizer. Yeykin joined the Komsomol while in the army because the Komsomol organization was very influential in his sub-unit. After demobilizing he come home full of hopes and because of his activism was elected secretary of the Komsomol organization at the railway division where he worked. He immediately began organizing different leisure events and Komsomol *subbotniks*.[35] He soon noticed, though, that the Communist officials repeatedly broke promises and cheated the young people. When Yeykin was elected candidate member of the *rayon* Komsomol committee and could see local Komsomol and Communist leaders at a closer distance, he understood that there was a big difference between what he was told and real life.[36] According to him, there were drinking parties, indecent behaviour, and other forms of debauchery—all at public expense. After one such occasion Yeykin clashed in public with the *rayon* Komsomol committee secretary and tore up his Komsomol membership card. Because of this he was 'invited' for a talk with the management where a KGB official was present and had to move temporarily to another city to avoid persecution.[37]

The above pattern of the evolution of attitudes towards Communist domination in society was not confined to provincial or grassroots 'democrats'. The Communist beliefs of a future leader of the 'democratic' movement, Gavriil Popov, also turned to doubt in the process of social activities. Popov writes that when he was a secretary of the Moscow University Komsomol he

---

[32] A kind of honour conferred in the Komsomol.

[33] Interview with Viktor Rybalko (Vladivostok, 23 Apr. 1994).   [34] Ibid.

[35] Voluntary labour heavily promulgated by official ideology as a manifestation of Communist morality, usually on Saturday.

[36] Interview with Vitaliy Yeykin (Orenburg, 22 Dec. 1994).   [37] Ibid.

disliked the glorification of Khrushchev and the necessity of doing things just for show. The shooting of striking workers by the army in his native Novocherkassk seriously upset him. In his case reality again contradicted earlier accepted beliefs. Popov writes: 'After becoming a Komsomol leader, for the sake of my career I had to trample all over my own beliefs about right and wrong. And I made my choice. Reluctant to give up my ideas and principles, I abandoned my Komsomol career.'[38] Instead Popov began an academic career.

As mentioned above, not all of the future 'democrats' actively believed all of the official dogma. But all of them, even those who did not pay much attention to politics or who would have been socially active under any regime, deeply felt the contradiction between officially advertised morality and the real behaviour of the authorities which they encountered daily at work or during their social activities. Many future 'democrats' were inclined to social activism and were natural leaders. Up to a point they were able to realize their potential within the official structures. But soon they crossed some invisible line and found themselves in conflict with the real power system or at least began to realize the contradiction between the system and the ideology. In many cases nothing more than a conscientious fulfilment of one's duties, a desire to work honestly, or to obtain a better education, or to improve performance at one's workplace—in line with the official ideology and even encouraged by it—in practice led to conflicts with the management and Communist Party officials, and even to being fired. Such was the outcome for several of the interviewees. In Krasnoyarsk the head of the *kray* architectural/construction inspectorate, Nikolay Klepachev, was (as noted earlier) fired because of his refusal to sanction the building of houses without the observance of construction rules, as was worker Sergey Loskutov for his attempts to introduce order at his factory and in a gardening partnership in accordance with what he understood to be right from his reading of the newspapers. In Moscow Mariya Sublina had problems with her superiors after criticizing the bureaucracy at the State Planning Committee, where she worked as an economist; in Penza a deputy head of the *oblast'* internal affairs department, Georgiy Didichenko, lost his job for attempting to deal with corruption among Communist officials in accordance with the law, as did Vladimir Yelistratov, the *rayon* party committee instructor, for trying to promote reforms.

Yelistratov, a teacher by education, for a long time could not join the Communist Party and thought this was unfair. He also noticed that many other things at his state farm contradicted official theories. Of the farm's Party leader he said:

---

[38] Gavriil Popov, *Snova v oppozitsii*, 19.

Our state farm was going downhill, but he, by the way, was one of the best Party committee secretaries of the *rayon*. And what struck me most was that the farm was falling apart but the Party committee secretary is the best. According to ideology it cannot be like that. Where ideology is the best, where personnel is the best the work should also be the best. Then for some reason they kept refusing my application to join the Party, when I suddenly decided to join: 'If you were a milkmaid or a herds-man . . . but you are a teacher. This is intelligentsia.' I became curious and pressed harder. I thought, all right, let's try. How can this be? If I work with children, but not with the herd, this is actually worse for the Party. However, at that stage they finally accepted me.[39]

Soon after Yelistratov joined the Communist Party he began working at the *rayon* Party committee and was actively trying to improve discipline and effi-ciency on the farms. He remembered that he was not so much defending the Party ideals as fighting for a simple principle so that words did not contradict actions. He maintained that he approached the situation as a teacher: 'if I said that this should be like that, it should be like that. Newton's law is Newton's law everywhere'.[40] His new knowledge of the reality of farming led to his disappointment with the Party leaders, though sometimes he found sympathy in some local Party officials. Yelistratov summed up the reasons for his dissat-isfaction:

At first it was interesting, of course, how the Party worked, when the farm went downhill and the Party committee secretary was the best in the *rayon*. This is one thing. Why is a person who works with children prevented from joining the Party while it is easier to join for somebody who works with cattle?

I took part in the preparation for the meetings of the *rayon* Party committee and its bureau, and I began speaking critically on various questions. The questions were mostly related to the defence of the interests of the working people, they were purely Party questions . . . For where does the Party stand? It claims that the working class is the vanguard, it should get the best and so on . . . But when I visited villages I saw that women worked in mud up to the waist and were paid very little, and sometimes didn't even receive their salary for months. Even in good years of 'stagnation' they did not receive their salary for three or four months.

I say: 'What kind of a manager are you, if your state farm lost twenty-five million?' But then it starts: 'Why did you interfere?', 'Why did you meddle with this?' 'What is this?' I think. They tell me: 'We sent people to check from one perspec-tive and you check from another.' But when you really check, and especially, when you speak about it, I found out that they start punishing you.[41]

Unlike Yelistratov, Lyudmila Antoshkina did not work at the Communist Party. Before moving to Orenburg, where she became an activist in Democratic Russia, she was the chairwoman of the territorial women's coun-cil in Samara *oblast`*. Soon after Gorbachev came to power the Moscow

---

[39] Interview with Vladimir Yelistratov (Belinskiy, 5 Apr. 1994).   [40] Ibid.
[41] Ibid.

authorities decided to put new life into the official women's councils and began to encourage their activities. Antoshkina was trying to solve the problems of the women who came to her council and appealed on their behalf to the Moscow authorities, including the CPSU Central Inspection Committee and various ministries and departments. She also opened a museum dedicated to the soldiers killed in Afghanistan and worked with juvenile delinquents. The Communist Party, despite the clear ideological appeals of official state doctrine, in practice far from encouraged her activities. According to Antoshkina 'relations with Communists . . . were somewhat complicated. Because whenever I tried to help somebody I ran into a wall of misunderstanding, a wall of indifference.'[42]

Stories of the attempts of future 'democrats' to fight for justice are strikingly similar. Mariya Sublina's experience was that 'when I began working I encountered the facts of pressure. . . . Somehow I began to rebel at the meetings and to speak out. When I joined the State Planning Committee the collective did not receive me very well, because I always spoke at meetings, spoke my mind. And once the department head even said: "You know, you are not one of us." '[43]

A worker from Krasnoyarsk, Sergey Loskutov, who later became an activist with the Krasnoyarsk Popular Front, also began by fighting problems and injustice within his factory. Loskutov particularly disliked widespread wastefulness, disregard for worker's interests' and violations of safety regulations. He remembered that 'at that time I was not engaged in politics, I did not know this politics but I was just selecting, so to speak, live examples and analysed them in my mind, what they could lead to'.[44] Taking seriously the official slogan that 'everyone should be an owner', Loskutov found lack of order everywhere and when others suffered injustice they often turned to him for help and advice. Loskutov explained the reason: 'I am just the kind of person that can tell every boss what I think'.[45] In 1971 Loskutov was sacked on a false accusation of drinking at work, despite the well-known fact that he was a teetotaller. After a long struggle he managed to get his job back by taking court action. But in 1978 he again found himself in conflict with the authorities because of taking official slogans literally:

At that time I joined a gardening partnership, I was doing gardening and read newspapers. At the partnership, again, things got into such a mess. Already in Brezhnev's time a decree had been issued on the necessity of an uncompromising crackdown on sharp dealers and rogues in gardening partnerships. The gardening partnership elected me chairman of the audit committee and we went ahead with an inspection. The chairman was a Party member, the bursar was also a Party member,

---

42 Interview with Lyudmila Antoshkina (Orenburg, 21 Dec. 1994).
43 Interview with Maria Sublina (Moscow, 28 Aug. 1993).
44 Interview with Sergey Loskutov (Krasnoyarsk, 21 Apr. 1994).   45 Ibid.

the money was stolen, false documents written, and I, so to speak, organized an investigation, contacted many organizations and found all the necessary papers. This was in 1978. But the case was dragged out until 1985. During that time the prosecutor and the investigator were sacked for wrongdoing. They, so to speak, tied up the case in red tape and dragged it on for two years. I show them the cashbook or some other document, and they steal it and say: 'You have not given us anything.' You see, what a nuisance! . . . As a result many prosecutor's offices worked on it and they gave me contradictory answers. I did achieve something, though: the plan appeared to be forged and I punished them and they had to return the money for the plan, but only in two years, a land regulator took the blame and in two and a half years he was sentenced to one year and had to pay a twenty per cent fine. He took the blame, the land regulator, but the chairman fled to the Crimea in 1980.[46]

Personal experience dealing with various rank-and-file bureaucrats made Loskutov totally disillusioned with their intentions. But in order to make broader generalizations he needed more information and a different general atmosphere.

An accountant from Nevinnomyssk, Valentina Knyazeva, encountered similar disappointments. Knyazeva, who called herself a 'truth-lover', had never been a member of the Communist Party, but always actively participated in public activities. According to her, she has 'never let herself lie to herself, or to others—or paid attention to officials'.[47] At the factory where she worked she was often elected a delegate to trade union conferences, and the party officials would 'even seat workshop Party secretaries at my side at meetings, so that I would not jump up on the stage to talk all about the problems of the collective'.[48] Given her independent character, many people asked Knyazeva for assistance with various problems, one of which was the fight against factory disposal of poisonous wastes into a river, damaging the health of many factory workers living nearby. Knyazeva was engaged in similar activities everywhere she worked.[49]

Generalizing to the national scale was done gradually. Future 'democrats' first saw the more obvious contradictions at the workplace or their local social organization, then they took notice of the disparity between 'Moscow' slogans and local practices and only then did they begin to question official ideology as a whole. This process was described by a gas engineer from Orenburg, Vladislav Shapovalenko, who at first actively worked in the official trade unions at the companies where he worked:

Everybody says one thing in the papers and from the rostrum and does another. I could well understand a person who, speaking at a Party meeting, told you how it should be . . . even in my native Gazprom, where I worked, or in the institute, but I saw quite clearly that the actions were different. So I was most indignant not at the

---

[46] Interview with Sergey Loskutov.
[47] Interview with Valentina Kaznacheeva (Nevinnomyssk, 5 Sept. 1994).
[48] Ibid.   [49] Ibid.

policies of those in Moscow, but at what was happening locally . . . When you witness so many small examples at your institute, in your town, you naturally transfer them to the level of Moscow and the country and you see the same things.[50]

Eventually Shapovalenko transferred his dissatisfaction to the top leaders. He already disapproved greatly of the tone of Khrushchev's policies, which became even more intense under Brezhnev. Despite having been brought up in the spirit of 'What are we going to do when Stalin dies?', Shapovalenko enthusiastically supported Nikita Khrushchev when the new leader criticized Stalin at the Twentieth Congress of the CPSU. However, as Shapovalenko put it, 'when I saw that Khrushchev continued the same personality cult . . . this was unacceptable to me, and my attitude toward Khrushchev was very negative.'[51]

A civil aviation pilot, Aleksandr Romanov, who was later to became the leader of Democratic Russia in Orenburg, also travelled the road from dissatisfaction with Communist domination in his own profession to broader generalization. He vividly described this road:

Our minister of civil aviation, Bugaev, had such an idea, he always repeated from the rostrum that the steering-wheel should be in the hands of a Communist. Those aimless Party meetings also got on your nerves—you sat there for no reason, just to show that you were present. Paying their dues, nobody knew how they were used, but we saw how, say, the first secretary lived, in fact much better. The first secretary can do what an ordinary person cannot and does not bear any responsibility for it. The same crime, for an ordinary person it was a crime, but for him it was nothing . . . Then, the very conditions themselves. The elite enjoyed privileges, but those who were entitled to those privileges, in practice could not enjoy them. Nothing was left for them, for such people as veterans, especially the disabled, who queued for a flat and could not get it, while, say, the son of a chairman of the executive committee of a city Soviet or of a secretary of a city or *rayon* Party committee, he could get such a flat, even though he did not have any merits or anything . . . And I saw many such cases.[52]

Describing the situation under Communist rule, Romanov remarked that 'officially, everything is perfect. What is written on paper—this is one thing, but what is being done—this is another . . . one thing is declared, another is done. But if we really want to do everything for the people, we should create a mechanism of doing it . . . of making people's work easier, of making people's recreation easier. But we did everything very differently. We declared one thing, but in fact it turned out to be directed against the people and such examples were numerous'.[53]

The shortages of food supplies, which affected everybody, especially in provincial towns, was also becoming a major source of discontent, often to a greater extent than more general political problems. This mood was described

---

[50] Interview with Vladislav Shapovalenko (Orenburg, 21 Dec. 1994).   [51] Ibid.
[52] Interview with Aleksandr Romanov (Orenburg, 22 Dec. 1994).   [53] Ibid.

by Shcherkin: 'Life in Pskov was very poor. We went to Moscow, Estonia, or Petersburg to buy sausages. Critical attitudes could have developed gradually. Everything was in the public eye. The people did not give much thought to what we did, say, in Cuba, or in Afghanistan. The Party does not care about us, one cannot buy anything in the shops, there are food tickets, many tickets, piles of them.'[54] Shcherkin himself had already found out the difference between ideology and the methods of the authorities when as a teenager he kept bad company: 'I knew that the militia, this embodiment of authority, violated the law, that unmanageable teenagers could be beaten there . . . But as for the lessons of social knowledge, of the fundamentals of the state and law, we were told different things.'[55] The discontent gradually accumulated and under certain conditions could develop into a desire to change the situation in the country fundamentally. However, these conditions were yet to come.

A special case of contradiction between official ideals and reality was connected to ethnicity. While official Soviet ideology declared all Soviet nationalities to be equal, real ethnic practice in the USSR was peculiar and contradictory. Some people, namely Russians, Ukrainians, and Byelorussians, were usually regarded by the Communist personnel experts to be 'normal' indigenous people and were not subject to discrimination when entering a university or applying for a job. Other peoples, such as those from the Russian North or from the Central Asian republics, enjoyed certain privileges, for example, in admission to Russian universities, and many official bodies were supposed to have a specific percentage of representatives of these nationalities. Other nationalities in different periods were seen as politically unreliable. These most often included Jews and the nationalities deported by Stalin: Chechens, Crimean Tartars, Meshetian Turks, Greeks, Germans, and others. These peoples were often subjected to semi-official discrimination when applying for a job, a place in a university, or permission to travel abroad.

It is not surprising that for the representatives of these 'unreliable' nationalities the constant suspicions of the authorities about their intentions were an additional source of doubts concerning the official ideology. This is clear from several interviews and documents. For example, Lyuboshits, discussing his reasons for disillusionment, highlighted the misfortunes he suffered after 1949 during the anti-foreign and anti-Semitic campaign against the so-called 'cosmopolitans'.[56] Gezentsvey also mentioned the existence of anti-Semitism in the USSR.[57] Gavriil Popov, an ethnic Greek, was several times asked hostile questions about his nationality by various bureaucrats and was once even advised to change it.[58] These experiences alone did not change Popov's

---

[54] Interview with Shcherkin.   [55] Ibid.
[56] Interview with Lyuboshits.   [57] Interview with Gezentsvey.
[58] Gavriil Popov, *Snova v oppositsii*, 11–12.

orthodox Marxist beliefs. As a 'genuine Marxist' he still thought that 'in future all nations will merge into one' and therefore he thought it unnecessary to study Greek.[59]

The Afghan War was another significant source of dissatisfaction with the situation in the country, especially among young people. Describing his mood during the Brezhnev era, Shapovalenko said: 'Those Kremlin elders, those anecdotes, and then that Afghan war, it made us think about where we were heading'.[60] The youngest 'democrats' often recalled how they took every precaution in order not to do military service during the war. For example, Shcherkin, in order to avoid being sent to Afghanistan, where his 'acquaintances . . . who began their service a bit earlier were being killed', moved to another city to enter a college where students were granted exemption from army service.[61] Ivlev admitted that he was evading the draft in Moscow, where he met the leader of the Democratic Union, Valeriya Novodvorskaya, and for the first time began to think seriously about politics.[62]

In any case real life, the encounter with Soviet reality, became the initial reason for most future 'democrats' to doubt the official Soviet ideology, both in Moscow and in the provinces, and the basis for this doubt, paradoxically, was the officially instilled moral beliefs. At the same time this basis was insufficient to proceed to more general conclusions about the Soviet system as a whole; and the discontent, however deep it may have been, usually was directed at specific individuals whose activities were thought to be inconsistent with the official theoretical image of socialism.

4.3. FAMILY EDUCATION AND FAMILY REMINISCENCES

It is widely accepted that the family plays an important role in political socialization. Studying the Twin Cities area (Minneapolis–St Paul) in the United States, Herbert McClosky and Harold E. Dahlgren concluded that 'the family is a key reference group which transmits, indoctrinates, and sustains the political loyalties of its members'.[63] In the USSR family and family reminiscences were also an important source for the formation of the belief system of Russian 'democrats'. There were hardly any model Communist families in the USSR, where children were allegedly educated in a purely Communist spirit. In fact, in almost every family members spoke about events or problems which were inconsistent with the official ideology. Some had relatives

---

[59] Ibid.
[60] Interview with Shapovalenko.
[61] Interview with Shcherkin.
[62] Interview with Ivlev.
[63] Herbert McClosky and Harold E. Dahlgren, 'Primary Group Influence on Party Loyalities', *American Political Science Review*, 53 (1959), 775.

who suffered political persecution, but whom they did not really think were 'enemies of the people'; some read old books which they inherited and which contained 'wrong' points of view; some believed in God; some expressed quiet dissatisfaction with Communist domination of professional matters at work or with social injustice, and everybody disliked endless queuing and shortages of commodities. Parents often tried to conceal their 'wrong' feelings from their children because of fear that children could unintentionally make these feelings known to strangers. Children, however, eventually found out about such feelings.

Many future 'democrats' spoke about the influence of the family, though criticism of the authorities varied widely. For example, Gezetsvey recalled that his father 'was a Communist. He believed that the future belonged to socialism, and that socialism could win throughout the entire world, but that it would be normal socialism, similar to "socialism with a human face" as it began to be called later'.[64] Didichenko claimed that his family implanted in him a hatred of Stalin:

> About Stalin I am quite frank with you and am telling you directly. I was about six and my grandfather, whom I respected a lot, once said when speaking to my father— and I remembered his words—I was sitting under the table and grandad said: 'You'll see, the time will come and people will find out who killed Kirov, it's Stalin who killed Kirov. People will find out that Russia was ruled by a Georgian who did not care about the Russian people.' And I had such a deep-seated hatred of Stalin from childhood. It especially developed when in 1948 I went to Sakhalin from Baku and saw my fellow-Ukrainians serving sentences for no crime, how they were tormented, but I knew already that I had to keep my mouth shut. . . . However, I almost cracked and nearly did . . . some silly things.[65]

Critical attitudes toward the authorities, especially toward Stalin, could often be found in peasant families. Fedor Vorob`ev, an arts teacher and a member of a discussion club in Belinskiy, came from such a family. His father fought in three wars and lost a leg during World War II. According to Vorob`ev, he was 'a democrat at heart' and saw 'the lies of our whole ideology'.[66] As a proof of his father's 'democratic' credentials Vorob`ev presented the words he remembered his father saying when he left for the army in 1942: 'It's a pity that I have to lose my life for that swarthy guy who's wiped out so many people.'[67] Recalling his own feelings at the time of Stalin's death Vorob`ev said: 'At heart I understood that a dictator had died. My father spoke of him a lot . . . We had a doctor and they were friends. I don't know why they were friendly, they both went fishing. Sometimes father drank and they talked a lot. I always heard a lot of negative things about Stalin. And then the period of dispossessing the *kulaks*. He said how the

---

[64] Interview with Gezentsvey.   [65] Interview with Didichenko.
[66] Interview with Fedor Vorob`ev (Belinskiy, 5 Apr. 1994).   [67] Ibid.

people were tormented, how they were dispossessed. Whole families were taken away.'[68]

Speaking about the sources of his negative attitude toward life in the Soviet Union, Yevgeniy Grachev, a researcher from a museum in Belinskiy, also mentioned the influence of his father, who 'was not a supporter of socialism' and 'already believed that socialism was a road to nowhere, a dead end'. According to Grachev, his father's opinions were influenced by his experience in Germany during World War II, where he 'saw how they lived in Germany'.[69] Grachev's father, like Vorob`ev's, often discussed sensitive questions with his friend, a geography teacher. Despite the fact that both men tried to ensure that children did not overhear their dangerous conversations, Grachev managed to listen in on some of them: 'Sometimes they went to the forest and told me to follow a hundred metres after them, so that I could not hear them speak. Their mood was that they did not believe in anything—in 1953, as well as before 1953.'[70] Dissatisfaction was also often expressed in Grinchenko's family, whose ancestors were dispossessed *kulaks* from the North Caucasus. According to Grinchenko, his elder uncle 'was a Communist but he was later blamed for being the son of a *kulak*. He was expelled from the Party but later his membership was restored. Already then, when I was perhaps just twelve or thirteen, he said: "Il`ya, if you ever decide to join the Party remember that it is a pack, a pack of wolves. And if you don't gnaw through somebody's throat, they will gnaw through yours." '[71]

Grinchenko's younger uncle, who was an officer in the strategic missile forces, could only rise to the rank of major because he 'conscientiously did not join the Party, so his promotion, naturally, was slowed down'.[72] The words and problems of relatives were imprinted into the memory of the young man.

The parents of Aleksandr Pavlov were exiled as *kulaks* in 1929 from Pskov to Tyumen` *oblast`*. His father's parents were also peasants, and though they did not suffer arrests or exile, they were deeply dissatisfied with the requirement to hand over all their possessions to the collective farm and join it. On the basis of his relatives' stories, Pavlov came to the conclusion that 'ordinary people, both in the 1920s and 1930s, never supported the regime. Perhaps they were afraid to speak up, but among themselves, in the family, people said whatever they wanted about the authorities and never supported them'.[73]

While the relatives of Grinchenko and Pavlov were peasants, Ol`ga Shul`cheva, an activist in Memorial and Democratic Russia from Orenburg, came from an exiled gentry family, which influenced her views.[74] The family

---

[68] Ibid.
[70] Ibid.
[72] Ibid.
[74] Interview with Ol`ga Shul`cheva (Orenburg, 22 Dec. 1994).

[69] Interview with Yevgeniy Grachev (Belinskiy, 5 Apr. 1994).
[71] Interview with Il`ya Grinchenko (Vladivostok, 24 Apr. 1994).
[73] Interview with Pavlov.

of Sergey Shokolenko, a Democratic Union activist from Vladivostok, was particularly hostile toward the Soviet powers. According to Shokolenko, his family

has been fighting this regime for seventy years. Some time ago my family owned a lot of real estate. Plus my grandfather fought in the army of Ataman Semenov. There used to be such an army here . . . When they finally confiscated everything from us in 1930 my grandfather took all his belongings . . . all his relatives went with him. They fled to Harbin. They were, let's say, petty merchants. They belonged to the bourgeois estate and did not take part in all that. Later my grandmother failed to cross the border with my father and my aunts. . . . They were caught at the border by the Red Army soldiers. Grandmother was put into irons and sent to the mines, father at ten was sent to a colony. . . . In 1945 the [Russian] people [in Harbin] were told either to go back or to leave for Canada or Australia. But my grandfather was already well informed, so he preferred to go to Canada. We received letters until 1968–69. So I naturally became saturated with all that. About my father, that's a whole epic. He also fought during that war, but on the wrong side. He is quite elderly now, but he can still get in trouble. And on my mother's side, it's even worse.[75]

Personal childhood and teenage impressions, like words and hints from elder relatives, often became another reason for questioning official dogmas. Lyuboshits, for example, recalled that when he was a child he witnessed arrests of neighbours and other people he knew. He explained: 'I lived in a house which was called the fourth house of the Moscow City Soviet, in front of the Yeliseev store in Gorkiy Street. . . . So, when I was a boy in 1937–38 the house was of a hotel type and there were thirty-eight flats on one floor. Occupants of seven or eight flats on each floor were arrested or exiled. Parents of most of my friends were arrested. . . . And Vyshinskiy[76] lived on the same floor with me.'[77] At first Lyuboshits accepted that those arrested were the enemies of the people, but later he stopped believing that.[78]

Valentin Manuylov was two generations younger than Lyuboshits and he could not find out from his own experience about the arrests and Stalin's Terror. He did not mention his family influence either. However, he met witnesses of the Terror who told him about that time:

I had a short stay in Moscow in 1984, then I often went there to work on my dissertation, and in 1986 I was taking advanced courses at Moscow State University where I happened to get acquainted with a man who still remembered his youth back in the 1930s very well. . . . He was an ordinary researcher, but he had such an interesting life. When he was a child he lived in a house with a Deputy People's Commissar, Lashevich. When he was a Komsomol member . . . he worked for two months at the NKVD, copied some papers there. Later because of that a friend gave

[75] Interview with Sergey Shokolenko (Vladivostok, 23 Apr. 1994).

[76] A. Ya. Vyshinskiy, Chief Prosecutor at the trials of 1937–8, later Soviet Prosecutor General and Foreign Minister.   [77] Interview with Lyuboshits.

[78] Ibid.

him an invitation to the trial of Bukharin, and what he was telling me at that time was kind of peculiar, but at the same time I remembered it and later all that was published in 1988, practically identical to what he was saying.[79]

Despite the presence of many similar recollections in the interviews, it would be wrong to assume that criticism of the authorities in families or by friends itself caused hostility toward, or even doubts about, the whole system of official ideology or its fundamentals. The case of Shokolenko was marginal. Many future 'democrats', especially during Stalin's rule, believed in official teachings even if their own relatives suffered persecution. Klepachev, for example, characteristically acknowledged that, despite the fact that both of his parents were exiled, for a long time he did not understand the real role of Stalin and believed him to be 'a leader, a teacher, our father and all that'.[80]

These examples show that realizing the contradiction between separate elements of the ideological system and reality did not necessarily undermine belief in the system as a whole. Without being put into a systematic context, fragmentary critical phrases and opinions or impressions of separate events which contradicted official claims could not seriously compete with generally consistent official beliefs. Since such an alternative context did not exist in the Soviet Union prior to Gorbachev, such opinions and events were usually interpreted within the context of the official Soviet belief system. In this way the crimes of the Stalin era, the arrests and persecutions, could be interpreted as serious but not fatal mistakes which were later corrected by the Party, and even an intense hatred of Stalin did not therefore necessarily lead to the rejection of Soviet Communism. The arbitrary actions of Communist bureaucrats could be understood as having been committed by politically backward Communists who entered the Party by deception to make a career. Shortages of food and commodities could be seen as the results of the war's destruction and of the mistakes of individual leaders. Few future 'democrats' turned from the criticism of shortages and isolated injustices to broader generalization before *glasnost*`. In most of their families the atmosphere was similar to that described by Shcherkin, who said that his parents 'definitely were critical enough. And were scolding. But this scolding did not go further than their kitchen. It was just making fun or telling jokes.'[81]

These conclusions are supported by the fact that family influences did not prevent Klepachev, Didichenko, Grinchenko, Pavlov, Lyuboshits, and many others from being active Komsomol or Party members who, at least for some considerable time, believed in the official ideology and fought for 'genuine' socialism. Finally, critical views were characteristic of only some families. Many parents themselves accepted the official teachings; some were not

---

[79] Interview with Valentin Manuylov (Penza, 4 Apr. 1994).
[80] Interview with Klepachev.   [81] Interview with Shcherkin.

interested in politics at all; and some managed to conceal their real beliefs from their children. Nevertheless, family impressions did not disappear without trace; often they were remembered and in the new conditions of greater information which emerged later these impressions could be reinterpreted and assist the formation of a critical attitude toward Soviet ideology and the Soviet political system as a whole.

4.4. OFFICIALLY PUBLISHED LITERATURE IN THE PRE-*PERESTROYKA* PERIOD

While the educational levels of members of 'democratic' groups differed, many of them were quite well read and managed to gain an impressive fund of knowledge from the books, journals, and newspapers which were officially published in the USSR. In fact official ideology encouraged the reading of approved publications on politics and society, especially newspapers, maintaining that a better educated citizen would be a more politically aware Communist supporter. Being politically aware, 'democrats' were naturally interested in this kind of literature, but they were usually also well read in works of fiction and social journalism, which touched upon questions of society, politics, or history, and they devoted a great deal of attention to the so-called 'thick journals'.

Thick journals were popular reading in the Soviet Union. They were traditionally the first to publish new, especially controversial novels, stories, and poetry and attracted particular interest when they contained articles in which well-known authors and public figures expressed independent opinions which could not be published in the more ideologically rigid official newspapers. Many interviewees noted that they were attentive readers of thick journals, the ones most often mentioned being *Novyy mir*, *Znamya*,[82] and *Inostrannaya literatura*.[83] In fact, 'democrats' were not alone in their interest in periodicals and shared it with the Soviet population as a whole.[84]

In a similar way, 'democrats', together with about 90 per cent of the entire population,[85] regularly read official newspapers. This was absolutely natural for people who were interested in the life of society. Many 'democrats' noted that before *perestroyka* official newspapers, along with radio and television, were the main sources of information both about the Soviet Union and the outside world and some limited their interest in politics to such reading. For

---

[82] Interview with Petr Popov.

[83] Interviews with Aleksandr Shubin (Oxford, 26 Jan. 1995) and Shapovalenko.

[84] According to one poll more than 70% of the entire population of the USSR and 70% of those with higher education read periodicals: Boris Grushin, *Svobodnoye vremya: aktual'nye problemy* (Moscow: Mysl`, 1967), 81.   [85] Ibid.

example, Shapovalenko said that he 'in general was always interested in politics, I mean reading newspapers'.[86] When reading the newspapers, 'democrats' tried to uncover the hidden meaning behind the official phraseology, or compared what they read with reality. One such scrupulous reader was Loskutov, who on the basis of reading newspapers came to the conclusion that reality did not match the high standards of official ideology:

> There was a time when I lived, so to speak, without any interests, I did not even read newspapers or anything else. Later somehow I began to read newspapers and, in fact, I began to get more information from the newspapers while before I only got it from talking to other people. So, I began to learn more from newspapers. And often while reading a newspaper I somehow analysed what was written there. Some people read and don't care, but . . . in my mind I thought of everything and I, for example, could not agree with what was written there. Or sometimes I saw a distortion of the heart of the matter or of the reality which was being discussed.[87]

Kryskin remembered that he also 'was keen on social and political journalism and read such articles making scrupulous marks with a pencil and hunting out meanings between the lines. It was the most interesting thing in life, to look for the concealed truth and dig it up'.[88]

Among various books the works of the 'classics of Marxism', as well as of 'progressive' (i.e. left-wing and USSR-friendly) foreign authors and materialist philosophers, were officially encouraged in the Soviet Union. General reading—for example, the reading of fiction and literary criticism—was supposed to be an indication of cultural growth and therefore a socialist achievement. The USSR was officially proclaimed the most widely read country in the world (which, according to some studies, was not a totally unfounded claim[89]). In different periods various works in philosophy and the social sciences were published in the USSR, many of which were not at all Marxist. With the exception of several 'politically unreliable' authors, such as Friedrich Nietzsche, virtually all major pre-twentieth-century social science literature was translated and published even during the Stalin period. Works by twentieth-century authors were published more selectively and those who were openly critical of Marxism, Communism, and the USSR were usually denied access to Soviet readers. However, in the post-Stalin period liberal Soviet scholars found a way of studying and presenting some of the ideas of even these foreign authors to the public in the form of criticism of their works. The only remaining absolute prohibition in the USSR was on the works of recent emigrants from the country and of Western specialists on the USSR.

---

[86] Interview with Shapovalenko.   [87] Interview with Loskutov.

[88] Interview with Kryskin.

[89] See Jenny Brine, 'Reading as a Leisure Pursuit in the USSR', in Jenny Brine, Maureen Perrie, and Andrew Sutton (eds.), *Home, School and Leisure in the Soviet Union* (London: George Allen and Unwin, 1980).

Even when such authors were criticized the censor exercised strict control to prevent any presentation of their genuine points of view.

Being socially active citizens, many 'democrats' were well read in both social science and creative literature which touched upon social problems. Their reading interests naturally differed according to individual level and character of education. Their range of reading can be generally described as relatively wide but not systematic. After finishing secondary school, which imparted a compulsory knowledge of many Russian and Soviet classics and of several specific works and quotations from the 'classics of Marxism', most 'democrats' searched for and read the kind of literature which corresponded most closely to their thoughts and experiences and interpreted it according to these thoughts and experiences.

This can be seen from the fact that in different periods different conclusions were drawn on the basis of the same books. For example, Krasulya, who wrote that he spent many evenings reading thick books with a pencil and a notebook, nevertheless believed in official slogans until the beginning of *perestroyka*.[90] He explains this as a result of having supposedly read 'the wrong books'. This, however, could hardly be the only explanation. He certainly did not have access to a number of books which were openly critical of the Soviet system. But in fact the official system of education led to a situation in which even books which were very far from Marxism were incorporated into the existing system of political beliefs and were interpreted as proving the general scheme. In the process of such interpretation, primary attention was paid to the facts and phenomena which supported and developed the original beliefs, while anything which contradicted them tended to be ignored or was taken to be of minor importance and therefore disregarded. The experience of an engineer from Vladivostok, Teodey Fel`dman, shows the workings of this mechanism of reading. Well before *perestroyka* Fel`dman read many philosophers and even learned German so as to be able to admire German literature in the original, some of which he knew by heart. He also volunteered to give a course in philosophical education to his fellow electricians after working hours (the course was encouraged by his superiors as a part of the political education of the staff). According to Fel`dman, the course covered philosophy 'from Heraclitus to Berdyaev' (despite the fact that the latter was not even published in the USSR at that time). However, the whole course was treated from the most orthodox ideological standpoints, which even caused surprise and disagreement among some of Fel`dman's less well read but more down-to-earth colleagues.[91]

The same mechanism also operated later, after the formation and stabilization of the 'democratic' political belief system. At that time, the reading of the same authors and works which earlier supported official beliefs began

---

[90] Krasulya, *Dissident iz nomenklatury*, 7–8.   [91] Interview with Fel`dman.

to be used in the 'democratic' way. Before *perestroyka* the works of various philosophers (who surely included Aristotle) did not in the least make Krasulya and Fel`dman hesitate about the truth of Marxism, Leninism, or the pronouncements of the Soviet leaders. However, in the late 1980s a member of the Democratic Union from Vladivostok, Oleg Obryadin, who studied law at Vladivostok University, interpreted Aristotle very differently:

I went even further. I read Aristotle. So I was arguing everywhere: if there was public property of everything, that would be the end. You say that in 1917 there was socialism. In fact, socialism existed earlier. Europe became clever enough for it. Take, for example, the fourth volume of Aristotle. It describes an interesting situation. People of Lenin's type were appearing. Like Lenin, Trotskiy, and others. Socialism for them was organized in one city. They were saying: create socialism, regulate prices and all that. That's how it happened. Historians know it. They created pure socialism. They distributed, divided everyone's share as they thought fit. But people ran away from such places . . . Aristotle argued with Socrates. Socrates said: 'There is land. If one gave it to several people they would all care for it and cultivate it. It would be ten times better cultivated since it would belong to society as a whole and everything would be better.' Aristotle said: 'No, Socrates is wrong. This land will be neglected since everyone will rely on everyone else and nobody will care about it. In the same way nobody will take care of the tools . . . He said: 'First, the bureaucrats will be wildly corrupt. There will be a mafia of bureaucrats, they will not care about anything, they will do nothing but grab since they will be elected from the poor, and will grab, grab, and grab.' This is the fourth volume of Aristotle. It says everything about socialism. And it was written so many centuries ago. There he said that a brutal system had to be created, like, say, the NKVD, although the wording was different, such a brutal system of people, who, in order to survive, had to, so to speak, stop the bureaucrats who went too far. All this was described.[92]

This confused account of Aristotle's writings resembles more the programme of the Democratic Union than the texts of the Greek philosopher, who never wrote about socialism, the NKVD, or the mafia, though he did write about the inviability of communal property (*Politics*, II. 3 and 5). Obryadin obviously not only uses some of Aristotle's ideas to back up his own beliefs but also attributes some of these beliefs to the ancient author.

Kryskin also found ideas in Aristotle's work which confirmed his own thoughts. In arguing for his point that having been brought up as good Soviet citizens he and his friends were rejected by the Soviet state, Kryskin maintained that the Greek philosopher supposedly wrote about this situation two thousand years ago: 'It seems that the same thing happened in ancient societies. He [Aristotle] said that a good state needed a good citizen. A bad state did not need a good citizen, he is harmful to it. So we were

---

[92] Interview with Oleg Obryadin (Krasnoyarsk, 21 Apr. 1994). The 'fourth volume of Aristotle' to which Obryadin refers is almost certainly Aristotel', *Sochineniya* (4 vols.; Moscow: Mysl', 1983), iv. It contains the *Nicomachean Ethics*, *Politics*, *Poetics*, and some other works.

created good citizens, but we lived in a bad state. The state appeared not to need us and we found ourselves thrown overboard.'[93]

Aleksandr Shubin interpreted in a similar 'democratic' way a book by Laurence Peter, *Why Things Go Wrong*, extracts from which were published in 1987 in *Inostrannaya literatura*, humorously describing the workings of bureaucracy.[94] Though Peter used examples mainly from Britain, the United States, and Australia, Shubin concluded that bureaucracy ruled not only in the West but also in the USSR. On the role of Peter's writings, Shubin said: 'I cannot say that he somehow determined our ideas; he gave concrete expression to them'.[95] In the same way Shubin evaluated the influence on him and his friends of the writings of anarchist and social-revolutionary theorists: 'In principle our ideas emerged from the study of the society around us, from some feeling that we were deceived. "Let's see what's really there!" And later they were given concrete expression by Bakunin, Chernov, Arshinin, Peter, and simply by conversations with various clever people whom we met'.[96] It can clearly be seen that in this case, as in many others, officially published literature was not an immediate source of 'democratic' beliefs, though it could provide additional proof and further convince those who were already moving in a 'democratic' direction.

The diary of the organizer of a discussion club, Dialog, in Belinskiy, Vladimir Yelistratov, discloses this process of illustrative reading. This diary of a schoolteacher from a tiny provincial town contains quotations from an impressive range of very different authors of various periods, including the classical Greeks Plato and Antisthenes; French writers Michel de Montaigne, Denis Diderot, François de La Rochefoucauld, Honoré de Balzac, Pierre-Augustine Caron de Beaumarchais, Jean de La Bruyère, Romain Rolland, and Anatole France; English authors William Shakespeare and George Halifax; the German Johann Wolfgang von Goethe; Russian writers and thinkers Mikhail Lermontov, Vissarion Belinskiy, Dmitriy Pisarev, and Vladimir Lenin; and Soviet authors and academics Vasiliy Shukshin, Yanis Raynis, and Dmitriy Likhachev.[97] The method of citation is distinctive. Before every meeting of the club, Yelistratov carefully selected only those thoughts of the authors he was reading which proved the point he was going to argue for in his presentation. His notes were therefore not a synopsis

[93] Interview with Kryskin.

[94] See L. Peter, 'Pochemu dela idut vkriv` i vkos` ili Yeshche raz o Printsipe Pitera', *Inostrannaya Literatura*, 1 (1987), 195–209 and 2 (1987), 175–89 (translation of Laurence J. Peter, *Why Things Go Wrong or The Peter Principle Revisited* [London: George Allen and Unwin, 1985]). Parallels with Russia and the Soviet Union were drawn in Yevgeniy Ambartsumov's afterword to the Russian translation.   [95] Interview with Shubin.

[96] Ibid.

[97] V. I. Yelistratov, diary and notes, unpubl. MS (Belinskiy, 1989–90), courtesy of the author. Yelistratov sometimes used quotations from secondary sources, some of which are mentioned in the diary.

resulting from thorough study of the works he read. The works were used as material to prove the predetermined point.

For example, the diary begins with materials concerning the creation of the club, in the process of which Yelistratov was obviously trying to prove the necessity of the club's existence by stressing the positive role of discussion. He therefore sought support from many authors for this idea of the positive role of discussion. He starts by referring to an article, 'Rules for Debaters', from an official Soviet journal, *Slovo lektora* (The Word of a Lecturer).[98] Later one can find the main idea which Yelistratov was to champion (explaining the aims of the club to potential members or to hostile authorities): 'Argument gives birth to truth.' It is followed by several quotations from various authors which prove the main idea, for example: 'A word is also a deed' (Anatole France); 'Conversation is the most fruitful and natural exercise for our minds' (Montaigne), etc. Yelistratov continues with his own conclusion: 'Let everyone express his own opinion without worrying that others think differently. One should be tolerant toward the opinions of others; it is impossible to make everyone think as you do.'[99] Apart from quotations from classical literature, this part of the diary also contains some formulas from contemporary *perestroyka* periodicals which were in line with Yelistratov's own thoughts. For example, a quotation from an official journal of the Central Committee of the CPSU, *Dialog* (formerly *Kommunist*), which shared its name with the discussion club, said: 'Let us pursue our dialogue for the triumph of civil peace.'[100]

Yelistratov's diary, which covers the period of 1989–91, shows the mechanism of the development of 'democratic' beliefs and of the emergence of 'democratic' activities. By the time of its writing Yelistratov was already convinced of the necessity and fruitfulness of free discussion. This idea in itself did not contradict official ideology, but Yelistratov, who worked in the apparatus of the Communist Party, knew only too well that in reality this idea could not be implemented, and that real freedom of discussion was not officially encouraged. To prove his point Yelistratov used official publications, as he had always done in his work as a political lecturer. But he did something which was unthinkable in earlier times: he put his belief into practice by creating an unofficial discussion group to pursue genuinely free discussions of pressing social questions. He depended upon the thoughts of famous people not for their own sake but to prove his own positions and actions, and he threaded them into the existing structure of his own beliefs.

Reading officially published literature surely broadened the range of interests of the future 'democrats', giving them new information which, under

---

[98] N. Stavskaya, 'Ustav dlya sporyashchikh', *Slovo lektora*, 10 (1989), 49. Yelistratov also refers to *Slovo lektora*, 1 (1989). [99] Yelistratov, diary and notes.
[100] Ibid.

certain circumstances, could play a role in changing their system of beliefs. For example, Anatoliy Zamyatin came to the conclusion that the USSR lagged behind the USA technologically while reading, during the time of his military service, a book on the American economy by the Soviet deputy trade minister, N. N. Smelyakov.[101] But in accordance with his previous beliefs Zamyatin thought that this lag could be overcome by the measures officially advanced by the Soviet leadership:

At that time I thought that it would have been great for our country to have the same level of development, but with justice, with equality and everything else . . . So my thought was typical of that time. I did not understand that people's psychology and the economy were interconnected . . . I believed that a person could be interested, that his enthusiasm could be raised, for example, by providing him with advanced technology, and he would work with it. Only now we can already see retrospectively that without personal interest no system would work. Any kind of machine, any kind of technology would be wasted.[102]

Only on the basis of new, 'democratic' beliefs, which he acquired later, would Zamyatin suggest a different solution to the problem. But he became aware of the actual existence of the problem from official Soviet literature.

Kryskin found out in similar fashion that planning in Japan was more efficient than in the USSR from an officially published translation of a book by some Japanese authors which he read in the early 1980s. According to Kryskin, the book argued that 'they in Japan had a research institute which was engaged in broad, large-scale planning. The difference was that these plans were implemented by private firms and companies. It did not regulate every tiny detail . . . But broad economic perspectives were being planned. And the head of this research institute or facility was the Japanese prime minister himself. . . . I thought that in such civilized countries the level of planning was higher than in our socialist country.'[103]

Alongside officially published newspapers and books, many 'democrats' mentioned films as a source of their beliefs. For example, the Soviet film *U ozera* (By the Lake), directed by Sergey Gerasimov, cautiously raised problems of environmental protection, in particular of the pollution of Lake Baikal, and criticized local authorities in Siberia for failing to address the problem. Authorities in the Siberian and Ural regions hurried to organize public meetings to prove that they had handled the problem properly. According to Shapovalenko, he and some interested friends once attended one of these discussion meetings, but were disillusioned, since all the speakers seemed to have been briefed in advance to criticize the film.[104] Other

---

[101] N. N. Smelyakov, *Delovaya Amerika*. Zapiski inzhenera (Moscow: Izclatel`stvo politicheskoy literatury, 967)
[102] Interview with Anatoliy Zamyatin (Penza 15 Aug. 1994).
[103] Interview with Kryskin.   [104] Interview with Shapovalenko.

'democrats' pointed out that they were influenced by foreign films which let them see life abroad and compare it with Soviet reality. For example, according to Romanov, 'life was becoming worse and worse every year, shortages began, but the party *nomenklatura* leaders were having a good life. While the ordinary people got worse they were told that we had a great life . . . And, as a contrast, some foreign films began to break through from abroad and we saw how they lived there and how we lived here.'[105]

On the whole we can conclude that even a deep study of the officially allowed Soviet literature and media by future 'democrats' could not in itself lead them to deny the official ideology. The same works and materials, under different circumstances, could reinforce a belief in the truth of this ideology or could undermine faith in it, depending on the original direction of the person's beliefs and on various other factors.

4.5. FOREIGN TRAVEL

Travel abroad was a privilege in the USSR. Only a few future 'democrats' managed to visit foreign countries and to see life there with their own eyes before *perestroyka*, when restrictions were gradually lifted. However, the impact of impressions of journeys abroad should not be underestimated, since many people returned to spread information among their colleagues and friends, and many 'democrats' who did not go abroad personally learned about foreign lands not only from the official media, but from those who visited them.

Of the sixty-seven 'democrats' interviewed for this study, only six travelled abroad before *perestroyka*, and they mostly visited 'socialist' countries of the Soviet bloc, which were not thought to be genuinely 'foreign'. For example, when asked about foreign travel, Loskutov said that he once went to Mongolia and asked if this should be counted as a foreign trip.[106] An activist in the Oktyabr`skiy District Union of Voters, Yuriy Belkin, who in the 1970s worked for a long time in Hungary and visited East Germany and Poland, quoted a Soviet saying: 'A hen is not a bird, Poland is not abroad' (which could be easily applied to any other Soviet-bloc country).[107] Their reasons for travel were usual for the USSR: army service during World War II and later, participation in official exchanges and delegations, and official tourism in organized groups. A greater number of 'democrats' were able to travel abroad after Gorbachev's reforms, and especially after the elections of 1989 and 1990, when many of them were elected or appointed to official positions.

When abroad, future 'democrats' first of all paid attention to the better

---

[105] Interview with Romanov.
[107] Interview with Yuriy Belkin (Moscow, 15 Sept. 1993).

[106] Interview with Loskutov.

living conditions there. This observation was often unexpected. For example, Lyuboshits, who was in Czechoslovakia, Austria, and Hungary with the advancing Soviet army during World War II, was especially struck by the high living standards of peasants in these countries compared to those on Soviet collective farms.[108] Those who went abroad later were startled by the fact that life seemed better even in those 'socialist' countries which were officially supposed to be less socially developed. Belkin, for example, felt every time he came home that he was returning 'to another planet, since the level of technology, living standards, and even the very pattern of life, the way of thinking there were different, this was a totally different civilization'.[109] Grinchenko, who became a ship telegraphist at the Far Eastern Shipping Company primarily to see the world, visited ports in many countries of the Far Eastern region and found out about the higher level of economic progress in Japan, Singapore, and Hong Kong.[110]

Nevertheless awareness of the contrast in living standards did not necessarily lead to the perception of life abroad as ideal and to the rejection of the Soviet system. The lower living standard of the USSR was often explained by reasons which did not imply the abandonment of official ideology: for example, by the belief that socialism in the USSR had not had enough time to show all of its potential, or by the influence of irresponsible people at the top, or by the consequences of the devastating war, or by the errors of particular leaders. Employing such explanations, many future 'democrats' did not see a contradiction between what they saw abroad and their beliefs of the time. Thus, Klepachev, who went to Hungary and East Germany when still working at the *kray* CPSU committee, saw the higher living standards there but did not think much about it. Moreover, he was critical of other members of the delegation who talked about this difference.[111] Gezentsvey was in Poland as part of a student exchange programme in 1968 when Soviet troops invaded Czechoslovakia. He saw the indignation of Polish students and together with them disapproved of the action. However, this disapproval did not lead him to reject Communist ideology as a whole. On the contrary, he thought this particular decision of his government to be 'non-socialist' and blamed 'some forces which have seized key positions within the party and are pushing the people into the abyss'. He believed that this decision could be corrected by genuine Communists.[112]

On the whole, while impressions of foreign travel gave new information to future 'democrats', these impressions considered separately, or even combined with previously discussed sources of new information, in most cases did not lead them to reject official Soviet beliefs. Usually the interpretations

---

[108] Interview with Lyuboshits.   [109] Interview with Belkin.
[110] Interview with Grinchenko.   [111] Interview with Klepachev.
[112] Interview with Gezentsvey.

employed, while not being absolutely in line with official ideology (which denied altogether that living standards in the USSR were lower than abroad), at the same time did not lead to its total rejection. This situation changed radically following the flow of new information during *perestroyka*. At that time, as will be shown in Chapter 7, many 'democrats' during their trips to the West began to find there the social ideal they were looking for. However, to be able to do this they first had to accept 'democratic' beliefs.

4.6. FORBIDDEN MATERIALS

It may seem logical to suggest that the decisive role in the denial of the official Soviet ideology by future 'democrats' was played by such openly anti-Soviet materials as foreign radio broadcasts in Russian, underground literature (*samizdat*), and literature by banned authors published outside Russia (*tamizdat*). However, this suggestion is not confirmed by this study. First, these sources were not widely used by 'democrats', most of whom familiarized themselves with them only after the beginning of *perestroyka*, when foreign radio was no longer jammed and many formerly banned writings were officially or semi-officially published.

Listening to foreign radio broadcasts, among which the most often cited were the Russian services of Radio Liberty, the Voice of America, and Deutsche Welle,[113] was relatively more popular than reading banned literature. Among this study's sixty-seven interviewees, twenty-six listened to foreign radio broadcasts. Only five did so regularly, while just eight people said they had read some underground literature before *perestroyka* began. The important thing, however, is not the figures (which may not be properly representative) but the impact of the openly anti-Soviet views these sources brought with them.

Among those 'democrats' who listened to foreign radio broadcasts, only a few said that they played a decisive role in the formation of their beliefs, and could say with Shcherkin: 'I was a victim of Western ideological aggression. I never turned off my radio.'[114] But even such 'victims' acknowledged that their beliefs were formed gradually under the pressure of broadcasts and the new ideas were confronted by the old ones. For example, Grachev, who listened to foreign radio broadcasts from 1960, eventually understood that 'our road is a road to nowhere. But this did not happen all at once. There was a duality, so to speak. On the one hand, Sakharov, Solzhenitsyn, and others.

---

[113] None of the interviewees specifically mentioned the Russian service of the BBC, which is usually regarded to have been popular in the USSR. However, it could sometimes be implied by such general terms as 'voices' (*golosa*) or 'radio'.   [114] Interview with Shcherkin.

On the other, we had been indoctrinated all the time and were always told that everything here was all right and but that their road was the road to nowhere.'[115]

Most listeners did not come to such an outright denial of Soviet ideology at that stage. For example, Zamyatin, who had also listened to foreign broadcasts since the 1960s, remembered:

We had that old Baltika radio and from that time I began listening to Radio Liberty. Radio Liberty was badly jammed, the Voice of America came through better. How did I listen? As one drinks a new drink, with caution. At that time they read Solzhenitsyn and Sakharov's statements. At that time all this seemed to me somewhat absurd. On the one hand, I was critical toward the system we had, but at the same time there was a kind of duality since I thought those people to be, let's say, ideological opponents. It was like that and it cannot be denied.[116]

Like Grachev, Zamyatin did not accept new beliefs immediately. They were at first repelled by the old ones, and later coexisted with them in one system, creating what both interviewees called 'duality', a result of an obvious contradiction between the old and the new information. Both Grachev's and Zamyatin's words show that in a political belief system, particular beliefs do not have to be logically connected and that the system itself is in a state of permanent evolution. Moreover, the impact of foreign radio broadcasts, even in conjunction with general dissatisfaction with the situation in the USSR, was not strong enough to make them fully accept the views propagated in these broadcasts. Kislov also described the same pattern of perception and acknowledged that foreign radio broadcasts led him to a similar duality of beliefs: 'Yes, I also listened to the Voice of America, but without much interest. By the way, about the situation with Sakharov—I did not bother to look into it seriously. Yes, official propaganda argued this way, . . . the other side argued differently. How should people have known where the truth was? So I believed both sides and was not really thinking it over.'[117]

Many 'democrats' admitted a similar lack of interest in foreign radio broadcasts in the pre-*perestroyka* period, which resulted in non-systematic listening. The reason for this was that the views propagated in the broadcasts were often too distant from the beliefs that future 'democrats' held at the time, and the problems discussed in the broadcasts were too distant from those which interested the listeners. For example, when Manuylov began listening to foreign radio broadcasts in the 1980s, he was trying to find a Marxist definition for bureaucracy and, not having been able to find anything helpful from the Voice of America or Radio Liberty, listened to them irregularly without much interest.[118] The same lack of interest was recalled by an engineer from Moscow and a future activist in the Democratic Platform, Vasiliy

---

115 Interview with Grachev.   116 Interview with Zamyatin.
117 Interview with Kislov.   118 Interview with Manuylov.

Shakhnovskiy, who, although listening to foreign radio occasionally before *perestroyka*, 'was no radical dissident' and was more interested in his professional activities than in politics.[119] The greatest interest among future 'democrats' was excited by those programmes which discussed ideas and concepts that were close to their own understanding of the situation in their country. For example, Kryskin, who listened to Radio Liberty regularly from the late 1970s, was particularly interested in a programme on law and legal problems presented by a well-known former Soviet barrister, Dina Kaminskaya, who acted as defence counsel for many dissidents and later suffered persecution herself. Kryskin explained his interest in terms of the main drift of Kaminskaya's arguments, which, according to him, maintained that 'the laws and the constitution of the Soviet Union are . . . very good, but the problem was that the Soviet power operates in such a way that Soviet bureaucrats do not carry out its own laws, and this is the main fault of the entire Communist system'.[120] It is quite clear that Radio Liberty presenters were unlikely to praise Soviet laws; however, it is important that among all their arguments, the idea that Soviet laws should have been implemented was the one which was accepted by the future 'democrat' from Penza.[121]

For the same reason, many future 'democrats' were particularly interested in radio programmes based on readings from banned authors or from works in which life in the Soviet Union was described in a realistic way, particularly the works of Aleksandr Solzhenitsyn. For example, Shapovalenko began listening to readings from Solzhenitsyn out of defiance, since he had previously read *One Day in the Life of Ivan Denisovich* and did not find anything special in it. So when everybody began criticizing Solzhenitsyn's *The GULag Archipelago*, he felt dissatisfaction: 'For some reason I was that kind of person: when everyone says one thing, I somehow . . . want to find out myself where the truth is'. However, he again failed to find much that was new, since he knew about the repressions and the wartime penal battalions from his father and uncle, who fought in the war against Germany and told him that 'almost half of Rokossovskiy's army consisted of penal battalions'.[122] Yelistratov and Grachev listened to radio readings of Solzhenitsyn's writings for the same reason. Yelistratov heard about them at official courses for propagandists at which Communist Party ideologists criticized the writer, and thought: 'So what about Solzhenitsyn? He used to be a normal person and then suddenly turned into a scoundrel and a villain.'[123] So he decided to find out what the writer was really talking about. According to Grachev, he became interested in the scandal surrounding Solzhenitsyn's deportation and at that time devoted all his evenings to listening to foreign radio programmes.[124]

---

[119] Interview with Vasiliy Shakhnovskiy (Moscow, 5 Jan. 1997).
[120] Interview with Kryskin. [121] Ibid.
[122] Interview with Shapovalenko. [123] Interview with Yelistratov.
[124] Interview with Grachev.

So despite some disagreement and lack of interest, the influence of foreign radio broadcasts should not be overlooked. Even those future 'democrats' who listened to what the official propaganda called the 'enemy voices' often used them as an alternative (and often the only alternative) source of information and comment on particular problems which interested them. Feeling that the official media did not give the whole picture or deliberately distorted the truth, they turned to foreign radio even though they often found new opinions there and did not always agree with what they heard. Thus for many, listening to foreign radio meant their first encounter with plurality of opinion.[125]

In any case, regardless whether future 'democrats' agreed or disagreed with foreign radio presenters, they were greatly dissatisfied with the attempts of the authorities to limit this source of information by jamming, which in fact only caused additional interest in it. An artist from Belinskiy, Fedor Vorob'ev, who had been listening to the Voice of America ever since his schooldays in Stalin's time, described what he once felt during a lesson at Penza Art College, where he was studying: 'We were discussing several paintings and one of them was called *The Voice of America*. There were young people listening to a radio. At that time it was thought to be, so to speak, "a frank approach". However, it is only natural for people to be curious. So I thought all this was disgusting. I wished that these lies and hypocrisy would end.'[126]

It is interesting that one of the institutions, where Russians were most often introduced to 'enemy voices' was the army. At least three of the interviewees, Valeriy Nikol'skiy from Pskov, Petr Popov from Orenburg, and Nikolay Klepachev from Krasnoyarsk, began listening to foreign radio when they served in the Communication Forces at radio-location or radio interception stations. The soldiers of the Communication Forces were cut out of other sources of information and listened to 'enemy' radio stations with great interest. As a result these soldiers, far from being a tool in the battle with the ideological opponent, often spread the opponent's views. According to Nikol'skiy, the radio interception station where he served even had to be closed because 'even the exemplary soldiers and sergeants, members of the Komsomol who were on duty there, literally after the first two or three months got outright anti-Soviet ideas'.[127]

Unlike foreign radio, banned written sources were known to only a very few future 'democrats' and only in some cities. Among the eight interviewees who said that they had read some banned literature before joining a 'democratic' group, five persons (Krivov, Belkin, Gezentsvey, Fadeev, and Shubin) came from Moscow, two (Zlotnikova and Shul'cheva) from

[125] Interviews with Ivlev, Petr Popov, Belkin, and Rybalko.
[126] Interview with Vorob'ev.
[127] Interview with Valeriy Nikol'skiy (Pskov, 24 Sept. 1994).

Orenburg, and one (Ivlev) from Pskov. At the same time other interviewees from the same cities, including Moscow, acknowledged that they had never seen or read underground literature. Apart from literature, another underground source which was known to some interviewees, but similarly not widespread, was the songs of some dissident singers, especially Aleksandr Galich.[128]

On the whole the interviews showed that forbidden literature had a limited circulation among future 'democrats' and was known mainly in Moscow. Because it was very dangerous to read this material and the reader if exposed could very easily end up in jail, even if such literature came to a provincial city it tended not to spread beyond a very close group of people who absolutely trusted each other. Grachev described this situation in Penza *oblast'* when he said that he had heard that the director of the Mikhail Lermontov Museum at the Russian poet's family estate had given some of his friends *The GULag Archipelago* to read, but Grachev himself did not manage to get hold of it and did not read it before it was published much later.[129]

The pattern of perception of forbidden literature and other banned sources was the same as in the case of foreign radio broadcasts: the only acceptable views were those that were close to the pre-existing beliefs and developed them. Ideas which were too alien were either rejected or for some time existed in an interviewee's belief system in a passive state and could be activated only later. For example, remembering his first perception of *The GULag Archipelago*, Gezentsvey said that the book did not destroy his reformist Communist beliefs since the book's 'anti-Communist ideas were not apprehended at that time. What was accepted was the humanist, humane idea. But as for anti-Communism: I thought what we had was not real communism, it was, so to speak, the faults of the project'.[130]

In some cases, reading forbidden literature could stimulate a radical shift in the belief system of a future 'democrat', provided such a shift had already been prepared by the person's own intellectual development. Andrey Krivov described such a revolution in his thinking, which he experienced after having been deeply impressed by the memoirs of the Soviet dissident Vladimir Bukovskiy. When he was studying at university he read Bukovskiy's book at night in bed under the blankets with a torch, keeping the activity a secret from his parents. However, Krivov was obviously prepared for such a shift in his beliefs by his previous reading of Solzhenitsyn and of some non-Marxist social scientists whom he studied at university, as well as by his conversations with opposition-minded friends.[131]

---

[128] Interview with Gezentsvey.
[130] Interview with Gezentsvey.
[131] Interview with Andrey Krivov (Paris, 22 July 1994).

[129] Interview with Grachev.

4.7. *PERESTROYKA* AND THE SWEEPING CONVERSION
TO 'DEMOCRATIC' VALUES

An analysis of interviews with members of 'democratic' groups and of other sources shows that the combined impact of family stories, personal experience, reading of officially permitted and banned literature, travel abroad, and listening to foreign radio broadcasts led only a very few future 'democrats' to accept 'democratic' beliefs. For the majority of them the world-view which resulted from official ideological education was too deep, strong, and systematic to be totally destroyed under the occasional blows of isolated beliefs and experiences which contradicted official dogmas. In most cases contradictory beliefs were accommodated within the structure of the pre-existing belief system and were interpreted within its framework. They could also exist within that structure passively, without being subject to analysis. At the same time, under the influence of new beliefs the system was undergoing constant evolution. By the beginning of *perestroyka* most future 'democrats', while not having become anti-Communists or anti-Marxists, nevertheless had come to the conclusion that the country was moving in a wrong direction and that many things should be changed. At the time most of them were not sure what exactly needed to be done, since the officially suggested measures obviously did not work but the possible alternatives were simply unknown. This pre-*perestroyka* mood of uncertainty was expressed by many interviewees:

[Vladimir Krylov, Vladivostok] I suddenly began to realize that life was organized somewhat wrongly, not as we were told at school. . . . Though I come from a workers' family, but nevertheless. . . . Of course, this was a slow process. In fact, until 1985, until the official start [of *perestroyka*], I did not understand that this was a system, because I did not have enough information.[132]

[Il`ya Grinchenko, Vladivostok] There was generally a feeling of discontent, everybody wanted something but it was unclear what exactly, but they did not want the Communists.[133]

[Mariya Sublina, Moscow] As an economist on the whole I believed that our life was not right. But I did not yet realize why. How should one live? We surely lived wrongly. And what was most important was that I saw that the human personality was not valued. We did not have personality. We lacked individual liberty.[134]

[Vasiliy Shakhnovskiy, Moscow] The thing is that as a more or less thinking person. . . . I was not satisfied with what we had in this country. Everybody was discussing things in the smoking rooms, telling anecdotes; in scientific circles especially this was widespread . . . But at the same time the country lacked a tradition of going out to demonstrations . . . Everything was discussed in smoking rooms or over tea.[135]

---

[132] Interview with Krylov.   [133] Interview with Grinchenko.
[134] Interview with Sublina.   [135] Interview with Shakhnovskiy.

[Aleksandr Romanov, Orenburg] We already wanted to change something. It was impossible to rule the state like that, it was impossible for everything to be openly stolen. We wanted a change. And only later did our other, broader and more consistent principles began to mature. Nobody becomes a democrat overnight.[136]

[Aleksandr Kislov, Penza] On the whole there was naturally dissatisfaction with the situation, all these kitchen conversations, irony toward the authorities. There was a general mood of dissatisfaction.[137]

[Aleksandr Yerasov, Penza] There was this unconscious criticism: we live badly, they live better abroad. . . . It turns out that unemployment is not so widespread there and the unemployed don't live so badly. . . . It was on that level . . . At the same time there were the sort of customary beliefs which were dinned into people's heads from childhood, so you believed that there would be communism sometime after the year 2000. . . . I think that people like academics in Moscow and in the centre, they were discussing on a higher level the exhaustion of natural resources and the impasse in the economy. . . . These discussions did not reach the small towns. So, people here spoke about what they saw and what they were dissatisfied with. Is that not right? Therefore discussions there were more intelligent: we are not moving in the right direction, this is useless, we cannot build anything this way but are only approaching a dead end. But here—just that the bosses are silly, that they pick people not for their intellect but for their loyalty, that there were no clever people at the top. But to argue that the whole country was moving in the wrong direction—this was unthinkable. . . . It seemed that the main thing was to stir everything up, that people just did not realize what to do, but that after such a shock everything would go on smoothly . . . So, on the whole life was too calm and some kind of agitation was needed.[138]

However, an influence emerged that made the majority of future 'democrats' renounce official dogmas and convert to 'democratic' values. It came with the cascade of new publications and information during the period of Gorbachev's *glasnost*`. This was a time when an influx of new theories and concepts, new facts about Soviet history, which left no doubt about the character of the Soviet regime and about the lies of its propaganda, became available in a freer atmosphere, a time when discussing unorthodox ideas was no longer dangerous. This influx stimulated the intellectual development of potential 'democrats' and pushed it in a clear and specific direction. Before the 1989 elections, when political debates moved to the official rostrum of the newly elected Congress of People's Deputies, the main sources of new ideas for members of 'democratic' groups were articles in popular newspapers and magazines and some formerly banned literary works which were finally published in the USSR. Many interviewees stressed the importance of specific articles and works which played a landmark role in the development of 'democratic' thinking. The importance of such works often depended not on the novelty of their ideas but on the fact that they made ideas which had

---

[136] Interview with Romanov. [137] Interview with Kislov.
[138] Interview with Aleksandr Yerasov (Penza, 3 Apr. 1994).

formerly been known to only a very few available to a mass readership at the right time. Such works included: an article by Yuriy Afanas`ev in *Pravda*, the first piece in the official Soviet media to argue that existing Soviet society was not really socialist;[139] Gavriil Popov's review of the novel *Novoye Naznachenie* (New Appointment) by Aleksandr Bek;[140] Bek's novel itself;[141] two articles by Sergey Andreev on bureaucracy;[142] a feature film by Tengiz Abuladze, *Pokayanie* (Repentance); a documentary on Soviet life by Stanislav Govorukhin, *Tak zhit` nel`zya* (It is Impossible to Live Like That); and periodic articles on the problems of Soviet society in reformist newspapers, magazines, and 'thick journals' like the *Moscow News*, *Argumenty i fakty*, *Ogonek*, *Znamya*, *Neva*, *Novyy Mir*, and others. The role of these new sources of information in his conversion to 'democracy' was stressed by Fel`dman:

So, everything began with *Argumenty i fakty*. . . . And the person to whom I am most thankful is Gavriil Popov, who, I believe, delivered the first blow, before Andreev . . . It was a short article and after that I read Aleksandr Bek's novel, I rushed to look for it as soon as I finished with the article, and found it. At that time I already realized something, began to realize. There was life around me which I did not understand, but when you see a book where everything is said beautifully and cleverly, that's what you need. And this was the plight of many intellectuals.[143]

Vorob`ev also stressed the importance of the press of the *perestroyka* period, by which 'many had understood that there were pure lies, pure hypocrisy. And suddenly we began to find so many things in newspapers and magazines . . . At last we were able to read the truth in newspapers.'[144]

The period of *glasnost`* was characterized by a real literary fever, and 'democrats' were naturally on the crest of the reading wave. Articles and books which had just come out were discussed in groups and clubs. Copies were produced by photocopier, by typewriter, or by hand and were studied attentively. Yelistratov's diary, for example, contains notes on and abstracts of several *perestroyka* articles, as well as cuttings of newspaper articles describing activities of groups from other cities similar to Belinskiy's Discussion Club.[145] According to Kryskin, at the meetings of the Penza Politklub its members discussed articles from *Literaturnaya gazeta* and Sergey Andreev's article in *Ural*. Gavriil Popov's review was discussed in almost every 'democratic' group and *Ogonek* readers' clubs began to multiply all over the country.

---

[139] Yuriy Afanas`ev, 'Otvety istorika', *Pravda*, 26 July 1988.

[140] G. Popov, 'S tochki zreniya ekonomista: O romane Aleksandra Beka "Novoe Naznacheniye" ', *Nauka i Zhizn`*, 4 (1987), 54–66.

[141] Aleksandr Bek, *Novoe naznacheniye. Roman* (Moscow: Sovetskiy pisatel`, 1988).

[142] Sergey Andreev, 'Prichiny i sledstviya', *Ural*, 1 (1988), 104–39; S. Andreev, 'Struktura vlasti i zadachi obshchestva', *Neva*, 1 (1989), 144–73.

[143] Interview with Fel`dman.          [144] Interview with Vorob`ev.

[145] Yelistratov, diary and notes.

Provincial 'democrats' often went to Moscow especially to get new publications and information, and to work in Moscow libraries.[146]

The flow of new information and ideas stimulated rapid change in the beliefs of 'democrats'. However, this change was not abrupt and the evolution from Marxism to 'democracy' was gradual. The first logical step usually consisted of a search for a better, real Marxism, a rejection of what was seen as Stalinist bureaucratic socialism in favour of 'genuine', Leninist democratic socialism. This step was described by Zamyatin, who was already serving in the army before *perestroyka*, and attempted to organize a non-orthodox Marxist group, since at that time he thought that the Soviet Union 'departed from the principles which had been elaborated by Lenin and Marx' and that 'on the whole society had become degraded and that there was a need to go back to something original and pure'.[147] The flow of *perestroyka* information pushed him further: 'Naturally during the years of *perestroyka* there was so much information to think over: radio, television, and so on. Here I moved ahead significantly. So I already understood that, let's say, a democratic form of socialism was needed which . . . would liberate people's political activism, would let them form various unions . . . At the factories there should be workers' self-management and the entire economy should move in the same direction.'[148]

Virtually every future 'democrat' went through a period of appreciation of the ideas of 'genuine Leninism', but some passed through it earlier, some later; some remained in it and some, like Yuriy Nikiforenko from Orenburg, who later joined Zyuganov's Communist Party of the Russian Federation, even went back to orthodox Communism.[149] Belief in genuine Leninism signified a rejection of the official dogmas that the situation in the Soviet Union was ideal, that the country was developing according to theory, and that the USSR, being more developed than the West, was getting closer to the ideal of communism. To abandon these dogmas was not very difficult, since they were in striking contradiction to Soviet reality and Gorbachev's leadership itself had gradually been giving them up.[150] At the same time the concept of genuine Leninism maintained an adherence to the basic tenets of the official theories of history and politics: thinking that the USSR at some point lost the right way did not mean that this way was wrong from the very beginning. Certain specific leaders could have simply committed an error which had to be corrected. Some 'democrats' came to this conclusion long before *perestroyka*. Vladimir Makhora and Grigoriy Chernetskiy from Vladivostok, Nikolay Klepachev from Krasnoyarsk, and Anatoliy Zamyatin from Penza

---

[146] Interviews with Yerasov, Kryskin, Grinchenko, and Ivlev.
[147] Interview with Zamyatin.   [148] Ibid.
[149] Interview with Yuriy Nikiforenko (Orenburg, 23 Dec. 1994).
[150] See, for example, Archie Brown, *The Gorbachev Factor* (Oxford: Oxford University Press, 1996), esp. ch. 4.

claimed to have formed or taken part in genuine-Marxist groups in Brezhnev's, Khrushchev's, and even Stalin's time. According to Makhora, 'The essence of all those movements before 1987 was a wish, so to speak, to understand original Marxism. We all believed in people's happiness . . . that the ideals were perfect and that the programme was elaborated well . . . What was needed was somehow to clean up the country.'[151]

Among early 'democratic' groups of the *perestroyka* period 'genuine Marxist' ideas became dominant. This was the situation in the Penza Politklub, which was described by one of its activists, Yevgeniy Kryskin:

> At that time our dissatisfaction was of a socialist character. We were supporters of improving socialism. This was in the years 1987–88. The direction was precisely towards improving socialism, perfecting it. But perfecting it how? To perfect oneself one should be shown one's shortcomings and for that *glasnost* was needed. This was the chain. So how do you create *glasnost*? Factions within the CPSU should be permitted. Or, and this was my most radical proposal, the CPSU had to be divided into two competing factions. I was thinking approximately like this: 'Capitalism existed in two forms, as bourgeois democracy and bourgeois dictatorship, but socialism has not yet appeared as socialist democracy. Socialism has always existed in all countries in the form of socialist dictatorship. So let's try socialist democracy in the form of a two-party socialist system. Why not try it?' I even had another thought: 'We have about twelve years left until the year 2000. This is the historical period during which multi-party democratic socialism must be tried. If in that period we do not use this opportunity to try democratic socialism, that will be it. Socialism as a whole will have to move to the side of the road, it will be forced out as non-competitive dictatorial socialism. If we do not try its democratic form it will be thrown to the side of the road of world history and everywhere only democratic capitalism will exist.'[152]

The mood in the Demokrat Club in Vladivostok in 1988–9, as described by member Yevgeniy Korovin, was similar:

> Yes, this was a period when we still believed that socialism could be improved. I remember that I watched reports from the Nineteenth Party Conference, when there were those attempts to democratize socialism with such feeling. This was also the period when transcribed copies of Yel`tsin's speeches at the plenum were circulated. At that time we thought that the CPSU could be renewed, democratized, and improved. And at that time we did not think that there could be another, in some way an alternative, party.[153]

His fellow-member Krylov remembered the evolution of his beliefs from genuine Leninism to anti-Communism in greater detail: 'The thing is that in the period of 1988–89 the development, especially of thinking, was very impetuous. I myself, at least, studied Lenin's writings, this was in the early

---

[151] Interview with Vladimir Makhora (Vladivostok, 23 Apr. 1994).
[152] Interview with Kryskin.
[153] Interview with Yevgeniy Korovin (Vladivostok, 24 Apr. 1994).

1980s, until 1985. And after that I joined the Democrat Club in March–April 1989, in the summer of 1989 we were already beginning to organize the DPR. . . . Generally in 1989 I was already agreeing with anti-Communist positions, but I still somewhat hesitated about Lenin.'[154]

The organizer of an independent human rights group from Penza, Georgiy Didichenko, also remembered his original Leninist position. Before *perestroyka* and during its first years he believed that order could be preserved in the country if leaders would adhere to the principles of socialist justice and legality.[155] Sergey Golovin later saw his position at the time of the formation of the Discussion Club in Orenburg as 'nomenklaturian'. According to him, he stood for 'socialism with a human face. . . . Meaning that the party, the Komsomol, and everything else should remain, but a multi-party system should be introduced. At that time this was terribly seditious'.[156] Acknowledging their former enthusiasm for democratic Leninism, many 'democrats' explained it by lack of information. This explanation was given by Shapovalenko among others

> I thought then—and this, perhaps, was not just my delusion—that if Vladimir Il'ich had not died, it would have been different since he did not want it . . . We would have had both private property and collective farms. The deviations were introduced by Iosif Vissarionovich [Stalin]. It was later, when I studied it closer, when I later read [the texts] again and again, that I found out that Iosif Vissarionovich also used nice phrases. But I could not find in the books which were available any earlier information about how the shooting of delegates of the Seventeenth Congress was ordered.[157]

This explanation can only be partly accepted. It was not just the lack of information but also the interpretation of available information in line with pre-existing beliefs that played a crucial role. New, often contradictory information stimulated many 'democrats' to re-analyse the situation, to think more about the society in which they lived, and aroused a new interest in the only theory they knew well, Marxism. In an attempt to find out what Marx, Engels, and Lenin really wrote, to verify the interpretations of the classics which were given by official ideologists and which often contradicted daily experience, many 'democrats' turned from reading school and university textbooks to careful and thorough study of these writings and Communist Party documents. The next step towards getting a more objective picture was to study the works of authors who were criticized or mentioned by the classics of Marxism.

This road is described by many of the interviewees. For example, Krylov, even before joining the Demokrat Club in 1989 and during his first period in the club, 'independently tried to understand what socialism was, because we

---

[154] Interview with Krylov.   [155] Interview with Didichenko.
[156] Interview with Sergey Golovin (Orenburg, 23 Dec. 1994).
[157] Interview with Shapovalenko.

had been indoctrinated for too long . . . I was trying to understand how Lenin understood socialism and what he said about it. So I was reading volume after volume, trying to understand everything, beginning with the 1890s'.[158] According to Krylov, at that time the club as a whole, far from rejecting Leninism, propagated Leninism against Stalinism and even organized discussions in support of what was thought of as genuine Leninism.[159] Many other 'democrats' spoke of a similar period of enthusiastic study of Marxist classics.[160]

The road of intellectual development led on to the works of authors who were not, strictly speaking, official but who were somehow connected with official Marxism or mentioned by official theorists. For example, speaking about the evolution of his own beliefs, Manuylov remembered that while studying the problems of state capitalism in the History Library in Moscow he 'studied thoroughly enough all the works of Vladimir Il`ich, studied Stalin' and turned to reading works by Bolsheviks of non-Stalinist orientations. He got hold of a book of a well-known Bolshevik economist Yu. Larin (whose daughter was married to Nikolay Bukharin) and of a Marxist historian, David Ryazanov, who was also close to Bukharin. Ryazanov's book contained quotations from Marx's articles on Russia which were not published in the Soviet Union because of Marx's criticism of Russian policy and his disbelief in the possibility of communism in such a backward country.

A member of the Stavropol` Popular Front, Alla Lipchanskaya, who wrote her dissertation on Engels' struggle with revisionism[161], began reading a German philosopher, Eugen Dühring, to whom Engels devoted the major work *Anti-Dühring*. In addition, while studying revisionism she managed to read some works by Czech 'revisionists' and by the Polish philosopher Leszek Kolakowski.[162] While reading discussions between Marx and Lenin with the anarchists and Russian populists and thinking over recently available information on the Bolshevik Terror, the future organizers of the Obshchina group, Andrey Isaev and Aleksandr Shubin, became interested in the arguments of Mikhail Bakunin, Petr Kropotkin, Nikolay Mikhailovskiy, Viktor Chernov, and other famous anarchists, Populists, and Socialist Revolutionaries. They began reading works by these authors and finally moved from progressive Marxism to non-Marxist Populist socialism and further onto anarchism after finding Marxist criticism of these concepts unconvincing.[163] A similar road has been travelled by many Russian 'democrats'. It led from Marx and Engels to Hegel, who was criticized by the

---

[158] Interview with Krylov.   [159] Ibid.
[160] Interviews with Yevgeniy Kutakov (Krasnoyarsk, 20 Apr. 1994), Vasiliy Krasulya (Stavropol', 2 Sept. 1994), and Manuylov.
[161] Term used in Marxism for deviation from the form of Marxism considered to be genuine.
[162] Interview with Alla Lipchanskaya (Stavropol`, 2 Sept. 1994).
[163] Interview with Shubin.

founders of Marxism; from Lenin's *Materialism and Empirio-criticism* to the Western classical and Russian religious philosophers who were attacked in Lenin's book; from criticism of banned authors to reading the very same authors. Under the influence of new information and new approaches the belief system of Russian 'democrats' was broadened and transformed, but in the first years of *perestroyka* most of them still did not totally reject many official interpretations.

Gorbachev's coming to power and the spirit of *glasnost*` and *perestroyka* at first coincided with the mood of the majority of future 'democrats'. Many of them considered the new and relatively young leader and his proclaimed policies to be the very measures the country needed. As a result of the loosening of political control 'democratic' groups multiplied all over the country. Depending on the local political situation they found themselves under greater or lesser pressure from local political authorities; however, even at this early stage they could not be disbanded. At first these groups, far from rejecting official ideology and Gorbachev's policy, actively supported them and tried to push their local authorities toward faster implementation of the proclaimed Moscow line. Many of the interviewees acknowledged that at first they believed Gorbachev and thought that 'there would be some changes for the better'.[164] For some it was the coming to power of Gorbachev that aroused interest in politics. As Kislov put it, 'the turning point came in Gorbachev's time. . . . At that point I became interested in politics and began thinking, comparing, analysing. . . . The coming of Gorbachev and his ideas overwhelmed me so much that I made notes while listening to his speech at, I guess, the January 1986 plenum.'[165]

For 'democrats' of the older generation the explanation given by Didichenko was typical:

I believed that all our shortcomings were caused not by the system, but by the people who governed. This was my serious mistake, and though I was no longer a boy, nevertheless . . . those dogmas dinned into our heads during our long years as Party members influenced people's consciousness and even their character. I thought that if Gorbachev, a young man while all of us were already old, came to power, he would be able to restore order soon. Surely, this was pure delusion.[166]

Younger 'democrats' thought the way an inventor and businessman from Penza, Aleksandr Yerasov, did. Yerasov enthusiastically welcomed *perestroyka* pledges to stimulate the initiative of the working people and expected 'that the initiative would be really supported, that I would be told: "You are a good boy to produce these things, but we did not realize this before. Previously you were under the threat of prosecution, but now we'll provide you with all the conditions necessary for your work." I somehow believed that

---

[164] Interview with Yeykin. [165] Interview with Kislov.
[166] Interview with Didichenko.

this could happen from the top'.[167] Some people previously dissatisfied with official policy now even thought it possible to join the Communist Party, which was proclaiming the reformist course. One such person was Gezentzvey, who explained his motives:

> For a very long time I didn't join the Party. But when Gorbachev came and announced *perestroyka*, it seemed that at last we could see what we should work for. We were given more freedom: form cooperatives if you wish, create, use your independence. I was one of the first to introduce the team method of work. So it became possible to presume that we had returned to the original, correct road . . . And with the consent of the workshop I called a workshops meeting and asked: 'Fellows, we are finally being given an opportunity to do openly what we have been fighting for here for four years. What do you think? Is it all right?' 'Yes, that's what we wanted.' 'So what do you think, what shall I do now?' They told me: 'Join the Party.' And in 1989 I joined the Party on the recommendation of the workshop, I was already forty-two at that time.[168]

Supporting *perestroyka*, 'democrats' often went one step further in their plans and proposals than the official position of the time, which was also evolving; and because of that they were always on the edge of what was officially acceptable. Given subsequent events many 'democratic' proposals can be seen as too modest. However, from the point of view of the authorities, especially local authorities, every time they were put forward they were much too radical. Kryskin, for example, gave a vivid account of the evolution of his proposals:

> We all supported *perestroyka*, the introduction of a multi-party system or as a minimum (since the multi-party system was at first seen as a seditious proposal) allowing free speech within the framework of the existing one-party system and within the existing control of the CPSU. Or, at least, as a next step, the creation of factions within the CPSU. For example, my personal opinion at the time was that the existing CPSU should be divided in a civilized fashion, not from below, not as a result of an explosion, but from the top. For example, a Party congress could adopt a civilized decision to introduce a two-party system. The existing CPSU would be divided into two parties. And let both parties work for building communism. For example, one half could be headed by, say, Ligachev, and it could be called the Traditional Communist Party, while the other party could be headed by Gorbachev and called the Party of Communist Renewal. And those two parties would compete with each other and use their own media in order, so to speak, to throw light on the other side.[169]

It is interesting that most of the proposals of 'democrats' either were part of Gorbachev's proclaimed programme, or, as it became clear later, were discussed by his circle as options. But Gorbachev usually rejected such proposals as too radical or, even after having agreed to them, backtracked

---

[167] Interview with Yerasov.   [168] Interview with Gezentsvey.
[169] Interview with Kryskin.

under pressure from the conservatives. For example, the plan to divide the CPSU into two parties, thought of by Kryskin (and surely not only by him) not earlier than 1988, was proposed by Aleksandr Nikolaevich Yakovlev to Gorbachev as early as 1985, but was rejected by the Soviet leader as premature, and obviously remained so in his opinion until 1991, when the CPSU was dissolved by 'democratic' leaders.[170] 'Democrats' were especially irritated by Gorbachev's indecisiveness, and by his refusal in many cases to accept responsibility, such as military actions in Azerbaijan, Georgia, Lithuania, and Latvia, when, in the view of 'democrats', he was playing the fool, pretending he did not know what was happening in the country under his leadership. Other indications of Gorbachev's weakness were his attitude toward the Five-hundred-day Plan, which he first accepted but later rejected, and his inability to cope with the deepening economic crisis against the background of the growing popularity of new leaders.

Gradually, with the development of the political situation in the country and the growing freedom of the media, the evaluation of the policy of the authorities by 'democrats' became more and more critical. New facts of Soviet history which had been unfamiliar to the general public became known, while previously known facts were reinterpreted in line with the new, rapidly changing public mood. This change influenced the beliefs of 'democrats'. The 'genuine Leninist' approach soon became insufficient for many of them and they moved toward anti-Leninist social democracy and some even much further: to classic liberalism and radical anti-Communism. As shown below, a swift transfer from one radical position to its radical opposite (devout Communism to radical anti-Communism) was often more typical than stopping in the middle. The very logic of the oppositional struggle stimulated radicalization of programmes. An important role in creating a radical uncompromising atmosphere was played by unofficial publications which were now being published by 'democratic' groups themselves. By 1989–90 the Democratic Union, the Social Democratic Association, Memorial, and other larger 'democratic' groups had found a way to print their newspapers, magazines, and leaflets by conventional means, usually in the Baltic republics, where opposition movements had already gained significant influence and controlled some printing houses. Smaller groups all over the country produced their materials on duplicating machines or photocopiers, or by photography, typing, or even handwriting. Many interviewees acknowledged the influence of such publications, which were usually discussed with colleagues who were more advanced in their anti-Communism. For example, Kryskin read an openly anti-Communist article for the first time in 1988 in *Svobodnoe slovo*, a newspaper of the Democratic Union Moscow

---

[170] On Yakovlev's 1985 memorandum to Gorbachev, see Aleksandr Nikolaevich Yakovlev, *Gor`kaya chasha: Bol`shevizm i Reformatsiya Rossii* (Yaroslavl`: Verkhne-Volzhskoe knizhnoye izdatel`stvo, 1994), 205–13.

organization. In the same year he often went to Moscow under different pretexts, where he met members of the Democratic Union and discussed political problems with them, and brought their materials back to Penza.[171] Rybalko, in his trade union activities at the Vladivostok cargo port, tried to use the experience of Polish Solidarity, of which he learned from the official Baltic newspapers *Sovetskaya Litva* and *Molodezh Estonii*, as well as from the materials published by Saudis (an opposition Lithuanian movement).[172] According to Krylov, he and his colleagues from the Demokrat club had already moved to anti-Communist views by 1989. He attributed this evolution to the influence of the 'informal' and official press and to the harsh reaction to their activities of the authorities, who banned their meetings and prosecuted activists, making them even more hostile toward official policies.[173] As a result of these influences many 'democrats' who earlier thought that changes were possible within the framework of the existing system gradually came to the conclusion that the entire Soviet system should be eliminated. This new mood was expressed by Yeykin, who said that soon after joining the 'democratic' movement in Orenburg he understood that 'we had this old bureaucratic, pro-Communist system which I simply called "the fascist regime" and that we will never solve any problems before we replace it'.[174]

New information and a new atmosphere led to a fundamentally new evaluation of the situation in the country and most 'democrats' gradually came to believe that 'the problem is not in particular leaders but one should look at its root and change the whole one-party totalitarian system'.[175] Naturally, this approach was based on a total disillusionment with the existing system, which was officially called socialist. Yelistratov vividly described this change of direction in his approach to the authorities:

> I was saying: 'That's it, fellows, we cannot go on like this.' What I saw, going from village to village for four years, was that we could not go on like that. Everything was a lie. The Party could not do anything positive any more. We had come to the brink. I did not know what it could do at the top, but here at the grassroots it could not do anything any more. The more they talked the worse the situation became. . . . I personally changed very much over that period. I did not believe any longer that we should live under socialism.[176]

The attitude toward Lenin also changed. The writings of the former idol were now read not to find a basis for liberal ideas but to get proof of the primordial viciousness of Bolshevism. Having this in mind Obryadin 'became absorbed in Lenin' and found out that the Bolshevik leader ordered killings and persecutions of innocent people.[177] Hatred toward particular

[171] Interview with Kryskin.　　　[172] Interview with Rybalko.
[173] Interview with Krylov.　　　[174] Interview with Yeykin.
[175] Interview with Yerasov.　　　[176] Interview with Yelistratov.
[177] Interview with Obryadin.

bureaucrats who slowed down reforms was transferred to Bolshevism, Communism, and sometimes socialism as a whole. Trying to define those who were now thought to hinder social progress, 'democrats' at first often used familiar official Soviet terminology. For example, Klepachev, who worked on the Communist Party committee and on soviet executive committees in Krasnoyarsk, remembered that he did not want to work in these organizations any more because 'I saw all the dirty practices there which were very different from what they announced from the rostrum'. Speaking at one of the Communist Party meetings in the presence of local party officials he openly hurled his accusations at them: 'You support Communism only from the rostrum but in your deeds you are enemies of the people.'[178] Only later was a useful concept of totalitarianism widely adopted (see Chapter 5).

Disillusionment with the Communist leadership naturally led to disillusionment with the personality of Gorbachev, who was now seen by 'democrats' at best as an irresolute chatterer who had fallen under the influence of the conservatives and was unable to push forward his own plans, or at worst as a cunning conservative himself who was trying to cover up his real plans with liberal talk. 'Democrats' looked for and found new idols and leaders who seemed more radical and resolute. Kislov thoroughly described many factors which led to a typical gradual disillusionment with Gorbachev by a provincial 'democrat' and to the growth in popularity of Boris Yel`tsin:

You know, Yel`tsin began to show himself from approximately 1986, when it was rumoured that this man, after becoming the first secretary of the Moscow Party committee, began to look into the irregularities in trade, to make the life of bureaucrats difficult, that he went by public bus himself and personally visited shops, in other words, that he was one of us, flesh of our flesh, a sincere man. . . .

Gorbachev came first; Yel`tsin followed and Yel`tsin did not tower above Gorbachev, he propped him up. . . . But then came the first disillusionments with Gorbachev. The first reason was that he was saying: 'Wait, everything will be fine in a year', then in two years, and everybody began to doubt: 'He just talks and talks.' And then this Raisa [Gorbachev's wife], she was always in the public eye, this caused some degree of irritation. And in this situation a person like Yel`tsin began to show himself, to rise. Copies of his interviews began to be disseminated here. His meeting with the students of Moscow University. . . . The interviews were strikingly sincere. Absolute sincerity, openness, radicalism of opinions. We were attracted by the arrival of a strong personality who could be a solid alternative to Gorbachev's empty talk, since we were already beginning to realize that Gorbachev was not exactly the kind of person he was trying to pose as. And while problems multiplied around Yel`tsin, his popularity grew. He suffered persecution and here in Russia those under persecution have always been sympathized with. And hopes grew that this man would really be able to do something. Gorbachev had done his job: he had made the announcement, he had opened the door, but that fellow meant business.[179]

---

[178] Interview with Klepachev.   [179] Interview with Kislov.

Yel`tsin's own beliefs also gradually moved from genuine socialism toward radical anti-Communism and because this evolution was similar to the general pattern of evolution of 'democratic' ideas his programme was well understood by 'democrats' and welcomed by them. Because of his previously high position in the CPSU, which, in the eyes of supporters, he did not hesitate to sacrifice to the course of genuine reform and justice, Yel`tsin was highly respected among most 'democrats' and was accepted by them as their leader. Not all of them, however, thought he was an ideal leader: some regarded him as too closely connected to the Communist regime, some were dissatisfied with the insufficient level of his education and intellectual ability, others thought his position was not anti-Communist enough. Such 'democrats', while usually not denying the role of Yel`tsin as a figure acceptable to a mass public, at the same time preferred other 'democratic' leaders: Gavriil Popov, Yuriy Afanas`ev, Andrey Sakharov, and even Valeriya Novodvorskaya of the Democratic Union, which at the time of deepest dissatisfaction with the regime (1989 to the beginning of 1990) gained considerable popularity, especially in some provinces.[180] In any case, by 1990 most 'democrats' had deviated from the official interpretation of socialism and the movement as a whole was heading towards a more and more radical anti-Communism.

4.8. CONCLUSIONS

This chapter has studied the main steps of the evolution of the political beliefs of Russian 'democrats' and its sources. It shows that these beliefs gradually moved towards radicalization, from belief in the official Soviet ideology or at least its passive acceptance to its full repudiation. This movement differed in speed and form in each particular case. Some 'democrats' went down this road faster than others; some never reached the logical conclusion of radical anti-Communism and stopped at the stage of 'genuine Marxism' or 'democratic socialism'. Some 'democrats' argued that they had always been anti-Communists, but this happened in very few cases which could be verified. The overwhelming majority of activists in 'democratic' groups, including those who subsequently endorsed radical anti-Communist views, accepted official ideology at some stage. This acceptance can be explained by the strength of the system of official ideological education and by the paucity and non-systematic character of sources of unofficial information before the time of Gorbachev's reforms.

Sources of alternative information, however, did exist in the USSR and they played some role in the formation of 'democratic' beliefs. The most

---

[180] Interviews with Obryadin, Pavel Borovik (Vladivostok, 25 Apr. 1994), and others.

important of these sources were family education, family reminiscences, and personal life experiences, which often contradicted official claims. The official education system presented Soviet society as an already achieved ideal. This claim caused dissatisfaction regardless of the real situation (which was surely far from ideal and deteriorating over the 1980s) because of the high level of theoretical expectation. At the same time, the officially inculcated 'active approach to life' instilled a constant desire to make 'real socialism' better so that it would correspond to the theoretical ideal of a socialism freed from deviations and shortcomings. Thus, paradoxical as it may seem, the confrontation of Soviet ideology itself with real life created reformers. While those 'democrats' who took the official ideal seriously naturally became active supporters of change, at first they supported a change within the framework of official socialism, therefore aiming at the perfection of the existing system. This was only natural since other possible aims of change were often simply unknown at the time.

Some understandings of different aims could originate from alternative sources available in the USSR. They included foreign radio broadcasts in Russian, officially published non-Marxist literature, banned literature, and impressions from trips abroad. The influence of these sources, though important for the gradual change of beliefs, only in a few cases led to renunciation of the official socialist ideal. In most cases it only partially changed the existing belief system; it brought new elements in, but new information was usually perceived within the framework of the pre-existing structure of beliefs, was distributed among its existing cells without breaking the structure itself. For a significant structural change a much stronger and systematic influx of new information was needed.

Such an influx came with the beginning of *perestroyka* and the information explosion of *glasnost`*. It fundamentally changed the old belief system of many individuals who were interested in politics and made 'democrats' of them. The flow of *perestroyka* ideas, which at first coincided with the wish to perfect existing socialism but rapidly became radical, was originally promoted by a relatively narrow group of Moscow and Leningrad intellectuals. But it soon spread to the provinces and captured wider circles of the population, changing old beliefs and making them more and more oppositional and anti-Communist. Thus, Communist education itself created a group of people who accepted the ideas of reform, which at first was aimed at the improvement of socialism. The landslide of information at the time of *glasnost`*, combined with Gorbachev's inability to improve the country's economic situation, gave new direction to the reformist movement. It took 'democrats' away from official Soviet ideals and from the belief in the possibility of improving the Soviet system, making them perceive this system as an obstacle on the road to reform and believe in the necessity of its total destruction in order to achieve a more perfect society. Gorbachev's policy, which, on the one hand, allowed freedom of information, and, on the other hand, produced a worsening in the living conditions of the population, inevitably led the beliefs of the politically active members of society toward rejection of the existing system and a more and more radical oppositional approach.

By the end of the 1980s this evolution had led to the formation of a system of 'democratic' beliefs which, while being sharply hostile toward official Soviet ideology and the beliefs that this ideology was trying to instil in the Soviet people, at the same time maintained many of this ideology's structural characteristics and even some particular beliefs which were typically Soviet. The following chapters study the contents of this new 'democratic' belief system, its correlation with official Soviet ideology as well as with its other sources and with contemporary Western understandings of 'democracy', and attempt to determine its place in the history of political culture in Russia and its influence on the country's subsequent political developments.

5

Hell on Earth: Attitudes toward the Existing Soviet State and Social Structure

5.1. FROM CRITICISM OF 'CERTAIN SHORTCOMINGS' TO FULL REPUDIATION

The beliefs shared by Russian 'democrats', like any other beliefs, were not static but developed in the course of time and events. One of the strands in this evolution can be characterized as 'growing criticism'. For many activists in the movement, it took only one or two years to transform themselves from supporters of 'true Leninism' into fighters against the 'totalitarian Communist dictatorship'.

However, it would not be correct to suggest that all of them passed through such a transformation, and fewer went all the way. Many of them did not change their views, others went halfway and then stopped, and the whole set of beliefs continued to exist within the movement at every moment of time. Furthermore, the pace of evolution was different between regions and within groups. Thus, it can only be said that at a particular moment, some opinions had become more popular than others or even prevailed, though no statistics are available. Therefore, this chapter, attempting to present a logical, rather than historical, model of the evolution of beliefs, emphasizes their main similarity. This similarity was the reason why the members of numerous 'democratic' groups' though declaring their association with very different sectors of the political spectrum, from anarchism to conservatism, none the less considered themselves as part of the same movement.

5.2. SHORTCOMINGS CAUSED BY 'DEVIATION FROM MARXISM'

The beliefs of the members of 'democratic' groups about the nature of state power in the USSR were rooted in the radical contradiction between the official state ideology and real practice. The official ideology proclaimed equality and social justice, democracy, the continuous improvement of living standards, and similar ideals, which evidently ran counter to existing realities. At the earlier stage of the 'democratic' movement, many members would identify these contradictions and demand their removal. This was the basis for the ideology and the activities of many early independent groups.

'Is it normal', wrote Pavel Novoselov, a member of the Krasnoyarsk Committee for Perestroyka,

that justice and equality, the Marxist-Leninist principles, have to be protected against the people who are assigned to be the leaders of the masses—the Party leaders them-selves?! Moral degradation, deaf hearts, and the selfishness of the superstructure of the Party and state: all these could not fail to work their effects on the spiritual level of our patient Soviet people, the people who made the Great Revolution and defeated fascism, but who so far have not been able to get rid of the heavy burden of the bureaucratic pyramid.[1]

At the early stages 'democrats' tended to see the reasons for the unsatis-factory situation in the personal mistakes and moral failings of the leaders: these were perceived as the explanation of their leaders' unwillingness to act in conformity with the official ideals. Gorbachev's first steps were perceived as an intention to make reality consistent with these ideals. 'Democrats' considered their own activities as contributions to Gorbachev's policy, and as the struggle against those who sabotaged it at the lower levels. Therefore, they studied the reasons for the contradictions between theory and reality. A mean-ingful point is that many such groups were called either committees, associ-ations, or popular fronts for *perestroyka*, acting in support of the official policy, or were discussion clubs on the theoretical problems of *perestroyka*.

5.3. THE NOTION OF THE ADMINISTRATIVE COMMAND SYSTEM

Later analysis of the situation brought about the need to define the system of relations that prevailed in the USSR and especially in the Soviet economy. This was actually the focus of criticism on the part of the reform-oriented leaders of the CPSU. The most popular definitions were the administrative command, the administrative, and the administrative instruction systems. The term 'administrative system' was coined by Gavriil Popov in his extremely popular 1987 article on Aleksandr Bek's novel *Novoye Naznacheniye* (New Appointment) and referred to the Soviet system of economic management. According to Popov, the system was based on complete subordination to the top leader and his complete control over his

---

[1] Pavel Novoselov, 'Real`naya democratiya—vlast` sovetam', *Pravo Golosa*, July 1988, 17.

subordinates. The crisis of the system, argued Popov, was caused by the inconsistency between such a style of decision-making and progress in science and technology. This resulted in the country lagging far behind the more developed economies.[2]

The term 'administrative system' and its derivatives were borrowed by many 'democratic' groups throughout the country and were widely used in their policy statements and informal publications. For example, the Declaration on the Establishment of the Penza Popular Front for Perestroyka reads as follows:

Rule by administrative command is throwing the country into the backwaters of world social progress; if the methods by which the national leadership is formed, are not made more democratic, in the near future the country will enter a period of economic humiliation on a global scale. The USSR has already been removed from the world's second position in industrial output; with German reunification and growth in India and Brazil, we shall be thrown down to seventh place and we will have to fight in order to sustain that.[3]

As we can see, the notion of the administrative system was transitional: while earlier the crisis in the USSR had been explained only by isolated faults, later the criticism was extended to the whole system of management, but was still applied only to the economic sphere. In his 1987 article, Popov, probably because of censorship considerations, mainly discussed economic management, but it appeared quite natural to extend this concept into the sphere of state structure and policy.

5.4. THE NEW CLASS

The 'democratic' movement, where many participants were no longer satisfied by such neutral definitions of Soviet society, made exactly such an extension. Somebody had to be responsible for administrative management. According to Popov's conclusions and the personal observations of theoreticians within the 'democratic' groups, decisions in the country were being made by a whole stratum of state and party bureaucrats whose power spread not only to the economic domain, but to the political as well. Speaking at the discussion of the Draft Law of the USSR on Public Associations held in early 1988 by the Democratic Perestroyka Club, radical activist Victor Kuzin said:

[2] Gavriil Popov, 'S tochki zreniya ekonomista. O romane Aleksandra Beka "Novoe Naznacheniye" ', *Nauka i Zhizn`*, 4 (1987), 54–66.

[3] 'Deklaratsiya ob obrazovanii Penzenskogo fronta v podderzhku perestroyki. Proekt' [Penza Dec. 1989], 10.

Such a euphemistic category as 'administrative system'—a category which is equally comfortable for the critics and for those under criticism—is no longer sufficient today. . . . The root of the evil cannot be found in the malevolence of a single person, however high that person's position. The continuation of 'villains' [in power] in our country, despite all the differences in their talents, indicates that there is an objective phenomenon. In this regard, it appears quite useful to study a problem which is totally ignored today: the problem of consistency between, on the one hand, scientific socialism (i.e. socialism which is based on the analysis and generalization of historical facts rather than a priori ideological dogma), and, on the other hand, the practice of monopolization, annexation, and forceful continuation in power, the right to dispose of the destiny of the people by one's own discretion, etc. It has long been the case already that the bureaucracy has replaced public opinion by its own opinion, the mechanism of free democratic election by bureaucratic appointments, and the will of the people as the essence of law—by the selfish voluntarism of the *nomenklatura*.[4]

Here we come to the notion of 'bureaucracy' as a social stratum that subjugated not only the economy but also the country's political power. Theoretical interpretation of this stratum was possible within the frame of the then most popular theoretical idea: Marxism. This could be done by defining the bureaucracy or bureaucratic stratum as a dominating class.

In Marxism, the main criterion of a social class is seen in its relation to the means of production. Hence, the bureaucratic class was recognized as the dominating one in Soviet society. V. Fedorov, writing in the magazine of the Moscow Popular Front, *Grazhdanskiy Referendum*, said in this regard: 'Certainly, the dominating class in Soviet society is the *bureaucracy* that has monopolized all functions of management in all spheres of social life, and relies on the broad network of totalitarian and power structures: party, state machinery, public associations (to be more precise, pseudo-public, as they are imposed from the top), and bureaucratically organized working collectives.'[5]

The term 'totalitarianism' gradually spread ever more widely among the Russian 'democratic' community. Abroad, the concept of 'totalitarianism' with regard to Soviet society was discussed by only one school of political science. Its application, at least to post-Stalinist Soviet society, was broadly criticized. In Russia, however, and within Russian 'democratic' groups it became popular to define Soviet society as totalitarian. Unlike the West, the discussion did not focus on whether there was totalitarianism in the USSR nor did it make the distinction observed by Western political scientists between totalitarianism and authoritarianism. Rather, it discussed what kind of totalitarianism it was and what the essence was of

[4] V. A. Kuzin, 'O kirpichakh i fundamente', *Otkrytaya Zona*, 4 (Feb. 1988), 31.
[5] V. Fedorov, 'Put` iz krizisa', *Grazhdanskiy Referendum*, 6 (1990), 3.

Soviet totalitarian society.[6] The discussion revealed the three major views addressed below.

5.5. THE SOVIET SYSTEM AS A POLITICAL REGIME

One of the options for the 'democratic' activists in trying to understand the Soviet system of power was to interpret it as a political regime. According to this option, the regime—most often characterized as totalitarian, but some-times also defined as an administrative system, a dictatorship of bureaucracy, Stalinism, or a Communist dictatorship—was understood as the usurpation, illegal seizure, and monopolization of political power by a certain political force carrying out a selfish 'anti-people' policy.

The milder version endorsed by the advocates of 'Leninist socialism' suggested that the power had been seized after demise of Lenin and the elim-ination of his associates. The anti-Communists dated this seizure of power to October 1917, and labelled the Bolsheviks one and all as usurpers. But in all of these options, the common feature was to refer to totalitarianism in the sphere of politics and power and to understand it as the imposition of the dominating political group's will upon the others.

'The totalitarian state', says Aleksandr Osovtsov, who later became a leader of the Democratic Russia Movement, 'is marked first and foremost by the fact that power (whether political, economic, or ideological—i.e. any power) belongs to one and only one force, group, team, whose programme of action is considered as the only correct one and thus necessarily worth real-ization, and whose norms and principles are announced as perfect and compulsory'.[7] According to Osovtsov, the antithesis of totalitarianism is pluralism.

Interpreted in such terms, totalitarianism has a lot in common with any dictatorship. The Russian 'democrats' could use this meaning of the term 'totalitarianism' as a synonym for dictatorship, autocracy, authoritarian-ism, Stalinism, a Communist regime, tsarist autocracy, or oligarchy, and thus no consistent and rigorous meaning was attributed to the word. In the

[6] The academic and public communities reached consensus on the 'totalitarian' character of Soviet society no later than 1989. The evidence is provided by the proceedings of the Moscow conference on totalitarianism as a historical phenomenon, published that year, where none of the participants, who represented Russia's prominent social scientists and various public groups, expressed any doubts about the very existence of totalitarianism in the USSR before and under Gorbachev. All of the participants proceeded from the common understanding that total-itarianism did exist in the USSR, and thus they simply analysed its essence. See A. A. Kara-Murza and A. K. Voskresenskiy (eds.), *Totalitarizm kak istoricheskiy fenomen* (Moscow: 1989).

[7] A. A. Osovtsov, ' "Totalitarizm umer!" Ili vse zhe "Da zdravstvuet totalitarizm!"?', in Kara-Murza and Voskresenskiy (eds.), *Totalitarizm kak istoricheskiy fenomen*, 155.

extreme case, totalitarianism was considered to be the most extreme form of dictatorship.

Certainly, the advocates of such an approach often drew parallels between the Soviet regime and every other form of dictatorship or authoritarianism known to the world; sometimes they included as totalitarian the rule of Ivan the Terrible and Peter the Great in Russia, the regime of General Franco in Spain, Nazi Germany, dictatorial regimes in South America, and, of course, all Communist regimes. The understanding of Soviet society as a society of 'one-party rule', a dictatorship by a group of 'partocrats', the rule of 'dictators worse than Hitler', was especially widespread among the rank-and-file activists of the 'democratic' movement.

5.6. THE SOVIET SYSTEM AS A SOCIAL SYSTEM

The interpretation of totalitarianism as merely a political regime represented the most superficial view of the problem. Raised in the Marxist tradition, in which the political arena was considered only part of the superstructure above the productive forces, the better-educated members of the 'democratic' movement tried to search more deeply for the roots of the Soviet regime. Their conclusion was that the basis of Soviet totalitarianism was to be found in the new, dominating bureaucratic class, which subjugated society and even influenced its 'economic basis'.

The claim that socialism generated the appearance of this new class was not a novelty for Marxism. Even Lev Trotskiy, expanding on the formation of a bureaucratic stratum in the USSR, called Stalin's ruling elite a 'parasitic oligarchy' and a 'totalitarian bureaucracy'.[8] Trotskiy's followers tended to consider bureaucracy as the ruling 'layer' or stratum in the system of 'bureaucratic despotism'.[9] Such ideas were certainly familiar to the well-educated Marxists in the Soviet bloc too. The textbook example is *The New Class* by former Yugoslavian Communist Milovan Djilas.[10] Basing his judgement mainly on the above ideas, Djilas, however, went far beyond them and characterized bureaucracy in Marxist terms as a social class that had usurped the right to possess the means of production. For a Marxist to define bureaucracy as a class, not just a layer, was important. While depriving a 'layer' of power (political revolution) is sufficient to improve the situation, a change of the entire

---

[8] Leon Trotsky, *In Defence of Marxism: Against the Petty-Bourgeois Opposition* (New York: Merit, 1965), 4.

[9] Ernest Mandel, *Power and Money: A Marxist Theory of Bureaucracy* (London: Verso, 1992), 26.

[10] Milovan Djilas, *The New Class: An Analysis of the Communist System* (New York: Praeger, 1958).

economic and social system (social revolution) is needed to overthrow an exploiting class. This was well understood by some more orthodox Western Marxists. According to Ernest Mandel, 'When one looks at the theoreticians of the "new exploiting class" (people like Djilas, Burnham, etc.) one finds that in most cases their revolt against Stalin and the post-Stalin Stalinists has resulted in skepticism towards the working class, adulation of bourgeois democracy, denial of Marxism. Their denunciation of the Kremlin has only turned them towards Washington.'[11] As it turned out later, in the case of Russian 'democrats' this accusation was largely true. However, to reject Marxism entirely Russian 'democrats' needed to undergo a long intellectual evolution.

While Djilas sometimes defined the Soviet system as a new despotism, he did not interpret it as a restoration of pre-capitalist social institutions. This was done by the Soviet émigré Mikhail Voslenskiy in his book *Nomenklatura: The Soviet Ruling Class*, which maintained that the ruling class of Soviet society was represented by *nomenklatura* bureaucrats in positions that could be filled only with the approval of the higher-level Party committee.[12]

These works circulated among Soviet intellectuals long before Gorbachev came to power. Nevertheless, as seen from the interviews, the activists of 'democratic' groups almost never borrowed the idea of the new class directly from publications prohibited in the USSR, whose circulation was too narrow. Many activists in Moscow, to say nothing of the provinces, were not familiar with *samizdat* 'Soviet underground publications' or *tamizdat* (foreign publications of banned authors). In many cases, the ideas of Marxist critics of the USSR were taken from articles published in official periodicals.

In terms of frequency of quotations, an article by Sergey Andreev, a young economist from Leningrad, had the strongest influence on 'democratic' activists. Published in the magazine *Ural*, the article considered the Soviet bureaucracy to be a class in terms of Marxist theory.[13] As was the case with the earlier publication by Popov, clubs and groups held discussions and seminars on Andreev's article, presented papers on it, and reprinted and reproduced the article's provisions in independent publications.

In fact, in comparison with the works written by Djilas or Voslenskiy, Andreev's article contained no news, but it had the advantage of being published in an official and popular literary magazine rather than an obscure academic journal, at a time when the reading public was attentively following every such publication. The conclusions of the article turned out to be extremely timely. An interesting point is that the article made no reference to the authors of

---

[11] Ernest Mandel, *On Bureaucracy: A Marxist Analysis* (London: IMG Publications, [1973]), 34.

[12] Mikhail Voslensky, *Nomenklatura: Anatomy of the Soviet Ruling Class*, tr. Eric Mosbacher (London: Bodley Head, 1984).

[13] Sergey Andreev, 'Prichiny i sledstviya', *Ural*, 1 (1988), 104–39. See also S. Andreev, 'Struktura vlasti i zadachi obshchestva', *Neva*, 1 (1989), 144–73.

the new-class theory, and the idea was presented as if the author had discovered it himself. It is difficult to say whether Andreev, who was himself a leader of a 'democratic' group, was aware of the other works, or whether he did not refer to them for tactical reasons, such as the censorship that was still being practised. However, it appears quite possible and even natural that a social scientist in the Marxist tradition should come to a similar conclusion independently.

Moreover, this idea had never died out in academic circles and, although publication was impossible, it was circulating from the mouth of one specialist to another. In addition, such conclusions could quite well be drawn via independent study of Marxist material, especially of less available earlier sources.

Valentin Manuylov, an activist in the Penza Political Club, said, for example, that he had come to similar conclusions when he was working on his dissertation on the period of transition from capitalism to socialism and communicating with liberal specialists on Marxist theory. In the course of his studies of what had been characterized by Lenin as state capitalism and the problems of the New Economic Policy (NEP), he scrutinized articles by Lenin and early Marxists and found in them the excerpts from Marx's works on Russia that had been unpublished in the USSR.

Addressing the then-fashionable problem of the 'contradictions of socialism', Manuylov concluded that the growth of bureaucratism was predetermined by the very character of modern production, in which an individual becomes a cog in a huge machine. Manuylov admits that he was influenced by talks with Yevgeniy Ambartsumov and Aleksandr Tsipko, the renowned liberal Marxists of that time, who could well have introduced him to the new-class theory. 'And evidently', says Manuylov,

all that communication, some discussions and intuition, coupled with the observations [that were possible before autumn 1987] on the activities of the Party bureaucracy—all that somehow led also to the conclusion that bureaucracy was a class. Even in 1987 we didn't consider it as something unique; I mean, it seemed quite natural that bureaucracy was a class or at least a class-like group. . . . The problem was to understand how hierarchical relations were built within that class or class-like group, who was playing a leading role there, and who was playing a less important role. It was clear that within the bureaucracy the Party was taking the leading positions *vis-à-vis* the economic bureaucracy.[14]

Certainly the CPSU was seen as the core of the dominating class and was blamed for the societal crisis. For example, the programme of one of the parties stated that 'not the individuals, but the whole system of partocracy has been a source of the people's troubles for the last seventy years'.[15] Even the

[14]   Interview with Valentin Manuylov (Penza, Apr. 1994).
[15]   'Deklaratsiya Demokraticheskoy Partii', in *Rossiya: partii, assotsiatsii, soyuzy, kluby. Spravochnik*, 10 vols. (Moscow: RAU-Press, 1991–2), ii. 10.

most extreme radicals did not consider all the members of the CPSU to be involved in the system of 'partocracy'. The ruling party was seen not as a political party as such, but rather as a special social institution, and membership was considered a social privilege. The institution appeared as a result of the actual convergence of the Party and the state, and thus the so-called state-class emerged. The Draft Programme of the Democratic Union defines the totalitarianism that dominated the USSR as 'the state system based on the monopoly of the partocratic state, represented by its bureaucracy: monopoly of power, ownership, ideological and cultural life, totalitarian nationalization of all spheres of social life and the elimination of civil society'.[16]

The observations most often heard were those to the effect that the ruling class included only the *nomenklatura* portion of the Party, while there was no difference between the rank-and-file Party members and the non-members. This judgement was to a large extent preconditioned by the fact that many activists of 'democratic' movements were themselves members of the CPSU. The analysis of the sources of dictatorship in the USSR made by Vasiliy Krasulya is a good case in point:

> The schemes and ideas, estranged from real life, could not become the life of the people and they were alien to the people. In order to realize those fantasies of the Party, a bureaucratic machine had to be built, the *nomenklatura* that gradually usurped the all and replaced political life in the country with their bureaucratic hustle and bustle. The bureaucracy has inevitably become punitive and repressive. .... Actually, a bunch of top Party workers ruled on behalf of the proletariat, and a dictatorship of the proletariat was transformed, as Trotsky said, into the dictatorship of the secretariat.[17]

The influence of Marxist terminology on the theory of new-class domination in the USSR is evident. Even when criticizing Marx, many activists continued to refer to Marxist, though previously prohibited, authors. While repudiating Marxism, 'democratic' activists maintained many Marxist approaches and basic Marxist attitudes toward the Soviet state and society. This trend is amply illustrated in one of the draft programmes of the SDPR:

> History has proved the utter failure of Marxism-Leninism. The realization of this teaching about the so-called dictatorship of the proletariat has ultimately led to the dictatorship of one tyrant, to unprecedented bureaucracy, and to the actual formation of the new elite class. .... The elite class has seized political power as well as the whole system of distribution of material and financial resources, and has thus obliterated the essentially more efficient market system.[18]

---

[16] 'Proekt programmy partii Demokraticheskiy Soyuz', in *Byulleten' soveta partii*, Feb. 1990, 8–9.

[17] Vasiliy Krasulya, 'Partiya: vchera, segodnya, zavtra. Tezisy k discussii', *Grazhdanin*, May 1989, 5, 11.

[18] V. Nyrko, 'Programma SDPR', in *K uchreditel'nomu s'yezdu Sotsial-demokraticheskoy partii Rossiskoy Federatsii. Sbornik materiyalov No. 1* (Tipografiya Minuralsibstroya, 1990), 45–6.

Marxist theory was not the only source of the perception of the state bureaucracy as a dominating class. According to Aleksandr Shubin, an activist in the Obshchina anarchist group, the theoreticians of this group took a somewhat different road. Having reached the conclusion of the class character of bureaucracy through the study of Marxist documents, they found substantiation of this theory in the works of Russian anarchists and Populists, especially Mikhail Bakunin. They were influenced by Bakunin's idea that collectivization and rule from a single centre—the measures proposed by Marx—would generate the appearance of a new, bureaucratic ruling class and a new state dictatorship. This idea, available in works of Bakunin officially published in the USSR, supported and developed the Marxist conclusions initially drawn by Shubin and his friends, and generated their interest in anarchism and the Populist movement. The works they subsequently read by the Marxist architects of the new-class theory, Shubin said, seemed correct, but of secondary origin.[19]

Whatever road a 'democratic' theoretician might follow, it included an understanding of Soviet society as divided into the new classes of exploiters and exploited and a common understanding of the Soviet social structure as a kind of social system. The 'democrats', raised by the Marxist theory to regard social and economic structures as successively changing in a 'progressive' direction, inevitably sought to define the place of that social system in the scale of social evolution.

5.7. THE SOVIET SYSTEM AS A HISTORICAL REGRESSION

Because the viciousness of the Soviet totalitarian system and its backwardness *vis-à-vis* capitalism were clear to the 'democrats', they quite naturally saw totalitarianism as a step back to the pre-capitalist level of development, or a historical regression. For example, Fedorov considered Soviet society to be divided into the classes of slaves and slave-owners and thus, in terms of its level of development, refers to it as a slave-owning society:

The economic system of state slave-ownership, where slave-owners are represented by the bureaucracy class and slaves by the working people such as labourers, peasants, and intellectuals, where bureaucracy faces direct competition on the part of the continuously reviving bourgeoisie and a stable economic opposition on the part of the petty bourgeoisie—such a system inevitably requires a political superstructure in the form of a totalitarian state, because otherwise such a system cannot be kept in balance. The progress of the surrounding civilized world inspires such a system to twist the screws of totalitarianism ever more tightly.[20]

---

[19] Interview with Aleksandr Shubin (Oxford, 26 Jan. 1995).
[20] Fedorov, 'Put` iz krizisa'.

This excerpt sets forth an important belief, widespread among Russian 'democrats': the interpretation of Soviet society as divided into two opposing classes—the bureaucracy (the class of exploiters owning all the nation's property) and everyone else (the exploited class of non-owners). This necessarily involves a repressive state, for which repressions are the only method of retaining the monopoly of ownership. However, the most significant point in such an analysis is its strict adherence to Marxist theory in relating such a society to the stage of pre-capitalist formation: in this case, to slave ownership.

Slave ownership as described by Fedorov has very little in common with slave ownership, for example, in ancient Greece. Because of the enormous role of the Soviet state, the USSR was most often compared to the ancient oriental societies. These ideas, too, are not at all a novelty in Marxism. As early as 1906, long before the victory of the Bolshevik Revolution, Georgiy Plekhanov, the first Russian Marxist, spoke at the Fourth Congress of the Russian Social Democratic Workers' Party against Lenin's proposal on the nationalization of land. Plekhanov characterized it as a 'dangerous,' 'anti-revolutionary', and 'reactionary' measure that would 'reverse the course of Russian history'.[21] His judgement proceeded from Marx's remarks about Asiatic despotism, based on the absence of private property.[22] Tending to see the old order in Russia as 'the Moscow version of the economic order that had been laid in the foundations of all great despotisms' when 'the land and landowners were the property of the state',[23] Plekhanov believed that the fulfilment of the Bolsheviks' programme would result in the restoration of the ancient Muscovite state order in Russia and in the new enslavement of peasants by 'Leviathan the state'.[24]

Quite naturally, after 1917, when Bolshevik rule was becoming ever more despotic, Plekhanov's ideas circulated widely among the Marxist critics of the Bolsheviks as well as the Bolshevist-oriented opponents of the hard-line regime. The latter group of critics, deprived of the possibility of writing openly about the government, were coming to their conclusions through the study of oriental countries, especially China. In so doing, they were warning the Bolshevik leaders against reverting to backward oriental despotism.

There was just one more step to be made before announcing that the system which had been formed in the USSR, especially after the Stalinist collectivization, was oriental despotism. This could be done both by those

[21] G. V. Plekhanov, 'Kagrarnomu voprosu v Rossii', in G. V. Plekhanov, *Sochineniya*, 24 vols. (St Petersburg/Leningrad: Gosudarstvennoe izdatel'stvo, 1923–7), xv. 31.

[22] See e.g. Karl Marx (letter to Engels, 2 July 1953), in K. Marx and F. Engels, *Polnoe sobranie sochineniy*, 2nd edn., xxviii (Moscow: Gosudarstvennoe politicheskoe izdatel'stvo, 1962), 215.

[23] G. V. Plekhanov, 'Kagrarnomu voprosu v Rossii', in Plekhanov, *Sochineniya*, xv. 31.

[24] Ibid. 36.

who continued to think within the frameworks of Marxism and socialism, and by those who opposed socialism. The only difference is that the advocates of socialism considered Soviet society to be a return to the pre-socialist or even pre-capitalist system and believed that real socialism had never been reached at all, while the opponents of socialism said that socialism as such meant a return to oriental despotism. Meanwhile, the very idea of oriental despotism, based on total state ownership, and the idea of the crucial difference between total state ownership and Western society, was in both cases the same.

That the same individual can undergo transformation from the former to the latter position is amply shown by K.-A. Wittfogel, an American scholar of German origin who started his studies of China in the early 1920s as a Marxist, and whose classic book, *Oriental Despotism: A Comparative Study of Total Power*, was published in the United States in 1957. Without seeing the USSR as the twentieth century's replica of his 'hydraulic society' or oriental despotism, Wittfogel argued that the Soviet system produced a combination of the major features of such a society, on the one hand, and modern technology and managerial bureaucracy on the other, resulting in the society of 'total political power as well as total social and intellectual control', which had never existed in the ancient Orient.[25]

Certainly, Wittfogel was aware of the notion of totalitarianism, which was undergoing elaboration by Western political scientists at about the same time, and according to which Nazi Germany and Communist USSR were considered as a new type of society of total control based on breakthroughs in science and technology.[26] What made Wittfogel's theory unlike the others was that he combined the concept of totalitarianism in Western political science with Marxist theories of the Asiatic mode of production, and emphasized the typological similarity between Soviet societal organization and traditional oriental societies, seeing them both as based on what he called 'total power'. Voslenskiy, evidently influenced by Wittfogel's ideas, simplified them and described Soviet society as a restoration of oriental despotism. According to Voslenskiy, the Soviet system was

a feudal reaction, a system of state-monopolistic feudalism. The essence of this reaction is that the ancient method of the 'Asiatic mode of production', the method of statization, is used for cementing feudal structures which had been shaken by an anti-feudal revolution. The archaic class of the political bureaucracy re-emerges as a 'new class'—the *nomenklatura*. It models its dictatorship on an unconscious prototype—theocratic oriental despotism. Thus, an old-fashioned reaction, disguised in pseudo-progressive 'socialist' slogans but which in reality was a mixture of feudalism and

---

[25] K.-A. Wittfogel, *Oriental Despotism: A Comparative Study of Total Power* (New Haven, Conn.: Yale University Press, 1957), 440.

[26] Carl J. Friedrich and Zbigniew K. Brzezinski, *Totalitarian Dictatorship and Autocracy*, 2nd edn. (New York: Praeger Publishers, 1966; 1st publ. 1956).

ancient state despotism, found its way into our time. Whatever this mixture is called—national socialism, real socialism, or fascism—it is one and the same phenomenon—totalitarianism, the plague of the twentieth century.[27]

Inside the Soviet Union, when liberal times arrived and censorship weakened, many believers in the Asiatic mode of production also began to include the Soviet Union in their analyses. Thus, an expert on ancient Chinese statehood, Leonid Vasil`ev, argued that 'Communist totalitarianism is merely a modification of the classical Oriental despotism with its arbitrary rule, suppression of human rights, strictly controlled market and strictly controlled private property. Incidentally, this is an extreme modification, i.e. one that out-despotized the classical Oriental despots.'[28] Like Plekhanov, Vasil`ev saw the system of government of ancient Russia as a part of the non-Western world. In his view, this system did not undergo any structural transformation under the Communist regime, let alone experience any substantial changes. On the contrary, 'the former command-administrative system based on the state-controlled mode of production ("Asiatic", as Marx called it) with its all-embracing system of centralized redistribution remained intact.' Communist policy made this Oriental system in Russia even more perfect by turning society, 'which already had in it the makings of a new system of government, of the European bourgeois democratic type, with its guaranteed personal freedoms, freedom of choice and private property ownership, into an absolutely rightless society with the ruling Party holding full sway over it.'[29]

Ideas similar to the theories of Wittfogel, Voslenskiy, and Vasil`ev can be found in abundance in the informal periodicals of the *perestroyka* period. The characterization of Soviet totalitarianism as a reversion to 'Asianism', or at least as a society 'covered by the shoots' of the Russian past, was widely shared by 'democrats' of various orientations. For example, the programme of the furthest left of all the micro-parties in Russia, the Socialists, said:

The attempt to build socialism in a backward country which did not have developed industry and which was isolated from the rest of the world and destroyed by a war lasting many years could not be successful. . . . In such a situation, revolutionary power inevitably took the form of a dictatorship that was initially supported by the working people but then more and more self-isolated itself from the masses. In the end, the rapid bureaucratization and degeneration of the regime resulted in the formation of a totalitarian dictatorship and the system of Stalin's personal power.[30]

[27] Volensky, *Nomenklatura*, 611–12. Voslenskiy elaborated these ideas in detail in the revised Russian edition of his book. See Mikhail Voslenskiy, *Nomenklatura: gospodstvuyushchiy klass sovetskogo obshchestva* (Moscow: MP 'Oktyabr`, 'Sovetskaya Rossiya', 1991), 611–12.

[28] Leonid Vasilyev, 'After Bankruptcy: What is Happening to the CPSU?', *New Times*, 49 (4–10 Dec. 1990), 7. [29] Ibid.

[30] [Sotsialisticheskaya Partiya], 'Put` k svobode. Programma Sotsialisticheskoy part ii. Proekt', unpubl. MS [Moscow, 1990], 4–5.

The Democratic Union, the party with the most radical anti-Communist orientation, gave an identical assessment of Soviet society:

After the October 1917 revolution, the Bolsheviks started to build a new state—the totalitarian system based on the state (Asiatic) mode of production characterized by them as socialist.

The totalitarian system organically integrated the industrial productive forces, quite modern for the twentieth century, and at the same time marked the further movement of the country along the 'Asian' path of the road of history; thus it was a successor to oriental despotic states. Unlike the latter case, however, communal structures under the totalitarian system are substantially destroyed and suppressed, while the [individual] personality is controlled not so much indirectly (i.e., through the community), but rather directly by the state and is thus much more thoroughly destroyed and impersonalized. . . .

The working people are alienated from the means of production and, even worse, they are no longer the owners of their labour and their intellects; due to the monopoly of the state as their only employer, they have become state serfs.

The slogan of proletarian dictatorship was used to establish the bloody dictatorship of partocracy. For the first time in history, the totalitarian party-state was built—in the USSR, where the Party structures have become the core of the state structure and have subjugated the latter.[31]

Certainly, the popularity of such ideas, previously expressed by Wittfogel, does not mean that many 'democrats' were familiar with his works. For most of the activists, Wittfogel's writings were not available. However, such ideas were actively discussed in the academic and especially orientalist community of Russia, within the discussion, restarted in the 1960s, on the Asiatic mode of production.[32] Though the advocates of this theory were not a majority among the researchers, they could publish their views and propagate them to students—at least as long as they acted as interpreters of Marxism and did not apply the Asiatic concept to the contemporary USSR. While such an application was prohibited, the sub-context of the discussion was absolutely clear. The following excerpt represents a typical 1970s academic description of Asian (in this case, Chinese) society:

The dominant class of Chinese despotism, supported by a certain unity between ownership and power, acted first and foremost as a collective exploiter, as a 'class and state'. Representing a certain degree of unity between the base and the superstructure, Chinese despotism not only was a powerful instrument of class domination, but exerted a substantial influence on the process of class formation; proximity to power became the major sign of social status. Antagonistic in nature, the despotic social and political structure at the same time fulfilled important functions of integration, as it consolidated the economically atomized society and contained its centrifugal trends. . . .

---

[31] 'Proekt programmy partii Demokraticheskiy Soyuz', 13–14.

[32] For detailed discussion of the history of the concept of the 'Asiatic mode of production', see Ernest Gellner, *State and Society in Soviet Thought* (Oxford: Basil Blackwell, 1988), ch. 3; V. N. Nikiforov, *Vostok i vsemirnaya istoriya* (Moscow: Nauka, 1975).

Despotism and the Chinese empire ever more broadly expanded their economic and social functions and ever more actively used their political power in order to contain the social and economic process that jeopardized the old system. The political monopoly, the political force had been able to suppress the opposition during a long period of history; however, in the conditions of the new epoch, it generated political impotence which doomed once-great China to full political subordination to capitalist powers.[33]

It was not very difficult to apply such conditions to Soviet society, to remove some Marxist phraseology and insert the prohibited term 'totalitarianism'. It was exactly this undertaking which was accomplished by the theoreticians of the Democratic Union and many of their colleagues. Their manoeuvre is clearly visible in their language: indeed, it is much easier to proclaim oneself a foe of Marxism than to stop thinking in the Marxist categories that one has studied since primary school.

For exactly this reason, the programmes of the Socialists and even of the more radical organizations contained such fundamental Marxist categories as 'class', 'exploitation', and 'mode of production', and even such *Soviet* Marxist terms as 'leading force'. In one of the draft programmes of the Social Democratic Party, the description of the Soviet system actually repeats in every major point the above description of 'Chinese despotism':

Set by the Communist Party, the initially vicious utopian objective was to build a single-system society, the 'single factory', ruled and planned in a totalitarian way. Such an objective inevitably required the mechanism of *diktat*, organized violence, and ideological indoctrination that provided for the domination of the new ruling stratum. The bureaucracy of the Communist Party has become the leading force of the bureaucratic system, the institutions of punishment, and the propaganda institutions. Power has become the major category in the new type of society, and the build-up and consolidation of power has become the main objective of the ruling oligarchy. Destruction of civil society, concentration of the able-bodied population in controllable collectives, nationalization of social life, and elimination of the opposition enabled the oligarchy to produce the historically unprecedented form of totalitarianism. There has emerged a hierarchical system: the bureaucratic state headed by the Party leaders, the latter ruling the socially uniform population, brought down to the position of state serfs or slaves.[34]

The perception of the Soviet system as the return to Asiatic despotism, despite its popularity, was not the only way to define the system's place in the scale of social evolution. Sometimes the Soviet system was defined as 'social-feudal' or 'state-feudal'; the left-wing anarchists, seeking to emphasize the

---

[33] A. V. Meliksetov, *Sotsial'no-economicheskaya politika Gomin'dana v Kitaye (1927–1949)* (Moscow: Nauka, 1977), 8–9.

[34] Sotsial-demokraticheskaya partiya Rossiyskoy Federatsii, 'Put' progressa i sotsial'noy demokratii. Osnova programmy SDPR. Vremennaya redaktsiya', unpubl. MS [Moscow, 1990], 4.

Soviet system's similarity to 'capitalism', tended to define it as 'state-capitalist'. However, in any case, the Soviet system was perceived as a historical regression or at least as a kind of historical slippage, while Western society was marching ahead on the road of social progress. For example, the platform of the Democrat Club in Vladivostok, adopted in 1989, repeated almost word for word the Moscow definitions and characterized Soviet society as 'social feudalism'.[35]

A good illustration of the above scheme is that the CPSU and its privileges were often seen as a restoration of estate and class privileges typical of pre-1917 Russia. The opinion was voiced that the monopoly power of the CPSU, as fixed by the Soviet Constitution, was 'a restoration of tsarist autocracy in new historical forms',[36] and that membership in the CPSU was merely a restoration of the class privileges that had existed in tsarist Russia. Pavel Poluyan, an activist in the Krasnoyarsk Committee for Perestroyka, wrote:

> Now, as is clear to everybody, the CPSU membership card is not evidence of either the moral level or even the ideological affinities of an individual. In fact, membership in the CPSU has become a sign of one's estate. . . . While the association with the Party estate cannot be inherited (by the way, this used to be the case for some categories of nobles, too), many signs of the division of estate are obvious. What matters is not even the gap between the 'haves and have-nots' (among Russian nobles, too, there used to be tsarist ministers and impoverished drunkards), but that the historical tradition turns out to be very, very impervious to.[37]

Kryskin, an activist in the 'democratic' movement in Penza, called the no-alternative elections 'feudal power privileges'.[38] Seeking to emphasize that the sources of Communist as well as fascist regimes were rooted in Asian despotism, he also labelled Hitler, Stalin, and Pol Pot 'Ghengis Khans of the twentieth century'.[39]

5.8. THE SOVIET SYSTEM AS A MODE OF THINKING

The documents and statements of members of 'democratic' groups contain another interpretation of the Soviet system, seeing it as based not on a certain social structure, but rather on a certain type of political thinking, one that has

[35] *Platforma kluba 'Demokrat'* (Vladivostok: 1989), 1.
[36] Vasiliy Krasulya, 'Nashi raznoglasiya', *Grazhdanin*, 5 (May 1989), 5.
[37] Pavel Poluyan, 'Ot byurokratii k demokratii', *Pravo Golosa*, July 1988, 20–1.
[38] Yevgeniy Kryskin, 'Kak penzenskaya nomenklatura sebya samoderzhit', in Yevgeniy Kryskin, *Demokratiya i antidemokratiga v Penze: nachalo protivostoyaniga* (Penza, 1992) (no publisher), p. 58.
[39] Yevgeniy Kryskin, 'Zastoynoe nachalo', *Listok Grazhdanskoy initsiativy*, 14 (5 Dec. 1989).

always existed in human society. For example, Andrey Isaev, the leader of the Anarcho-syndicalists, identified three types of political thinking—authoritarian, anarchist, and liberal—each of which determined a specific political ideology and that, if victorious, would contribute to the development of the corresponding type of society. In Isaev's view, a type of thinking is primary in relation to a given ideology, and predetermines the programme and specific action of political groups. Isaev supports his judgement by saying that

in the same political situation, people with the same type of thinking would behave in a similar way, irrespective of their political doctrines. For example, the Marxist Mensheviks and Marxist Bolsheviks found themselves on opposite sides of the barricades, but the Bolsheviks' allies included people who were either very far from Marxism, such as the Jacobite wing of the Socialist Revolutionary Party, or the anarchic Communist Zheleznyak, who dissolved the Constituent Assembly, or General Brusilov. It was the authoritarian type of thinking that brought all those people together in the same camp. Exactly this type of thinking forged their belief that the 'decisive' action of the Bolsheviks was correct, and ideological substantiation of that action was a matter of the lowest priority.[40]

Isaev sees the core elements of authoritarian thinking as the following: the belief that power is the only efficient means to reach both greater and smaller social objectives; seeing individuals and even entire groups and classes as a means to attain abstract objectives; and readiness to sacrifice specific individuals for the sake of building the ideal 'progressive' human society.[41] He argued that exactly such thinking had prevailed in Russia in 1917 and become the basis of Soviet social realities.

There is no doubt that the type of thinking which served as the basis for the Soviet system was perceived by the members of 'democratic' groups in the most negative terms, i.e. as the least acceptable one. Based on this type of thinking, the authoritarian regime, or totalitarianism, in their view, began to distort the personality, depersonalized the human psyche, and transformed human individuals into slaves—slaves not only in terms of their social status, but conscious slaves who were satisfied with their subordinate position and considered it quite normal.

This resulted in a peculiar anti-world that confronted 'normal' society. 'In its essence, totalitarianism is a phenomenon of mentality rather than being,' wrote Democratic Union ideologist Aleksandr Eliovich. 'Under totalitarianism, there is no being in the philosophical sense, and it represents the ideal kingdom of non-being.'[42]

Accepting the above social and economic attitudes toward the Soviet

[40] A. Isaev, 'Filosofskie razmyshleniya o gnusnosti liberalizma i prichinakh, po kotorym intelligentnyy chelovek ne mozhet ne byt` anarkhistom', *Obshchina*, 35–6 (1989), 14.
[41] Ibid. 15.
[42] A. Eliovich, 'Perestroyka i psikhoanaliz', *Vpolgolosa*, 3 (June 1991), 8.

system, Eliovich sees its major feature as the absence of the 'economic sovereignty of the personality, when all people are lumpenized and totally depend on the state structures.'[43] However, he suggests that such a structure produced an entirely new situation in the sphere of thought in which one could see 'not only a fertile soil for manipulation, but also the basis that makes such manipulation inevitable'. Therefore, totalitarianism, victorious in the USSR, became an ideal anti-world, the absolute evil, 'the kingdom of Hades', 'the kingdom of the dead', where one could find nothing positive, not even the logic typical of 'normal' society.[44]

Seeing the Soviet regime as an 'anti-world' that had changed people's mentality became more prevalent in the later period of *perestroyka* reforms, when some 'democrats' felt disappointed as they saw that neither the destruction of the totalitarian political regime nor the elimination of the bureaucratic state-class was leading to democracy. In the view of the supporters of the 'anti-world' theory, even in the conditions of free choice available as a result of the destruction of the totalitarian empire, the totalitarian personality would nevertheless choose a new totalitarianism. Thus, repudiation of a specific political ideology such as Communism would not change the essence of the social system and could even be useful for the elite. Eliovich continues: 'Because there exists a totalitarian structure of mentality, i.e. because the border between good and evil is erased and the two somehow converge into the same whole while people know that good is not the same as evil, there appears a surprisingly organic system that, unfortunately, has a very great potential for development.'[45]

This, argued Eliovich, posed a threat even more serious than before to the USSR and the whole world. Furthermore, it became more difficult for the outside world to see the distinction between good and evil. While previously the West perceived Communism as an enemy, now, 'in our country, from everyone—from the Democratic Union to [hard-line CPSU Politburo member Yegor] Ligachev—one can hear the words "democracy", "human rights", "*perestroyka*", and a situation has appeared in which it is not clear what the West should protect itself from. And we see that in our country people slaughter one another fiercely in the name of different understandings of human rights.'[46]

On this view, as a result of *perestroyka*, totalitarianism in the USSR was in fact consolidated and acquired new anti-Communist forms. Having thrown away the Communist-style clothes that are so unpopular in the outside world, the renovated 'totalitarianism' acquired even better opportunities to converge with 'the prosperous countries of the West, which have not learned [to recognize it] well enough',[47] and thus tended to take the social democratic

---

43 Eliovich, *Vpolgolosa*, 3 (June 1991), 8.   44 Ibid.
45 Ibid. 10.   46 Ibid. 11.   47 Ibid.

approach to the nationalization of the economy, as well as gaining greater influence in the countries of the South, which had a system based on the same ethnocratic and nationalist principles.

5.9. METHODS OF STRUGGLE

Analysis of the beliefs developed by Russian 'democrats' concerned with the state and social organization of the USSR provides a key for better understanding their concrete political actions as well as the strategy and tactics of their struggle against the regime. The logic of struggle by Russian 'democrats' proceeds directly from the logic of their view of the world, and especially their understanding of the major target of their activities, Soviet reality. Discussion of three aspects of this struggle follows.

First, the interpretation of the Soviet system as an ordinary dictatorship, i.e. a certain form of political regime, does not provide any insight into the tactics-of-struggle context. Such an interpretation led to the belief that the mere toppling and replacement of the regime would immediately result in the victory of 'democracy'. This belief, in its isolated form, almost never existed anywhere in the 'democratic' movement, and in their general tactics the activists were guided by the understanding of the Soviet system as a more fundamental phenomenon.

Second, the Russian 'democrats' saw the target of their struggle neither as individual dictators nor the political party, or even the organs of state power, but as a monolithic political and economic giant: the state-class, which possessed all political and economic power in the country and which restored the order of the distant past, thus slowing down or reversing the nation's development. Thus, any reforms were understood as measures to deprive this giant of political, economic, cultural, and other powers. Political reforms would withdraw political power first from the CPSU, and then from the whole class of exploiters headed by the Party. In the economic field, this implied the elimination of the system of control over enterprises; in the sphere of culture and education, it implied denationalization of art associations, schools, and universities.

The 'democrats' clearly realized that the dominating class would cling fiercely to its privileges, so the process of reform was viewed as the persistent struggle between state and society, the haves and the have-nots; only victory in this struggle and the elimination of the dominating class would turn the country in the direction of 'normal' development. Therefore, it was not coincidental that the Marxist term 'to eliminate as a class' (in this context, the bureaucracy) appeared in many documents, such as this one from 1989: 'Elimination of the *nomenklatura* as a class through the election of economic managers and other leaders is the only way to get out of the deep crisis, comparable to that of 1917. Conservative forces confront the reforms, and the outcome of the struggle against these forces will predetermine the wealth or poverty of our descendants.'[48]

Various methods were proposed for such elimination, but the rejection of violence and the acceptance only of peaceful forms of protest was the most dominant opionion. The more cautious 'democrats', most often of the social- ist, social democratic, or 'stateship' orientation, proposed to use the more gradual, evolutionary methods. To support their judgement, they argued that however bad the system was, its sudden destruction, followed by the rapid institution of freedom and a market economy, would bring chaos and trans- form Russia into a Third World country.[49] In this context, they emphasized the need to undertake broad measures of social protection, as the resultant threat of the lumpenization of a substantial part of the population might cause a social explosion.[50]

A noteworthy point is that the same danger was mentioned by the authors of the Democratic Union's draft programme, who believed that 'the crisis of totalitarianism can lead to the total collapse of all party and state structures, and—in the absence of civil society—to the restoration of totalitarianism'. As for their remedy, however, they proposed 'to build the infrastructure of civil society, the system of alternative public power' that at some future moment could replace the 'illegal' and 'totalitarian' power structures and open up 'the possibility of escape from the blind alley of social development'.[51]

Very few 'democrats' found violence acceptable, though such views did exist within the most extreme wing of the movement. For example, the Democratic Union leader Valeriya Novovdodskaya writes in her memoirs that she was ready to prefer the elimination of the USSR along with its entire population to the continued domination of totalitarianism, as such a measure would be beneficial for the rest of the world and global development as a whole:

In August 1968 I became the real enemy of the state, army, navy, air force, Party, and Warsaw Pact bloc. I walked the streets as a clandestine figure in occupied terri- tory. It was precisely then that I decided that for all those deeds (I already knew about Budapest, too) there was only one form of punishment: the destruction of the state. And now, when it is half-destroyed and lies in blood and mud, when it appears quite possible that it will die together with the entire people, I feel neither pity nor repen- tance. Damn the day when the USSR was born! Better to let it become a common

---

[48] 'Deklaratsiya ob obrazovanii Penzenskogo fronta v podderzhku perestroyki. Proekt', unpubl. MS [Penza, Dec. 1989], 10.

[49] Interview with Shubin, Rumyantsev, and Shakhnovskiy.

[50] For example, this view has become the essence of the 'Basic Programme of the SDPR'. See 'Put` progressa i sotsial`noy demokratii', 19.

[51] 'Proekt programmy partii "Democraticheskiy soyuz" ', 16.

grave for all of us, rather than come back from the graveyard at night as a vampire and suck the blood of those still alive, who have never been in the USSR, or have been there for only a short time and, like the Baltics, have the chance to survive.[52]

Such views should not be seen as an attempt on the part of an excited radical to shock the public. The belief that the USSR was the centre of the world's evils, and that its elimination by whatever means would be useful to all mankind, was quite popular in educated society as well. Novodvorskaya recalls that during a conversation with her literature teacher at school, she heard for the first time that she lived 'in a country so terrible that if the atomic bomb was dropped on it and killed us all but at the same killed the system, this would be a desirable outcome'.[53]

Certainly, views as radical as Novodvorskaya's were not heard very often. However, as a result of political developments in the last years of the USSR, the 'democratic' opposition developed increasingly radical sentiments that rapidly shifted to favouring harsher measures in order to eliminate the 'totalitarian' regime, the regime that was being accused of destructive activities, including standardization or even elimination of human personality. As the Soviet power structures were perceived as a giant beast whose only mission and natural interests were 'to suck the blood' of their downtrodden subjects, and as that perception was based on a unique mix of life experience and anarchism-populism, Marxism, and contemporary theories in political science, politica and everyday life was seen as a universal confrontation between two poles: the authorities and society, 'democrats' and Communists, East and West, reaction and progress, Us and Them.

Such a confrontation was addressed more from uncompromising moral positions than from the point of view of the real political art of the possible. 'I always believed that there must be "either, or". Either them or us. Either the KGB or the possibility of publishing a book like this. Either the Party bureaucracy in power, or our freedom', writes Novodvorskaya.[54] Every concession on the part of the regime, every one of its attempts to carry out democratic reforms, was perceived as an act of weakness that had to be used to finish it off, while the regime's weak attempts to demonstrate force were understood as further evidence of its destructive objectives.

Certainly, this does not at all mean that every participant in the 'democratic' movement took their beliefs to such a drastic conclusion. However, by the early 1990s the 'democratic' movement was ever more enthusiastic about the idea of a decisive struggle against the regime. To some extent, this circumstance can throw light on the course of events that followed. The most radical free-market ideas of the Chicago model, as well as the liberal anti-state theories of the Friedrich von Hayek school and the plans to eliminate the 'empire'

---

[52] Valeriya Novodvorskaya, *Po tu storonu otchayaniya* (Moscow: Novosti, 1993), 22.
[53] Novodvorskaya, *Po tu storonu otchayaniya*, 19.   [54] Ibid. 9.

(of which even the CIA could not have dreamed)—all these turned out to be most popular in the 'democratic' community and were finally approved by President Yel`tsin, and not only because of political considerations.

Another reason was that it was these theories which were the most consistent with the anti-totalitarian beliefs of the Russian 'democrats' who sought to eliminate the state-class rapidly, and who considered privatization and the sovereignty of the republics as the liberation of more and more properties, territories, and people from the power of their adversary. The problems which emerged later as a result of this policy—the collapse of the state, conflicts between nationalities, the growth of crime, and others—when they were discussed in the 'democratic' movement, were seen as a result of the preservation of the totalitarian regime, rather than as a possible result of its decisive elimination.[55]

Third, this position resulted in the interpretation of the Soviet system as a mentality that had brought about the anti-world on Earth. In the sphere of practical action, advocates of such an approach usually rejected the direct anti-state struggle and asserted the need to change the totalitarian mentality through time-consuming, meticulous work. Seeing that the direct attack against the regime and even its social fundamentals did not result in any major changes, supporters of such views became quite sceptical about Western methods of anti-totalitarian struggle and became interested in the ideas of moderate populists and social revolutionaries, anarchists, Chayanov's theories of cooperation, and the theories of non-violent transformation in Gandhi and in Christianity.

These teachings seemed attractive because they preached the possibility of changing human mentality through new forms of social coexistence, mutual assistance, and cooperation. According to such views, the new society should grow up from the bottom, via new forms of popular self-government, and thus should be based on such social structures and renovated thinking in order to provide a worthy alternative to the status quo. Given such an evolution of 'democratic' ideas after the disintegration of the USSR, many 'democrats' started to criticize Yel`tsin's policy, the aim of which, in their view, was to leave power with the former *nomenklatura* and to sustain the domination of the former totalitarian stereotypes.

Some such critics, following populist or anarchist ideas, were moving closer to the left or to the previously criticized ex-official Soviet trade unions, as well as to various forms of alternative people's movements, like the Greens, self-government committees, or independent trade unions. These

---

[55] It was widely believed that 'the unprecedented power of the mafia in our country objectively proceeds from the one-party form of government and is fuelled by the super-centralized state economy' (*Grazhdanin*, 9 (Apr. 1990), 14), and that 'the imperial policy of the centre, which ignored national peculiarities and suppressed national identity, is currently aggravating the nationalities issue' ('Put` progressa i sotsial`noy demokratii', 10).

groups were seen as the real and visible shoots of the people's self-government which were restoring the spirit of cooperation, and thus were capable of changing the totalitarian mentality and improving the situation in the country. It is of interest that today many former anarchist leaders work in the Federation of Independent Trade Unions, a former official Soviet organization, while many former leaders of the socialists and even of the Democratic Union openly cooperate with the Communist Party of the Russian Federation and other radical groups of Communist and even ultra-nationalist 'patriotic' orientation.

5.10. CONCLUSIONS

Notwithstanding the substantial differences in the interpretation of the Soviet system among the members of 'democratic' groups, there were several basic beliefs about its characteristic features which were shared by all or at least most of the 'democrats'. All or some of these features were usually mentioned when members of a 'democratic' group discussed the Communist regime or Soviet totalitarianism:

1. The division of society into two opposing classes: the rulers, or collective owners of property, and the ruled, who lacked even the most basic rights;
2. Repression—an inherent policy of the rulers preconditioned by the need to secure their domination as the Soviet Union lagged ever further behind the outside world;
3. The basic defectiveness of such a system as compared to the more efficient Western system—the system itself was seen as the major reason for the nation's crisis;
4. The basic similarity between this system and the totalitarianism of Nazi Germany, pre-capitalist Asian and African societies, and in some cases pre-revolutionary Russia;
5. The destructive effects which the Soviet system inflicted on human personality and thinking.

Definitions of Soviet society based on such characteristics, were widely disseminated in the policy statements of 'democratic' groups throughout the country. While differing in details, the main contents followed the above formulations.

This analysis of the attitudes of Russian 'democrats' toward the state and social organization of the USSR leads to the conclusion that such beliefs emerged as a result of the mixed influence of official Soviet Marxism and contemporary Western ideologies. However, while the influence of the latter

in most cases manifested itself in terminology and name-changing, the influence of official ideology led to the maintenance of many elements of its structure. This conclusion can be drawn on the basis of the analysis of five main
features of the 'democratic' attitude toward the Soviet state and social structure:

1. The division of society into two classes has as its clear source one of
the central postulates of Marxism, namely Marxist class theory. While the
specific classes in the portrayal of the Soviet Union by the 'democrats' (the
state rulers and the masses) were different from those envisaged by official
Soviet ideology, they were quite standard in writings within the Marxist tradition broadly understood. Therefore, in this case the influence of 'democratic'
theories cannot be traced at all.

2. The belief that repression is the determinative characteristic of Soviet
society can be understood as a result of direct life experience. However, it was
part and parcel of the official Soviet ideology to see repression against the
'working people' as a distinctive trait of the capitalist West and to an even
greater extent of the worst imperialist regimes, such as Nazi Germany or
'fascism' in general. The Western media and some Western theories of Soviet
society viewed repression as one of the main traits of Communism. All three
influences could have played a role in this case and here it is possible to speak
of a mixture of sources for this particular belief of the 'democrats'.

3. The third belief can be understood as the complete reverse of the official Soviet dichotomy of real socialism and capitalism, in which socialism
was superior as a higher stage of social development, while capitalism was
historically bound to decay and give way to socialism.

4. Equating the Soviet regime with Nazism was primarily based on the
postulate in Soviet ideology that Nazism was the worst possible social
system, and only on a secondary level on Western theories of totalitarianism,
which were made easier to accept precisely because of this well-known postulate. However, the very necessity of such an equation came from life experience and from the eagerness to justify political struggle against the
Communist regime. Comparisons of the USSR with Asian societies and pre-
1917 Russia were common in non-orthodox Marxist writings, some of which
(such as those of Georgiy Plekhanov) were published in the USSR. So when
similar comparisons came to Russia from Western literature, in which they
were also quite common, their acceptance was already well prepared.

5. The belief about the destructive impact of the Soviet system on human
personality was to a great extent the inversion of the official Soviet concept
of the creation of a new man under socialism, but it was also partly influenced
by concepts of totalitarianism and some modern psychological theories.

The greatest deviation from official Soviet ideology, as well as from most
earlier Russian anti-government movements, that can be found in the beliefs

of most Russian 'democrats' about the Soviet state and social structure is their suggestion regarding the tactics of political struggle, namely their rejection of violence. Revolutionary violence was advocated by a majority of pre-1917 Russian opposition movements, including the Westernizing ones. This was the case not only in the nineteenth century, when revolutionary violence was commonly advocated by opposition movements in Europe, but also at the beginning of this century, when terror and armed rebellion were openly supported by most anti-government parties. Even the most pro-Western and liberal of them, the Constitutional Democrats, while not supporting terrorism, at the same time refused to reject it openly. At the time such a refusal could not be accepted by any Western liberal. Although, as shown above, some Russian 'democrats' of the *perestroyka* period at times spoke in favour of violence and armed struggle, they were a tiny minority; the vast majority of them, continuing the tradition of Soviet 'dissidents', rejected violence, which they saw as a distinctive feature of totalitarianism. However, as will be argued in Chapter 8, rejection of violence was only partially a result of the influence of Western liberalism; to a great extent, it was a position which Russian 'democrats' shared with the dominant Soviet political culture.

6

The Ideal Society: Interpretations of Democracy

6.1. 'DEMOCRACY' AND 'COMMUNISM' IN THE LATE SOVIET PERIOD

The term 'democracy', unlike many other terms which were widely used by the Russian 'democrats', like 'totalitarianism', 'nomenklatura', 'partocracy', and others, was not officially banned in the USSR as a way of defining the Soviet political system. On the contrary, the Soviet political system was officially considered to be democratic, and the kind of democracy practised in the USSR was supposed to be its highest form: socialist democracy. Because of this, the use of the term by 'democrats' did not mean open confrontation with the authorities. By contrast, the use of the term 'totalitarianism' with respect to the USSR immediately signified open opposition. Practically everybody in the USSR during the *perestroyka* period, from Stalinists to members of the radically nationalist Pamyat`, declared themselves supporters of different forms of democracy. However, not everyone called himself a 'democrat'.

According to official Soviet ideology, 'democracy', like all other social phenomena, was considered to be a 'class category'. This meant that the character of democracy, a political regime which was supposed to exist at various levels of social development, was determined by the ruling class of the given society. Thus, in keeping with the theory of social evolution, ancient or slave democracy was replaced by feudal and later bourgeois democracy, and they in turn were bound to be replaced by socialist democracy. The class character of democracy determined the fundamental difference between socialist democracy, which allegedly flourished in the countries of the Soviet bloc, and the bourgeois democracy of Western capitalist states. While the latter was considered to be a mere cover for the domination of the bourgeoisie, the former was seen as an expression of the self-government of the working people and a transitional period to communism, when, according to Karl Marx and Friedrich Engels, 'the free development of each is the condition of the free development of all'.[1]

---

[1] Karl Marx and Frederick Engels, 'Manifesto of the Communist Party', in Karl Marx and Frederick Engels, *Selected Works* (Moscow: Progress Publishers, 1969), i. 127.

The official Soviet notion of 'communism' is vital for the understanding of the Russian 'democratic' approach to democratic society. This official concept was quite unclear in its own right and, especially in the post-Stalin period, was based not so much on the multiple and often contradictory descriptions of the final stage of human development by Marx and Engels but more on its definition given in the Programme of the CPSU which was adopted by the Twenty-second Congress of the CPSU and contained characteristic features of Khrushchev's utopianism. According to this definition, which had to be learnt by heart by every Soviet schoolchild and university student,

Communism is a classless social system with one form of public ownership of the means of production and full social equality of all members of society; under it, the all-round development of people will be accompanied by the growth of the productive forces through continuous progress in science and technology; all sources of public wealth will gush forth abundantly, and the great principle 'From each according to his ability, to each according to his needs' will be implemented. Communism is a highly organised society of free, socially conscious working people in which public self-government will be established, a society in which labour for the good of society will become the prime vital requirement of everyone, a necessity recognised by one and all, and the ability of each person will be employed to the greatest benefit of the people.[2]

Four main components of this official definition of communism were the most important. Communism was seen as the perfect society, a society: (1) based on the continuous progress of science and technology; (2) of freedom, based on social awareness and active participation in self-government; (3) of full social equality and social justice; (4) of material prosperity for all (where all sources of public wealth will gush forth abundantly); (5) of spiritual perfection (the wholistic development of the person); (6) of collectivism and a high level of organization. The following analysis shows that in their understanding of 'democracy' Russian 'democrats', while rejecting Soviet collectivism, maintained and developed all the other main components of the official understanding of a perfect society.

6.2. THE DEMOCRACY OF 'CIVILIZED' SOCIETY AND SOCIALIST DEMOCRACY

The most important difference between the understanding of democracy by Russian 'democrats' and that of the supporters of 'real socialism' lay in the

---

[2] *Programme of the Communist Party of the Soviet Union (Draft)* (Moscow: Foreign Languages Publishing House, 1961), 51.

former's transcending the class interpretation. Their new interpretation was, in turn, a result of disillusionment with the contemporary state of Soviet society, contrasted with the, in every respect more successful, 'Western' or 'civilized' society. Dissatisfaction with one's own society, common to all members of the opposition, resulted in the questioning of its official theoretical basis. The supremacy of 'civilized' Western society, deeply rooted in the thinking of the opposition, prompted it to turn to the ideology which provided the underpinnings for such a society as a positive example. As the programme of one of the 'democratic' groups put it: 'It is obvious today that the theory and practice of "building Communism" (and its first stage—socialism) have proved to be totally groundless. In all democratic countries people live more freely, more prosperously, and more honestly.'[3]

If everything was that much better in 'democratic' countries, it was only natural to think that the USSR needed the same kind of democracy, and not its homespun socialist democracy, which had not resulted in anything positive. From that point it was only one step to the acceptance of democracy as something capable of 'transcending class' and 'transcending the nation'. This step did not necessarily mean a rejection of socialism, which could be understood as a form of society even more 'progressive' than Western 'capitalism', as official Soviet ideology claimed. But the 'democrats' rejected the claim of Soviet officials that existing Soviet society had already reached this highest stage of social development. 'Real socialism' was moved either to the West or to the future. Though the acknowledgement of democracy as something which transcends class did not automatically lead to a rejection of socialism, it did lead to a decisive rejection of the CPSU. At the first stage, the search for 'genuine' democracy was conducted within what was understood as Leninism or Lenin's ideas, from which Stalinists supposedly departed later on. One of the authors of a bulletin of the Krasnoyarsk Committee for Assistance to Perestroyka, Pavel Novoselov, put it this way: 'We were mistaken, led by the politically blind. To take the right road we should go back to the original source—to Lenin, to the ideas of building socialist society on the basis of full democracy and people's power.'[4]

Later, with the accumulation of information on Lenin's real policies and his attitude toward democracy, Leninism was interpreted more and more as a direct source of Stalinism and thus was also blamed for the country's straying from the path of world civilization and for its backwardness. Arguing with those 'democrats' who still saw the reasons of the crisis in a departure from Leninism Kryskin asked: 'Is it not too late? The system is morally (as well as

---

[3] 'Programma Demokraticheskoy partii Rossii', in Rossiysko-amerikanskiy universitet, Institut massovykh politicheskikh dvizheniy, *Rossiya: partii, assotsiatsii, soyuzy, kluby. Spravochnik*, 10 vols. (Moscow: RAU-Press, 1991–2), ii. 12.

[4] Pavel Novoselov, 'Real`naya demokratiya—vlast` sovetam', *Pravo Golosa*, July 1988, 18.

materially) exhausted and it is not possible to revive it by any "return to pure Leninism", to the so-called "sources". The global experience of political and economic democracy, of economic and political freedom, is our main and most important contemporary leader and teacher.'[5]

For these Russian 'democrats', the ideal to follow was no longer the socialism of Lenin's theory, the abandonment of which was initially thought to be the reason for the crisis of 'real socialism', but the political system of real capitalism, which was associated with the 'civilized' 'Western' world. It is no coincidence that people like Kryskin described Western democracy in terms which Soviet ideologists used to describe only Lenin, Stalin, or the Communist Party, calling it 'our leader and teacher'. The non-critical attitude toward the 'highest' ideology survived, though the ideology itself changed. Since 'socialist democracy' could not ensure prosperity, did not fulfil its own promises, since the official Marxist theory failed to achieve its aims, that theory and that form of democracy were abandoned, but the ideals remained.

6.3. DEMOCRACY AS AN AIM AND AS A MEANS

The understanding of democracy as a means of achieving these lofty purposes, as a tool in the struggle for a more progressive society, is an important feature of the world-view of the Russian 'democratic' movement. The main aim here was not political democracy as such, but a more perfect society. Though the democratic organization of such a society was considered to be one of its important traits, it did not constitute the main reason why the movement aimed at this ideal.

'Democracy' in a broader sense meant the social ideal itself. Various descriptions of democratic society by 'democratic' activists make it possible to pick out four main elements of their concept, which can be provisionally identified as: (1) freedom (sometimes interpreted as 'democracy' in the narrow sense); (2) justice; (3) well-being; and (4) spiritual and moral perfection. The most evident differences among 'democrats' of different trends (for example, between socialists and supporters of 'Western capitalism') can be found in the interpretations of freedom and justice. Well-being was generally understood in a similar way as high living standards based on an efficient economy. Such an abstract idea as 'spiritual and moral perfection' is hard to define. However, it can be mentioned that Christian Democratic groups tended to stress the necessity of a return to faith while socialists had in mind the realization of one's creative abilities. In any case, despite the differences,

---

[5] Yevgeniy Kryskin, 'Apriornost` marksistskoy futurologii', in Yevgeniy Kryskin, *Demokratiya i antidemokratiya v Penze*, p. 64.

all four elements can be found in most variants of 'democratic' political subculture.

The analysis of people's understandings of democracy is hampered by the fact that sometimes the term was used in a broader sense, and all the above-mentioned elements were included in it, while in other cases 'democracy' was used as a synonym of one of them. In the narrow sense 'democracy' could also mean the methods for achieving this ideal society. Thus, one can find two different usages of the term: (1) to indicate specific political procedures and structures which were worked out in the 'Western' or 'civilized' world; (2) to indicate an ideal 'progressive' society, for which one should strive. It is interesting that in everyday usage a third meaning also existed: the very activities which were aimed at achieving this ideal, the whole way of life of a democrat, could also be called 'democracy'. A 'democrat' was someone who was 'doing' democracy. Thus, according to the Democratic Union activist from Krasnoyarsk, Oleg Obryadin, he was expelled from university for 'being engaged in democracy'.[6]

6.4. DEMOCRACY AS FREEDOM FROM STATE CONTROL

Freedom was understood by Russian 'democratic' activists first of all as freedom from state control, as the antithesis of 'non-freedom', which prevailed in a Soviet society most often referred to as totalitarian.[7] Since totalitarian 'non-freedom' was viewed as the rule of a bureaucratic 'state-class', it is only natural that the opposite situation of freedom was perceived as liberation from this rule. The process of democratization was therefore seen as a struggle with the all-embracing state and the liberation of the whole of society, step by step, from its rule. In its most radical form this argument ran as follows: while previously the society was totally subordinate to the state, now the state should become categorically subordinate to society. The programme of the Democratic Party formulated this idea very clearly:

To secure genuine people's power the state must become subordinate to society, must become an exponent of its interests and must be guided in its legislative activities by the democratically expressed people's will. The development of self-government in economic and political life, reform of economic mechanisms, securing the independence of enterprises and the rights of working collectives are particularly important.[8]

---

[6] Interview with Oleg Obryadin (Krasnoyarsk, 21 Apr. 1994).

[7] For a fuller account of the meaning of 'totalitarian' in the Russian 'democratic' political subculture, see Alexander Lukin, 'Interpretations of Soviet State and Social Structure: Perceptions of Members of the First Russian Democratic Political Groups, 1985–1991', *Demokratizatsiya*, 3 (1995), 365–91.

[8] 'Programma Demokraticheskoy Partii', in *Rossiya: partii, assotsiatsii, soyuzy, kluby*, ii. 4.

Yefim Lyuboshits' formulation of this idea was even more clear-cut: 'Democracy is when the government depends on the people, not the people on the government'.[9]

It was not by chance that the first independent groups started by defending their own rights, by creating and widening a sphere of activities which was independent of the influence of officialdom. Oleg Rumyantsev, a leader of one of these groups, the Moscow club Democratic Perestroyka, wrote: 'Our politicians should have long ago renounced dogmatic interpretations of interests under socialism and acknowledged the real existence of a pluralism of group interests and opinions. . . . And—as an unavoidable consequence—to a certain extent demonopolize the mechanism of power of the administrative apparatus by transforming it into a more democratic organ of public power, based on a political alliance of the major social forces and movements.'[10]

At the beginning of 1988, Rumyantsev, like the majority of 'democratic' activists, did not visualize his aim as putting the entire administrative apparatus under the control of unofficial organizations. He even reassured Communist leaders that within his envisaged union of the CPSU and the new social forces, the Communists would retain their leading position. As long as Gorbachev's policy was seen by 'democrats' as progressive, they argued that their activities supported 'reformist forces within the CPSU'. But the aim of this support from the very beginning was to create a system of independent public control over state power.

An integrated programme for this sort of democratization was put forward by the Democratic Perestroyka activist and founding member of the Memorial society, Yuriy Samodurov.[11] In substance it advocated the creation of civil society by the introduction of freedom of speech and the press. However, such terminology was still avoided, possibly for tactical reasons, as being too 'bourgeois' and likely to cause a sharp reaction on the part of the authorities. Eventually these terms did come to be used, but their usage did not in itself mean total opposition to the CPSU leadership. At first, even the introduction of a multi-party system was grounded on the necessity of an alliance with the 'reformist forces within the CPSU'. However, the target for this alliance's struggle was still the same: what the 'democrat' saw as the all-embracing system of totalitarian state power. Introduction of a multi-party system was seen as the next step in withdrawal from such rule. As Vasiliy Krasulya stated: 'Freedom of speech and the press and the activities of socio-political organizations, independent from the Party apparatus, form one of the conditions of the development of a multi-party system. Civic initiatives and social movements, by acting as opponents of the Party apparatus, help

---

[9] Interview with Yefim Lyuboshits (Moscow, 18 Sept. 1993).

[10] Oleg Rumyantsev, 'O nekotorykh politicheskikh i pravovykh aspektakh dvizheniya samodeyatel'nykh klubov', *Otkrytaya zona*, 4 (Feb. 1988), 8.

[11] Yu. V. Samodurov, 'Zaglavnoe zveno demokratii', *Otkrytaya zona*, 4 (Feb. 1988), 23–4.

progressive forces within the Party itself. For its spiritual revival the Party needs to rely on independent civic movements, such as, for example, popular fronts.'[12]

Not all 'democrats' regarded the introduction of a multi-party system as the basis of democratization. For example, one of the theorists of the Krasnoyarsk Committee for Assistance to Perestroyka, Pavel Poluyan, proposed not the introduction of multi-party elections, but the conducting of general elections to CPSU committees. Poluyan called on people to acknowledge an obvious situation: that the real organs of state power in the USSR were the organs of the CPSU, not of the soviets. By acknowledging that the Communist Party is really the power within the state, he argued, it was possible to democratize the existing system without an abrupt destruction of state power. According to this plan, the CPSU would have retained the right to put forward candidates. This would maintain the Party's ruling position, and keep experienced profession-als in power. At the same time genuine campaigning by several candidates for a single seat would move the system away from stagnation and make the candidates look for ways of devising more effective policies. Poluyan did not reject the multi-party system, but he believed that its 'thoughtless' introduction in Soviet conditions would lead to the destruction of the existing system of power without creating a more effective one. He wrote:

It is possible to achieve the success of *perestroyka* only through the ability of the people to directly influence the ruling apparatus. Bureaucratic reforms can once more leave the people outside of real politics and are utopias, based on the imagi-nary selection of the 'best people'. Again, the projects of socialist parliamentarian-ism are based on the idea of 'introduction' (and in its 'pseudo-revolutionary' variant), without taking into account in the slightest the real mechanism of power which had been developing in our country throughout history. We need to find a third way: where the mechanism of effective control over the ruling bureaucracy is practically implemented and where the expression of the popular will would find its proper place.[13]

The moderate suggestions of Poluyan were directed at the same goal: introduction of public control over the activities of the state apparatus. However, the increasingly radicalized 'democratic' movement chose a differ-ent path. Retaining the CPSU in power and even cooperation with it was becoming less and less popular, while freedom and democracy were more and more understood as the total liquidation of single-party rule and of the entire system of state power connected to it. The DPR programme pointed out:

[12] Vasiliy Krasulya, 'Partiya: vchera, segodnya, zavtra, Tezisy k diskussii', *Grazhdanin*, 4 (May 1989), 12.
[13] Pavel Poluyan, *Ot byurokratii k demokratii* unpubl. MS [Krasnoyarsk, n.d.], p. 9, cour-tesy of the author.

The remaining monopoly of power of the CPSU, and the system created by it, not only prevented the finding of a way out of the deadlock, but by instigating tensions, by preventing democratic reforms, was swiftly leading the country and its economy towards collapse. The absence of a strong, well-organized, constructive, democratic opposition, which would be able to compete with the CPSU in the struggle for power, could make the situation desperate.[14]

Eventually the idea of defeating the supporters of official policies at the elections was becoming more and more popular. The policy of Gorbachev's leadership itself, which, after the failure of its attempts to democratize the CPSU, turned to the tactic of reducing its power by transferring authority to the soviets, only contributed to this trend. The elections to the soviets were gaining practical significance since the possibility of defeating the CPSU had emerged. To achieve this, the introduction of a whole system of democratic rights and freedoms was needed. Gradually such demands became an integral part of the programmes of 'democratic' organizations, which aimed at the total destruction of the 'totalitarian' system. For example, the electoral programme of the major movement Democratic Russia, which openly called for the 'dismantling of totalitarianism',[15] included the following immediate political demands to the RSFSR Congress of People's Deputies:

1. adoption of a new RSFSR constitution, which should not contradict the UN Declaration of Human Rights and other international agreements on human rights, and the adoption of laws which would guarantee the implementation of these rights;
2. elimination of the CPSU monopoly on power by the abolition of Article 6 of the RSFSR constitution, which provided for this monopoly; elimination of all forms of Communist control at enterprises and institutions; an end to Communist activities in the army, in law enforcement organs, and in the diplomatic service;
3. a guarantee to every Russian citizen of an unconditional right to join parties, organizations, and associations;
4. abolition of the two-level Parliament (Congress of People's Deputies and Supreme Soviet), which was seen as disrupting direct communication between the highest organ of legislative power and the voters;
5. movement from the toleration represented by *glasnost`* to genuine freedom of speech and the press, secured by law;
6. introduction of real freedom of conscience by extending the rights of social organizations to religious communities;

[14] 'Programma Democraticheskoy partii Rossii', 13.
[15] See 'Dvizhenie "Democraticheskaya Rossiya" ' and 'O zadachakh 'Deklaratsiya dvizheniya Democraticheskaya Rossiya', in *Rossiya: partii, assotsiatsii, soyuzi, cluby*, ii. 35 and 37 respectively.

7. reducing the functions of the KGB to the tasks of defence from outside threats and terrorist activities, and effective control of the elected bodies of power over the KGB, Ministry of Defence, and Ministry of Internal Affairs.[16]

Many other programmes contained similar demands, often with reference to international human rights documents.

All these demands may seem very similar to those of liberals all over the world. However, it is hardly enough merely to point out this superficial similarity; the particular beliefs of Russian democrats can be understood only within the broader context of their belief system. It is impossible to understand the fate of the notion of 'democracy', the evolution of the interpretation of this term, and the attitudes of the contemporary Russian political elite toward it without a clear understanding that this set of demands was seen not only as an ideal, though the idealization of democracy was also an important element of attitudes towards it; it was also seen as a tool in the struggle with the contemporary power structure within the framework of the 'statoclasm' or, more precisely, the 'totalitarianoclasm' of Russian 'democrats'. At this stage it was thought that in the process of the struggle it was possible not only to create new groups independent from the 'totalitarian' system, but to chop off from this system certain state organs—for example, the soviets—and to direct them against the system itself. The 'democratic' idea was being formed not on the basis of theoretical knowledge or an acquaintance with existing democracy, but on the basis of the attitudes toward 'totalitarianism' as the focus of evil. 'Democratic' freedoms became an antithesis to the total control of the 'totalitarian', 'bureaucratic' 'class-state' over society. That is why the fundamental point of political reform in the programme of Democratic Russia was described as the 'state for the people, but not the people for the state; the priority of the individual over the interests of the state'.[17]

It is not a coincidence that the right freely to elect and be elected, as well as freedom of speech and public gatherings, which were meant to secure free elections, were often thought to be the most important of all rights and liberties. They were supposed to secure the 'dismantling of totalitarianism'. These very rights were put in first place in most 'democratic' programmes where democracy was discussed. The programme of the Kaliningrad *oblast'* Union of Democratic Forces defined democracy in the following way:

By democracy, according to established interpretations, secured by international agreements, we understand a form of political power which can be characterized by the following features:

—people's rights are guaranteed by freely choosing the form of state power and electing its bodies;

---

[16] 'Predvybornaya programma Izbiratel'nogo bloka "Demokraticheskaya Rossiya" ', in *Rossiya: partii, assotsiatsii, soyusy, kluby*, ii. 42–3.   [17] Ibid. 42.

—the equality of every citizen under the law, which rules out discrimination on the grounds of nationality, social background, religious beliefs, or political views.[18]

The idea that the right to elect is the basis of democracy was deeply rooted among Russian 'democrats'. Valeriy Fadeev, an active member of many Moscow 'democratic' groups, formulated the idea most clearly. He argued that democracy was a 'possibility for the people of a country to take part in making decisions as much as possible. Moreover, on an equal basis. Or, simply put . . . general direct elections by secret ballot'. According to Fadeev, the separation of powers is only a specific form of democracy, and such forms can be different. He argued: 'I would insist on proceeding from the sources, from the origins, from the genesis, from the genealogy of democracy. Democracy emerges at the moment when people put their secret ballot into the ballot box, when we, supporting this or that programme, this or that person, all take part in an act of electing. And everything else. . . . I mean that this form can be a constitutional monarchy, anything you like. But the main thing is elections.'[19]

In a similar way Vorob`ev regarded as democratic a system where people are allowed to choose between several parties and thus express their opinion. Therefore he thought that democracy was indivisible from a multi-party system.[20]

However, elections according to the rules of the system were not considered to be an ideal option for every occasion. Some 'democratic' groups eventually came to the conclusion that elections within the framework of the 'totalitarian' system could only lead to the strengthening of the system, and proposed the creation of other power structures, which would constitute an alternative to the existing 'illegal' organs of the Communist regime. Such an evolution was experienced by the Democratic Union, which began by acknowledging the necessity of transferring power to the existing soviets and finished with a boycott of elections to these soviets and a call for elections to an alternative Constituent Assembly. Anarchist groups from the very beginning did not recognize these bodies of the 'totalitarian' state and called for elections to such alternative organs as gatherings or councils of working people, which were supposed to form higher-level soviets by delegating representatives. The place of the existing 'unitary centralized state', according to anarchists, should be taken by a 'federation of autonomous self-governed communities'.[21] Some even proposed to put aside elections

---

[18] 'Programmnoe polozhenie o deyatel'nosty Ob'edinennogo demokraticheskogo dvizheniya Kaliningradskoy oblasti', *Vestnik 'Solidarnosti'*, 29 (Nov. 1989), 2.

[19] Interview with Valeriy Fadeev (Moscow, 13 Aug. 1993).

[20] Interview with Fedor Vorob`ev (Belinskiy, 5 Apr. 1994).

[21] 'Programmnyy dokument Konfederatsii Anarkho-Sindikalistov', in B. I. Koval` (ed.), *Rossiya segodnya. Politicheskiy portret, 1985–1990* (Moscow: Mezhdunarodnye otnosheniya, 1991), 257. See also 'Deklaratsiya moskovskoy organizatsii Anarko-kommunisticheskiy revolyutsionnyy soyuz', in ibid. 264–5.

altogether, since 'the majority opinion is not always the truth'. They argued that 'in the event of actions by communities of people, decisions should not be adopted by voting, but initiatives should be supported *individually*'.[22]

However, the dominant opinion was that democracy was a system based on implementing the majority will, as opposed to minority rule, which was characteristic of 'totalitarianism'. One activist, rejecting the interpretation of democracy as a guarantor of minority rights, wrote: 'Democracy is, however, the right of the majority to assert its position, to build their life in the way they feel comfortable. The rights of the minorities in this situation may be guaranteed to a higher or lower extent or not guaranteed at all. The latter situation would indicate the imperfection and vulgarity of democracy. But no minority rights must suppress the right of the majority—or this will be a retreat from democracy.'[23]

That is why the idea of elections was put forward. Even the Democratic Union and the anarchists, refusing to take part in the state-conducted elections, which in their view could strengthen the 'state-bureaucratic system', called for elections to alternative bodies of authority and did not reject the idea of elections itself. In some cases, however, the utilitarian attitude of Russian 'democrats' toward 'democracy' as a means of achieving an ideal could well lead to a paradoxical rejection of specific democratic procedures in order to secure the advent of 'freedom' and 'democracy' as an ideal. Valeriya Novodvorskaya, the Democratic Union leader, made this step very early. Novodvorskaya rated the destruction of the 'totalitarian' state and her own ideal of freedom 'as it exists in the West' higher than democratic procedures as they are known in the West. She was afraid that the majority of the population could vote in general elections against 'democrats' and for a return to 'totalitarianism'. In her opinion, the danger was too grave to permit free elections in the country before a certain degree of stabilization and development of civil society took place. According to Novodvorskaya, 'The stakes are too high, and now there is no time to care for trifles. To care for the right of the people to decide on its fate. It was decided in 1918 in this country and in 1933 in Germany. By constitutional means . . . It is too much of a good thing'.[24] Such moods, which were quite rare at the time, became widespread after 'democrats' came to power and it was feared that the reforms were not supported by the majority of the population.

This fear of elections was based on the belief of some 'democrats' in the low level of political awareness of the population of the Soviet Union (often as opposed to that of the 'civilized world'). Thus, Yevgeniy Grachev argued

---

[22] 'Pis`mo A. Karpova. Sotskomitet (Leningrad)', *Informatsionnyy byulleten' Sotsial-demokraticheskoy Assotsiatsii*, 22 Mar. 1990, 2.

[23] P. Fishman, 'Sotsial-demokratiya i klassoviy podkhod', *Kaplya*, 11 (2 June 1990), 10–11.

[24] Valeriya Novodvorskaya, *Po tu storonu otchayaniya* (Moscow: Novosti, 1993), 263–4.

that while 'clever people think about this and that, our people are basically like sheep: they go where their herd is led.'[25] According to Mariya Sublina, however developed democracy may become, the people cannot and never will rule directly, so they should be directed by good leaders: 'In fact, the people should work. For all that, they still should be led by some kind of instructors, leaders should direct them. But the leaders should be extremely upright with respect to the people.'[26] It is quite clear that these decent and upright people could not be corrupt Communists, but only 'democrats'.

While there existed a consensus among practically all 'democratic' groups in seeing political freedom as part of democracy, they differed in their approach to 'democratic reforms' in the economy. Members of the Socialist Party proposed to transfer property from the 'state-class' to the local soviets, since, in their view, this would mean the spread of democracy to the economic sphere. The Socialists believed that the road to the liberation of man proceeds through the liberation of labour, and to achieve this aim it was necessary to overcome economic and social alienation. This is impossible to achieve in a society where state-bureaucratic or private-capitalist forms of property dominate. To overcome alienation they proposed the introduction of 'industrial and public self-government, which is based on collective forms of property and public-state regulation of the economy'.[27] The term 'alienation' was directly borrowed from the writings of Marx.

Anarcho-syndicalists called for 'the transfer of the means of production to the full disposal of working collectives'.[28] They based this demand on the understanding of freedom as the right of the individual to take part in making decisions that concern him or her, including economic questions, and on the idea that any mediators, either state or private owners, were intolerable. Competition was permitted only as a necessary evil and its 'victims' were thought to have the right to receive assistance from society.

The supporters of 'Western capitalism' believed that the 'economic freedoms of a citizen' could only be secured by a 'market economic system' and 'private property'. This belief was based on the idea that 'since a free individual himself bears the responsibility for his fate, in a free society of free people the state should not strive to solve any of the problems of its citizens, and should be guided by the principle: the freedom of an individual finishes where the freedom of another individual begins. As for everything else— food, clothes, accommodation, and work—a free man should worry about himself'.[29] Despite such differences in the understanding of economic

[25] Interview with Yevgeniy Grachev (Belinskiy, 5 Apr. 1994).
[26] Interview with Mariya Sublina (Moscow, 28 Aug. 1993).
[27] [Sotsialisticheskaya Partiya[, 'Put` k svobode. Programma Sotsialisticheskoy partii. Proekt' unpubl. MS, [Moscow, (1990)], 10.
[28] 'Programmnyy dokument Konfederatsii Anarkho-Sindikalistov', 257.
[29] 'Programma Demokraticheskoy partii Rossii', 14.

democracy, all 'democratic' groups shared one fundamental belief: property rights should be removed from the centralized 'state-class', from the 'bureaucracy', which was seen as a collective owner of all means of production. Economics should be cut loose from the totalitarian monster. As long as the 'state-class' existed and was trying to keep property in its hands, the 'democrats' could all work together. The disappearance of this common enemy, and the necessity to solve the question of whom the property rights should belong to, would inevitably lead to a split.

In the same way 'democratic' freedom was associated with reducing territory under totalitarian control and destroying totalitarian 'order'. That is why for many Russian 'democrats' the term 'democracy' implied the idea of the division of the 'empire' and a certain amount of 'disorder' which would replace the totalitarian 'order'. This can be seen in the discourse of one of the most active members of the 'democratic' Inter-regional Group of Deputies, Vladislav Shapovalenko, who admitted that he could not call himself a pure 'democrat' because he wanted Russia to stay united: 'Despite all my theoretical democratic credentials, I do not want Russia to become just Novgorod and Moscow. Though Siberia was conquered by Yermak, I believe it also to be Russia. I have not been a good democrat. I have not been a good Communist either. I want both and sometimes I catch myself thinking that I want democracy and order at the same time.'[30]

This 'democratic' belief that promoting the unity of the country and its orderly development—indeed, all questions of national pride and national interests—were the prerogatives of the opposing camp of Communists or 'patriots' (of the 'red and brown' as they were labelled by 'democrats') made it very difficult for any 'democratic' group to include such questions on its agenda. Those who tried to do it, like the DPR under the leadership of Nikolay Travkin, the RCDM under Viktor Aksyuchits, and the CDP–PPF under Mikhail Astaf ev, were attacked by the majority of the 'democratic' movement for betraying 'democracy' and siding with 'patriots' and later in fact found themselves in the 'patriotic' camp. The situation changed only much later, when President Yel`tsin and the new Russian leadership, well after coming to power, gradually began incorporating 'patriotic' positions into their agenda, claiming that 'democrats' could promote Russia's national interests and protect its territorial integrity.

6.5. DEMOCRACY AS JUSTICE

Alongside freedom, justice was a fundamental ideal of the members of the 'democratic' groups. Justice was understood first of all as social justice,

---

[30] Interview with Vladislav Shapovalenko (Orenburg, 21 Dec. 1994).

which in the Soviet context meant depriving the 'ruling bureaucracy' of privileges. In this sense the term 'social justice' was either used as a synonym of 'democracy', or was understood as its integral part. Political democracy, elections in particular, were often seen as a method of eliminating the unjust system of distribution, of the 'feudal' system of privileges of the 'ruling class'. As Novoselov put it:

The block over which people were stumbling and which no society could overcome is the unjust distribution of material wealth. The surplus product must become the property of society but not of the 'servants' of the people, who leech off it. The removal of the privileges of the ruling strata is the main task that should be implemented first of all! Just distribution should be implemented by the people itself, who entrust this function to its elected representatives. The material basis of society— under the strictest control of the people! As long as there are people in the leadership whose interests are in contradiction to the ideas of *perestroyka*, one cannot expect genuine democratization and social justice. Only people's power can move *perestroyka* further.[31]

Striving for the elimination of injustice in the system of distribution as the main task of democratization was widespread throughout the 'democratic' movement. In many cases the demand for an end to the privileges of ruling officials became the basis for the growth in popularity of new independent groups which had disclosed the existence of these privileges and demanded 'the return of what was stolen to the people'. This was fuelled by a growing awareness of social inequalities, despite official claims about general equality under socialism. A draft declaration by the Penza Popular Front for Support of Perestroyka shows this very clearly:

Today we, under the present circumstances of the thawing of social relations, confirm the task of limiting and ideally of eliminating the revivified socio-political inequality. It is the fifth year of *perestroyka* already, but the fulfilment of the tasks of social justice and democratization is as distant as ever; the election of authorities is more the exception than the rule; and at a time when all other segments of the population feel the lack of ordinary products and normal services, within the administrative-command elite the shameful system of food distribution and special medical service is still in practice. To engage the population in the collective appointment of personnel to state positions, including the positions of People's Deputies, to remove the atmosphere of secrecy from this most important task—what can be more important for the Fatherland at this moment?[32]

The elimination of privileges in this sense was seen as a key to democratization and as the main goal of the struggle of the oppressed class, which had nothing to lose. On the contrary, as one 'democratic' editorial put it, those

---

[31] Novoselov, 'Real`noye narodovlastie—vlast'sovetam', 16.

[32] 'Deklaratsiya ob obrazovanii Penzenskogo fronta v podderzhku perestroyki. Proekt', *Penzenskiy Grazhdanin*, 10 (Dec. 1989), 10.

who dislike us and call us the supporters of a 'bourgeois way of life' have something to lose, namely those privileges, about which at some time it will be said what character they possess, either bourgeois, or, perhaps, feudal, and what contradictions in society they produce. These contradictions exist, they permanently manifest themselves, obviously or latently, and more or less permanently push us towards confrontation, which will not disappear unless social justice, declared some time ago, triumphs, and the severe monopoly of certain uncontrolled groups on power and information in the country vanishes.[33]

Though naturally not everyone thought that the fight against privileges was the main task of reforms and democratization, practically all 'democratic' groups included such demands in their programmes because of their extraordinary popularity. According to a less radical camp only 'unjustified' privileges should be abolished, and these would die out automatically if property were removed from the ruling apparatus. Pavel Poluyan, for example, believed that

the levelling demands like 'Deprive the apparatchiks of their privileges!'—with their moral zeal—are nevertheless illusory. Political power will always be connected with certain privileges. It is only necessary that the people know who can do what, and that the privileges are gained not by bureaucratic rank, but by productive political activities, and are commensurate with the responsibility of the post. It is precisely for this that a democratic, legally fixed evaluation procedure for those who enjoy privileges is needed.[34]

Both positions agreed on one point: the law should be higher than the whims of the leaders and even if somebody was to enjoy privileges, his or her right to do so should be fixed by law. Demands for adherence to the law became one of the important components of the 'democratic' programme for securing social justice. The source of these demands was often not a theoretical belief in the necessity of the 'supremacy of law' as the basis of democracy, but the dissatisfaction of many 'democratic' activists, including those who worked or used to work in high official positions, with the immunity from normal jurisdiction enjoyed by Communist officials and with the flouting of the law by the ruling *nomenklatura*. This immunity sharply contradicted the official Soviet concept of 'socialist legality'. Moreover, as noted in Chapter 3, many informal groups started their work by defending persons who had been illegally fired or otherwise oppressed for political activity, and were even headed by people who were waging a lengthy struggle with the authorities for their own rights. In that struggle they had only one basis—the law—while the authorities were using illegal methods of exerting pressure.

Belief in the rule of law was fundamental to 'democratic' thinking. Vladimir Yelistratov, for example, recalled that 'when I nominated myself as

[33] 'Redaktsionnaya', *Penzenskiy Grazhdanin*, 1 (Mar. 1989), 3.
[34] Pavel Poluyan, 'Ot byurokratii k demokratii', *Pravo Golosa*, July 1988, 22.

a candidate to the *oblast*' and town soviets I argued that I saw my activities as a deputy not as managerial or administrative, but as legal: my task would be to check on the enforcement of laws. I understood democracy as people's power which was manifested in the power of the relevant elected body. By the way, all these ideas were formulated at the meetings of this club during its three years of activities.'[35] According to a Democratic Russia activist from Orenburg, Aleksandr Romanov, 'in democratic society all laws must be enforced and the majority of the population take part in administration by voting for a legislative assembly'.[36]

However, in 'democratic' thinking belief in the rule of law was indivisible from the concept of social justice. The rule of law was seen not as a value in itself, but as an instrument for fighting the corruption and privilege of the ruling elite or for the promotion of an abstract moral or spiritual ideal (see below). Thus, Klepachev stressed that even before organizing a democratic group he thought that social justice should be implemented: 'everyone should be equal before the law and nature'.[37] An activist in the Oktyabr`skiy District Union of Voters in Moscow, Yuriy Belkin, suggested his own criterion for the democratic character of a state's laws: 'If these laws are conducive to human needs, I regard such a state to be democratic. But if these laws contradict human demands or morality, then by no means can it be called democratic.'[38]

The criteria of democracy here are not formal, but moral and idealistic. The same criteria were suggested by Yeykin, who maintained that while freedom, which constitutes the basis of democracy, meant the equality of everyone before the law, laws at the same time 'should be just'.[39]

It is only natural that securing justice should have become one of the important factors in the activities of such groups. The idea of 'a law-based state' as an integral part of democracy fell on well-prepared ground. Those who in pre-*perestroyka* times would have become classic Soviet fighters for social justice, spending their lives in the waiting-rooms of numerous offices and in courtrooms in hopeless attempts to get reinstated in their former jobs or to prove their cases, adopted a new tactic after getting acquainted with democratic ideas from the *perestroyka*-era press. They readily declared themselves supporters of democracy, precisely because democracy proposed equality before the law. The interpretation of a 'law-based state' not only as a theoretical concept, but as an effective tool in the struggle with bureaucracy and arbitrary rule, can be seen in many programmatic documents of 'democratic' groups. The programme of the Democratic Party, for example, stated:

[35] Interview with Vladimir Yelistratov (Belinskiy, 5 Apr. 1994).
[36] Interview with Aleksandr Romanov (Orenburg, 22 Dec. 1994).
[37] Interview with Nikolay Klepachev (Krasnoyarsk, 19. Apr. 1994).
[38] Interview with Yuriy Belkin (Moscow, 15 Sept. 1993).
[39] Interview with Vitaliy Yeykin (Orenburg, 22 Dec. 1994).

The formation of a law-based state cannot be separated from the development of democracy. The self-government of the people can only be implemented under the supremacy of law, which excludes arbitrary rule and anarchy, or any manifestations of wilfulness by the officials. The law-based state is not only one of the highest social values, meant to establish the humanistic foundations of civilized society, but is also a practical tool for securing and defending the freedom, honour, and dignity of the individual, a means of struggle against bureaucracy and the excessive power of regional and departmental authorities [*mestnichestvo* and *vedomstvennost`*], a way to implement genuine people's power.[40]

Here one can see a combination of external sources (one of the highest values of civilized society) and internal Soviet ones (a practical means of struggle against such domestic Soviet shortcomings as bureaucracy and the conflict of interests between different regional and departmental authorities, a struggle in which the concept of the law-based state takes the place of 'socialist legality'). The interpretations of the law-based state as an alternative to the lawlessness of 'totalitarianism' led to an understanding of the supremacy of law first of all as a means of struggle against the party-state system. Thus, the programme of the Democratic Party identifies as potential lawbreakers only the Party and state organs: 'In a law-based state a law which has been adopted by the supreme body of power cannot be repealed, changed, or suspended either by departmental orders, including government decrees, or by a decision of party organs. All party organizations and their organs must act on that basis and within the framework of the USSR constitution, within the framework of law.'[41]

Observance of the law was demanded first of all of the 'partocratic' state, since this state was believed to be the main obstacle to establishing law and democracy, i.e. it was unjust. But should 'democrats' themselves observe the law, especially if it is clearly 'anti-democratic' and 'unjust'? This question was debated within the 'democratic' movement, and with the radicalization of the movement a belief that it was necessary to observe the law only if it was 'democratic' and 'just' became more and more popular. For 'democrats' law was not a value as such, but legality ought to be based on justice, and since justice, in their opinion, was inseparable from democracy, the laws should be 'democratic'. This idea was clearly expressed by one of the most educated 'democrats', Leonid Volkov, at a meeting of the Democratic Perestroyka Club. The meeting was devoted to supposedly undemocratic decrees on demonstrations, designed to limit and regulate them. In Volkov's opinion,

the main point of the idea of a law-based state is connected to the fact that it is a social system where the law stands not only above the citizen, not only above the society, but also above the state, above state power, and where legality even stands above specific laws. Because the Law is not just specific laws, but, as was well understood

---

[40] 'Programma Demokraticheskoy partii', 4.   [41] Ibid.

already by the creators of the code of Justinian, is above all wisdom and justice. In a legal state a law submits to the constitution, the constitution submits to the deeper moral demands and social needs of the citizens, and the servants of the state submit to the law and only to the law.[42]

Such an understanding of law unavoidably leads to the conclusion that 'unjust' laws, i.e. laws which do not meet 'moral demands and social needs', are 'illegal'. Since these needs were understood as the elimination of 'totalitarianism' and the establishment of a 'democratic' society, in the opinion of many 'democrats', any law which did not work toward this aim could be set aside. Galina Rakitskaya, a Democratic Perestroyka activist, defended this idea at the meeting:

Only half a year ago we were thinking and saying that democracy was, above all, legality. We associated our hopes with the restoration of the force of law in our country, since for years our people had lived in the conditions of arbitrary rule and lawlessness. The Constitution was not ensured by laws which would have guaranteed the rights and freedoms of citizens. And what do we see now? We see that the laws which are being worked out and adopted are non-democratic. This means that we will have to fight not for legality, but against the laws. Such a struggle is revolutionary. As long as there is no law, one can blame an individual person, an individual bureaucrat, an individual official for wrongdoing. But if laws are undemocratic, dictatorial, laws which are characteristic of a totalitarian state, it becomes clear that the people are confronted by the system as a whole. And a struggle with the system as a whole, but not with individual bureaucrats, is a revolutionary struggle.[43]

Rakitskaya put forward as a task of the 'democratic' movement the creation of alternative structures, like the popular fronts in the Baltic republics and Armenia, 'which in fact are reviving the soviets of the old, revolutionary type . . . If we do not succeed in transforming the existing soviets into organs of "democratic" power, then the way of the revolution, of revolutionary *perestroyka*, should be the creation of alternative power and governmental structures'.[44]

The very course of this discussion is interesting. The proposals of Rakitskaya caused quite a stormy reaction at the meeting, both negative and positive. It is important, however, that the necessity of pursuing the struggle within a legal framework whatever the circumstances was mostly defended by invited specialists in law and social movements from academic circles, who did not belong to 'democratic' groups. For example, a specialist on the labour movement, Professor Leonid Gordon, warned that the denial of legality led to revolutionary violence and that since Russia had already suffered from the revolutionary disease it should be clear that 'there exist only legal

---

[42] 'Problemy pravovogo gosudarstva v SSSR: o prave na sobraniya i demonstratsii' in *Otkrytaya zona*, 9 (April 1989), 40. [43] Ibid. 42.
[44] Ibid.

and non-violent ways'.[45] Igor` Klyamkin, holder of a doctorate in philosophy, legal expert and member of the Human Rights Committee of the Supreme Soviet of the USSR, agreed with Gordon's view. However, every member of a 'democratic' group who took the floor supported the acceptability of refusing to obey 'undemocratic' laws. Aleksandr Shubin, for example, pointed out that it was observance of the existing laws that was prolonging the crisis and leading to a destructive revolt, while non-violent disobedience could save the situation. A member of the Club of Social Initiatives, Gleb Pavlovskiy, argued that 'time was running out and by the evolutionary method we can achieve nothing but a transformation of the reform into a counter-reform'.[46]

The presentations at this meeting clearly show that the idea of a 'law-based state' was perceived by Russian 'democratic' activists as a weapon of struggle with the existing system of 'unjust' and 'immoral' power. The fight for 'just' 'democratic' aims, including paradoxically both 'legality' and a 'law-based state', did not have to be bound by 'undemocratic' laws. Rejecting Bolshevism in general, some more outspoken 'democrats' acknowledged the continuity of this attitude with Bolshevik tactics and even praised the latter. For example, Novodvorskaya stated at the First Congress of the Democratic Union: 'Political struggle should be uncompromising. We can take an example here from the Bolsheviks, who had one virtue: they never compromised with their enemy, autocracy.'[47] Outright rejection towards the official legal system had by 1990–1 become overwhelmingly predominant within the 'democratic' movement. The main method of struggle of the major part of the movement, Democratic Russia, was organizing mass rallies, ignoring official bans.

The understanding of democracy (and of legality as its essential part) as a means to the introduction of justice is highly characteristic of Russian 'democrats'. In this line of argument the notions of 'justice' and 'legality' came before the notion of 'democracy' and were more fundamental. Such an understanding contained the possibility of disillusionment with democracy itself in the event that it did not lead to justice. Not surprisingly, many supporters of social justice and legality left 'democratic' groups and some did indeed become disillusioned with democracy when, after the coming to power of Boris Yel`tsin's 'democratic' leadership, it became clear to them that the politics of the new leadership did not lead to the elimination of privileges and the arrival of justice. On the other hand, putting 'justice' above formal law resulted in neglect of the law by many 'democratic' politicians who found themselves in a position of power if, in their view, the law did not lead to a 'just' settlement of a problem.

---

[45] *Otkrytaya zona*, 9 (April 1989), 49.   [46] Ibid. 53.
[47] 'Den` pervyi: doktrina', *Khronograf*, 4 (18 May 1988), 2–3.

6.6. DEMOCRACY AS PROSPERITY

The understanding of democracy as a means of achieving well-being and as a society of prosperity did not cause any serious differences among 'democratic' activists. Everyone agreed that in 'democratic' countries people enjoyed a life not only of 'greater freedom' and 'greater honesty', but also of 'greater prosperity'. This belief was maintained regardless of whether the existing 'Western' 'democratic' society was interpreted as a perfect ideal, or as a society which was not perfect, but at least closer to this ideal than the real Soviet system. In both cases Soviet society was considered to be relatively poor. Andrey Shcherkin lucidly explained this belief in the prosperity of democratic society by the showcase effect of Western economic success:

We received a very strong stimulus. We could look at, speaking figuratively, the showcase of the Western society of consumption, and we saw it. We believed that political freedoms in the end would provide the Western level of consumption. This was a simplistic view but it explains why the movement at first was quite popular. Literally in a year's time we found out so many bad and unpleasant things about the regime, which was misanthropic and totalitarian, and at the same time we saw the result which had been achieved by the democratic countries.[48]

Sometimes the belief in Western prosperity was expressed quite directly, as in the highly questionable claim that the official income even of the leaders of the Soviet regime 'does not exceed the wages of a skilled worker in the developed countries and according to their criteria are somewhere close to the poverty line'.[49] Such an idealization of 'Western' prosperity was partly caused by the fact that the main source of understanding of the outside world was in most cases not personal experience but second-hand information. Another important source of this view was the impulse to reject official Soviet propaganda, the falsity of which resulted in a belief that the truth was directly opposite to it, as well as in a great desire to find an alternative to Soviet 'poverty' in 'democratic' society.

The connection between 'democracy' and prosperity in the belief system of Russian 'democrats' contained the seeds of contradiction. If Russian 'democracy' did not lead to prosperity, if 'democratic' Russia remained 'poor', a wish to achieve prosperity by other means could emerge. This was exactly what happened after the coming of the 'democrats' to power. When some of them found out that 'democratic' reforms were unable to secure the level of prosperity of the 'democratic West', theories about the possibility of

---

[48] Interview with Andrey Shcherkin (Pskov, 25 Sept. 1994).

[49] P. V. Kulikov, 'Programmnye orientiry SDPR', in *K uchreditel'nomu s`yezdu Sotsialdemocraticheskoy partii Rossiskoy Federatsii. Sbornik materiyalov No. 1* (Tipografiya Minuralsibstroya, 1990), 30–1.

reaching prosperity by an authoritarian leap towards the market became popular. A temporary abolition of 'democracy' was advocated for the sake of 'democracy' itself. The logic of these arguments was as follows: because of social polarization, which emerged as a result of the market economy, people could vote against reforms. But swift implementation of reforms would lead to a rise in living standards and in the future democracy would gain a strong foothold. In this respect some Russian 'democrats' began to take a positive attitude toward Chilean experience and the figure of General Augusto Pinochet, and changed their views of China, which gradually turned from a symbol of bloody dictatorship into a symbol of successful authoritarian reforms. Novodvorskaya, for example, wrote in this connection: 'I cannot accept political repressions, the limitation of the rights of self-expression. I am not talking of the right to elect. This right to choose between totalitarianism and democracy I am not ready to grant. The risk is too high. Freedom of speech, press, rallies, and gatherings—this is sacred. But everything else— later. After the creation of the middle class, the class of owners, after the victory over the reds, after the past is finally destroyed.'[50] After the collapse of the Soviet Union many former members of 'democratic' groups brought such ideas with them into the organs of power.

6.7. DEMOCRACY AS A 'ROAD TO PERFECTION'

The view of democracy among members of 'democratic' groups as the road to moral and spiritual perfection is hard to define. However, an analysis of the documents of 'democratic groups' and of the discourse of their members shows that an inseparable part of the 'democratic' political subculture was a belief that life in a democratic society was not only 'just', 'prosperous', and 'free', but was also characterized by a deeper meaning, by a possibility of realization of the creative abilities inherent to persons, by a higher level of spiritual and moral feelings, by life without lies and vice. Democracy was understood as a panacea, which could save not only society, but also every single individual, from troubles and misfortunes, from every sin of 'totalitarianism' and 'bureaucratic dictatorship', and bring joy and happiness.

To understand the 'democratic' approach to democracy it is important to bear in mind that the official definition of communism, which already was quite unclear and utopian, became even more obscure and idealistic when transformed by popular beliefs. Kryskin, for example, described what he made of it in the following words:

---

[50] Novodvorskaya, *Po tu storonu otchayaniya*, 262.

The goal of communism is to create the highest culture. This is its main programmatic aim. It is to create the highest level of culture in human society, when people would deliberately refrain from committing crimes and prisons would not be needed. . . . In the 1960s, after the programme of building communism was adopted, this was the opinion one could often see in the newspapers. One person was worried: 'Where will I go when I'm old? I work in the militia, but there won't be any criminals, so I'll be unemployed.' And such things were being seriously discussed.[51]

Kryskin directly compared these feelings of the 1960s about communism with the enthusiasm about the advent of democracy of the *perestroyka* period in 1989–90. He recalled that 'People found themselves in an euphoric state similar to that of Chapaev when he said in the movie: "Eh! You, Pet`ka, are young, you will be happy, and the coming life will be so good that you will never want to die." '[52] It is important to note that in this quotation from the classic Soviet film *Chapaev* (1934) its main character, the Red Army commander Vasiliy Chapaev, is clearly talking about communism, not democracy.

Definitions of 'democratic' society given by 'democratic' activists also described it as heaven on earth, where everyone would live happily, though this happiness was seen to be based on very different foundations from those of communism—not on collectivism but on the rule of law and political freedom. These components of democracy combined the 'democratic' understanding of democracy with some of the official Soviet perceptions of an ideal society.

On this interpretation democracy was again seen as a direct antithesis to the existing Soviet social and state structure. The necessity of finding new principles, new concepts, the implementation of which would lead to a perfect society, was keenly felt in 'democratic' circles. 'Marxism-Leninism gives birth to the "vanity of vanities", and it offers false ideals and ideas. A new theory, a new teaching on the development of mankind must be able to comprehend the existence of a higher reality, which cannot be grasped by common human feeling or reason and which alone gives meaning to our life', wrote Taisiya Kaznacheeva, a member of the Stavropol` Popular Front. Such a theory, in her view, should help to develop the best human qualities:

We must become free people, and above all, begin to feel this in our soul, to wake up from paralysis. And this means returning life to life, human warmth to ideals, light to the soul. Freedom of soul is a manifestation of the Highest Law and Highest Perfection. There are already teachings on earth that can transform people into highly developed beings. Theory must be united with the spirit, which brings shining purity and warmth, and not class intolerance and violence, and does not, to quote Daniil Andreev, 'mix deadly poison with the communion wine'.[53]

---

[51] Interview with Yevgeniy Kryskin (Penza, 3 Apr. 1994).   [52] Ibid.
[53] Taisiya Kaznacheeva, 'Nad propast'yu vo lzhi', *Grazhdanin*, 9 (Apr. 1990), 20.

'Democracy' had become this 'new theory' for Russian 'democrats'. At the beginning they tried to prove, without rejecting the CPSU leadership's goal of building socialism, that the level of 'democracy' inherent in 'existing social-ism' surpasses the level of 'democracy' inherent in 'capitalism', and this would lead not only to higher living standards, but also to a higher morality, and would even wipe out 'lies'. Kryskin asked in this connection:

Let us ask a question: how can we *out-democratize* the West—in the sense of surpass-ing them in the field of genuine democracy?

Only after having adopted such a maximalist goal, which is not sabotaged by a hypocritical postulation of the priority of state interests over private interests, and on the way to this goal, having surpassed the rich capitalist world, having eradicated crime and lies, and having got the economy going, is it possible to call ourselves the inhabitants of a genuinely socialist, but not a social-feudal, not a *nomenklatura-*bureaucratic, world.[54]

The change in attitudes toward the leadership of the CPSU only strength-ened the understanding of democracy as a means of achieving a better, more moral, indeed perfect life. It was democracy which was believed to be the remedy that was able to cure society and individuals of many shortcomings. In an open letter of the Krasnoyarsk Committee for Assistance to Perestroyka one can read: 'Bureaucratism, in particular Communist bureaucracy, is the main obstacle at the moment to the development of democracy and *glasnost`*, which can cure us from our disgusting vices, lies, deception, hypocrisy, corruption, and bribery, and from the tradition of silencing the victims.'[55]

The Russian 'democrats' believed that democracy, because of its pluralist nature, always leads to the selection of the best option as a result of an 'honest' competition of ideas, projects, or economic systems. Such competi-tion was thought to be in sharp contrast to the selecting of 'unwise' and 'harmful' variants as a result of subjective decisions which were being taken in the interests of the ruling bureaucratic class under 'totalitarianism'. Alexander Sukharev, one of the Orenburg organizers of the 'informal' move-ment, wrote about the mechanism of pluralism: 'We recognize victory in a free competition of opinions, positions, actions of free citizens as the only criterion of the correctness of our path, of the verifiability of our attitudes toward the world and toward Russia's place in it'.[56] Kryskin points more particularly to the 'two-party system' as a trait of democracy, which, in his opinion, brings to light 'all the sins which are being committed in a society'.[57]

---

[54] 'Slovo o pol`ze demokratii', *Listok 'Grazhdanskoy initsiativy'*, 4 (24 Mar. 1989), 1.

[55] Krasnoyarskiy komitet sodeystviya perestroyki, 'Otkrytoe pis'mo Krasnoyartsam', unpubl. MS [Krasnoyarsk, 1989], 1; courtesy of Nikolay Klepachev.

[56] Aleksandr Sukharev, 'SDPR. Nashi sovmestnye tsennosti', in *K uchreditel`nomu s`yezdu Sotsial-democraticheskoy partii Rossiskoy Federatsii*, 57.

[57] Kryskin, 'Apriornost` marksistskoy futurologii', in Yevgeniy Kryskin, Demokratiya i antidemokratiya v Penze. Nachab protivostoyaniya (1989–99 gg.) (Penxza, 1992), p. 64.

The Russian social democrats more than once asserted that 'democratic socialism', which differed from the 'existing socialism' in the Soviet Union by embracing the widest democracy, could bring more than just a rich, free, and just life. 'Our goal is a society of democratic socialism, which we understand as a society of the people's self-government, based on a harmonious combination of developed productive forces with social relations that secures for everyone the living standards appropriate for a worthy life and at the same time a society that creates the conditions for a full realization of the creative potential of the individual in any form of human activity,' wrote Aleksandr Obolenskiy, one of the leaders of the Social Democratic Party of Russia (SDPR), a People's Deputy of the USSR, and a founding member of the Voluntary Society for Assistance to Perestroyka in the town of Apatity in Murmansk *oblast*.[58] Another SDPR activist, USSR People's Deputy Nikolay Tutov from Orenburg, proposed the inclusion of the following words in his party's programme: 'The movement towards democratic socialism is an international movement for *freedom*, social *justice*, and solidarity, which aims at building a society where every individual is able to live a life full of meaning, with an unlimited opportunity to develop his own personal qualities and talents and with a guarantee of the realization of civic and human rights.'[59]

The purposes which are being realized through the democratization of the political system are combined here with an abstract moral ideal, a wish to give a person a chance to live 'without lies', to live 'a life full of meaning', to 'fully realize his creative potential', etc. In the opinion of many social democrats, this very ideal could be reached by the combination of democracy and socialism, by including 'Western' democratic political methods in the process of building socialism.

This understanding of democracy was not characteristic only of those who called themselves social democrats. A description of democracy suggested by Ol`ga Shul`cheva shows this combination very clearly:

I think that at that time I understood democratic society as a society which provides man with a space for self-development and for the development of his qualities with no need to fear, to look back, to be too thoughtful. This development should not be limited by anything but law. So, I thought that democratic society was a society which could give man space for developing his essential powers, that is to say of the human essence, it probably cannot be put in a simpler way.[60]

When Shul`cheva, a lecturer in Marxist philosophy, rejected the Soviet regime as 'totalitarian' and 'half-fascist'[61] she also rejected the regime's

---

[58] A. M. Obolenskiy, 'Deklaratsiya o provozglashenii Sotsial-demokraticheskoy partii Rossiyskoy Federatsii', in *K uchreditel`nomu s`ezdu Sotsial-demokraticheskoy partii Rossiyskoy Federatsii*, 26.

[59] N. Titov, 'SDPR, Programmnye orientiry', in *K uchreditel`nomu s`ezdu Sotsial-demokraticheskoy partii Rossiyskoy Federatsii*, 42.

[60] Interview with Ol`ga Shul`cheva (Orenburg, 22 Dec. 1994).   [61] Ibid.

communist ideal. In the process of converting to 'democracy' she obviously transferred her earlier view of the ideal communist society to her new, 'democratic' ideal. At the same time she incorporated into her perception of this new ideal a 'democratic' demand for the rule of law. Within the framework of the resulting synthesis the law had to be just and law was seen not as a value in itself but as means of promoting an ideal society which would provide the conditions for the self-fulfilment of all its members.

Similar definitions of 'democracy' could often be heard from former 'democratic' activists. For example, Mariya Sublina defined the civilized democratic world as the one where people were upright and decent and respected each other.[62] According to Belkin, in a 'democratic' state 'no wishes and needs of one person contradict the wishes and needs of society as a whole. There people have every opportunity for self-expression in creative work, in particular personal aspirations, in the possibility of putting ideas and plans in practice and nobody hinders the realization of these opportunities. In short, anyone can realize his potential. And there are no parties or social forces which can negatively influence the life of society.'[63]

Grigoriy Rayzman described his political ideal at the time of joining the 'democratic' movement in Orenburg in very similar terms. He saw it as a society where 'everyone has a real, absolutely unlimited opportunity to realize his potential, which would depend only on himself, a possibility of exhausting one's potential.'[64] In his view a democratic society was a society where 'such laws operate as promote this goal' and where 'all society, regardless of a person's position in it, implements these laws be they good or bad'.[65] Rayzman's words show the mixture of the instrumental approach to law characteristic of official Soviet ideology with the concept of the rule of law: on the one hand, everyone should obey the laws regardless of status or moral consequences ('be they good or bad'); on the other hand, laws should serve the purpose of promoting a social ideal, i.e. in a way be 'good'. This was not regarded as a contradiction by most 'democrats'.

Many 'democrats' recognized the connection between their understanding of the 'democratic' ideal and the official representation of communism by stressing that the communist ideal was not bad and was not different from the social ideals of previous liberalizing movements, but had not been implemented properly. Thus, according to Rayzman, the essence of the communist ideal was 'Freedom, Equality, Fraternity' but this slogan was 'somehow being wrongly implemented. And then there was a sort of kitchen question. When I saw what they ate and what everyone else ate, despite the propaganda. . . . So I believe we came not to overthrow these ideals but to find another mechanism.'[66]

---

[62] Interview with Sublina.
[63] Interview with Belkin.
[64] Interview with Grigoriy Rayzman (Orenburg, 21 Dec. 1994).
[65] Ibid.
[66] Ibid.

Romanov went even further, arguing that communist ideals were perfect and were borrowed from the Bible and from Athenian and Roman democracy. The problem with them was that they were empty declarations. Romanov argued that many communists who sincerely wanted these ideals to be implemented could be called democrats and this, in his view, explained why many communists gradually joined the 'democratic' movement.[67] Not every 'democrat' however, thought positively of the communist ideal. As shown above, some believed that 'democratic' and communist ideals were very different, even opposite. However, the analysis of the understanding of 'democratic' society, even of those 'democrats' who thought that they had completely rejected the official social ideal, shows a significant element of continuity.

The understanding of democracy as a road to building a perfect society and to the creation of a perfect humanity contained in itself the possibility, or even inevitability, of disillusionment after the coming to power of forces which proclaimed that they were putting democracy into practice. The Russian 'democrats' expected so much of democracy that it could hardly be fulfilled under any social system. In fact the realization of at least some of these expectations was not a matter for society at all, but of a personal attitude toward life. At the same time such unreserved expectations can lead to condemnation of any society which does not meet all of them, and any society which is only 'half-democratic' or imperfect can be considered as not democratic at all. That is why many former members of 'democratic' groups did not and still do not recognize any democratic elements in Russia after the collapse of the Communist system and sometimes call Yel'tsin's rule a 'dictatorship' which is even worse than the Soviet regime.

6.8. THE INTERNATIONALISM OF RUSSIAN 'DEMOCRATS'

The internationalism of Russian 'democrats' of the *perestroyka* period was based on their understanding of their struggle against 'totalitarianism' and for 'democracy' not as an internal Russian task, but as a part of the international movement for the 'democratic' ideal. One of the 'democratic' declarations claimed: 'Democracy is our nation, and we are its citizens! In defending the nation of Democracy we are internationalists with those who think the same way in this country and in the entire world.'[68]

This understanding is inseparable from the beliefs of Russian 'democrats' about the historical process in general, according to which 'democracy' is

---

[67] Interview with Romanov.
[68] Yevgeniy Kryskin, 'Slovo o pol'ze demokratii', *Listok 'Grazhdanskoy initsiativy'*, 4 (24 Mar. 1989).

seen as the final stage of social development, the crowning achievement of the world's social progress. Basing themselves on this idea, representatives of various trends of the 'democratic' movement did not look for the sources of their views solely in a narrow ideological concept for which they declared their support, but preferred to consider themselves the heirs of all freedom and humanistic movements and ideas both in Russia and in the outside world, of all ideologies which, in their opinion, favoured social progress, which they understood as movement towards democracy. For example, an SDPR draft programme claimed:

In our activities we base ourselves on national and international traditions, and consider ourselves the successors of the popular movement for social dignity, of the best features of liberalism. Among our spiritual sources are the ideas of European humanism and Enlightenment; the spiritual experience of humanistic religions, in particular Christianity; the strivings of thinkers who were trying to comprehend the laws of thinking and of social development; the richest theoretical and practical inheritance and experience of international Social Democracy. We consider ourselves the heirs of the best traits of Russian liberalism, the Populists [*narodniki*] and Social Democrats (the Mensheviks), of the anti-totalitarian movement for liberation.[69]

According to this understanding, Russian 'democrats' proclaimed their union with the 'democratic' movements of the entire world, and they cared about the encroachment on democratic rights in the countries of Eastern Europe, and even in China, Africa, and Latin America, no less than about the breaking up of a rally in their own town. Moreover, the events in the USSR and abroad were seen as parts of a single process of worldwide historical struggle between the forces of progress and reaction, of 'democracy' and 'totalitarianism'. They adopted declarations and petitions in support of their colleagues all over the world, considering their struggle as part of their own. One such petition, drawn up by a district voter's club in Moscow, declared:

We, the voters of Proletariat District No. 20 of the city of Moscow, are alarmed by the multiple manifestations of uncontrolled violence in our country and in neighbouring Bulgaria and China. We ask you, the People's Deputies of the USSR, to adopt a Declaration of the Congress on the non-violent settlement of all political problems in the USSR and also demand that the Congress should express its attitude toward the suppression of a peaceful demonstration of students in Beijing on 3–4 June 1989.[70]

Quite revealing in this respect was the reaction of Russian 'democrats' to the suppression of the student movement in China in 1989. Every rally and meeting organized in Russia by 'democratic' groups to support 'democratic'

---

[69] Sotsial-demokraticheskaya partiya Rossiyskoy Federatsii, 'Put' progressa i sotsial'noy demokratii. Osnova programmy SDPR. Vremennaya redaktsiya', unpubl. MS [Moscow, 1990], 16.

[70] 'Obrashcheniye kluba izbirateley Taganskogo i Proletarskogo rayonov k narodnym deputatam SSSR', unpubl. MS, Moscow, 7 June 1989; courtesy of Valeriy Fadeev.

deputies of the First Congress of People's Deputies condemned the Beijing authorities. The events in China were seen as similar to the past actions of the Soviet authorities and the Soviet leadership was called on to condemn the Beijing authorities, to cancel meetings with Chinese leaders, and even to apply economic sanctions.[71]

These demands were based on the belief in a natural unity of 'democratic' forces throughout the world, which was the point of departure for the entire foreign policy programme of the Russian 'democratic' movement. The attitudes of the Russian 'democrats' toward foreign policy were characterized by the belief that such traditional concepts of international relations as 'national interests', 'balance of power', and others were outdated and were even being used as a cover for 'totalitarian' interests. If ideas of the 'end of history' have found an appreciative audience anywhere, it was surely in the 'democratic' group of Russia, where the understanding of 'democracy' as an ideal society and a universal means of peaceful and mutually beneficial settlement of conflicts was transferred to, among other spheres, foreign policy.

'Democrats' were ready for any sacrifice, for sanctions against 'totalitarian' regimes which were economically disadvantageous to their own country, if these sacrifices could assist the development of democracy as a world phenomenon, since, in their view, this development was beneficial in the last analysis to the USSR as well. They believed that in a 'democratic' world, where everyone respects human rights, there could be no ground for conflicts, since the main conflict in the international arena was between the forces of 'totalitarianism' and 'democracy'. According to this view respect for 'democratic' principles and human rights was considered a 'solid guarantee of trust between peoples, which is the main condition of peace and friendship between them'.[72] Even those groups which proposed to take into consideration 'national interests' understood these interests as above all the democratization and 'civilization' of Russia, its entry into the world of 'civilized' nations. This was supposed to solve all international problems by itself, since 'civilized countries do not threaten each other'.[73] This orientation towards a union with all the 'anti-totalitarian' forces in the world is clearly formulated in the draft programme of the Democratic Union:

The Democratic Union reaffirms its solidarity with the forces of democracy all over the world and stands for complete respect of human rights in all countries. The Democratic Union declares its solidarity with all peace-loving forces in other countries, international human rights groups, ecological and pacifist groups. Respect for

[71] See Alexander Lukin, 'The Initial Soviet Reaction to the Events in China in 1989 and the Prospects for Sino–Soviet Relations', *China Quarterly*, 125 (1991), 119–36.
[72] 'Proekt programmy partii Demokraticheskiy Soyuz', *Byulleten' soveta partii*, Feb. 1990, 44.   [73] 'Programma Demokraticheskoy partii Rossii', 12.

human rights and the securing of basic freedoms should become the main criteria of providing aid to any state, either East European or "Third World".[74]

In its most radical form this position could lead to recognizing the possibility of 'exporting democracy', sometimes even by the use of military force. Though few members of the 'democratic' movement supported these methods of 'democratization', such views did exist. For example, the manifesto of the Revolutionary Liberals, one of the factions of the Democratic Union, declared: 'Revolutionary liberals, at the first demand of conscience, are ready at any day or hour to protect freedoms and humanism by both peaceful means and, under certain circumstances, by the use of arms. The ideas of Revolutionary Liberalism are worthy of subject to export to every corner of Earth where this need arises.'[75]

While proposing military aid to democrats all over the world, some Russian 'democrats' were also ready to accept such aid from 'democratic' states at critical moments, with no doubt that aid could be granted. The Democratic Union declaration of 19 August 1991 (the first day of the anti-Gorbachev coup) proposed to 'demand the sending of US, UN, and EEC troops to the territory of this country and to fight side by side with the soldiers of Western democracies against our domestic fascism and the putschists.'[76] Some 'democrats' might have regarded this invitation to foreign troops by the most radical group in Moscow to be somewhat excessive. However, this proposal would certainly have been supported by a 'democrat' from Penza, Yevgeniy Grachev, who believed that the best way to develop 'democracy' in the Soviet Union was to voluntarily accept the trusteeship of the United Nations or even occupation by a 'civilized' power. Grachev, who called himself a supporter of the British-style two-party system, saw the reason for the rapid development of West Germany and Japan as rooted in these countries' occupation by the United States. Therefore, he thought, the backward Soviet Union also needed occupation by a member of the civilized world: the United States or Germany. Grachev also said that he would appoint a 'punctual German' prosecutor in every *oblast*` and district, since 'this would be much better for the observance of laws than appointing our own prosecutors'.[77]

The internationalism of Russian 'democrats', their ideas of world solidarity among 'democrats' and even of the possibility of exporting 'democratic' revolution, was reminiscent in many respects of the official internationalism of official Communist ideology and its teaching on 'proletarian internationalism'.

---

[74] 'Proekt programmy partii Demokraticheskiy Soyuz', 44.
[75] 'Manifest revolyutsionerov-liberalov', in *Rossiya: partii, assotsiatsii, soyuzy, kluby*, ii. 151.
[76] 'Vstavay, strana ogromnaya, vstavay na smertnyy boy', in *Rossiya: partii, assotsiatsii, soyuzy, kluby*, ii. 91.   [77] Interview with Grachev.

While the goal of the worldwide struggle for goodness and the very under-standing of goodness of this struggle remained. While 'proletarian interna-tionalism' is surely a Marxist concept, some authors have pointed out that in Russia it was welcomed because of certain traditional beliefs. Whatever the sources of the new 'democratic' internationalism might be, the study of this internationalism provides an opportunity of better understanding Russian foreign policy after the collapse of the USSR. There it manifested itself in the effort to unite with the 'civilized' 'democratic' world, which was based on a sincere confidence that unconditional support for the 'democratic world' in the international arena, and above all for the USA as its natural leader, would lead to similarly unconditional and massive aid from that world to 'democra-tic' Russia. The subsequent changes in this policy could also be partly explained by deep disillusionment, caused by confrontation with the realities of international politics and by understanding of the fact that the introduction of 'democracy' did not automatically lead to the resolution of every interna-tional problem.[78]

6.9. METHODS OF STRUGGLE FOR 'DEMOCRACY'

As was shown above, the belief that breaking 'undemocratic' laws was justi-fiable dominated the Russian 'democratic' movement, at least after 1988. Discussion of the use of violence took a different turn, though it also devel-oped in the same direction of radicalization. An overwhelming majority of 'democratic' groups declared themselves supporters of non-violent methods of struggle with the regime. Even the most radical of them stressed in their programmes that their task was to effect a non-violent change of the political and economic system of the USSR.

This can be partly explained by tactical reasons, since open acceptance of violent methods would have resulted in denial of official registration and in criminal prosecution. It is likely, however, that in most cases the rejection of violence was not just a tactical device, but reflected one of the important beliefs of Russian 'democrats'. In their view, violence was one of the main characteristics of 'totalitarian' regimes, and democracy, as an opposing system, should be characterized by its absolute rejection. In the opinion of most members of the 'democratic' movement, the new, 'democratic' society should be based on the principles of humanism, and all conflicts should be settled peacefully, by the discussion of different positions, as a result of which the most reasonable decision would always be chosen. 'The Democratic Party

[78] For a more detailed analysis, see A. Lukin, 'Predstavleniya "democraticheskikh" grupp o vneshnem mire', *Mirovaya ekonomika i mezhdunarodnye otnosheniya*, 8 (1995), 104–13.

rejects violence not only because it is morally unacceptable, but also because any violent action is a people's tragedy which does not lead to the humanization of society,' argues the programme of the Democratic Party.[79] The Social Democratic Party also declared itself a democratic party which as a question of principle rejected any form of dictatorship, leadership cult (*vozhdizm*), and violence.

Even those groups who supported actions which contravened the law usually believed that such actions should be non-violent. For example, the Anarcho-syndicalists, who called for the creation of alternative organs of self-government, propagated the ideas of Mahatma Gandhi. The Democratic Union as a whole also supported the principle of non-violent civil disobedience. Declaring a policy not of reforming and modernizing the 'totalitarian' regime, but of its 'full dismantling and replacement by a system based on principles of pluralist democracy', the authors of the Democratic Union draft programme wrote: 'Our Way is a moral, civic, and political opposition to the totalitarian system, and therefore non-participation in Evil and non-cooperation with Evil, civil disobedience and non-violent resistance to the criminal and illegal system. . . . The Democratic Union openly declares its goal to be the changing of the USSR state system in a non-violent, civic way.'[80]

Violence was thought by the majority of 'democrats' to be the main means by which the 'totalitarian' state maintained its power and the main obstacle to democratization. Therefore, the categorical rejection of violence became the key to the practical implementation of 'democracy'. Because of this, the determination to refrain from any form of violence was so strong that sometimes quite radical projects were put forward. One of the documents proclaimed: 'Considering violence to be the source of all distortions of political power in the direction of personal rule or in the direction of the abolition of democratic freedoms of speech, the press, meetings, rallies, and demonstrations, we declare our rejection of violence as a means of solving political problems'. Further, the author insisted on refusing all calls to armed struggle against the existing system, including terrorist acts and armed demonstrations, threats to use arms when disputes arose within an organization or between two or more organizations, torture or the infliction of physical injury as well as the arrest and kidnapping of members of one's own or another organization, and even the organization of security groups and the use of bodyguards.[81]

Such proposals represented the opinion of the great majority of Russian 'democrats', who did not look on them as too abstract or far-fetched. Being

[79] 'Programma Demokraticheskoy partii', 10.
[80] 'Proekt programmy partii Demokraticheskiy Soyuz', 8.
[81] 'Sovmestnoe zayavlenie o neprimenenii nasiliya v reshenii politicheskikh problem. Proekt', unpubl. MS [Moscow, (1989], 1–2; courtesy of Valeriy Fadeev.

addressed not only to Russian groups, but to independent organizations in other Soviet republics, they were based on the fear of the spread of conflicts between opposition factions as a result of ethnic and other disputes, which had already begun in some non-Russian republics. The events in the Trans-Caucasian and the Central Asian republics showed that former allies in the struggle against a Communist regime could well fight each other and even start a war. Besides, the Communist authorities, in the opinion of the 'democrats', were also widening the sphere of the use of force. As one Moscow-based group put it: 'It is clear that in such a situation, when violent methods of solving political and other problems have become the main ones, the democratic movement is confronted by a single task: not to let violence spread beyond the borders of the few places where it exists and to eliminate it in these places, since fanning the flames of violence cannot but lead to military dictatorship.'[82]

However, a mood in favour of violence also existed in the Russian 'democratic' movement. Because of the possibility of criminal prosecution, few were ready to support it openly. Therefore it is even more important that such arguments could nevertheless be heard. For example, differences in their approaches to violence became the reason for a split in the Democratic Union, which occurred after the publication of the 'Letter of the Twelve' of its members. The letter condemned the use of troops by the authorities in Tbilisi, Baku, and Vilnius, and compared President Gorbachev with the Nicaraguan dictator Somoza, Stalin, Hitler, and Ceauşescu, arguing that the Soviet leader deserved the fate of the Romanian tyrant. The letter argues: 'From now on the people have the right to overthrow the criminal power by any means, including military uprising. The political regime which is flooding the country with blood must be overthrown and the Kremlin butchers should share the fate of the criminals who were prosecuted at the Nuremberg trials or were killed by the members of the anti-fascist resistance in the occupied territories.'[83]

Such views elicited protest even in the most radical parties and were not supported by the majority. But the opinion that the use of force was necessary and justified, if not to fight against the regime, then at least to defend 'democracy', was gaining popularity, and at the time of the August 1991 putsch caused few doubts among 'democrats'. After the putsch the former defenders of the Russian parliament formed a special para-military group in Moscow, Zhivoe Kol'tso (Live Ring), which declared a wish to 'maintain readiness to come out at any time against any attempts to set up a dictatorship'.[84]

---

[82] Dvizhenie za svobodu i demokratiyu, 'Obrashcheniye k demokraticheskim silam strany', unpubl. MS [Moscow, 1989], pp. 2–3; courtesy of Valeriy Fadeev.

[83] Quoted in Novodvorskaya, *Po tu storonu otchayaniya*, 179–80.

[84] 'Ustav Soyuza "Zhivoe kol'tso" ', in *Rossiya: partii, assotsiatsii, soyuzy, kluby*, ii. 145.

6.10. CONCLUSIONS

Despite some differences between various trends in the 'democratic' move-ment, the understanding of democracy by Russian 'democrats' can generally be summarized in the following points:

1. Real, civilized democracy was seen to be fundamentally different from the so-called 'socialist democracy' which was promoted by official Soviet ideology. The main difference was that in the eyes of the 'democrats' real democracy transcended class.

2. Democracy was seen at the same time as a social ideal of a 'civilized, democratic society' and as a set of procedures which constituted a means of achieving this ideal.

3. Democratic society was seen as free, where freedom was seen first of all as freedom from excessive control by the state over society.

4. Democratic society was seen as just, where justice was understood as the equality of the rights of government officials and the rights of ordinary people, and the absence of legal and distributive privileges for the ruling elite. Some 'democrats' interpreted equality of wealth as the absence of privileges in terms of distribution of wealth.

5. Democratic society was seen as the one which ensured the highest possible prosperity for the people.

6. Democratic society was seen as guaranteeing for the people a life full of meaning and as providing the conditions for achieving personal perfection.

7. This society was to be achieved by 'democratic' means, that is to say generally through elections and other manifestations of the people's will (such as strikes, rallies, referenda, etc.). Despite some 'democratic' voices in favour of the possibility of the use of force, especially as a reaction to the violent or openly illegal actions of the authorities (such as the military actions in Tbilisi, Baku, and Lithuania, and the August 1991 coup), the majority of 'democrats' strongly advocated non-violent protest. At the same time such protest did not always have to be legal. On the contrary, as the 'democratic' movement grew, more and more 'democrats' began to reject the official legal system,which they believed to be outdated and totalitarian, and to advocate disobedience to the laws of the Communist 'centre'.

Analysing the sources of these beliefs and the mechanism of their forma-tion, one can come to the following conclusions:

1. The view that democracy transcended class and was a value 'common to all mankind' was a distinct deviation from Soviet ideology in its classical form. However, this idea was already widely in use among the Soviet media and liberal Soviet officials, including Gorbachev himself, towards the end of

the 1980s. The acceptance of this belief by 'democrats' did not need direct Western influence.

2. The understanding of democracy as both the ideal society and the means of creating it closely resembles the understanding of communism (and its first stage, socialism) in official Soviet ideology as first of all the ideal society but also as a means of constructing this society. It was Lenin's famous idea, which he formulated in discussion with more traditional Marxists, that to build communism the revolutionary party should not wait for economic circumstances to improve under the old regime, but should seize power and create these conditions itself.[85] The transitional period to communism was later called socialism, which was at the same time supposed to be the first, less developed stage of communism. Just as the Bolsheviks endeavoured to build communism by Communist (i.e. violent, non-democratic) means, 'democrats' thought democracy attainable only by 'democratic' means.

3. The fight for freedom, understood as the weakening or even the elimination of the state, was the chief aim of most opposition movements in Russia. The Bolsheviks were not an exception. In his famous book *The State and Revolution*, written in the summer of 1917, Lenin, in accordance with Marxist theory, wrote that the state under communism could be expected to 'wither away'.[86] However, after attaining responsibility for the state themselves, Russian Communists soon changed their minds and official Soviet ideology adopted a dubious concept of the withering away of the state through its strengthening. The anti-statism of Russian 'democrats' was a natural reaction of the opposition to the excessive role of the state and the state's suppression of freedoms under Communist rule. Life experience and the aims of the struggle are in this case more obvious explanations of the interpretation of freedom by Russian 'democrats' than the influence of earlier Russian anti-government movements, the exact programmes of which were hardly known to most 'democrats'. The official idea of freedom within an all-powerful state was reinterpreted as freedom with a weak state or no state at all. The reason for the obvious similarity between the understanding of freedom by Russian 'democrats' and pre-1917 anti-government movements is that, as before, Russian 'democrats' were confronted by a powerful state. The Western notion of 'democracy' was used to legitimize this goal of fighting for freedom.

4. Understanding justice as equality before the law, elimination of privileges, and a welfare system equally accessible to everyone has always been an official position of Soviet ideology,[87] explicitly confirmed by the

---

[85] See e.g. V. I. Lenin, 'Our Revolution', in V. I. Lenin, *Collected Works* (London: Lawrence & Wishart; Moscow: Progress Publishers, 1966), xxxiii. 478–9.

[86] V. I. Lenin, *The State and Revolution*, in Lenin, *Collected Works*, xxv. 381–492.

[87] See e.g. A. P. Butenko (ed.), *Sotsializm: sotsial`naya spravedlivost` i ravenstvo* (Moscow: Nauka, 1988); V. I. Davidovich, *Sotsial`naya spravedlivost`: ideal i printsip deyatel`nosti* (Moscow: Izdatel`stvo politicheskoy literatury, 1989).

perestroyka leadership. Speaking at the Twenty-seventh Congress of the CPSU in 1986, Gorbachev claimed:

Socialism has eliminated the main source of social injustice—exploitation of man by man, inequality in relation to the means of production. Social justice characterizes every facet of socialist relations of production. It is in the real power of the people and in the equality of all citizens before the law, in the practical equality of nations, in respect for the individual, in the creation of conditions for their all-round development. It also is broad social guarantees: guaranteed work, accessibility of education, culture, medical services, and housing, concern for the elderly, for maternity, and for childhood. Strict implementation of the principle of social justice is an important condition of the unity of the people, of the political stability of society, and of dynamic development.[88]

It can clearly be seen that social justice, understood very broadly, was seen by official ideology as one of the central achievements of the Soviet system. The problem was that its claims strikingly contradicted reality. Therefore the fight for social justice by 'democrats' did not even have to contradict Soviet ideology. As will be shown in Chapter 8, this understanding was generally shared by 'democrats' with the population as a whole, so the influence of the dominant Soviet political culture is evident. In fact, at an early stage many 'democrats' saw their fight for social justice as part of the struggle to improve socialism, as was their support for *perestroyka* leaders, whom they regarded to be genuine Communists, against local and middle-level bureaucrats. Later, after gradually becoming disillusioned with official *perestroyka* ideas, 'democrats' transferred this understanding of justice to their ideal of democracy.

5. Like social justice, prosperity and creating the conditions for the perfect life and the self-realization of every individual had always been official ideological goals of the Soviet authorities. In the same way, these goals were largely shared by the population as a whole and were regarded by the 'democrats' as clear examples of what the state had failed to achieve. These aims were likewise transferred to the 'democratic' ideal.

6. The roots of the rejection of violence were discussed in detail in the previous chapter. The relative disregard for existing law was surely also a 'tradition' of Russian opposition movements. However, in the case of the 'democratic' belief system it is more logical to see its immediate source in the official Soviet concept of the class character of law, according to which law was instrumental to the class aims of the more progressive movement. While the 'democrats' regarded a different group as progressive, the concept of instrumentality itself remained.

---

[88] Mikhail Gorbachev, 'Politicheskiy doklad TsK KPSS XXVII s`ezdu KPSS' in *Materialy XXVII s`ezda Kommunisticheskoy Partii Sovetskogo Soyuza* (Moscow: Izdatel`stvo politicheskoy Literatury, 1986), 44.

Research on the attitudes of the members of the 'democratic' movement in Russia towards democracy is also useful for attempting to understand some of the subsequent political developments in Russia, especially in 1992–3, when the policies of President Yel`tsin were highly influenced by the ideas of 'democrats'. These developments are sometimes met with surprise by those Western specialists whose analyses are based on their own understanding of democracy, which differs substantially from its interpretations in Russia. For example, one can understand a disillusionment with democracy itself which is based on the inability of the Russian leaders to create a 'richer', 'just' society 'with no lies', where 'life is full of meaning', only in the light of Russian attitudes towards democracy as a moral and social ideal, and not just as a system of political institutions. Moreover, such an understanding of democracy made disillusionment inevitable, since even if the 'democratic' leaders could improve the living standards of the population, they would never have been able to realize all the hopes that were placed on 'democratic' society. The use of force by the supporters of 'democracy' against political opponents, which took place, for example, in October 1993 during the conflict between the parliament and the president, and later in Chechnya, caused comment abroad that the Russian leadership had moved away from democracy. This is one of the most striking examples of different interpretations of the notion of 'democracy', since armed struggle against the enemies of 'democracy', against the supporters of 'totalitarianism', was possible from the point of view of at least one interpretation of democracy in Russia, and from this standpoint was not a deviation from 'democratic' principles. As for the belief in the possibility of ignoring laws for the sake of 'democracy' (a most common practice in post-Communist Russia), it was, as shown above, widespread among the Russian 'democrats'.

The Bi-polar World: Soviet Totalitarianism and Western Civilization

7.1. THE WORLD OF 'DEMOCRACY' AND THE WORLD OF 'TOTALITARIANISM'

The majority of Russian 'democrats' saw the world as divided into two parts: the zone of 'democracy' and the zone of 'totalitarianism'. Society in the countries of the 'democratic' zone was also defined as 'Western', 'normal', or 'civilized', these terms usually being used as synonyms. In contrast, societies in the 'totalitarian' zone were linked to 'dictatorship', 'despotism' (or 'oriental despotism'), 'Communist regimes', 'partocracy', etc.

It was noted above that the main feature of 'totalitarian' society was seen in the opposition between the ruling 'state-class' and the *déclassé* population which was deprived of all rights. The state of 'totalitarianism' was most often understood in 'democratic' circles not as an accidental evil, but as a fundamental deviation from the natural course of history, as a 'dead end of social development'.[1] Within the framework of this belief system 'democratic' society was its direct antithesis. The original source of this antithesis was a deeply seated belief that life in 'democratic' societies is better, fairer, and more prosperous than in 'totalitarian' societies. The fact that the Soviet Union, with which 'totalitarianism' was most closely associated, found itself in a dead end of history was naturally associated with government policy, and more broadly with the Communist theory by which the government claimed to be guided. Typical was the opinion of Mariya Sublina, who thought that the Soviet Union 'has lagged behind the rest of the world—at least the civilized world'.[2]

If life in the USSR was seen to be worse than in the 'democratic' world, then the first logical conclusion was that 'democracy' was a preferable, 'progressive' system. On this basis the main goal of the Democratic Party of Russia was formulated as 'the transformation of Russia into a civilized country': 'We give an unequivocal "no" to Communist ideology. Putting forward

---

[1] Sotsial-demokraticheskaya partiya Rossiyskoy Federatsii, 'Put` progressa i sotsial`noy demokratii. Osnova programmy SDPR. Vremennaya redaktsiya', unpubl. MS [Moscow, 1990], 7.   [2] Interview with Mariya Sublina (Moscow, 28 Aug. 1993).

a democratic alternative to the totalitarian system we seek to attract the attention of Russians to the fact that apart from the socialist choice with a Communist perspective there exists another choice which has been made by almost the whole of world civilization.'[3]

Unlike 'totalitarianism', 'civilized' society, for which one should strive, was seen as the final goal of world social progress or at least as the highest stage yet achieved. The struggle of groups and parties for 'democracy' and 'civilization' was understood and justified as an effort aimed at Russia's return to the main line of 'world civilization', on the rails of 'normal', 'natural' development, at leading it out of a historical dead-end. This aim was explicitly expressed in the programme of the SDPR, which called on Russia 'to rejoin the currents of world civilization'.[4] This return should take place in the form of a fundamental change in the old Communist policy, which was seen not only as driving the country away from civilization, but as attempting to turn back the advance of history. According to the SDPR draft project, written by Leonid Volkov, 'Communism and its Russian form, Bolshevism, showed in practice what peculiar consequences can be produced by an anti-historic experience of the practical implementation of a theoretical utopia. . . . In contrast to these anti-historic aspirations and the inhuman practice of the Bolshevik regime which was formed under their influence, social reformism has always followed the real course of history.'[5]

7.2. 'DEMOCRATIC' GEOGRAPHY

Geographically 'totalitarianism' was associated first and foremost with the USSR, the countries of the Soviet bloc, and other countries with Communist and pro-Soviet regimes. They included the Communist states of Eastern Europe before their 'liberation from totalitarianism', the People's Republic of China, North Korea, Vietnam, Ethiopia, etc. In some cases countries with non-Communist but aggressively anti-Western regimes, such as Iran and Libya, were also defined as 'totalitarian'. The social and political systems in these countries were seen as similar to that of Soviet 'totalitarianism', the perception of which by Russian 'democrats' was discussed in Chapter 5.

[3] 'Programma Demokraticheskoy partii Rossii', in Rossiysko-amerikanskiy universitet, Institut massovykh politicheskikh dvizheniy, *Rossiya: partii, assotsiatsii, soyuzy, kluby. Spravochnik*, 10 vols. (Moscow: RAU-Press, 1991–2), ii. 12–13.

[4] Sotsial-demokraticheskaya partiya Rossiyskoy Federatsii, 'Put` progressa i sotsial`noy demokratii', 13.

[5] L. Volkov, 'Deklaratsiya printsipov SDPR. Proekt', in *K uchreditel`nomu s`yezdu Sotsial-demokraticheskoy partii Rossiskoy Federatsii. Sbornik materiyalov No. 1* (Minuralsibstroy: Tipografiya, 1990), 52.

In contrast the main features of the 'civilized' West were seen by 'democratic' activists to be 'freedom' and 'democracy'. It was also seen as a place where people are wealthy, where political and economic systems work as a perfect mechanism, and sometimes as a place where people live a full and happy life. The idea that everything works splendidly in 'democratic' Western society was expressed very clearly by many 'democrats'. Pavel Poluyan, for example, gave as an alternative to the Soviet political system a 'parlamentarianism based on a multi-party system', where 'the functions of the people—to choose a worthy candidate by voting—are self-evident. It is also known that in the West this political system functions effectively: foreign and domestic policy are constructively elaborated, unwise decisions are improved as a result of taking into account criticism by the opposition, etc.'[6] An activist from Stavropol`, A. Novikov, expressed similarly idealistic views on the 'democratic' economic system: 'If the president of the United States spoke on the radio and called on his fellow-citizens to work better, fulfil the five-year plan, and monitor the quality of production, Americans would think that the president had gone mad. Effectiveness and profitability are inherent in the American economy, and nobody could ever think that it is possible to make the economy work better by certain artificial actions of the government.'[7]

It is clear that this picture of the United States, where in fact governments often use 'artificial' actions to improve the economic situation and presidents do occasionally call on fellow-citizens to work better, is based on the reality of the Soviet, not the American, economy. This image of the American economy was constructed as an idealistic opposite to the Soviet economic system: if under evil totalitarianism everything is regulated then under good democracy nothing should be regulated; if in the Soviet Union the leaders tell their people what to do, under democracy they should not tell the people anything at all. This pattern of the construction of the Russian 'democratic' ideal was especially characteristic of those 'democrats' who rejected socialism in all its forms and who found their ideal in non-socialist Western countries, particularly in the United States. As shown later in this chapter, sometimes this ideal contradicted the reality of the United States, which visiting Russian 'democrats' confronted during their visits. They did not find in the United States the absence of government they expected and this puzzled them greatly.

It is only natural that a world where people live 'more freely, more prosperously, and more honestly' was considered to be the only normal and possible one. Among Russian 'democrats', the socialists' view of existing Western society was less idealistic and the members of anarchist groups even thought it to be in many ways similar to that of the Soviet Union, especially in the

---

[6] Pavel Poluyan, *Ot byurokratii k demokratii*, unpubl. MS [Krasnoyarsk, n.d.], 4.

[7] A. Novikov, 'Perestroyka—eto otkaz ot vsyakoy perestroyki', *Grazhdanin*, 5 (May 1989), 20.

sphere of suppressing civic initiative. However, even the most radical 'leftists' very decisively preferred the Western alternative to Soviet society, believing that even if the former was not absolutely perfect, it was surely closer to the ideal than was the latter. Socialists saw the advantage of Western society in the presence of socialist elements to a greater degree; anarchists saw virtues in the reduced role of the state and greater civic initiative.

It is not easy to draw the geographic borders of the 'democratic' West as perceived by Russian 'democrats', for, as with 'totalitarianism', their notions of 'democracy', 'civilization', and even 'the West' itself were not geographic, but social. This is indicated by the fact that the West included not only the countries of Western Europe, the USA, and Canada, but also Japan. For obvious reasons the example of Japan was particularly popular in the Soviet Far East, where its economic prosperity was often compared with its own former poverty, as well as with the ineffectiveness of the Communist Soviet Union and North Korea. For example, a Vladivostok 'democrat', Sergey Shokolenko, was impressed by the example of neighbouring democratic Japan. Shokolenko found out about life in Japan from the stories of people who visited the country on board Soviet ships. The impression was that Japan, which was quite backward after World War II, had made amazing progress, and Shokolenko, as a patriot, wanted Russia to become at least as rich.[8]

'Democratic' groups saw the centre of the zone of the 'democratic' West in two main places. Socialists, social democrats, and anybody who either by conviction or for tactical reasons sought to prove that the Soviet social system was not socialist and that real socialism could be achieved only on the basis of democracy, saw the centre, or the most 'progressive' part of the Western world, in the countries where social democrats had controlled the government for a long time and/or where state and public property played a major role in the economy. Often the opposition of 'genuine Western socialism' to the Soviet system was deliberately used to exert pressure on the Soviet leadership. Russian 'democrats' wanted to convince Gorbachev, who had proclaimed democratization and high standards to be the goals of 'socialist construction', that these goals had already been achieved in some countries of the 'civilized' world and therefore the Soviet Union should follow their example.

By all accounts the most important symbol of 'civilized' socialism was Sweden, which was thought to have achieved the highest living standards, at least in Europe, during the rule of the social democrats. The example of some other countries, especially Finland, Austria, Switzerland, France, and Spain, were also often used. For Russian social-democrats the experience of these countries proved that socialist ideals should be preserved and combined with democracy. A member of the SDPR from the town of Kovrov, L. V. Kulikov, argued:

---

[8] Interview with Sergey Shokolenko (Vladivostok, 23 Apr. 1994).

In the course of the development of social morals worthy beliefs about the future of humanity have been elaborated, which to a great extent manifest themselves in socialist ideals and should not be subjected to a fundamental revision. The fact that Communist parties parasitized these ideals and did everything possible to vulgarize and discredit them cannot be a basis for their rejection, especially while socialism in the form in which it exists in the developed countries (Austria, Canada, Sweden, Finland, and others) is a natural stage of the development of society which it unavoidably reaches in the process of evolution.[9]

Finland, which once was a part of the Russian Empire and could be compared with its other parts of the empire which remained under Moscow's control during soviet time, presented especially useful material for the 'democratic' argument. One of the editorials of a magazine in the Stavropol` Popular Front, *Grazhdanin* (Citizen), agreed with the opinion of a well-known writer, Chengiz Aytmatov (which he expressed in his speech at the First Congress of People's Deputies in 1989), that socialism had already been built in many countries, in particular, in Sweden, Denmark, Switzerland, and Spain. The editorial comments: 'Perhaps they have also done so in Finland, which used to be on Russia's national periphery. And this was done contrary to [Marxist] science and without the leading role of the Communist Party'.[10] Sweden was cited as an example of real socialism by democratic activists in many places: Il`ya Grinchenko, the leader of Democrat Club in Vladivostok; Yevgeniy Kryskin, one of the leaders of the group Civic Initiative in Penza; Vladislav Shapovalenko, former leader of the Orenburg 'democrats'; and many members of Moscow groups. Kryskin and Grinchenko were attracted by the combination in Sweden of freedom and the active role of the state in the economy.[11] Kryskin also found such traits of socialism as strong government support for economic development in Japan and South Korea, though he did not call these countries purely socialist and argues that they combined the best elements of Marxism and the market economy.[12] Shapovalenko explained that, on the basis of the information he had at the time, he thought Sweden to be an 'ideal variant'. He thought that a combination of cooperation and private property would make Russia 'a lot richer'.[13] A member of the Oktyabr`skiy District Union of Voters in Moscow, Yefim Lyuboshits, also thought that Sweden was a real socialist country, 'where society strongly supports the poor'.[14]

But Sweden was not a positive example for all 'democrats'. The supporters

---

[9] P. V. Kulikov, 'Programmnye orientiry SDPR', in *K uchreditel`nomu s`yezdu Sotsial-democraticheskoy partii Rossiskoy Federatsii*, 33.

[10] 'Otredaktsii', in *Grazhdanin*, 6 (1989), 2.

[11] Interviews with Yevgeniy Kryskin (Penza, 3 Apr. 1994) and Il`ya Grinchenko (Vladivostok, 24 Apr. 1994).   [12] Interview with Kryskin.

[13] Interview with Vladislav Shapovalenko (Orenburg, 21 Dec. 1994).

[14] Interview with Yefim Lyuboshits (Moscow, 18 Sept. 1993).

of individual capitalism regarded socialism as the reason for the Soviet crisis and found negative traits in the Swedish experience. In their opinion, Sweden was experiencing an economic crisis because 'the individual to a great extent was not respected there' any more and that people there 'became obsessed over distribution'.[15] The Russian supporters of individualism and the 'minimal state' favoured other European countries, but most of all the United States, as positive examples of countries where individual rights are best protected and the state does not interfere in the affairs of citizens. An activist in the Oktyabr`skiy District Voters Union, Il`ya Gezentsvey, put it this way: 'I visited America and it impressed me a lot. . . . Everyone is to a great extent dependent on oneself rather than on the state. . . . The state virtually never interferes in one's life, in determining one's status'.[16]

It is quite interesting that, according to this Russian 'democratic' activist, his idealistic views on American society were contradicted by many Americans. He says: 'I was astounded, though, that in America I was confronted many times by people who said that capitalism was bad and that what they had was bad. And what is funny is that we came there as open anti-socialists, anti-Communists and met Americans who wanted to depart from the freedom which they were to a great extent fed up with.'[17]

Gezentsvey explained this by the fact that freedom of choice was a great burden for a person and therefore many people want the state to solve some questions for them, for example, in the sphere of medicine and education. However, he did not think this right and considered American society to be even more progressive than the 'more socialist' French society.[18]

Grigoriy Rayzman also thought that the United States was the country closest to democracy, though he meant by democracy and ideal to which reality could only approximate. This ideal society should be free of all forms of violence, including state violence. According to Rayzman, the fact that many Americans pay their taxes voluntarily (he gave a particular example of his American friend, whom he met when he visited the USA) demonstrates that the American system is close to pure democracy.[19] Aleksandr Romanov, who also thought that the United States should be an example for the Soviet Union, admired the protection which the American state gave to its citizens when they had trouble abroad, while, in his view, 'our state tries to conceal it or hush it up if somebody is killed abroad'.[20] Andrey Shcherkin also argued that at the time of his 'democratic' activities he and his colleagues thought that Russia should become 'like America or like Europe'.[21]

Despite the differences between the American and Swedish variants of

[15] Interview with Il`ya Gezentsvey (Moscow, 27 Aug. 1993).   [16] Ibid.
[17] Ibid.   [18] Ibid.
[19] Interview with Grigoriy Rayzman (Orenburg, 21 Dec. 1994).
[20] Interview with Aleksandr Romanov (Orenburg, 22 Dec. 1994).
[21] Interview with Andrey Shcherkin (Pskov, 25 Sept. 1994).

democratic society, they were none the less seen as a united whole, as a part of the world where a high level of freedom, justice, prosperity, and even spirituality had been achieved. All other countries were seen as being between the two poles, closer either to 'democracy' or to 'totalitarianism'. Since the opposition between democracy and totalitarianism was seen as an opposition between 'development' and 'backwardness', the countries with regimes similar to that of the Soviet Union were understood as at the same time the most backward or even primitive. Thus, according to Kryskin, 'history shows that backward societies, like Ethiopia, are the first to be infected by *nomenklatura*-feudal Communism. Their primitive structure and psychology is adapted to its reproduction. The road from one bondage to another turned out to be the shortest. At the same time developed, so-called bourgeois democracy has shown an "unexpected" ability to go much further along the road of social progress.'[22]

The aspirations to emulate the Soviet 'totalitarian' system, its backwardness, was seen by Russian 'democrats' as harmful but temporary, since the movement of world history towards progress had to be realized sooner or later. As a positive example of overcoming backwardness the countries with pro-Western orientation were usually cited. The character of the regime in such countries often did not matter since, according to the view of Russian 'democrats', their international orientation in itself was a guarantee of progress and, in the last analysis, of democratization. In this respect all of the international victories of the Soviet and Soviet-style regimes were considered to be short-lived. Kryskin argued:

The Afghan massacre is already useless because even after a kind of relative victory of the Marxists, socialism will not come to Afghanistan, as it did not come to Egypt, Tanzania, or Indonesia. Faced with Islamic opposition it will soon begin to dissolve, as it is dissolving now under different conditions in Hungary, Poland, and China. Or, under a ruthless dictatorship of the Cambodian or Laotian-Vietnamese type, it will come to a dead end which will be evident against the background of the dynamic development of Singapore, Malaysia, Thailand, and Pakistan.[23]

It can be concluded from the above that the basis for the beliefs of the Russian 'democrats' about the outside world was the official Soviet theory of international relations. According to this theory, two worlds, those of socialism and capitalism, confront each other in the international arena in the process of class struggle. The more progressive socialist world is bound to win in the end, thus spreading socialism all over the world. All countries which are not obviously members of either camp are called 'developing' or

---

[22] Yevgeniy Kryskin, 'Apriornost' marksistskoy futurologii', in Yevgeniy Kryskin, Demokratiya i, an tidemokratiya v Penze', p. 63.
[23] Yevgeniy Kryskin, 'Strashnaya godovshchina', *Penzenskiy grazhdanin*, 10 (Dec. 1989), 12.

sometimes 'Third World', and were divided into those of socialist and capitalist orientation. Capitalist-orientated countries were supposed to be doomed to stagnation because of the capitalist world taking advantage of their resources and pursuing neo-colonialist policies, while socialist-oriented countries were privileged to have the opportunity of jumping over the capitalist stage of development and proceeding directly from feudalism to socialism.

This scheme was retained by the 'democrats', but the poles of progress and backwardness were reversed. Now the 'democratic', 'developed', 'civilized' West, not the failed socialism of the Soviet type, was seen as the highest stage of social development. Some developing countries with the most pro-Western regimes, such as the members of ASEAN, could be presented as having already caught up and even passed the USSR in levels of development. Such countries were presented as a positive example to the Soviet leadership. Most other 'Third World' countries, which were not able fully to assimilate Western values, and especially those centuries which orientated their policies toward the USSR, were considered the most backward. Whole continents could be regarded as zones of backwardness, and, as 'democrats' often pointed out, the failure of the USSR to take the road of 'civilized' development might result in its turning into an 'African' or 'Latin American' country. In this case the use of the terms 'African' and 'Latin American' (however offensive this might have seemed to the peoples of those continents, who sometimes expressed their reservations) designated social, not geographic or ethnic, phenomena.

7.3. THE ADVANCE OF HISTORY

The majority of Russian 'democrats' understood history as a forward movement, a development from simple forms to more complicated ones, from barbarity to civilization, from imperfection to perfection. Again, as in the case of their 'democratic' map of the world, their views on history were influenced by the official Soviet ideology. According to this ideology, which was based on a simplified version of Marxism, societies were directly advancing from the primitive communal system through slave ownership, feudalism, and capitalism to communism, 'real' Soviet socialism being the first stage of the latter. This scheme was taught in every Soviet educational institution beginning with the first years of school. It was rejected by the 'democrats' but this rejection, not surprisingly, continued to exert its influence on their ideas. This influence manifested itself in their pattern of rejection, which was again based on the principle of the looking-glass reflection.

The rethinking of this theory proceeded in stages. In most 'democratic' concepts of the time only its surface level was changed, the level of the definition of the ideal society towards which social development was heading. Soviet socialism and even more perfect communism was replaced by democratic society in its different variants: socialist Sweden for the supporters of genuine socialism, American individualism for the 'liberals', and a society of self-ruling communes for the anarchists. However, the core tenets of the official Soviet theory of history, such as the ideas of the forward movement of history, of social progress, and of the inevitability of every society passing through specific stages of development, stayed in place. These tenets were doubted only by a few. A Russian 'democrat' could disagree with the official theory on specific stages of social development, but not on the postulate that this development goes forward. For example, Russian totalitarianism was understood by the 'democrats' as a temporary 'historical retreat', but similarly to the official theory's understanding of the victory of 'fascism' in Germany and Italy as a historic retreat from the advance towards communism. The fundamentals of the official theory of history were rarely questioned.

Even their criticism of Bolshevik policies was usually based on these quasi-Marxist beliefs. Taking the side of the Mensheviks in their discussions with Lenin, S. Zybin wrote in the magazine of the Stavropol` Popular Front:

the Bolsheviks failed, despite Lenin's plans, first to seize power and *then* create the conditions for the construction of socialism, including the creation of corresponding productive forces and the rise of general culture (including political culture). These conditions were known to have been created within the old society, i.e. within capitalism. Unfortunately, in this case Lenin appeared not to be a dialectician (or, perhaps, was too much of a dialectician?), ignoring the *natural course of the development of history*, and tried to jump the stages of historical development.[24]

The prognoses for the future were also based on this understanding of history. As Kulikov argued:

The collapse of the Communist system and the return of its former member-states to human civilization should be regarded as the determinative characteristic feature of the historic process. The debate between capitalism and Communism has been solved quite clearly in favour of democratic systems, based on pluralism of property and ideas, freedom of the individual and the priority of universal human values. All these the bankrupt Communist ideologists and politicians attempt to present as a renewed model of socialism. Indeed, the new is the well-forgotten old.[25]

The echo of the concept of 'the main contradiction of the contemporary epoch' between capitalism and socialism, which was supposed to be solved by the final victory of the latter, is heard hear quite clearly. Of the core concepts of the official Soviet theory of 'scientific communism', only the

---

[24] S. Zybin, 'Chto zhe my postroili?', *Grazhdanin*, 4 (March 1989), 32.
[25] Kulikov, 'Programmnye orientiry SDPR', 29.

evaluations and the prospective winner changed places, while the scheme itself remained intact.

7.4. THE ROAD TO CIVILIZATION

On the basis of these beliefs about the world, Russian 'democrats' regarded the principal goal of their country to be 'the return to world civilization'. This goal was set in most of the programmes of 'democratic' parties and groups, regardless of whether their orientation was 'socialism' or 'capitalism'. Thus, the Social Democratic Party of the Russian Federation defined its official goal as the 'return of Russia into the international community'.[26] The Democratic Party of Russia, which rejected the 'socialist choice', set the task of following a course of 'non-violent change of the political and economic system and the turning of Russia into a civilized country'.[27]

The specific political developments in the Soviet Union were approached by the 'democrats' from the point of view of this worldwide struggle between the forces of barbarity and civilization. As Kryskin put it: 'Right now a devilishly sophisticated struggle is going on at the very top. The result of this struggle will determine not only the fate of this country but of the entire world: are we to be united in its advanced ranks in alliance with the civilized West or are we to oppose it in alliance with barbarians in the mould of Pol Pot, Khomeini, and the like, condemning the planet to attrition and destruction?'[28] The author quite obviously sees the struggle for democracy in his country as the centre of world history, the field of the decisive battle for world progress.

Such a high evaluation of Russia's role came from the official Soviet understanding of Russia as the bearer of Communist ideas, which made her the front-runner of world progress. Just as Soviet propagandists spoke of the 'worldwide historical significance' of the Bolshevik victory in Russia, since it turned a vast country and later a significant part of the world into the base for world progress, the 'democrats' saw their struggle as of more than only national importance. The Soviet Union was not seen as the only country which departed from civilization. It had fellow-sufferers, such as other countries with Communist, pro-Soviet, or anti-Western regimes (like Iran or Libya). What they were all believed to have in common was having deviated

---

[26] 'Put` progressa i sotsial`noy demokratii. Kratkiy variant programmy SDPR', in V. Savel`ev (ed.), *Malaya entsiklopediya rossiyskoy politiki. Osnovnye partii i dvizheniya, zaregistrirovannye ministerstvom yustitsii* (Moscow: Verkhovnyy Sovet Rossiyskoy Federatsii, Parlamentskiy Tsentr, 1992), 212.

[27] 'Programma Demokraticheskoy Partii Rossii', 12.

[28] Ye. Kryskin, 'Na Kipre pravit Kassio?', *Penzenskiy grazhdanin*, 5 (July 1989), 7.

from 'normality' or 'civilization' and having joined the world of barbarity. The defeat of Communism in the Soviet Union would mean a fatal blow to barbarism, since as a result the main force of the barbaric world would join civilization. Therefore the struggle for democracy in the USSR was not seen as a narrow concern of the Soviet people, but as a final battle that could solve the problems of the entire world. These beliefs of Russian 'democrats' are another example of how official Soviet ideology, turned upside down, can get close to the most extreme and simplistic Western political theories, thus fertilizing the soil for their spread in 'democratically'-minded circles in Russia. In this case Russian 'democrats' came very close to Fukuyama-type ideas of the 'end of history' and the coming victory of Western liberalism.

7.5. THE UNITY OF THE WORLD AND GLOBAL VALUES

The term 'normal society' was often used in the documents of the 'democratic' groups as a synonym for 'civilized society'. This can be explained by a fundamental belief that it is Western society which is based on natural principles, normal for human society, and that totalitarianism is only possible as a result of the loss of these principles. The declaration of the Democratic Party argued: 'A man is born free and no ideology or social ideal can compensate for the loss of this freedom. The primordial human right is the right to doubt, to disagree with the majority, to be mistaken and to dispute one's theories. . . . Millions of victims sacrificed to totalitarianism and the tragic experience of many countries have shown that there is no alternative to the social system of democracy.'[29] Thus, the basis for the return to civilization, from which Russia 'fell away' as a result of the Bolsheviks' victory, was understood as the acceptance of the values of civilization, which were also defined as 'natural', 'normal', 'universal human', and therefore 'global' values.

A major part of this terminology was borrowed by 'democrats' from the *perestroyka* writings of liberal academics and journalists which were appearing in official reformist publications.[30] In fact, from 1987–8 Gorbachev himself accepted notions of 'universal human' or 'global' values, thereby limiting the classical Marxist class approach. However, 'democrats' went much further than Gorbachev.[31] In contrast to Gorbachev, the 'democrats'

---

[29] 'Deklaratsiya Demokraticheskoy Partii', in *Rossiya: partii, assotsiatsii, soyuzy, kluby*, ii. 9.

[30] See Alexander Dallin, 'New Thinking in Soviet Foreign Policy', and T. H. Rigby, 'Some Concluding Observations', in Archie Brown (ed.), *New Thinking in Soviet Politics* (London: Macmillan, 1992).

[31] M. S. Gorbachev, 'Sotsializm i perestroyka', *Pravda*, 26 Nov. 1989, 1–3. See Archie Brown, *The Gorbachev Factor* (Oxford: Oxford University Press, 1996), 220–5.

denied the existence of any positive experience in the USSR and argued for full acceptance of civilized (i.e. Western) values. In their view this did not mean a capitulation to the West or the abandonment of traditional Russian values, as their 'patriotic' opponents argued. 'Democratic' views were based on a deep-seated belief in the existence of 'global values' applicable to any part of the world, which formed the basis for world civilization and for the fundamental unity of the world. Therefore, in rejecting Soviet values, they saw them not as something positive or unique, and therefore worth keeping, but as constituting a narrow, barbaric class approach to global ideals. These natural global values were understood to be the same as Western values, since the West had never departed from the road of progress, bound to be sooner or later accepted all over the world.

The belief about the 'unity and interdependency of the world, about the common fate of humanity which on the contemporary stage needs to unite its efforts in order to solve global problems'[32] was shared by most 'democratic' groups. This belief emerged first of all as a result of the class morality of the Bolsheviks. The programme of the Democratic Union, for example, argued that the theory and practice of Bolshevism was based on the following principles:

—a confrontational view of the world, absolutization of the class approach, stretching the idea of the dictatorship of the proletariat to seizing and holding power at all costs;
—the fetishization of the role of the state, turning the state into an exclusive subject of all social relations, the primacy of the state over society and the individual;
—rejection of universal human values, moral relativism, devaluation and destruction of the personality, abolition of human rights and freedoms.[33]

It is clear that the authors rejected a class approach and strongly believed in the existence of universal moral values, and that their realization in politics would mean understanding the importance of worldwide unity, reducing the power of the state, and promoting the role of society and individual rights.

The leader of the Civic Dignity group, Viktor Zolotarev, enumerated the universal values which, in his view, should be the essence of any politics. He argued that 'politics can and should be based on the firm foundations of a humanist morality of contemporary civilized society' and included among these fundamentals: 'the primacy of humanism and a non-violent approach to the world and relations in the world; the proclamation of the unity of aims and the means used to achieve these aims; conscious rejection of deception, duplicity, and pure utilitarianism'.[34] According to Zolotarev, a 'return' to

---

[32] *Put' progressa i sotsial'noy demokratii. Osnova programmy SDPR. Vremennaya redaktsiya* (Moscow and Sverdlovsk: [publisher], 1990), 24.
[33] 'Proekt programmy partii Demokraticheskiy Soyuz', in *Byulleten' soveta partii*, Feb. 1990, 13.
[34] V. Zolotarev, 'Nravstvennaya deklaratsiya Grazhdanskogo Dostoinstva. Proekt', *Byulleten' obshchestvennoy organizatsii Grazhdanskoye Dostoinstvo*, 18 (Feb. 1989), 4.

these values was necessary for the successful development of his country. He wrote:

All of the actions of the authorities in the USSR over the last seventy years have been conducted under the circumstances of a total loss of moral, ethical, and humanist guidelines, which were replaced by considerations about the highest interests of the implementation of Marxist-Leninist ideas. This established the dangerous tendency of a purely opportunistic approach to the events of life and politics. Overcoming this inheritance is a necessary condition for democratic development and for the moral and humanist revival of the country.[35]

Though the moral principles declared by 'democrats' were sometimes the opposite of those of the Communist class morality, the very idea of a society based on a new morality was quite similar to that of the rejected Soviet Communist theory, with its concept of a 'new man' and the 'code of a constructor of communism'. In this case again the core belief was kept, while its contents were changed to those of its opposite. New Russia and the world was now to be based on still universal, but very different, principles, the bearer of which was not the USSR, but the democratic Western world.

7.6. THE 'DEMOCRATIC' FOREIGN POLICY

Russian 'democrats' directly connected the character of foreign policy to the character of the social system of the state. The programme of one of the most radical opposition groups, the Democratic Union, argued: 'A country's foreign policy, its principles and essence, is a continuation of the principles and character of its internal policy'.[36] This phrase, which is in fact a paraphrase of one of Lenin's famous dicta, could well be endorsed by any Marxist. However, as the evaluation of the internal policy of different countries became the opposite of what it had been before, so did the evaluation of their foreign policy. According to 'democratic' beliefs the foreign policy of Soviet totalitarianism was seen as a continuation of its repressive internal policy and as a direct cause of all major conflicts and problems in the international arena. A rejection of Soviet internal policy was to lead to a radical change in foreign policy. The programme of the Democratic Party described the foreign policy of the USSR in the following way:

The history of Soviet totalitarianism is the history of intensifying international tensions, of distrust between the peoples of the USSR and of the rest of the world. The disregard for human rights inside the country, the unwillingness to take into consideration the

---

[35] Zolotarev, *Byulleten` obshchestvennoy organizatsii Grazhdanskoye Dostoinstvo*, 5.
[36] 'Programma Demokraticheskogo Soyuza', in *Rossiya: partii, assotsiatsii, soyuzy, kluby*, ii 64.

international agreements on this matter, claiming the absolute character of the chosen road of development for the country—which was called socialist—the erroneous idea that all peoples and countries should take this road—all this led to the expansionist foreign policy towards the countries of Eastern Europe and of other regions. The implementation of this policy constituted a threat to the forces of democracy, peace, and humanism, and caused the militarization of the economy and the constant attempts at military and political expansion against other countries.[37]

Soviet military actions aimed at the suppression of people's movements in the GDR, Hungary, and Czechoslovakia and the Soviet invasion of Afghanistan were interpreted by the programme as the 'external manifestations of totalitarianism'.[38]

The pattern of 'democratic' foreign policy was constructed by the 'democrats' in direct opposition to that of totalitarian foreign policy. The programme of the Democratic Union argued that 'a democratic foreign policy means equality in international relations, respect for the rights and sovereignty of nations and observation of their right to freedom and to choose their own path'.[39] It was implied, however, that the right to choose the path of development and the rejection of imposiition of a political system on other countries was significant only in the case of the relations between totalitarian powers, principally the USSR and nations oppressed by totalitarian powers. There was no real choice for free countries, since they were believed to have naturally chosen the 'normal' road: the road of Western civilization. Only direct or indirect totalitarian pressure could prevent them from doing so. Since the bearer of universal human values for the Russian 'democrats' was Western civilization, the new, 'democratic' foreign policy of the USSR would in their logic have meant fully rejecting the totalitarian course and uniting with the Western world in support of its aims and the goals of its leaders, since they were seen as the leaders of world democracy.

The West was not expected always to be absolutely altruistic in its defence of the universal interests of civilization. In some cases the essence of Western foreign policy was interpreted as a struggle for power, for hegemony over the East. This opinion was expressed, for example, by Valeriy Fadeev. He admitted that in its foreign policy the USA defended its own economic and other interests, but, in his view, Russia's interests coincided with those of the United States. According to Fadeev, Russia should join the West because Western civilization and values were closer to those of Russia and in Russia, 'after all, Western civilization dominates, beginning with Christianity and all its values'. Fadeev argued that since Russia was on the 'periphery of the Western world', it was in its interests to play the role of a buffer between the

---

[37] 'Programma Demokraticheskoy Partii', in *Rossiya: partii, assotsiatsii, soyuzy, kluby*, ii. 7.   [38] Ibid.

[39] 'Programma Demokraticheskogo Soyuza', 64.

West and the East, protecting the West from 'less cultured forms of life', towards which Muslim fundamentalism, for example, was leading. Russia could receive technical and financial aid for playing this role.[40]

Though hopes for unity with the Western world were high, there were some doubts concerning the ability of the West to understand that its fundamental interest was not in achieving purely materialistic gains but in assisting world progress and therefore in assisting Russian democracy. Because of this, the programme of the Social Democratic Party of the Russian Federation suggested explaining this to the Western public. The programme argued that it was necessary 'to convince public opinion in Western countries that their fundamental interest is not so much in material benefit from joint economic projects as in securing the conditions for the advance of civilization'.[41] The source of these expectations of Western help was the Soviet idea that the USSR, being the centre of world Communism, should promote Communism and progress all over the world. In 'democratic' thinking the centre of world progress was moved to the West and Russia became its underdeveloped periphery, which should be helped by the more progressive and stronger democratic brother. There was little doubt that in the end massive Western help would come in every area, since democratic Russia would sincerely fulfil its obligations as a junior 'democratic' partner in the fight against the remnants of totalitarianism all over the world.

This led the majority of Russian 'democrats' to believe that a 'democratic' foreign policy should be aimed not just at rapprochement with the West, but at adopting its international policy, which was understood as a united 'democratic' policy of civilized nations. This implied the full acceptance of the aims of this policy as one's own. To adopt such a new 'democratic' foreign policy the 'totalitarian' foreign policy of the Soviet Communist rulers not only had to be changed, but to be reversed.

This construction of the foreign policy agenda on the basis of the rule of opposites can be seen clearly in the programme of the Democratic Party. It envisaged the following measures:

a) rejection of the policy of expansion; withdrawal of all foreign troops from foreign territories;

b) observation of human rights as a guarantee of trust between peoples, which is the main condition for peace and friendship among them;

c) observation of human rights in all countries; solidarity with the peace-loving forces of other countries, and with international human rights, ecological, and pacifist organizations. The main criteria for providing assistance to a country must become its record on securing human rights and major freedoms.[42]

---

[40] Interview with Valeriy Fadeev (Moscow, 13 Aug. 1993).
[41] '*Put' progressa i sotsial'noy demokratii*' 26.
[42] 'Programma Demokratcheskoy Partii', 7.

Despite the claim that the new 'democratic' foreign policy should be ideology-free, a new 'human rights' messianism was taking the place of Communist messianism. So was 'democratic' internationalism, from whose roots in the former Communist internationalism come such phrases as 'solidarity with the peace-loving forces of other countries', and the idea of providing assistance to friendly countries. However, the reverse pattern of the interpretation of official ideology manifested itself in the opposite character of the foreign policy (expansion—withdrawal), the opposite basis for solidarity (class similarity—human rights) and the opposite groups defined as friendly (human rights, ecological, and pacifist groups as opposed to Communist parties and pro-Communist trade unions).

Similar demands were put forward in the first programme of the Democratic Party of Russia. The programme argued that Russian foreign policy should be free from ideology and based on securing Russia's national interests and human rights. But Russia's national interests were interpreted from the internationalist point of view, and to secure these interests Russia was to become part of the world community: 'The world of humanity is one, regardless of beliefs, race, or nationality. There should be no place for confrontation, military or ideological, in it. We, together with all free citizens of Russia, want to live in an open and prosperous society, based on the priority of universal human values.'[43]

The combination of the belief in the direct connection between a country's economic situation and its foreign policy, and the interpretation of the contemporary Soviet economy as being in deep crisis—a result of totalitarian mismanagement of the economy—led to demands for radical reductions in military spending. The 'democratic' vision of the future of international military cooperation was quite idealistic and impractical. The programme of the DPR continued:

As for military doctrine, it is becoming evident that a continued arms race will be in more and more striking contradiction to our economic abilities. The current official doctrine of military sufficiency is beyond the abilities of this ruined country. In recent decades it was we who posed the main danger to peace, therefore it is we who should make the first step towards peace by suggesting the creation of joint UN armed forces. These forces would be a guarantee against the possible growth of local conflicts into a world war, especially under the conditions of constant threat on the part of fanatical dictators in some countries.[44]

The idealistic view of the post-Communist world is very obvious here. Most 'democratic' foreign policy programmes show a striking lack of awareness of specific questions of the international situation and the mechanisms of international organizations. They are also usually written very vaguely,

---

[43] 'Programma Demokraticheskoy partii Rossii', 16. [44] Ibid.

without discussing specific problems of relations to a specific country or region and without suggesting specific measures for addressing these problems. However, the lack of awareness and vagueness were not solely the result of ignorance (though of course very few 'democrats' were experts in international relations). The main reason was the belief that after the defeat of totalitarianism in the USSR it would not be necessary to go into much detail about foreign policy, since it would be simple. The greater part of the world would be 'democratic' and there could be no conflict among democratic countries. Therefore there was no need to be very subtle in elaborating foreign or military policy towards them. As the programme of the DPR put it: 'Our variant of the military doctrine is this: civilized countries do not threaten each other'.[45] Another reason for the fact that 'democratic' foreign policy programmes were not very elaborate was that in most cases the prospect of influencing decisions in this sphere was seen as remote and the main task was believed to be the destruction of 'totalitarianism' inside the country. This would automatically 'democratize' foreign policy. Despite all the differences, four main points of the 'democratic' international agenda can be found in most of the documents of 'democratic' groups and statements by their activists which concerned foreign policy:

1. granting the republics of the USSR the right to independence and building future relations with them on the basis of equality, as with any independent state;
2. rejection of expansionism and withdrawal of troops from all foreign territories;
3. reduction (including unilateral reduction) of the armed forces, of military production, and of the influence of the military on foreign policy;
4. active support for human rights abroad, and making the level of democracy and of the observation of human rights the main criterion of granting assistance to a country and of the general attitude toward that country.

7.7. CONCLUSIONS

This chapter's study of the beliefs of Russian 'democrats' about the outside world and Russia's place in it show that official Soviet ideology was the immediate source of these beliefs, just as it was for most other elements of Russia's 'democratic' political culture. The pattern of constructing 'democratic' beliefs was also similar: official ideological dogmas were not directly borrowed but in

---

[45] 'Programma Demokraticheskoy partii Rossii', 16.

most cases changed to their opposites. The most important official concepts which underwent this transformation in 'democratic' thinking were:

1. the division of the world into two opposites: the progressive Communist camp and the regressive capitalist or imperialist camp;
2. the understanding of international politics as a struggle between these two opposites in which, in the end, despite some possible setbacks, the progressive Communist world was destined to be victorious and spread its system all over the planet;
3. the perception of all countries which do not directly belong to one of the two camps as a field of struggle between capitalism and Communism; all these other countries sooner or later would have to choose between the two camps and should be judged according to this choice;
4. the understanding of world history as a forward movement through stages, from primitive socio-economic systems through capitalism towards communism;
5. the belief that all classes have their own ideologies, but that Communist (Marxist-Leninist) ideology is the only true ideology since communism is the most progressive and the final stage of social development;
6. the role of foreign policy as a means of achieving communism all over the world and in this way promoting world progress.

In 'democratic' political culture these concepts respectively turned into:

1. the division of the world into progressive 'capitalist' or 'democratic' and regressive 'Communist' or 'totalitarian' systems;
2. the understanding of world politics as a struggle between the 'totalitarian' and 'democratic' camps in which 'democracy' was bound to win;
3. the perception that countries which do not belong to either camp are confronted with a choice between 'democracy' (which leads to progress and prosperity) and 'totalitarianism' (which leads to social and economic collapse);
4. understanding world history as moving from primitive social organization through different forms of non-capitalist and non-democratic organizations (totalitarianism being one of them) to 'democratic' society as the highest and most perfect form of human society;
5. the belief in the existence of universal values, common to all classes, which in fact meant a rejection of Communist values and a recognition of the predominance of 'capitalist', 'Western', or 'democratic' values;
6. the role of foreign policy as a means of promoting 'democracy' all over the world.

This pattern of creating 'democratic' beliefs about the outside world does not mean that these new beliefs were a mere borrowing or rephrasing of previously existing themes. What was new was not the tendency to use Western terminology, to see Russia broadly as part of Western civilization, or to see Western values as global and therefore the only possible values applicable in Russia. These ideas have existed at different periods in Russian history, at least from the time of Peter the Great, and were parts of the belief systems of such different intellectual groups and political movements as the Enlighteners of the eighteenth century, the Decembrists and Westernizers of the nineteenth century, and the early Russian Marxists and social democrats. There is, however, an area in which the international vision of the Russian 'democrats' of the 1980s was unique. Never before had Russia's foreign policy interests been seen as making Russia the junior partner of the West, of submitting Russia to the broader Western foreign policy, which was understood as progressive and united. Previous generations of Westernizers, beginning from Tsar Peter, saw Westernization as a means of creating a greater and mightier Russia and of promoting Russia's influence, and as the best way of confronting Western powers. Therefore the most intellectually 'liberal' or pro-Western governments in Russia, such as the governments of Peter the Great, Alexander I, Alexander II, and the Provisional Government—especially when its foreign policy was in the hands of prominent Westernizer Pavel Milyukov—were at the same time the most active in the international arena, and supported foreign expansion and territorial gains and did not hesitate to confront specific Western powers at a time when the West did not yet see itself as united by sharing universal democratic values.

In contrast, the Russian 'democrats' of the 1980s saw Russia's interests not in strengthening the country's military power or international role, but tied democratization tightly to supporting every specific international policy of the West. Naturally, this course was not understood subjectively as anti-Russian by the 'democrats' themselves (as nationalist critics suggested). On the contrary, the fundamental Russian interest was seen to lie not in maintaining a great international influence and military might, but in becoming a 'normal', modest, but 'civilized' player in the international arena, one which respected its more experienced and credible democratic partners and listened to their advice. The basis of this idea was a new understanding of international reality according to which the centre of world progress was not in Russia but in the West and an exclusively Russian international role could only hinder democratization in the world.

Being a reaction to Communist claims that the Soviet Union was the centre of world progress, this concept in fact resembles some early ideas of Russian Marxists. When Russian Marxism was still an ideology of radical Westernization, the Western capitalist world was seen by Russian Marxist activists as more progressive than Russia's 'feudalism', and Russia was urged to develop capitalism in order to create the conditions for communism.[46] There was no doubt at that stage that communist revolution was first going to happen in the more developed West. Even immediately after coming to power in 1917 Lenin continued to wait for the world revolution. Writing in 1920, he defined the international significance of the Russian revolution as 'the historical inevitability of a repetition, on an international scale, of what has taken place in our country' and argued that when this happens and the proletarian revolution wins in 'at least one of the advanced countries . . . Russia will cease to be the model and will once again become a backward country (in the "Soviet" and the socialist sense)'.[47] However, since Western workers failed to meet the expectations of Russian Marxists, Russia was proclaimed to be socialist (Communist) and therefore more progressive and began to be seen as the centre of world progress.

The early ideas of Russian Marxists indicate that advocating a policy of subordination to the West in international politics was one of the options for Russian Westernizers. However, it could become overwhelmingly popular among Russian Westernizers only in the last decades of this century, after the belief in Western democratic unity and global values had become dominant in the West itself and in this form had penetrated Russia. This led to the rejection of the Communist project of creating the centre of world progress in the Soviet Union and of turning it into a militarily powerful and at the same time economically effective country.

[46] G. V. Plekhanov, 'Nashi raznoglasiya', in G. V. Plekhanov, *Sochineniya* (St Petersburg/Leningrad: Gasudorstvenhoe izdatel`stvo, 1923), ii; V. I. Lenin, 'The Development of Capitalism in Russia', in V.I.Lenin, *Collected Works* (London: Lawrence & Wishart; Moscow: Progress Publishers, 1966), iii. 21–607.

[47] V. I. Lenin, ' "Left Wing" Communism—An Infantile Disorder', in Lenin, *Collected Works*, xxxi. 21.

8

The Political Culture of Russian 'Democrats': the New and the Old

The aim of this concluding chapter is to put the political culture of Russian 'democrats' into a broader context by analysing its similarities to, and differences from, political concepts and beliefs in the West (above all those which form the basis of modern political science as an academic discipline); and also by comparing it with Russian and Soviet political theories of earlier periods and the political culture of the Soviet Union as a whole. This will permit a more precise definition to be made of the elements of continuity and innovation in the political subculture of Russian 'democrats', in order to determine the mechanism of innovation and of the maintenance of tradition, and to see how Western ideas were reinterpreted on Russian soil. It should be noted that some of this comparison will necessarily be preliminary given the contemporary state of the study of Western and, particularly, Russian and Soviet political cultures and political thought, which leaves much to be desired.

While a study comparing the belief system of Russian 'democrats' and beliefs that existed in Russia in earlier periods is limited by the lack of serious studies of the history of Russian beliefs, the comparison of the belief system of Russian 'democrats' with theories and concepts of contemporary political science is further complicated by a different problem. Beliefs which constitute a political culture do not necessarily consist of coherent concepts and often are not connected with each other logically; they can sit uncomfortably with each other or even be logically incompatible. It should be remembered that political culture is but an analytical model which consists of those beliefs typical of or most popular among the members of a social or political group. Unlike a concept or theory, it cannot be found in full in one or even several documents, it is not coherently formulated in any one book or article, and no member of the group believes in every single one of its components. Therefore conclusions such as 'the political culture of Russian "democrats" is a new version of the liberalism of John Stuart Mill' or 'of Friedrich von Hayek' are meaningless since theories such as Mill's and Hayek's are the views of individual thinkers, committed to paper in a highly structured and developed way (though not necessarily consistent in every detail), and it would be unreasonable to expect to find a view present in the same way in such an amorphous structure as a political culture of a group.

However, several methods of comparison are possible. Three methods will be used in this chapter. First, one can point to those elements of theories or concepts that were used and adapted by a political culture and analyse why it was that these elements were selected. Second, one can compare the political culture of Russian 'democrats' with broad ideological trends, such as classical Western liberalism, conservatism, or democratic socialism as a whole, provided that these trends effectively became parts of the political culture of different social and political groups in a specific period. Third, since, as shown by Leites, it is often difficult to determine what is allowed within the framework of the code of a given political culture, it is possible to determine its borders by finding out what it forbids or makes unacceptable. All three methods are used in this chapter.

8.1. DEFINING SOVIET SOCIETY: WHY 'TOTALITARIANISM'?

As shown above, to define Soviet society and the Communist regime, Russian 'democrats' often used terms from Western political science which were either not employed in official Soviet political literature or were banned from application to Soviet reality. The term 'totalitarianism' was probably the most popular among them. In the opinion of 'democrats', the definition of Soviet society as totalitarian did not contradict other definitions, such as 'party dictatorship', 'partocracy', 'administrative command system', 'dictatorship of bureaucracy', etc. In fact all these terms were often used as interchangeable synonyms of totalitarianism to emphasize a particular trait of the system. Characterizing their society as totalitarian, Russian 'democrats' were convinced that they were using terminology which was accepted in Western social science, and they knew very little or nothing at all about alternative Western approaches (except, perhaps, some of the approaches of those Western authors who thought the USSR to be a kind of socialist state and whom Russian 'democrats' believed to be victims of Soviet propaganda). Ironically the concept of 'totalitarianism' gained in popularity among Russian 'democrats' after it had come under strong criticism within Western political science and its application to the post-Stalin Soviet Union had lost many supporters.[1] What was the reason

---

[1] For an important account of Western and Soviet approaches to political power and the state in the USSR, see Archie Brown, 'Pluralism, Power and the Soviet Political System: A Comparative Perspective', in Susan Gross Solomon (ed.), *Pluralism in the Soviet Union* (London: Macmillan, 1983), 61–107.

for this popularity of the idea of totalitarianism in Soviet opposition circles, to the neglect of other Western concepts?

The approach of Russian 'democrats' towards their own country was far from theoretical; therefore one should look for the roots of the popularity of the idea of totalitarianism not in Western theoretical treatises but in their critical attitude toward the existing system, their idealization of the 'anti-totalitarian' West, and in the whole system of their political beliefs. For 'democrats', the Soviet state with its system of state power and social relations was a bitter enemy, not an object of academic analysis, while the West became an ideal to be imitated. It is natural therefore that to define this enemy they picked the concept which in the West was used by the most uncompromising critics of Soviet Communism and which, as was acknowledged by Western theorists themselves, became 'not merely an essentially contested concept on the model of liberty or democracy, or a value-laden normative idea in the fashion of all significant political ideas, but a term the primary meanings and uses of which are exclusively ideological'.[2]

It was particularly important for the penetration of the concept of 'totalitarianism' into Russia that, unlike most other theories of Communist regimes, the notion of totalitarianism had by the 1980s become a cliché in the Western mass media, including those broadcasting to the USSR in Russian. These broadcasts, and not the theoretical works of Western political scientists, were the main source of new ideas about Soviet society for Russian 'democrats'.

Accessibility and wide dissemination were not of course the only reasons accounting for the success of the concept of totalitarianism in Russia. The main reason was still that while Russian 'democrats' were hostile to the Soviet 'totalitarian' state, the main points of Western analysis (which reached Russian 'democrats'—often in a distorted form—through the main mass media and the writing of some of the famous authors of the period of *glasnost*), were met by Russian 'democrats' with sympathy and understanding, since they matched their own experience, beliefs, and wishes. Among these traits the most obvious was a fundamental opposition of totalitarianism to Western liberal democracy and to Western civilization as a whole, their absolutely antipodal character, which was clearly formulated and long stressed by the founders of the concept.[3] The idea of the opposition of two worlds and two civilizations was familiar to Russian 'democrats', who had

---

[2] Benjamin R. Barber, 'Totalitarianism', in David Miller, Janet Coleman, William Connolly, and Alan Ryan (eds.), *The Blackwell Encyclopaedia of Political Thought* (Oxford: Basil Blackwell, 1987), 526.

[3] See F. A. Hayek, *The Road to Serfdom* (London: Routledge, 1944), esp. 8–17; Karl R. Popper, *The Open Society and its Enemies* (London: Routledge & Kegan Paul, 1945). This idea was borrowed by the liberal enemies of totalitarianism from the Italian authors of the term, who invented it to describe the Italian fascist state as a positive alternative to liberal civilization. The term was later used in the same way by some of the Nazi ideologists. See Leonard Shapiro, *Totalitarianism* (London: Macmillan, 1978), 13–14.

been taught the official Soviet concept of the fundamental opposition of the socialist and capitalist worlds.

The parallels drawn by Western political scientists between the Soviet and Nazi regimes, in virtue of which the Soviet regime began to be thought of as totalitarian, were also perceived by Russian 'democrats' within the framework of this concept of the opposition between absolute good and absolute evil. For Russians these parallels contained significant value and emotional elements. To argue that the ruling Communist regime was fascist[4] or close to fascist in the USSR, where every child from nursery age knew that there could be nothing worse in the whole world than fascism, meant in practical terms not just academically to define the system, but to say that the USSR (Nazi Germany having long since been defeated) was the centre of the world's evil.

Russian 'democrats' were also sympathetic to the claim that there was a difference between the Soviet regime and an ordinary dictatorship. Theorists of totalitarianism argued that modern technology made totalitarianism a new, more stable, and more dangerous form of autocracy.[5] There are several reasons why Russian 'democrats' agreed with this view. First, defining the ruling regime as not just an ordinary evil (compared to a free, democratic society), but as an extraordinary, unique evil—the struggle against which should also be of extraordinary, unique importance—served very well the task of legitimizing this struggle and providing its participants with self-esteem. Second, defining the Communist regime as totalitarian made it possible to find periods in Russian history which could be put forward as better alternatives; for example, while tsarist autocracy, especially after 1905, was obviously not democratic from the point of view of 'democrats', it was still far more liberal than Communist totalitarianism and could therefore be a source of useful borrowings.[6] It also supported the belief that Russia in principle was moving in the right direction before the Bolsheviks' seizure of power and to remove their successors from power would put it back on the common path of world civilization.

[4] The term 'fascist' was usually used in the Soviet Union to describe the regimes of both Nazi Germany and Fascist Italy, and the term 'Nazi' was rarely used.

[5] This argument is very clearly developed, for example, in Carl J. Friedrich and Zbigniew K. Brzezinski, *Totalitarian Dictatorship and Autocracy*, 2nd edn. (New York: Praeger, 1966; 1st publ. in 1956), 3–13.

[6] This point of view was influenced by the well-known writings of Aleksandr Solzhenitsyn, who described tsarist authoritarianism as in every aspect superior to Soviet Communism. However, unlike most 'democrats' Solzhenitsyn dismissed parallels between the Russian past and the Soviet present and, at least at one stage, regarded Russian authoritarianism (and authoritarianism in general) to be superior to Western-type democracy precisely because 'weak' democracy is more likely to give way to totalitarianism. See e.g. Alexander Solzhenitsyn, 'As Breathing and Consciousness Return', in Alexander Solzhenitsyn (ed.), *From Under the Rubble* (London: Fontana/Collins, 1976; first publ. in Russian as *Iz pod glyb* (Paris: YMCA Press, 1974)).

At the same time the understanding of totalitarianism by Russian 'democrats' differed greatly from its Western interpretations, including those accepted in political science. It is not that a Russian 'democrat' would not agree that totalitarianism had certain specific characteristics noted by Raymond Aron or Carl Friedrich and Zbigniew Brzezinski in their descriptive definitions. Among these characteristics, first formulated by Friedrich in 1953, the 'totalitarian syndrome' consisted of: (1) an official ideology, which everyone living in the society is supposed to adhere to and which is focused on a 'perfect' final state of mankind; (2) a single hierarchically organized mass ruling party typically led by one man; (3) a technologically conditioned and near-complete monopoly by the party and bureaucracy of the effective use of all weapons of armed combat; (4) a technologically conditioned control over all means of effective mass communication; and (5) a system of terrorist police control.[7] In a later book, written jointly with Brzezinski, a sixth factor was added: central control and direction of the entire economy.[8] Aron, whose interpretation of totalitarianism was arguably the most popular in Francophone political science, formulates a similar 'five-point syndrome': one-party monopoly, an ideology which becomes the official truth of the state, monopoly on the means of coercion and persuasion (mass media) by the state and its representatives, state control over most economic and professional activities, the ideological transfiguration of all possible crimes, and in the end police and ideological terrorism.[9]

One-party rule, a total ideologization of society, a state monopoly on the mass media, state control over economic and social life, political terror, and the 'cult of personality' were surely seen by Russian 'democrats' as characteristics of their society. However, they approached its analysis from a rather different angle: not from an empirical (or, as in the case of Hannah Arendt, historical) position, but from the postulates of Marxism, and first of all its class theory, which were very familiar to them. From this point of view all the above-mentioned characteristics of totalitarianism had one common basis: the class domination of bureaucracy (the *nomenklatura*, partocracy, etc.).

Therefore the descriptive works on totalitarianism, like those of Friedrich and Brzezinski or Aron, which from the point of view of a member of the Russian opposition were only registering facts that were obvious to the Russians themselves, could not but fail to be very popular. George Orwell's *1984*, which got to the root of the phenomenon in describing the absolute

---

[7] Carl J. Friedrich, 'The Unique Character of Totalitarian Society', in Carl J. Friedrich (ed.), *Totalitarianism*, (New York: Grosset & Dunlap, 1964; 1st publ. 1954).

[8] See Friedrich and Brzezinski, *Totalitarian Dictatorship and Autocracy*, 22.

[9] Raymond Aron, *Democracy and Totalitarianism* (London: Weidenfeld and Nicolson, 1968, 194; 1st publ. 1965 in French). For a thorough discussion of the concept, see Shapiro, *Totalitarianism*.

domination of the new bureaucratic class, was even more popular for this very reason, and not just because of its literary form.

The only thing in theoretical works on totalitarianism that could attract Russian 'democrats' was seeing Soviet Communism and German Nazism as one phenomenon, which for them had not theoretical, but 'condemnatory', significance. This was only natural since the 'democratic' movement consisted not of theorists, but of political activists who put forward the concrete political aim of the elimination of the ruling regime. (This does not mean of course that the concepts of Western theorists of totalitarianism were uninfluenced by their own political views.[10])

The fact that the Russian opposition needed the concept of totalitarianism as an instrument of their criticism of the Soviet regime is clearly shown by the well-known dissident Vladimir Bukovskiy, who, although not a member of any 'democratic' group during the period under study (he was deported in 1976), was respected by many of them.[11] Bukovskiy begins his article on totalitarianism with the following explicit argument:

In order to define what totalitarianism is, one is usually forced to write a lengthy theoretical treatise or an equally lengthy description of the governmental structures and social institutions of a totalitarian state. This is a difficult and thankless task, for apart from being incomprehensible to a non-specialist, such scholarly definitions fail to convey the very essence of the subject: its utter inhumanity; its danger for mankind; and the degree of horror and desperation experienced by those unfortunate nations which are trapped by it.[12]

What mattered for Russian 'democrats' in a theory was not a cold analysis of the sources and characteristic features of totalitarianism, but its capacity for moral condemnation capacity. They used 'class analysis' of Soviet totalitarianism not only because such an approach was familiar to them, but also because the façade of academic terminology concealed its open moral condemnation.

Keeping this in mind it is easier to explain why other theories of Soviet society, such as pluralism, corporatism, or industrial society, did not impress Russian 'democrats' or the Soviet opposition in general. The earliest of these alternative theoretical approaches, the theory of industrial (or the new industrial) society, and the idea of the convergence of the two systems, was applied to the Soviet Union as early as the 1950s by Inkeles and Bauer, who noted some fundamental similarities between Soviet and Western societies.

[10] See e.g. Barber, 'Totalitarianism', 526.

[11] One of the groups of 'democratic' deputies of the Moscow City Council attempted to nominate Bukovskiy for the mayorship of Moscow against the *nomenklatura* candidate Yuriy Luzhkov after Gavriil Popov resigned in 1992, but the elections were cancelled.

[12] Vladimir Bukovsky, 'Totalitarianism in Crisis', in Ellen Frankel Paul (ed.), *Totalitarianism at the Crossroads* (New Brunswick, NJ: Transaction, 1990), 9.

According to them, despite the fact that the mechanism of power, the political regime, and the situation with respect to individual rights were very different, these differences were less fundamental than the historical movement toward industrial development, which characterized both systems. It was assumed that with the passage of time the more superficial political differences would disappear and the more objective laws of industrial development would push the societies of both types in one direction.[13]

According to the theory of convergence future society would have traits not only of Western democracy, but also of Soviet Communism, and therefore not only should the USSR move in the direction of Western freedoms, but also Western society, with its free-market economy, should move in the direction of more planning, increased state regulation, and the continuing greater concentration of the economy. From the point of view of most Russian 'democrats' (except most extreme leftists and anarchists, who were in a considerable minority) any theories that understood the USSR and the Western world as belonging to the same type of society and as developing in one direction obscured the fundamental opposition between good and evil.[14]

Paradoxically, the acute feeling on the part of Russian 'democrats' of the opposition of the two systems, which was rooted in their Marxist education and fuelled by their struggle to do away with the Soviet regime, was structurally very close both to most right-wing Western approaches to the USSR and to official Soviet ideology: both considered the two systems to be fundamentally different and bound to oppose each other. The Soviet authorities were sympathetic to many of the Western adherents of the theories of convergence and the new industrial society; the latter usually supported Brezhnev's policy of détente, which they saw as a practical step towards the rapprochement of the two societies. Therefore, although these theories were officially labelled as 'bourgeois falsifications', the works of their authors were translated and published in the post-Stalin Soviet Union.[15] At the same time the term 'totalitarianism' remained banned as a description even non-Soviet-bloc countries until *glasnost*`. Russian opposition activists as a consequence avoided the concept of convergence; the banned concept of totalitarianism became even more popular.

For similar reasons, a later attempt to use the concept of pluralism for theorizing about Soviet society could not be attractive to Russian 'democrats'.

[13] Alex Inkeles and Raymond A. Bauer, *The Soviet Citizen: Daily Life in a Totalitarian Society* (Cambridge, Mass.: Harvard University Press, 1959), 246–8.

[14] Some Russian opposition activists were initially sympathetic towards the theory of convergence but later their views evolved in a more pro-Western direction. For a most prominent example, see Andrey Sakharov's *Progress, Coexistence and Intellectual Freedom* (London: Deutsch, 1968) and his subsequent writings.

[15] For example, *The New Industrial State* (New York: Penguin, 1968), the work of John K.Galbraith, one of the chief proponents of convergence, was translated and published in the Soviet Union by Progress Publishers.

Though this theory did not imply a movement of Western society in the direction of Soviet Communism, by its application of the term 'pluralism', which has been long associated with democracy in Soviet society, it in fact also saw the two systems as belonging to one species. One of the most active proponents of this application, Jerry Hough, claimed to find 'pluralist aspects of Soviet society'[16] and argued that 'if the Soviet and Western political systems are each visualized as types of pluralist systems, then we are led to explore the respective impact of those aspects of pluralism which they have in common and those which differ'.[17]

The use of the notion of pluralism to define Soviet society had certain distinctive aspects. Political scientists suggest several definitions of pluralism. It is quite clear that the narrowest among them, according to which a 'pluralist state' is 'a situation in which there are many politically significant groups with cross-cutting membership',[18] does not fit Soviet reality. But even the attempts to apply to the USSR a broader version of Dahl's 'organizational pluralism', and similar concepts of 'institutional pluralism' or 'bureaucratic pluralism', or Hough's 'institutionalized pluralism', which while putting Soviet and Western societies under one rubric, at the same time pointed at significant differences, still could not satisfy the needs of Russian 'democrats'. For example, according to Dahl, institutional pluralism is 'the existence of a plurality of relatively autonomous (independent) organizations (subsystems) within the domain of a state'.[19] In the view of the majority of 'democrats', to say this of the Soviet system would be to conceal the total domination of the bureaucratic *nomenklatura* class. It is noteworthy that official Soviet ideologists before *glasnost`* similarly considered pluralism to be a bourgeois theory aimed at concealing the class domination of the bourgeoisie.[20] 'Democrats' differed from official ideologists in regarding existing Western democratic society as the real and only possible pluralism, but they obviously inherited some fundamental principles of the analysis of social reality from official Soviet Marxism.

Another aspect unacceptable to 'democrats' was the idea that the USSR in its development is moving in the right direction along with the rest of the world, which was implied by the theories of pluralism and the new industrial society. This is easily understood in terms of their political position. The demand to intensify the struggle against the regime and to use ever more radical methods, as derived from the inner logic of the development of the movement, would be impossible to justify under a theory which predicted that the

---

[16] Jerry Hough, *The Soviet Union and Social Science Theory* (Cambridge, Mass.: Harvard University Press, 1977), 5.   [17] Ibid. 14–15.

[18] D. Nicholls, *Three Varieties of Pluralism* (London: Macmillan, 1974), 56.

[19] Robert A. Dahl, *Dilemmas of Pluralist Democracy: Autonomy vs. Control* (New Haven, Conn.: Yale University Press, 1982), 5.

[20] See Archie Brown, 'Pluralism, Power and the Soviet Political System', 80–1.

detested society would improve with or without their struggle. The arguments of many supporters of the theory of totalitarianism, according to which Khrushchev's and even Gorbachev's reforms were aimed at deceiving public opinion and at maintaining the totalitarian regime, and were therefore not much different from Stalin's policy, suited the demands of the opposition much better. That is why, as shown above, the documents and speeches of 'democratic' activists often contained arguments that under Gorbachev the Communist regime did not reject its old ways and methods, as well as the yet more radical opinion that Gorbachev was no better or was even worse than Stalin or Brezhnev.

Paradoxically the Marxist theoretical inheritance, combined with the logic of their struggle, pushed Russian 'democrats' closer to the most right-wing Western approaches and points of view. It is not by chance that the authors and supporters of the theory of totalitarianism in the West (such as Brzezinski) most often supported a tough right-wing policy towards the USSR while adherents of convergence and pluralism (like Galbraith and Hough) stood for détente and greater cooperation.[21]

For similar reasons, attempts to apply other theories and concepts to Soviet society, such as 'corporatism', 'pressure groups', 'elite competition', etc., did not find sympathy among Russian 'democrats'. Corporatism, for example, is defined by Philippe Schmitter as

a system of interest intermediation in which the constituent units are organized into a limited number of singular, compulsory, non-competitive, hierarchically ordered, and functionally differentiated categories, recognized or licensed (if not created) by the state and granted a deliberate representational monopoly within their respective categories in exchange for observing certain controls on their selection of leaders and articulation of demands and support.[22]

This definition, like that of pluralism, was not originally designed for the USSR but was applied to Soviet society by several authors, notably Bunce and Echols.[23] Russian 'democrats' could argue that it implied far too much freedom of the separate institutions of state power from the central leadership, suggesting that Soviet society was similar to any other dictatorial or authoritarian regime. This was not very appealing to those who saw their struggle

---

[21] Hough explicitly points to the direct connection between these two conceptions of Soviet society and these two foreign policy stances toward the USSR: see *The Soviet Union and Social Science Theory*, pp. vii–viii. For a discussion of this question, see Aleksandr Lukin, 'Angloyazychnaya sovetologiya i obshchestvennye nauki v Rossii', *SSHA: economika, politika, ideologiya*, 9 (1995), 38–50.

[22] Philippe Schmitter, 'Still the Century of Corporatism?', *Review of Politics*, 36 (Jan. 1974), 93–4.

[23] V. Bunce and J. M. Echols III, 'Soviet Politics in the Brezhnev Era: "Pluralism" or "Corporatism"?', in Donald R. Kelly (ed.), *Soviet Politics in the Brezhnev Era* (New York: Praeger, 1980), 1–26.

against the Soviet regime as a battle against the world's major force of evil, comparable only to Nazi Germany.

The search for 'pressure groups' and 'competing elites'[24] could not appeal to 'democrats', since it, like the search for pluralism and corporatism, saw in the USSR a greater decentralization of power and a growing role for different factions and groups. 'Democrats' saw Soviet society as distinctly divided into two opposing groups: the generally united bureaucratic class, which enjoyed monopolistic control over all property, means of production, and power, and the oppressed 'people', wholly deprived of their rights. Thus, the term 'elite', was usually used by 'democrats' not to designate a faction within the ruling class but the entire 'class' of party and state bureaucracy.

The spread of the use of the term 'totalitarianism' among Russian 'democrats' did not mean, of course, that they were widely familiar with political science concepts of Soviet society and that they made a conscious choice. These theories most often became known to them through the mass media, official Marxist literature, or Soviet *perestroyka* writings, often in a distorted and unsystematic form. However, their choice was by no means accidental and was conditioned by their pre-existing beliefs and how they perceived the aims of their political activities.

8.2. THE BELIEFS OF RUSSIAN 'DEMOCRATS' AND CONTEMPORARY THEORIES OF DEMOCRACY

A comparison of 'democratic' beliefs with contemporary theories of democracy faces two difficulties. First is the difficulty of comparing a vague belief system which can be reconstructed only as a model with structured and developed theories. The other difficulty is the absence of one prevailing theory of democracy. The situation remains as Robert Dahl described it in 1956: 'there is no democratic theory—there are only democratic theories'.[25] Though the study of democracy has greatly advanced since that time, there is as much disagreement in this field as there was then.[26] Nearly forty years on, Dahl

[24] See e.g. G. Skilling and F. Griffits (eds.), *Interest Groups in Soviet Politics* (Princeton, NJ: Princeton University Press, 1971); Terry Cox, 'Democratization and the Growth of Pressure Groups and Post-Soviet Politics', in Jeremy J. Richardson (ed.), *Pressure Groups* (Oxford: Oxford University Press, 1993). For 'elite pluralism', see H. G. Skilling, 'Interest Groups and Communist Politics', *World Politics*, 18:3 (Apr. 1966), 435–51.

[25] Robert Dahl, *A Preface to Democratic Theory* (Chicago, Ill.: University of Chicago Press, 1956), 1.

[26] For a discussion of different theories of democracy in political science, see e.g. Howard P. Kainz, *Democracy East and West: A Philosophical Overview* (London: Macmillan, 1984); Anthony H. Birch, *The Concepts and Theories of Modern Democracy* (London: Routledge, 1993).

reflected that democracy 'is not so much a term of restricted and specific meaning as a vague endorsement of a popular idea'.[27] In a recent study James Hyland points out that 'while the very terms "democracy" and "democratic" carry with them the honorific connotations of legitimacy, there are widely divergent and sometimes incompatible accounts both of the nature of democracy and of the reasons why democracy is such a desirable form of government'.[28]

In his fundamental study Giovanni Sartori points to several quite different usages of the term 'democracy', depending on whether it is used as a part of such concepts as *political democracy, social democracy, industrial democracy*, or *economic democracy*. According to him, the latter three notions are inventions of recent times: 'The word *demokratia* was coined in the fifth century B.C., and from that time until roughly a century ago it has been a political concept'.[29] Sartori attributes the first analyses of social democracy to Alexis de Tocqueville and James Bryce, who understood democracy as a state of society or as 'an ethos and a way of life' (in Bryce's case) rather than a political form, social democracy being, according to this understanding, 'a society whose ethos requires of its members to conceive of themselves as being socially equal'.[30] Social democracy in this sense is connected to *primary democracy*, that is, 'small communities and voluntary organizations that may flourish throughout a society, thus providing the societal backbone and infrastructure of the political superstructure'.[31] In this respect Sartori points to the difference between social democracy, the characterizing element of which is its spontaneity and its endogenous nature, and socialist democracy, which is 'a policy enforced by a socialist state upon society'.[32]

The term 'industrial democracy', which was formulated by Sidney and Beatrice Webb at the end of the nineteenth century, stresses the necessity of workers' self-government and the importance of the management of a factory or a plant by workers themselves as the basic unit of democracy. 'Economic democracy' can be used in a similar way, meaning equality of control over the productive forces. However, it is also used with a different meaning, denoting a democracy 'whose policy is the redistribution of wealth and the equalization of economic opportunities'.[33]

Even if it is used in the political sense democracy is understood by political theorists very differently. Dahl, for example, distinguishes three types of concepts of democracy: Madisonian democracy, which stresses the importance

[27] Robert A. Dahl, *Democracy and Its Critics* (New Haven, Conn.: Yale University Press, 1989), 2.

[28] James L. Hyland, *Democratic Theory: The Philosophical Foundations* (Manchester: Manchester University Press, 1995), 36.

[29] Giovanni Sartori, *The Theory of Democracy Revisited* (Chatham, NJ: Chatham House Publishers, 1987), 8.   [30] Ibid. 9.   [31] Ibid.   [32] Ibid.
[33] Ibid. 10.

of a system of constitutional checks and balances designed to prevent 'the tyranny of the majority'; populist dictatorship, which envisages unlimited strengthening of popular control over the government by the broad application of the majority principle; and polyarchal democracy, which encourages social rather than constitutional checks and balances.[34] Barry Holden depicts five types of theories of democracy: radical democratic theory, which includes classical Greek approaches; new radical democratic theory, which denotes the new radicalism of the 1960s; pluralist democratic theory, developed particularly in the writings of Dahl; elitist democratic theory, as formulated by authors like Schumpeter; and liberal democratic theory, which covers the writings of authors from John Locke to Tocqueville and John Stuart Mill.[35]

In many cases the preferences of different political theorists are closely connected to their political allegiances. Thus, adherents of contemporary Western systems, like Joseph Schumpeter, equate democracy with existing institutions and procedures. Schumpeter's well-known definition describes the democratic method as 'that institutional arrangement for arriving at political decisions in which individuals acquire the power to decide by means of a competitive struggle for the people's vote'.[36]

While this definition is precise and provides 'a reasonably efficient criterion by which to distinguish democratic governments from others',[37] its application, combined with Schumpeter's suggestion that society itself could decide who constituted the people, leads to the denial of the right of ancient Athens (where most of the offices were filled by lot) to be called democratic and at the same time to a possibility of defining as democratic any society which is ruled by more than one person, if the ruling group itself elects its leaders.[38]

When comparing the positive attitudes of Russian 'democrats' towards democracy with various theoretical concepts of democracy, detecting differences becomes more difficult. As noted in Chapter 6, Russian 'democrats' associated democracy with freedom, social justice, prosperity, and perfection. The preceding brief outline of theories of democracy shows that all these characteristics of democracy can be found in at least some of these theories. However, there is a significant difference. While one usually meets these interpretations of democracy in different theories, some of these theories contradict and criticize each other. Consequently, those who, for example, see democracy chiefly as a system designed to preserve liberalism very often, though not always, argue with those who put justice or perfection above

[34] Dahl, *A Preface to Democratic Theory*.
[35] Barry Holden, *The Nature of Democracy* (New York: Harper & Row, 1974).
[36] Joseph A. Schumpeter, *Capitalism, Socialism, and Democracy* (New York: Harper, 1942), 269. [37] Ibid.
[38] For a discussion of these problems see Dahl, *Democracy and its Critics*, 121–2.

everything else. In the case of Russia all these beliefs coexisted within one political subculture. Of course there were discussions of what role the state should play in a democracy and how centralized power should be, and all these sorts of questions would be part of the political struggle in a contemporary democracy. However, the differences in answers to these questions by various groups of Russian 'democrats' did not form the lines of organizational division, or at least did not (or did not yet) prevent different groups from taking part in the common struggle for 'democracy' and against the existing regime. The line of division in Russian politics of the time was not between the supporters or critics of a significant state role in the future democratic Soviet Union, between the supporters and critics of a welfare state, or between those who saw democracy as unlimited liberty and those who interpreted it as stateless self-government of the people or fulfilment of each person's creative potential, but between those who supported and rejected the existing regime.

Therefore it was not uncommon to see in one and the same 'democratic' group or 'party' those who would be called socialists, anarchists, or new liberals in the West and who, as members of very different groups, most probably would be bitter political enemies. A 'democrat' was a 'democrat' as long as he or she rejected 'totalitarianism' and therefore stood for 'democracy'. The particular kind of democracy he or she stood for was not of course totally insignificant, but was less significant than a firm anti-totalitarian position, and in most cases was not the reason for joining a particular group. What mattered was the level of opposition to the authorities and the acceptance of a particular kind of oppositional activities. For example, the most cautious and moderate 'anti-totalitarians' joined groups like the Democratic Platform of the CPSU, which in many (but not all) cases did not mean sharing views with each other about Communism, socialism, the planned economy, or even the welfare state, but rather that at least at that stage they believed in the possibility of cooperation with the reformists within the CPSU. In contrast, those who were totally disillusioned with the authorities and preferred direct action, rallies, demonstrations, and hunger strikes joined the Democratic Union.[39] In fact such contradictory beliefs (from the Western, or theoretical, point of view) could well characterize the views of one person, for whom possible contradictions either did not exist or seemed of minor importance compared to the grand and urgent task of toppling totalitarianism. It is also important that only in Moscow (and perhaps Leningrad) was there a real choice of 'democratic' groups with different names, making it possible to choose

---

[39] For example, by virtue of their views on the future of Russia both Vladimir Lysenko and Valeriya Novodvorskaya can be called radical liberals. However, since Lysenko at a certain stage thought it possible to reform the CPSU he stayed in as the head of the Democratic Platform, while Novodvorskaya became one of the leaders of the radical Democratic Union, which united radical Marxists, socialists, and liberals alike.

between reformist Communists, socialists, anarchists, and liberals. In most other cities and towns the choice was either limited or did not exist at all. As a result, to oppose the regime one had to join a group whose name was selected either by chance or, as in the case of the Vladivostok branch of the Social Democratic Party of the Russian Federation (who were in fact radical liberals and later always supported Gaydar's reforms), was chosen in order not to challenge the authorities too bluntly.[40]

The possibility of the coexistence of potentially contradictory ideals and goals within one belief system was possible because of the domination of the strongest belief over the others, according to which the lack of freedom, justice, prosperity, and self-perfection were all caused by the existence and policy of the totalitarian state. The elimination of that state would open the way to change. This belief naturally influenced the interpretation of these components of democracy by Russian 'democrats' and made them distinctive.

If we use Isaiah Berlin's famous division of all concepts of liberty into negative and positive, it can be seen that Russian 'democrats' advocated negative liberty, since for them liberty, as discussed in Chapter 6, was freedom from coercion by the totalitarian state. However, to say this is not to define their attitude to liberty in full. According to Berlin, negative political liberty 'is simply the area within which a man can act unobstructed by others. If I am prevented by others from doing what I could otherwise do, I am to that degree unfree; and if this area is contracted by other men beyond a certain minimum, I can be described as being coerced, or, it may be, enslaved'.[41]

The Russian 'democratic' interpretation differed from this definition in its emphasis on state coercion. While Berlin's Western interpretation of negative freedom does not distinguish who coerces the individual—the state, another individual, or a group—Russian 'democrats' saw the primary source of coercion in the state, which they were used to and indeed had been subjected to from childhood, and only the most socialist-minded of them on rare occasions might discuss the highly remote and purely theoretical possibility of individuals or non-state groups becoming a source of coercion. Moreover, since official Communist propaganda emphasized the coercive role of private monopolies and the capitalist class in Western democracies, Russian 'democrats', who saw these democracies as their ideal, tended to disbelieve the authorities and to disregard the possibility of 'private coercion' at all.

Since the main obstacle to freedom was understood to be the totalitarian state, the flourishing of freedom following its removal did not have to be seen as in any way contradictory to justice or equality. Though an anti-state and anti-totalitarian vigour of a Hayekian type was very popular among Russian

[40] Interview with Il`ya Grinchenko (Vladivostok, 24 Apr. 1994).
[41] Isaiah Berlin, 'Two Concepts of Liberty', in Isaiah Berlin, *Four Essays on Liberty* (Oxford: Oxford University Press, 1969), 122.

'democrats', Hayek's emphasis on the contradiction between freedom and equality was not widely known:

The great aim of the struggle for liberty has been equality before the law . . . Equality of the general rules of law and conduct, however, is the only kind of equality conducive to liberty and the only equality which can be secure without destroying liberty. Not only has liberty nothing to do with any other sort of equality, but it is even bound to produce inequality in many respects. This is the necessary result and part of the justification of individual liberty: if the result of individual liberty did not demonstrate that some manners of living are more successful than others, much of the case for it would vanish.[42]

As shown in Chapter 6, Russian 'democrats' understood democracy as based on a far broader equality than just equality before the law. In fact economic equality was one of their core demands; it was this demand which earned them public support. However, Russian 'democrats' approached questions of economic and political equality from a very different perspective to those Western theorists who lived in a situation of competition among individuals (which from the point of view of some of them was only just coming under threat from growing state power). Life under total state control gave birth to very different beliefs.

The attitudes of Russian 'democrats' to equality should be understood within the general framework of their perception of the society they lived in. According to this perception the chief abuser of both freedom and equality was the totalitarian state and in the case of equality this abuse was manifested in the creation of the ruling *nomenklatura* class, members of which were granted privileges in both the legal and economic spheres. These two types of privileges could hardly be seen by 'democrats' as in any way different or separate: the privilege of a high Party or government official of being exempt from the jurisdiction of an ordinary court was all of a piece with the privilege of buying better food from special shops at a cheaper price and of going to special resorts for holidays. The replacement of totalitarianism by democracy was understood by Russian 'democrats' as the abolition of class or status privileges; therefore it was difficult for them to understand why, as Hayek claims, 'any policy directly aiming at a substantive ideal of distributive justice must lead to the destruction of the rule of law'.[43]

This does not mean, of course, that most of the Russian 'democrats' were social democrats in the Western sense, though some of them were sympathetic in a purely academic manner to the idea that economic democracy should follow political democracy and that material inequalities should be limited and the poorest should be helped by society. However, that was not tantamount to being a social-democrat or a conservative in the contemporary

---

[42] F. A. Hayek, *The Constitution of Liberty* (London: Routledge & Kegan Paul, 1960), 85.
[43] Hayek, *The Road to Serfdom*, 59.

European sense (or a liberal or a right-winger in the contemporary USA), involving a conscious choice between increasing or decreasing the economic role of the state. To make these choices one needs to see and understand these alternatives and for this some experience of living in a market situation is needed. Russian 'democrats', regardless of whether they saw themselves as liberals or social democrats, did not really see this alternative or give it much thought; this kind of choice was not on their agenda. They differed in their preferences on the way democracy should be created: 'liberals' might advocate the ultimate destruction of the state, thinking that the new democratic structure would emerge naturally by itself; 'socialists' might argue that a smoother transition and some use of existing state structures was needed. But this was more a tactical than ideological difference. It did not mean that 'liberals' consciously chose more freedom and the formal rule of law at the expense of equality, because they agreed with Hayek that to 'produce the same result for different people it is necessary to treat them differently'.[44] They believed that only a radical destruction of the old system was the best and fastest way to create democracy, which was freedom (from state coercion), equality and the rule of law (since the privileges of the *nomenklatura* would disappear), and either they were reluctant to see much danger in the possibility of private encroachments on liberty or of private inequalities, believing them to be deliberately exaggerated by official propaganda, or they thought that these problems would somehow be solved by themselves in the future heaven of democracy, as had supposedly happened in the successful West. In this respect it can be argued that the idea of social justice, which was the core demand of both Russian Communists and Russian 'democrats', was turned upside down by the 'democrats': from the demand for equality among individuals in relation to each other which should be promoted by the Communist party-state as the arbiter it became a demand for the equality of the oppressed class in relation to the oppressor state. State-promoted egalitarianism became radical anti-statism.

The radical rejection of the old state did not, however, necessarily mean that the state was rejected as such. Some 'democrats' spoke of the necessity of a strong democratic state. However, among 'democrats' there were also supporters of a minimal state. The question was not vital: as since victory over the all-powerful totalitarian state seemed remote, it mattered less which kind of state to create after that victory had been achieved.

This led to a unique situation: belief in a Nozickian minimal state[45] and Rawlsian 'justice as fairness',[46] in a liberal *Rechtsstaat* (law-based state) and

---

[44] Ibid.

[45] See Robert Nozick, *Anarchy, State and Utopia* (New York: Basic Books, 1974).

[46] See John Rawls, *A Theory of Justice* (Cambridge, Mass.: Harvard University Press, 1971).

a *gerechte Staat* (the just state, the term of National Socialist legal theorist Carl Schmitt)[47] could very well coexist in one and the same Russian 'democratic' programme, among members of one group, or even within the belief system of a single 'democrat'. Only after the first 'democratic' attempts at introducing the market and limiting the state's role did questions of contradiction between efforts to make Russia 'like the West' (as it was understood) and radical demands for social justice become an issue for 'democratic' activists. And even then the continuing presence of the main enemy kept 'democrats' together; the real problems and splits over the choice between 'more equality' or 'more freedom' began after the start of Gaydar's reforms, which created inequalities unheard of in the USSR.

The ideals of prosperity and perfection were approached the same way. It was believed by Russian 'democrats' that the totalitarian state was the only obstacle to achieving these goals. Just as the Communists believed that prosperity or self-realization follows from the removal of the class of capitalist oppressors, and just as modern utopians posit that the development of modern technology will give people greater leisure time to reflect on the vital questions of their life, Russian 'democrats' believed that everything was possible after the removal of the totalitarian state oppressor. Therefore it would have been difficult for a Russian 'democrat' to accept the attempts of some Western theorists to separate democracy from individual freedom or individual freedom from prosperity, or to understand how there can be 'no necessary connection between individual liberty and democratic rule',[48] or that 'we may be free and yet miserable'.[49] For them democracy was not only a procedure, but the whole way of life of what they called 'Western civilization', which they saw as free, just, prosperous, and creating the best possible conditions for people's self-realization and happiness at the same time.

It is noteworthy that such a broad understanding of democracy led to an uncritical acceptance of democratic procedure as a part of this way of life, which for many constituted its basis. In this respect Russian 'democrats' were closer to those Western theorists who advocate the maximization of democracy through a fuller application of the principle of majority rule and are not worried about the dangers of the tyranny of the majority. The line of argument against unlimited majority rule, which runs from Aristotle and Plato through Madison, Tocqueville, and John Stuart Mill to contemporary theorists such as Schumpeter and Dahl, and which warns of the dangers of a simple application of the principle of majority rule and offers different measures for limiting and balancing it, could not be accepted or even carefully considered by Russian 'democrats', whose primary concern was to topple the system of

[47] See Hayek, *The Road to Serfdom*, 59.
[48] Berlin, 'Two Concepts of Liberty', 130.
[49] Hayek, *The Constitution of Liberty*, 18.

unjust minority rule. It was only logical to oppose such a rule by the principle of the rule of the 'people', and it was believed by 'democrats' that the 'people', if given a chance to choose, would naturally choose democracy, since 'democrats' thought it to be not only just, preferable, and more effective, but also natural and historically inevitable.

At the same time it was not exactly true that the principle of majority rule was in all cases advocated by Russian 'democrats'. The question of minority rights did arise. However, it is important to note that when these rights were opposed to majority rule, the reason was usually not, as in the above-mentioned theories, the fear of the tyranny of the majority. As with every preference of the 'democrats', putting forward either of these principles was instrumental to their primary aim: the destruction of the existing regime. For example, since the population of both the Soviet Union and the Russian Federation were likely to vote against the Kremlin regime, 'democrats' strongly advocated elections and referenda on almost any major policy question. However, this did not apply to the question of secession of the union republics from the USSR or of the autonomous republics from the RSFSR. Since secession was seen by some as diminishing the territory of totalitarian rule and therefore a blow against it, they criticized Gorbachev's proposals of organizing referenda on the question of the secession in the whole of the country, and not only in the republic concerned, since the population of the USSR could have voted against the secession of, say, Ukraine. They also were very critical of the reasonably democratic proposal of the Kremlin to launch three successive referenda in the republic concerned over a period of fifteen years, since, in their view, the process would be uncertain and would take far too long. In some cases arguments were put forward even against a single referendum in a republic, whose population might not understand well enough the importance of weakening totalitarianism in Moscow by proclaiming independence from it. Generally, the 'democratic' attitude toward referenda was instrumental to their general goal of the destruction of Soviet 'totalitarianism' and the Communist 'empire'.

A revealing example of this argumentation is a discussion between two leading members of the Democratic Russia faction at the Supreme Soviet of the RSFSR, Mikhail Astaf'ev and Anatoliy Shabad. Their positions on the future of the USSR and Russia were diometrically opposed. Astaf'ev stood for maintaining a united state which would consist of 'at least today's RSFSR, Ukraine, Byelorussia and Kazakhstan'.[50] He also supported the position of the First Congress of the People's Deputies of the RSFSR that autonomous republics should obtain independence from Russia only as a result of an affirmative decision of an all-Russian referendum and that the Russian government

---

[50] 'Rossiya: nedelimaya ili "delimaya" ', *Demokraticheskaya gazeta*, 7:13, (10 May 1991), 9.

should give equal self-government rights to both ethnic republics and Russian *oblast*'s and *krays*. Shabad's position on all these questions was the absolute opposite. He argued that apart from the 'great idea' of the equality of everyone regardless of nationality, 'there are also rights which result from one's nationality'.[51] Therefore he argued that ethnic republics should be given more rights than Russian regions and backed Gorbachev's Union Treaty giving the same status to Russian autonomous republics and the Soviet Union republics (including the right to secede).

How could two such different people work in one and the same movement? It was possible so long as, apart from the beliefs that separated them, there existed a stronger belief that they shared. This was a belief in 'democracy'; that is, according to their interpretation, the necessity of finishing off the old Soviet totalitarian state and building something in its place (though this something was seen very differently). If one reads the arguments of both 'democrats' carefully, one can see that both regarded their position as a better way of achieving this aim. Astaf ev argued that the independence of the RSFSR from the Union was nonsense so long as all of the resources, including the army and state finances, were controlled by the Union government. Therefore, he argued, decentralization should be gradual, with rights of self-government granted step by step to republics and regions. Otherwise these rights could be seized either by the old local *nomenklatura*, or by so-called 'national democratic' forces, which, according to Astaf ev, were those whose 'first priority is nationalism, with democracy only second or third'. An example is Ukraine's Rukh, whose representatives revealed to Astaf ev their plans to introduce the compulsory use of Ukrainian even in Russian-speaking areas of the republic and who opposed referenda on the autonomy of these areas. In contrast, Shabad stood for the immediate and abrupt destruction of the empire. He recognized that the local Communist elites could hijack the autonomous rights which were being given to autonomous republics according to the Union Treaty, but he thought that if these new rights were not granted, such elites would gain even more legitimacy by presenting themselves as the force which expressed national sentiments. Unlike Astaf ev, he was not worried about non-democratic tendencies in the 'national democratic' movements and saw them as an ally of the Russian 'democrats', since for him the main indication of their democratic character was their anti-imperialist or anti-centrist potential.[52]

While Shabad's and Astaf ev's positions on the future of Russia and the Soviet Union were very different, both shared a belief in democracy (as they understood it) and in the necessity of the destruction (whether faster or slower) of the non-democratic totalitarian centre. As long as this centre existed, they could work together, but when it disappeared and the main question became

---

[51] *Demokraticheskaya gazeta*, 7:13, (10 May 1991), 9.　　　[52] Ibid.

not destruction but what to build, they were bound to discover that they did not have anything in common any more. This in fact happened and while Shabad became one of the most radical of Gaydar's supporters, Astaf ev joined the nationalist camp.

The existence of several understandings of democracy within the 'democratic' political subculture did not mean that every single Russian 'democrat' believed with equal intensity that democracy would bring freedom, social justice, prosperity, and self-perfection interpreted in the way discussed above. Some could do so; others chose to emphasize some of these ideals; and some strongly believed in a single item, like social justice or freedom. But even the latter did not see a major contradiction in believing in the whole set at once and surely did not see those who emphasized a different aspect of democracy as their opponents, since they were allies in the struggle against totalitarianism, which at that stage mattered much more.

The same idealistic attitude toward democracy determined the differences between Russian 'democratic' and Western theoretical approaches to foreign policy. As discussed in Chapter 6, Russian 'democrats' refused foreign policy interests any existence independent from the interests of internal and world democratization. Such ideas as security interests, geopolitical calculations, the balance of power, and national interests, which in most theories of international relations are seen as more or less independent of a country's domestic policy or the character of the ruling regime, were either disregarded by 'democrats' or were seen as dependent on the task of democratization. Since 'democratic countries do not threaten each other', the only possible national or security interests of Russia would be creating democracy and joining the democratic world. It was believed that success in fulfilling this task would automatically lead to the solving of international problems.

Despite the obvious similarities between particular beliefs of Russian 'democrats' about Russian society or 'democracy' and contemporary Western theories of democracy, the 'democratic' belief system in its totality was very different from any single Western theory. Even if the terminology of Western political science or concepts common in Western political philosophy were used, they were reinterpreted and their meaning in the Russian context differed.

8.3. CONTINUITY, CHANGE, AND RUSSIAN POLITICS

At the very inception of Russian historiography scholars tried to ascertain the extent to which foreign theories and cultures determined the beliefs of Russians. Russia, in contrast to certain civilizations of Asia and America which for a long time developed without significant outside influences, has always been open to different cultural influences, including those from the West. It is very difficult to define any originally Russian or even Slavonic basis of Russian culture. In fact only pre-Christian pagan culture can arguably fit into this category, but despite growing interest in the study of this period, with a number of scholars finding pagan influence in some popular practices of later centuries up to very recent times, it is very difficult to draw any conclusions about the political beliefs of the pagan period because of the virtual absence of any written sources.[53]

The first half-mythical political act of the people of the ancient Russian state to be mentioned in a chronicle, namely the invitation of the Varangians, became the source of the discussion of the correlation between indigenous and borrowed elements in Russian political culture. The Norman theory of the origin of the Russian state, which was dominant in Russian historical theories from the eighteenth century, was subsequently largely disproved and today most specialists agree that the influence of Viking culture on ancient Russian society was quite limited.[54]

The adoption of Christianity meant a fundamental cultural transformation—the borrowing of a whole set of cultural categories and cultural language from the Orthodox Byzantine empire. However, this did not mean that Russian culture became Byzantine. As Vladimir Val`denberg wrote in his classic analysis of ancient Russian political thought, Byzantine influence

could not consist of a mere transfer of ready-made notions and could not give birth to just a *single* trend which could be named Byzantine. Byzantium could give Russian thinkers a stimulus for development and material for the substantiation of very different theories of the power of the tsar—all of which with equal reason can be called (or not called) Byzantine.[55]

If this is true for such an early period, when Russian civilization was not yet mature, it should be even more true for later Western influence. The forced dissemination of Western values and forms under Peter the Great, as a result of which Russian political culture adopted European political language and terminology, did not at all mean its full Westernization.

Moreover, the Western culture of the time was even less unified than Byzantine culture, and Russian thinkers were able to use very different, and even at times opposing, Western theories to substantiate their own ideas which they thought proper for Russia. As in ancient Russia, the theoretical

---

[53] See e.g. B. A. Rybakov, *Yazychestvo drevney Rusi* (Moscow: Nauka, 1987).

[54] See Nicholas V. Riasanovsky, 'The Norman Theory of the Origin of the Russian State', in Nicholas V. Riasanovsky, *Collected Writings: 1947–1994* (Los Angeles: Charles Scholacks, 1993); V. A. Riazanovskiy, 'Vopros o vliyanii normanov na russkuyu kul`turu', in *Historical Survey of Russian Culture* (New York: L. Rausen, 1947).

[55] Vladimir Val`denberg, *Drevnerusskie ucheniya o predelakh tsarskoy vlasti. Ocherki russkoy politicheskoy literatury on Vladimira Svyatogo do kontsa XVII veka* (Petrograd: Tipografiya A. Benke, 1916), 81.

sources of very different trends in Russian political thought could be found in the West,[56] but the sources of their specific political demands and proposals derived from the Russian political realities of the time.

There are many indications that Western political ideas have been adapted by modern Russian political thinkers and political activists in the same way as foreign political culture was adapted in earlier times. For example, while Russian Populists (*narodniki*) were bred on Western socialist literature and had some similarities with romantic revolutionary movements of the time elsewhere in the world, there is little doubt as to the uniqueness of their movement and the peculiarity of their interpretation of socialist theories. In her memoirs, Vera Figner, one of the leaders of the most radical terrorist Populist group, Narodnaya Volya, described very clearly how this interpretation was influenced by previous beliefs. According to Figner, who specifically wrote about how she was influenced by Marx's *Das Kapital*, which she first read in 1881,

> The book had an exceptionally powerful impact upon me; this was, one might say, my second baptism in socialism. Marx's impassioned eloquence imprinted whole pages upon my memory in words of fire . . .
>
> The knowledge that we feeble individuals were backed by a mighty historical process filled one with ecstasy and established such a firm foundation for the individual's activities that, it seemed, all the hardships of the struggle could be overcome.
>
> I did not reconsider all my previous views or all the earlier influences; I did not readjust my ideas on the basis of Marx's theory. The previous views remained as the underlying stratum above which was deposited everything learnt from *Capital*. These two layers never intermingled, but in some mysterious fashion they fused together and doubled the power of conviction and the determination to struggle and to fight—to fight now, immediately, using those weapons which were at hand and which were called for by the reality around us.[57]

Again, as in the case of Byzantine culture, Russians saw in a foreign theory, which was far from consistent in its own way, a proof of the correctness of their views and plans, despite the fact that these views and plans could be very different and even diametrically opposite. Radical revolutionaries, like Figner and Populist terrorists, and later Lenin and the Bolsheviks, overlooked the 'scientific' part of *Das Kapital*, Marx's arguments about the necessity for capitalism to mature naturally in order to become fit for transformation into socialism. At the same time moderate Populists, like Georgiy Plekhanov, who became moderate social democrats (Mensheviks), stressed this 'scientific' part of Marxism and tended to downplay his calls for

[56] On Western influences on Slavophiles, see N. I. Tsimbaev, *Slavyanofil'stvo* (Moscow: Izdatel'stvo Moskovskogo universiteta, 1986), 145–6.

[57] Vera Figner, *Polnoye sobraniye sochineniy*, v (Moscow: Izdatel'stvo politkatorzhan, 1919), 427; tr. in Tibor Szamuely, *The Russian Tradition* (London: Secker & Warburg, 1974), 382–3.

immediate revolution. The interpretation of external intellectual trends thus depended on the previous beliefs and on the already existing vision of present society and the means of its improvement. This is not to say that these previous beliefs and vision were eternally Russian or that this pattern of interpretation was characteristic only of Russia. On the contrary, it seems that Figner, like Val`denberg, described a very natural way of adapting new beliefs which is highly unlikely to be peculiar to Russians: it is very difficult to imagine a situation in which anyone would read, for example, *Das Kapital* without having previously acquired some other beliefs which would naturally influence their understanding of the new ideas. However, it shows that to understand a belief system it is not enough to point to an outside influence, since this influence can at the same time be found in very different belief systems. A study of the previously existing beliefs and the form of their 'fusion' with the new ones is very important.

Therefore it is not enough for a student of contemporary Russian political subculture to point to the obvious fact that it has its sources in both earlier Russian and Western political thought. It is necessary to define the exact contents of the different influences and the forms of continuity and change, the forms of that very fusion which Figner calls mysterious.

If one looks at the political subculture of Russian 'democrats' within a broader context of Russian history, it should surely be catalogued as an extreme form of Westernism. In this sense it is easy to see that some of its elements are similar to the beliefs of such Westernist political movements as the Petrine reforms, the Decembrist movement, the liberalism of the Kadets, and even Russian Marxism (especially the early social democrats and later Mensheviks). All these very different movements shared some fundamental beliefs: an understanding of history as the forward movement towards more perfect social forms, a perception of the West as having achieved a more advanced stage in its development along this road and as developing in the right way, and the perception of Russia as lagging far behind or even as having diverged from the development of world civilization.[58] As the first theorist of Russian Westernism, Petr Chaadaev, put it in his famous first philosophical letter in 1829:

But, you will say, are we not Christians, and is there no way of being civilized other than European? Certainly one can be civilised without being civilised in the European way. Is that not true of Japan, even more so than Russia, if we are to believe one of our compatriots? But do you think that the Christianity of the Abyssinians and the civilization of the Japanese will bring about that order of things I have spoken about,

---

[58]   On the general history of Russian political thought, see e.g. Vasiliy Zen`kovskiy, *Istoriya russkoy filosofii* (Leningrad: 1991; 1st publ. 1948); Thornton Anderson, *Russian Political Thought: An Introduction* (Ithaca, NY: Cornell University Press, 1967); Isaiah Berlin, *Russian Thinkers* (London: Hogarth Press, 1978).

which is the final destiny of the human species? Do you think these absurd aberrations of divine and human truths are capable of bringing Heaven down to earth? . . . Thus, despite all the imperfections, faults, and vices of European society as it is today, it is nonetheless true that the Kingdom of God finds itself in some sort realized there, because it contains the principle of continuous unlimited progress and harbors in embryo all the necessary elements for [God's Kingdom] one day to be finally established upon earth.[59]

It was thought by most Westernizers that Russia needed to leap forward to catch up with the West and, since Russian culture was the main reason for Russian backwardness, to do this the country needed to borrow and use forms of Western culture and civilization. These forms could be understood differently, depending on what was seen as central to the success of the West. Peter the Great mainly wanted to use Western technology and Western educational and military systems. The Decembrists (like later liberals) wanted to destroy tsarist autocracy and to introduce Western constitutionalism and other governmental forms. Chaadaev connected Western progress with Catholicism. Marxists such as Plekhanov and even Lenin at an early stage held that it was the remnants of feudalism and autocratic rule which hindered Russia's economic progress and stressed the need for the development in Russia of the economic forms of Western capitalism.[60] However, the belief that the borrowing of Western cultural forms was necessary for a historical leap forward was always present.

It is easy to see even greater similarities to the ideas of Russian 'democrats' in the beliefs of those Westernizers who regarded the authoritarian Russian political system, with its lack of constitutionalism and democracy, as the main obstacle to such a leap. For example, the Decembrist Count Sergey Volkonskiy said that after seeing Europe during the campaigns of 1813 and 1814 he understood that 'Russia significantly lagged behind in its social, internal, and political way of life'.[61] Petr Borisov, a member of the Society of the United Slavs, remarked in 1826 that from his youth he 'was blinded by the love of democracy and freedom'.[62] These themes were developed by Westernizers fifty and even a hundred and fifty years later.

Such similarities, however, do not mean that the beliefs of earlier Russian

---

[59] Peter Chaadaev, 'Filosophiches kie pis´ma. Pis´mo pervoe', 1 Dec. 1829) tr. in Mark Raeff, *Russian Intellectual History: An Anthology* (Brighton: Harvester, 1978), 169, 171.

[60] Lenin later changed his mind and argued that capitalism was already developed in Russia to a level sufficient for the immediate transfer to socialism. See G. V. Plekhanov, 'Nashi raznoglasiya', in G. V. Plekhanov, *Sochineniya* (St Petersburg/Leningrad: Gosudarstvennoe izdatel´stvo, 1923–7), ii; V. I. Lenin, 'The Development of Capitalism in Russia', in V. I. Lenin, *Collected Works* (London: Lawrence & Wishart; and Moscow: Progress Publishers, 1966), iii. 21–607, and Lenin's subsequent works.

[61] Quoted in V. I. Semenovskiy, *Politicheskie i obshchestvennye idei dekabristov* (St Petersburg: Tipografiya Pervoy spt. trudovoy arteli, 1909), 207.

[62] Quoted in ibid. 551.

Westernizers were directly borrowed by Russian 'democrats', whose historical knowledge was, as a rule, limited to school and university textbooks. Therefore, it is only possible to speak of the influence of Russian historical beliefs through the official ideology, within which they were usually reinterpreted in a way that made them very different from the original. Russian 'democrats', after getting acquainted with democratic ideas, might think that they were continuing the task of the Decembrists or the Kadets but in fact their image of this task was distorted by their previous ideological education.

This does not mean that the postulates of the official ideologies of these earlier movements were uncritically borrowed by 'democrats'. On the contrary, sometimes these postulates were different or (as in the case of the Kadets) even the opposite. But the very form of perception of these ideas was conditioned by existing beliefs, which were highly influenced by official Marxism.

Therefore it is important not to look for direct influences of earlier Westernism on the political subculture of Russian 'democrats', but to study the correlation of this subculture with official Soviet Marxism as the ideology in which they were socialized and with the dominant Soviet political culture of which they were a part. This study shows that these were two main sources of the structure of the 'democratic' political belief system, while certain beliefs could well have come from other sources.

This conclusion does not exclude an element of continuity in Russian political culture. While determining that the immediate source of the beliefs of the Russian 'democrats' was not pre-revolutionary ideas but official Soviet ideology and the dominant Soviet political culture, this study shows that continuity with Soviet political culture, at least in this particular case, manifested itself not in direct borrowing of traditional beliefs but in patterns of adaptation of new ideas.

What can be said about this pattern? Students of political socialization have discovered that political beliefs within a culture are adapted by both obverse and reverse imitation. The latter, according to Richard E. Dawson and Kenneth Prewitt,

sometimes takes place among adolescents, as they seek to shape an identity which differentiates them from parents and other authorities. Under certain conditions (when politics is highly salient to both the rebel and the ones rebelled against), this process can significantly alter the political self . . . The basic dynamics of rejecting the values of the imitated are similar to those taking place when the values are adopted.[63]

Both obverse and reverse imitation were surely characteristic of the pattern of political learning of Russian 'democrats'. But it was not limited to them.

---

[63] Richard E. Dawson and Kenneth Prewitt, *Political Socialization* (Boston, Mass.: Little, Brown and Co., 1969), 75.

Otherwise, the 'democratic' belief system would have been either another form of the official Soviet ideology or as authors like Sergey Cheshko claimed, its exact mirror image. This book shows, however, that this was not the case, since the system included many distinctly new elements, some of which came from Western sources.

Combining internal and external influences into one belief system was not an unfamiliar phenomenon in Russia. The most obvious example was Bolshevism itself, which later evolved into official Soviet ideology. According to Geoffrey Hosking, if 'one regards Populism and Marxism as two separate traditions, Bolshevism must be seen as a synthesis of the two, Marxist in its original impulse, but borrowing from the Populists the ideas of the peasants as a revolutionary class, of leadership by a small group of intellectuals and of overstriding the bourgeois phase of social evolution to reach the socialist revolution directly.'[64]

Russian 'democrats' combined Western liberal ideas with official Soviet ideology in a similar fashion. This combination cannot be a result of just imitating and reversing previous ideas. Studying cultural change in Russia up to the end of the eighteenth century, Yuriy Lotman and Boris Uspenskiy found two such patterns:

1) The deep structure which evolved in the foregoing period is preserved. But it is subjected to drastic renaming while still maintaining all the basic features of the old structure. In this case *new texts* are created while the archaic cultural framework is retained.

2) The deep structure of the culture is itself changed. But in this process it reveals its dependence on the previous cultural model since it is constructed by turning the old culture 'inside out', by rearranging what has previously existed but with a change of signs.[65]

The patterns of renaming and rearranging are both clearly seen in the case of the Russian 'democratic' political subculture. The whole process of democratization, like *perestroyka* itself, was seen as a revolution, just as the Bolsheviks' coming to power in 1917 was so interpreted by official Marxism. But the purpose of the 'democratic' revolution was to be the opposite: whereas the 1917 revolution created the Communist regime, the 'democratic' revolution was meant to destroy it. Democratic procedures, which in Western democratic cultures are regarded as the essence of democracy, were seen by

---

[64] Geoffrey Hosking, *Russia: People and Empire (1552–1917)* (London: HarperCollins, 1997), 365. On the correlation between Bolshevism and Populism, see also Nicolas Berdyaev, *The Origin of Russian Communism* (London: Geoffrey Bles, 1955, 10; 1st edn. 1937); and Szamuely, *The Russian Tradition*, 287–415.

[65] Ju. M. Lotman and B. A. Uspenskij, 'The Role of Dual Models in the Dynamics of Russian Culture (up to the End of the Eighteenth Century)', in Ju. M. Lotman and, B. A. Uspenskij, *The Semiotics of Russian Culture*, ed. A. Shukman (Ann Arbor, Mich.: Michigan Slavic Publications, 1984; 1st publ. in Russian, 3).

'democrats' as a means of attaining an ideal 'democratic' society, and to better fulfil this role democratic procedure could be modified and limited. An objective process formed the basis of the development of society, but Bolshevik and Soviet Marxism treated this process as a tool which could be manipulated by the revolutionary party, first for the creation of the conditions for revolution and then for achieving the ideal communist society.

The ideal society, as in official ideology, was seen as just and prosperous and as providing the conditions for a perfect life, but since total nationalization, an unlimited role for the state, and the utter subjection of the individual to the collective failed to achieve this aim, it was now to be achieved by total denationalization, unlimited individualism, and the destruction of the 'totalitarian' state. The ideal itself was reinterpreted: It was now not the future communist society, but its opposite in the official ideology: the 'rotten' capitalist West became the civilized democratic world. The idea of internationalism, of a worldwide alliance in the fight for the ideal, also remained, but this time it was not a Communist, but an anti-Communist 'international', an alliance not of the 'reds' but of the 'whites'.

Though all these opposite values and beliefs sounded Western, in fact their interpretation was based not on Western theories, but on a reversal of official ideas about what was socially negative, on their distorting mirror image of Western democracy. Since this idea of the 'socially negative' included not only the West but the Russian past, a great interest emerged in Russian anti-Bolshevik ideas from before 1917.

The foregoing analysis of the attitudes of Russian 'democrats' of the *perestroyka* period shows that a 'democratic' political subculture developed in the last years of the USSR under the influence of official Soviet ideology, the dominant Soviet political culture (which in turn developed on the basis of some earlier Russian beliefs), and Western liberalism. However, this does not exclude similarities between the 'democratic' and earlier cultures—although those similarities were not a result of direct borrowing. To the degree that official Soviet ideology itself can be interpreted as a product of a similar reinterpretation of earlier Russian culture, the deeper roots of Russian 'democratic' thinking are to be found. For example, some authors find that looking at the West as a social ideal was common at certain periods of Russian history. In pre-Petrine times, to prove the legitimacy of their power and faith the Muscovite princes, especially Ivan the Terrible, stressed a direct blood relationship with the Roman emperors and described Rome as an ideal state.[66] According to Lotman and Uspenskiy, Peter I himself reinterpreted the formerly dominant belief about the contemporary West as a

---

[66] Yu. M. Lotman and B. A. Uspenskij, 'Echoes of the Notion of "Moscow as the Third Rome" in Peter the Great's Ideology', in Lotman and Uspenskij, *The Semiotics of Russian Culture* (1st publ. 1982 in Russian); 53.

sinful and harmful place, embracing its opposite by ascribing to the enlightened West, from where the light of reason must come to Russia, some of the properties of the formerly holy lands (the East).[67] Describing the Russian Westernism of the nineteenth century, Berdyaev interprets it as 'more of an Eastern phenomenon than a Western', since to Western peoples 'the West was a reality and not infrequently a repugnant and hateful reality' while to Russian Westernizers 'the West was an ideal, it was a vision'.[68] For Berdyaev, Marxism in Russia was at first itself a form of radical Westernism since, according to classical Marxism, the economically developed West was closer to the projected future society than backward Russia. However, the Bolsheviks reinterpreted this notion, saying that Russia, because of the very weakness of its capitalism, was more capable of building the ideal society and that the capitalist West would be the one to resist. So Westernizing Marxism turned to its opposite: radical anti-Westernism.

The understanding of an ideal society as just and prosperous and as providing the conditions for personal perfection can also be found in Russian culture well before Bolshevik Marxism came into being. In the same way, Official Soviet internationalism can be seen as a transformation of earlier ideas of the formation of worldwide alliances to fight for the true Christian faith. The idea of individualism and the understanding of freedom as liberation from the satanic state can be found in many Russian belief systems, from those of the Old Believers and peasant insurrectionists of the seventeenth and eighteenth centuries to the anarchist revolutionaries of the nineteenth century like Mikhail Bakunin, and even in liberal opposition to tsarism such as the Kadets.[69]

The similarities of 'democratic' attitudes towards the state to certain earlier Russian beliefs are also obvious. Reconstructing the traditional Russian attitudes toward the state and state power, many authors pointed to some similarity in critics' approaches to the Russian state. According to Nikolay Berdyaev, the idea of struggle against the Russian state first appeared in the period of the church schism. Berdyaev recounts that after the fall of the

---

[67] Lotman and Uspenskij, 'The Role of Dual Models in the Dynamics of Russian Culture', 25.

[68] Nicolas Berdyaev, *The Russian Idea* (London: Geoffrey Bles, 1947; 1st publ. 1946 in Russian); 56.

[69] On the Old Believers see Serge A. Zenkovsky, *Russkoe staroobriodchestvo: dukhovyke dvizheniio semnadt satogo veka* (Munich: Wilhelm Fink Verlag, 1970). On the ideas of 19th-century revolutionaries, see: B. S. Itenberg *Dvizhenie revolutsionnogo narodnichestva* (Moscow: Nauka, 1965); V. Bogucharskiy, *Aktivnoe narodnichestvo semidesyatykh godov* (Moscow: Izatel`stvo M. I. S. Sabashnikovykh, 1912); Franco Venturi, *Roots of Revolution: A History of the Populist and Socialist Movements in Nineteenth Century Russia* (London: Weidenfeld and Nicolson, 1960; 1st publ. in 1952 in Italian); and Berlin, *Russian Thinkers*. On Kadets and Russian liberalism see: V. V. Leontovich, *Istoriya liberalizma v Rossii* (Paris: YMCA Press, 1980; 1st publ. 1957 in German); and George Fischer, *Russian Liberalism: From Gentry to Intelligentsia* (Cambridge, MA: Harvard University Press, 1958).

Byzantine Empire, within the greatest Orthodox state in the world 'there awoke in the Russian people the consciousness that the Russian Muscovite state was left as the only Orthodox state in the world and that the Russian people was the only nation who professed the Orthodox Faith.'[70] This idea was expressed in the monk Philopheius's renowned theory of Moscow being the Third Rome, supplementing the second Rome, Constantinople. Nikon's reforms resulted in a crisis in the national mentality when the existing state was no longer perceived as a religious ideal: 'A suspicion awoke in the Russian people that the Orthodox kingdom, the Third Rome, was being impaired, that a betrayal of the true faith was taking place. Antichrist had seized on the hierarchy of Church and State alike. Popular Orthodoxy broke with both.'[71] The social and religious ideal, the idea of a sacred kingdom was transferred from the real Russian state to the sphere of ideas, but the willingness to bring that kingdom, back on Earth was preserved.

Turning to the beliefs of Russian intellectuals in the late tsarist period, Berdyaev notes that they preserved the characteristic features of Orthodox dissident thought—especially the perception of the state as an absolute evil and the willingness to realize a social and moral ideal in Russia. The idea began to circulate together with socialism, but, according to Berdyaev, its broad popularity in Russia was possible because the theory of the ideal socialist or communist society and the state-directed rejection of capitalism were perfectly compatible with 'traditional' social and religious beliefs. In this context, the opposition considered the existing Russian state, counterposed against the ideal, as the evil against which the struggle was necessary. The idea was expressed in the most extreme terms by Vladimir Pecherin, a writer and philosopher of the nineteenth century, who wrote such verses as: 'How sweet it is to hate one's native land, and eagerly await its annihilation.'[72]

These conclusions are supported by others such as Vasiliy Zen`kovskiy, who traces the influence of Orthodox Christian social beliefs on the evolution of world views undergone by many ideologists or intellectuals who shared socialist ideas: Belinskiy, Stankevich, Dobrolyubov, Chernyshevskiy, and Bakunin. This does not involve borrowing the beliefs of the Old Believers, but rather developing them: the extension of the Orthodox social ideal from Russia to the outer world—in this case, to the future—while preserving the belief that Russia is the most proper country for the realization of this ideal. Certainly, it is not incidental that many ideologists of Russian socialism discussed by Zen`kovskiy were raised in priests' families and received religious education.[73]

Given the absence of serious contemporary studies on the ideology of

---

[70] Berdyaev, *The Origin of Russian Communism*, 10.   [71] Ibid. 11.

[72] Quoted in Berdyaev, *The Russian Idea*, p. 38.

[73] See Zen`kovskiy, *Istoriya russkoy filosofii*.

Russian religious dissent and Russian socialist thought, this concept cannot be accepted unconditionally. However, many of its elements are relevant to the present study. Attitudes toward the state and the social organization of the USSR which were shared by Russian 'democrats' of the *perestroyka* period can be interpreted as a further development of certain traditional attitudes toward the Russian state.

These attitudes, developed by the members of 'democratic' groups, towards the Russian state as an absolute evil and even as an anti-world counterposed to the social ideal (located either in the West or in the future) actually follow the approach of the pre-1917 Russian socialists. However, as was the case with the Old Believers, this does not at all imply any automatic borrowing. On the contrary, these ideas, even when developed by those 'democrats' who identified themselves as socialists or social democrats, were based on the rejection of the pre-1917 ideology of radical Russian socialism and especially its most consistent form, Bolshevism. So in this case it would only be correct to speak of similar patterns of approach and similar types of attitudes toward the state.

At the same time, the continuity in Russian attitudes towards the state should not be over-emphasized. The traditional attitudes toward the state, which in essence were an integral whole, underwent considerable transformation in the Russian 'democratic' community under the influence of new beliefs, especially those of the official Soviet Marxist ideology and of liberal Western concepts that infiltrated the USSR. In particular the Marxist concept of the state as a legitimate institution of violence was certainly not a new theme in Russia.

The Marxist understanding of socialism and communism as a perfect society extended the social ideal to the future. The Russian 'democrats' in turn extended it to the West or to the future (the future being nearer to the West than to Russia). This meant a deviation from the Leninist-Populist belief that Russia was closer to the ideal than was the rest of the world (Leninist, because Russia represented the 'weak link of imperialism', and Populist because of Russia's alleged special 'communal' system).

Lenin's interpretation of Marxism, by which it was necessary to destroy the old state to seize power and then to build the ideal state, survived in the form of the attitude that the state was the absolute evil, suggesting the need for its destruction. The interpretation of the social essence of such a state as based on the exploitation of the people by the dominant class is also borrowed from Marxism, though in order to apply the idea to the USSR a new class unknown in Marxism was 'introduced': the *nomenklatura*.

The ideas that are conventionally called Western liberalism also underwent several transformations on their way to Russia. This can be explained by the indirect character of the sources used by the Russian 'democrate'. Any official criticism of the West was turned on its head by the 'democrats'. For example, if the capitalist state was presented by the Soviet mass media as an exploiter ridden with social conflicts, then the future opposition 'democrats', who did not believe the official media, thought that the West lived in complete social peace and harmony; exploitation was a characteristic of the USSR. Thus, Soviet literature indirectly supported the impressions produced by foreign radio broadcasts. The few 'democrats' who had a chance to visit the West, normally in short-term delegations, saw only the exterior of the 'society of abundance' and looked at the West through their belief system.

Western liberalism, especially on the ideological and public opinion level, understands 'Western democratic society' as a social ideal or at least as capable of evolving into such an ideal. This belief in its extreme form corresponds very well with Russian pre-revolutionary and Marxist traditions. The Russian 'democrats' of the right moved their social ideal to the West and tried to prove that Western society had already become the ideal. On this point their opinions matched those on the right in the West. Socialists and anarchists among Russian 'democrats' thought that the ideal was not the contemporary West, but a society of the future, to which contemporary Western society was closer than the Soviet Union. Here they agreed with the Western left. However, such similarities in opinions could only mislead both sides, since the total belief systems of Western and Russian political activists were very different.

At the same time the existence of superficial similarities between the belief systems of Russian 'democrats' and of earlier Russian political movements do not mean that nothing changes in Russian political culture. Certainly these are differences between the overall belief system of Russian 'democrats' and that of Russian Bolsheviks or Westernizers of the nineteenth century. The Russian 'democratic' political subculture included and assimilated many new beliefs which simply did not exist in Russia before. Some came from the West, others from official ideology, still others from personal experience, and only a part through family education, which could transfer traditional 'eternal Russianness'. But even this family education is greatly conditioned by contemporary experience, under the influence of which traditional patterns can change. For example, as will be discussed below, one of the most significant new features of the political culture of Russian 'democrats', namely their strong belief in the peaceful resolution of conflict, was not characteristic of any previous Westernizer movement (including even the Kadets, who refused to openly condemn revolutionary terror), and most probably has as its source not Western political ideas, but the dominant Soviet political culture as a whole.

As with any culture, Russian culture changes gradually and while it is easy to find many similarities between two cultures when one is an immediate source for the other, or some similarities between cultures which are separated from one another by decades, it is very difficult to find much in common between the Russia of the twentieth century and, say, the Russia of the fifteenth century. Attempts to find specifically Russian analogies (and not features common to all humanity) in such cases are bound to find far-fetched superficialities and are usually guided by non-academic goals. The present study shows how misleading it may be to look only at the surface level of discourse when analysing the problem of continuity in Russian culture, where 'the historical tradition . . . often became active at the point where a break with tradition was subjectively taken for granted and innovation sometimes took the form of fanatic adherence to artificially constructed "traditions".'[74] This feature of Russian culture (and not necessarily Russian culture alone) makes quantitative survey studies only partly useful, since they pick up only separated attitudes, leaving aside the whole network of interrelations which make culture a relatively consistent system of beliefs. A casual glance at the Russian political stage will give the impression that the most radical anti-totalitarians, anti-statists, and supporters of absolute individualism and private initiative are the most untraditional people in the country. But a closer look at Russian political culture and political tradition will lead one to different conclusions. Thus, Russian 'democratic statists', who argued for a realistic balance between state power and individual rights and who were labelled by some scholars as 'liberal nationalists', and even those anarchists and social democrats who supported less radical and socially costly economic reform, were perhaps more innovative and less traditional for Russian political culture than those radical 'democrats' who called for the total and immediate destruction of the 'totalitarian' state and the absolute domination by the individual over the state and collective (even though the former often used historical argument to support their position).

8.4. THE RUSSIAN 'DEMOCRATIC' POLITICAL SUBCULTURE AND THE DOMINANT POLITICAL CULTURE OF THE SOVIET UNION

The influence of the dominant Russian political culture on the political beliefs of Russian 'democrats' is quite understandable since the 'democratic' political subculture itself, despite its peculiarities, was one of its parts. For a detailed analysis of the dominant political culture of the Soviet Union, or even of Soviet Russia, separate studies would be needed. However, the parts of it which most influenced the beliefs of the Russian 'democrats' must be described. The problem with describing Soviet political culture is that while there are dozens of works which touch upon this culture, very few serious

---

[74] Lotman and Uspenskij, 'The Role of Dual Models in the Dynamics of Russian Culture', 28.

studies are devoted to it. Though the term 'political culture' had existed in the USSR since Lenin and the concept because increasingly widespread after 1970, Soviet usage was very different from that of the West, and most studies by Soviet authors until the very end of Soviet rule were highly politically biased.[75] Although some survey-based studies were conducted in the Soviet Union before *perestroyka*, especially in the relatively relaxed atmosphere of the 1960s, most of them were controlled by the authorities, who either did not allow the results to be published or published a 'corrected' version.[76] At the same time, foreign specialists were deprived of the possibility of pursuing broad research projects in the USSR and of deploying the methods which are usually used in studies of mass political beliefs. However, it is possible to base an analysis of Soviet political culture on at least some empirical information, using materials which became available outside the USSR and on some studies in the later Soviet Union.

On the basis of study of the documents from the Smolensk archive which were moved to the West during World War II, Merle Fainsod noted relatively widespread popular discontent and dissatisfaction with the authorities in the USSR before the war, which, however, was not expressed in any organized form. According to Fainsod, the documents provided 'unimpeachable evidence of widespread mass discontent with Soviet rule'.[77] Though Fainsod's conclusions could be too strong since he mostly used the reports of the NKVD informers, who for career purposes, especially in the late 1930s, could have exaggerated the level of discontent and the number of the enemies of the regime,[78] it was an important contribution since it ran contrary to the arguments of official Soviet propaganda and of some Western scholars that the Soviet regime had been successful in creating a new man and that everyone in the USSR accepted official values. However, Fainsod did not study in detail the real values of the Soviet population.

This task was addressed in *The Soviet Citizen* by Alex Inkeles and Raymond Bauer, whose study was based on interviews with Soviet emigrants and was pursued within the framework of the Harvard Project on the Soviet Social System. Their book, published in 1959, contained data mainly on the Stalin period. The authors point to several important traits of the political culture of the Stalinist USSR.

First, there existed a stable belief that Soviet society was divided into two

---

[75] See e.g. E. M. Babosov (ed.), *Dve kul`tury—dva obraza mysli* (Minsk: Nauka i tekhnika, 1985).

[76] See V. A.Yadov (ed.), *Sotsiologiya v Rossii* (Moscow: Izdatel'stvo Instituta sotsiologii RAN, 1998), 572–9.

[77] Merle Fainsod, *Smolensk under Soviet Rule* (Cambridge, Mass.: Harvard University Press, 1958), 449.

[78] For more on this, see Lukin, 'Angloyazychnaya sovetologiya i obshchestvennye nauki v Rossii', 46.

main groups: there was the ruling and privileged group of Communist officials and there was everyone else.[79] What was surprising was that some emigrants, sometimes after several years of living abroad, expressed quite positive opinions about certain aspects of Soviet reality. They were especially in favour of the Soviet state systems of education, health, and welfare, which they regarded as superior to those in the United States. Paradoxically, they did not regard these positive features to be a result of the efforts of the communist authorities but took them for granted. In other words the aspects of Soviet society which people liked did not translate into any endorsement of the authorities. Moreover, life experience in market conditions led emigrants to more positive views about Soviet society generally. According to the authors, 'refugees of all social groups respond to contact with American society with a renewed desire for the welfare provisions of Soviet society.'[80]

Most emigrants strongly rejected Soviet state terror and supported the idea of a state which guarantees individual rights and the rule of law. However, most people believed that these rights should be limited by the general interests of society. For example, only one third believed that citizens should be free to openly criticize the government and less than a third said that the authorities had no right to interfere in a meeting critical of the state. At the same time almost everybody believed that a citizen should have the right to travel freely in the country, to choose employment, and to be protected by law from arbitrary arrest.[81]

The Soviet state was seen by the majority as just such an arbitrary and unjust state. As a result, from 40 to 60 per cent of those interviewed (in different social groups) said that if the Bolsheviks were overthrown their leaders should be executed, and from 44 to 70 per cent deemed the Bolsheviks worse than the Nazis. While these proportions should not be directly applied to the total Soviet population of the time, this analysis none the less shows the tendency of the development of popular beliefs, especially in the situation of personal experience of broader political and economic freedom. This tendency can be briefly described as the growth of dissatisfaction and hatred towards the Communist regime and the expectation of a successor government to fulfil the promises of the Communist regime more effectively.

During later Soviet times, until the late 1980s, serious empirical studies of Soviet political culture in the USSR itself still could not be pursued. However, for this period we have several other studies based on surveys of emigrants which, though narrower than the Harvard Project, support some of its findings and show some tendencies in the development of the political beliefs of the Soviet mass public. Probably the broadest of these studies was the Soviet

---

[79] Inkeles and Bauer, *The Soviet Citizen*, 301.   [80] Ibid. 238.
[81] Ibid. 248–9.

Interview Project (SIP), the results of which were published in 1987.[82] Unlike
the Harvard Project, which used interviews mainly with Russians and
Ukrainians, SIP interviewees were mostly Jewish emigrants. In the late 1970s
and early 1980s Jews were allowed to emigrate, and they constituted the main
stream of emigrants. There were also significantly more educated, urbanized
respondents than in the Harvard Project. It was expected that they would be
very hostile to the Soviet system. However, the results were not that simple.
The study showed that most of the respondents praised the same features of
Soviet reality as their predecessors had done thirty years earlier. Evaluating
different aspects of their 'last normal period of life' in the USSR, more than
two-thirds of the respondents said that they were somewhat satisfied or very
satisfied with their standard of living, their job, their housing, and public
medical care. Only in response to a question on the availability of goods was
less than a majority either somewhat satisfied or very satisfied; less than one-
fourth said they were somewhat satisfied or very satisfied with the availability of goods.[83]

   The answers to the question of what should be preserved in the present
Soviet system virtually repeated the findings of the Harvard Project. The most
popular aspects of the Soviet system were again education and medical care.
Half spoke in favour of state ownership of heavy industry while more than
half strongly supported the privatization of agriculture.

   The Harvard findings were also echoed in the sphere of political freedoms.
A significant portion of the interviewees supported the broadening of rights
and freedoms, but not without limit and not in every sphere. For example,
they stood for the elimination of residence registration (*propiska*) and for
giving workers the right to strike, but only about a quarter rejected the idea of
protecting the rights of society, 'even if an innocent person (accused of a
crime) sometimes goes to jail'. On the whole the political beliefs of Soviet
citizens showed a significant level of continuity over a period of some three
decades. This continuity also manifested itself in the absence of a positive
correlation between the favourable evaluation of some aspects of the Soviet
system and support for the regime as a whole. According to Brian Silver,

there is a residue of strong support for parts of the system even among those who are
strongly antipathetic to the whole. For example, among those who volunteered that
'the U.S. can learn nothing from the USSR,' 48 percent give the strongest possible
endorsement to state ownership of heavy industry. This may testify to how people's
historical experience, that is, their socialization within a given political system, has
shaped their fundamental beliefs about how the government *ought* to organize its

---

[82] James R. Millar (ed.), *Politics, Work and Daily Life in the USSR: A Survey of Former
Soviet Citizens* (Cambridge: Cambridge University Press, 1987).
[83] Brian D. Silver, 'Political Beliefs of the Soviet Citizen', in Millar (ed.), *Politics, Work
and Daily Life in the USSR*, 105.

work. In particular, support for collective control is not substantially lower among those hostile to the system than among the respondents as a whole.[84]

As in Stalin's time, Soviet citizens of the Brezhnev period, while being hostile towards the regime, were not in favour of the Western and especially radical libertarian patterns (though they might prefer the Western to the Soviet system). On the contrary, their hostility was caused by the inability of the Soviet regime to fulfil its own ideological goals and meet the moderate and mixed social ideals of the population. These conclusions are generally supported by data from other studies.[85]

The available analyses of the beliefs of Soviet citizens about international relations show even deeper agreement with the official line. Inkeles and Bauer, for example, noted that most seem to have accepted the main outlines of the official image of foreign affairs disseminated by official media. They see the United States government as dominated by powerful groups who

seem committed to waging a war of destruction against the Soviet Union and other countries. They imagine a vast conspiracy by the West to prevent colonial and under-developed areas from attaining their independence and achieving their rightful national aspirations for peaceful economic development. They take substantial pride in Soviet strength and the image they have of the USSR as a leading world force. They believe the Soviet government to be a champion of peace and a defender of the small and the weak. They are eager for peace and the smaller burden of arms a stable world order would yield.[86]

One should not forget that these conclusions were made on the basis of the answers of people who were generally very hostile to many aspects of the Soviet regime. It seems that foreign policy was not a source of hostility, at least at that time. This support for the general ideological principles of Soviet foreign policy does not exclude, however, the opinion that some of the specific acts of the Soviet government in the international arena are inconsistent with its peaceful policy and therefore to be subjected to criticism. Unfortunately, the studies of the political beliefs of the Soviet people of the Brezhnev period do not contain full data on foreign policy attitudes. At the same time data from the SIP show that the beliefs of Soviet citizens that military spending and assistance to 'friendly' regimes should be cut persisted thirty years later.[87]

When in the late 1980s both Soviet and foreign scholars had the opportunity to conduct large-scale surveys in the USSR, their findings generally supported the conclusions of earlier studies of Soviet emigrants. Foreign

[84] Ibid. 114.
[85] See e.g. Stephen White, *Political Culture and Soviet Politics* (London: Macmillan, 1979).
[86] Inkeles and Bauer, *The Soviet Citizen*, 382.
[87] See Linda L. Lubrano, 'The Attentive Public for Soviet Science and Technology', in Millar (ed.), *Politics, Work and Daily Life in the USSR*, 156.

scholars, analysing data from the first such surveys, were initially astonished to see in the Soviet population the kind of aspirations for freedom and individual independence which were usually found in Western democracies. However, differences soon began to emerge. For example, on the basis of the results of a sample survey in the European part of the USSR conducted in May 1990, James Gibson and Raymond Duch concluded that the 'people extended fairly broad support to competitive electoral structures, and they were quite willing to claim a variety of rights of democratic citizenship'.[88] At the same time the authors found that support for other sub-dimensions of the constellation of democratic values was more mixed. Gibson and Duch concluded that

there is some evidence that not everyone was willing to embrace liberty if its cost is social disruption. To the extent that democratic politics allows the open expression of unpleasant, disruptive, and offensive views, many Soviet people did not have much allegiance for democracy. This is especially the case when we examine political tolerance. The Soviets were quite unwilling to allow their most-hated enemies to compete for political power. Citizens were willing to claim rights for themselves, even if they were not yet willing to extend the same rights to others.[89]

As in previous studies, Soviet citizens indicated that they accepted freedom limited by the interests of society as a whole, as they understood these interests. However, it was not the lack of rights and freedoms that was considered by the majority to be the country's main problem. As was the case with emigrants, new surveys showed that they thought the main problem of the government was its inability to solve social problems and to raise living standards.

The differences in the attitudes of members of 'democratic' groups and the population as a whole can be seen from a comparison of a survey conducted by the All-union Centre for the Study of Public Opinion (VTsIOM) in November 1989 with a survey of two hundred participants in a discussion conducted by the Perestroyka Club in Moscow in April 1988. When answering the question 'What does a Soviet citizen lack most today?' almost 57 per cent of the VTsIOM respondents pointed to material prosperity and less than 15 per cent to political rights. Asked to name the main task which society faced, 38 per cent of the respondents pointed to the necessity of securing material prosperity for the people, 29 per cent to the establishment of genuine justice without privileges, 24 per cent to the need to revive the village, agriculture, and the rural way of life, and only 19 per cent (fourth place) to the task of building a free democratic society.[90] It is clear that the fulfilment of

    [88] James L. Gibson and Raymond M. Duch, 'Emerging Democratic Values in Soviet Political Culture', in Arthur H. Miller, William M. Reisinger and Vicki L. Hesli (eds.), *Public Opinion and Regime Change: The New Politics of Post-Soviet Societies* (Boulder, Colo.: Westview, 1993), 87.   [89] Ibid. 88.
    [90] Yu. A. Levada (ed.), *Sovetskiy prostoy chelovek* (Moscow: Mirovoy okean, 1993), 280–1.

these tasks would be expected from a new government. At the same time, when answering the question 'What kind of socialism is needed by the people?' more than 70 per cent of the participants in the Perestroyka Club discussion said that its most important feature should be social justice, 65 per cent respect for personal rights and freedoms, and only 12 per cent mentioned higher living standards.[91] It is clear that while 'democrats' shared the concerns of the population about social injustice (though giving it much more attention), they saw political liberalization as a priority task of reform, while the population as a whole, while not objecting to some liberalization, gave first priority to more material wealth and higher living standards.

A comparison of the dominant Soviet political culture with the political subculture of Russian 'democrats' can lead to the following conclusions. The hostility of 'democrats' to the Soviet regime in the last years of the Soviet Union was very similar to that of the population as a whole and probably differed only in being more intensive and better articulated. This was the reason for the growing popularity of the 'democrats' by 1990–1. The social structure of Soviet society and the reasons for the system's failure were seen very similarly by 'democrats' and the population as a whole: both saw society as divided into two groups, the privileged Communist *nomenklatura* and the masses; both blamed the Communists, specifically the leaders, for the country's misfortunes. The privileges of the ruling elite, its indifference to the needs of the people, and the open contradiction between the announced goals and the ability to achieve them were especially detested both by 'democrats' and the population as a whole. That is why 'democratic' theories of the 'new class', the all-mighty *nomenklatura* ruling over the masses, were well understood and supported by the population. However, not all of the measures of eliminating injustice which were proposed by 'democrats' were supported by the public. Moderate proposals to deprive the 'partocracy' of power, and to put the legal rights Party officials on the same level as those of other citizens, or to deprive the CPSU of its monopoly on power, were close to what the majority of the population thought was necessary. But the demands of the most radical 'democrats' to ban the CPSU, to define it as a criminal organization, to put the Party on trials of the Nuremberg type, or to introduce a ban on the appointment of former Communist officials to high state positions were unlikely to gain the support of the population, which on the whole did not believe every Communist to be equally responsible for the situation in the country.

The same can be said about the correlation between the political ideals of 'democrats' and the population as a whole. The general goal of 'democrats' to change the country's political system was surely backed by the majority of

---

[91] 'Nekotorye resul`taty oprosa uchastnikov discussii v clube "Perestroyka" 25 aprelya 1988 g.', unpubl. MS; courtesy of Oleg Rumyantsev.

the population. But there were significant differences as to what kind of society should be built in its place. The majority of the population believed that privatization in some spheres of the economy, especially in those which had most obviously failed in the USSR, such as agriculture, light industry, and services, was possible and necessary. At the same time most regarded as normal and useful state control over heavy industry and were very much in favour of state-run education, medical, and welfare systems. Thus, it can be said that public opinion was close to the economic views of moderate 'democrats' of social democratic and communitarian orientation but not to the most radical privatizers and Westernizers.[92]

Some of the liberalization suggested by 'democrats' could, though, be supported by the public, since the majority of the Soviet population strongly rejected the excesses of the Soviet regime: terror and persecutions and the unaccountability of repressive state organs. The 'democratic' slogans of building a law-based state and solving all conflicts in society through discussions and consultations, not by force and repression, found support in a population which remembered the violence of Stalin and the Nazis. At the same time, the population regarded political freedoms to be a less important objective than the improvement of economic conditions and approached them not as rights but more as means of improving society. While believing that a certain level of liberalization and the abolition of the government's monopoly on information were necessary and desirable, the majority of the Soviet people would not object to placing certain limits on such liberalization in order to ensure the interests of society. Taking this into consideration it can be argued that radical marketeers and libertarians among the 'democrats', who regarded political freedoms to be inalienable rights of the individual or suggested immediate and total marketization regardless of the social consequences, could hardly expect support from the majority of the population. At the same time the position of more moderate 'democrats' of communitarian, statist, or social democratic persuasions was much closer to the expectations of the mass public and therefore their suggestions did not meet with stronger support.

The differences on foreign policy were even more striking. While in this sphere even more moderate 'democrats' at that time were in favour of a radically pro-Western policy, public opinion was ready to accept only limited change. A small number of foreign policy measures suggested by 'democrats' could be accepted by the population, such as the cutting of the military budget, the cessation of military involvement in conflicts abroad and the withdrawal of

---

[92] For example, in a VTsIOM all-union survey conducted in Nov. 1990, 58% of the respondents maintained that the state should care more about the people and only 23% said that the people should take the initiative and care about themselves. Most people prefered to have a small but stable salary to a bigger but insecure income. See Yu. A. Levada, *Sovetskiy prostoy chelovek* (Moscow: Mirovoy okean, 1993), 62, 52.

troops from abroad, and the granting of independence to the former satellites. However, a total subordination of Soviet foreign policy to Western interests or a kind of partnership where, according to some 'democrats', the Soviet Union should be a junior partner of the West, together with what was traditionally thought to be Russia's and Soviet achievements, would not find much enthusiasm among the population to the degree that foreign policy issues were held to be important.

Thus, despite significant similarities between the dominant Soviet political culture and Russian 'democratic' subculture, there were significant differences, and the suggestions of the most market-oriented and pro-Western 'democrats' went far beyond what was acceptable to the majority of the population.

9

Conclusions: The Political Culture of Russian 'Democrats' and Russian Politics

Awareness of the differences between Soviet political culture and the 'democratic' subculture is important for understanding political developments in Russia after 1991. Despite the later arguments of some less fortunate 'democrats' that the 'democratic' movement as a whole did not come to power in Russia, an objective analysis would suggest that politicians who shared 'democratic' beliefs partially ruled the Russian republic from the election of the Russian parliament in spring 1991, and almost solely from early 1992 for a period of about one year. During the latter period 'democratic' activists and their supporters not only controlled the most important federal institutions, but also held sway in the country's three most populous cities (Moscow, St Petersburg, and Ekaterinburg). At that time almost all Russian leaders, including President Yel`tsin, considered themselves 'democrats' and stood for 'democratic' policies. For example, the first real head of the post-Soviet Russian government (and later state secretary) Gennadiy Burbulis,[1] who in early 1992 controlled all Kremlin appointments, had himself been part of a 'democratic' group in Sverdlovsk[2] and was later active in the Democratic Platform of the CPSU, Democratic Russia, the Inter-regional Group, and the Democratic Party of Russia. Other 'democrats' who held powerful positions included: Sergey Shakhray (deputy premier), Mikhail Poltoranin (deputy premier); Sergey Stankevich (political adviser to the president); Galina Starovoitova (presidential adviser on ethnic policy); Gavriil Popov (mayor of Moscow); and Anatoly Sobchak (mayor of St Petersburg). Deputies from the Democratic Russia Movement enjoyed a majority on the city councils of Moscow and St Petersburg, and despite being a few votes short of a formal majority in the Russian Congress of People's Deputies, they twice managed to have their candidate elected as its chairman (first Boris Yel`tsin and later Ruslan Khasbulatov). All of them joined and actively worked in either the

---

[1] The formal chairman of the government at this time was the president, but Burbulis as his first deputy effectively headed the government until his appointment to the post of Secretary of State in May 1991.

[2] In 1987 Burbulis was one of the organizers of a political club in Sverdlovsk, Diskussionnaya tribuna.

Inter-regional Group of Deputies or the Democratic Russia Movement (or both) and were widely regarded by grassroots 'democrats' as their leaders.

Burbulis's choice for the role of the architect of economic reforms, first deputy and later acting premier Yegor Gaydar, though he personally did not take part in a 'democratic' group, was one of the prominent *perestroyka* writers on the Soviet economy whose ideas were very popular among 'democrats'. In his 1995 book, *The State and Evolution*,[3] one can find a whole set of 'democratic' beliefs of the most radical pro-Western type, which match very well the model of the 'democratic' political culture reconstructed in this book, stated systematically and comprehensively. There are the familiar notions of the fundamental division of the world into the two opposing systems of a normal Western society based on private property and an unnatural oriental system based on the domination of state property. Gaydar writes positively of the theory of the Asian mode of production; he understands Russia as a culture in between the West and the East which has been unsuccessfully trying for centuries to keep up with Western civilization; he defines the rule of Bolshevism as a historical regress to the East and recommends making a historical leap to join Western civilization by eliminating state control over the economy and by introducing rapid privatization.[4] The respective mayors of Moscow and Leningrad, Gavriil Popov and Anatoliy Sobchak, were active members of the Inter-regional Group and were acknowledged leaders and theorists of Democratic Russia and of the 'democratic' movement as a whole. Anatoliy Chubays, who became the architect of the Russian privatization programme, was close to the 'democratic' circles in his native Leningrad. Foreign Minister Andrey Kozyrev, though not part of the 'democratic' movement before his appointment, actively joined the 'democratic' group in the leadership immediately upon becoming minister and supported the most radical 'democratic' pro-Western course. When he changed almost the entire leadership of the foreign ministry of the USSR, he appointed many of his supporters among whom were 'democrats' and even former dissidents.[5]

While leading 'democrats', like ordinary members of the movement, agreed on the necessity of fighting the Soviet regime, they differed on many specific policies. The first leadership of independent Russia, which came to power in early 1992, generally shared the beliefs of the most radically pro-market and pro-Western part of the movement. Therefore their policy ran violently counter to the political culture of the majority of the population.

Some more far-sighted 'democratic' leaders saw this contradiction between the aims of the 'democrats' and the aspirations of the population at quite an

---

[3] Yegor Gaydar, *Gosudarstvo i evolyutsiya* (Moscow: Yevraziya, 1995)—an obvious allusion to the fundamental *The State and Revolution* by Vladimir Lenin. [4] Ibid.

[5] For example, Kozyrev's deputy Fedor Shelov-Kovedyaev was a Democratic Russia activist and the Head of the Department of Human Rights was a former dissident, Vyacheslav Bakhmin.

early stage. For example, Popov, just several months after becoming the mayor of Moscow, noted that 'now we must create a society with a variety of different forms of ownership, including private property; and this will be a society of economic inequality. . . . The masses long for fairness and economic equality. And the further the process of transformation goes, the more acute and the more glaring will be the gap between those aspirations and economic realities.'[6]

But the Burbulis–Gaydar group claimed that the success of their policy would raise living standards and eventually lead to approval of this policy by the population. In reality the implementation of Gaydar's reforms led to an even greater gap between government policy and public opinion, which then interpreted this variant of 'democracy' as the only one. In the eyes of the population the 'democrats', headed by the 'democratic' president, were in power and they were now to blame for all the failures of the leadership and for social hardship.

This situation prompted an inevitable split within the 'democratic' movement. When the CPSU was removed from power and the common enemy of all of the 'democrats' disappeared, the chief goal of their struggle which had united everybody disappeared with it. Immediately differences between various tendencies in the 'democratic' movement began to surface, in some cases turning former allies into bitter enemies. While the ruling group was consistently implementing the ideals of the radical-market group, communitarian 'democrats' started criticizing them for deviating from the equally 'democratic' ideal of social justice. Ironically, the demands of both groups fitted the model of the 'democratic' political culture described in this book. The first sought the dismantling of the Soviet empire since in their view it was easier for smaller territories to break with the totalitarian past, to implement immediate and full privatization, and to pursue a Western orientation. This group did not feel restrained by the formal rules of outdated 'totalitarian' law. The other group stood for strict legality, put social justice ahead of privatization, and wanted to preserve the union since its break-up entailed the destruction of the Soviet economic system and the emergence of nationalistic regimes in the former Soviet republics.The goals of the first group were well formulated by Burbulis, the chief ideologist of reform:

The social-economic goal of the reform, from my point of view, can be expressed as follows: to create the institution of private property. People should live in a society where they can acquire and freely possess private property of any kind. The experience of history teaches this: nothing that better corresponds to human nature has been invented over the last ten thousand years. The system is not ideal, but normal. And this system somehow suits Europe, Asia, America and does not efface national characteristics.[7]

[6] Quoted in Anthony Arblaster, *Democracy*, 2nd edn. (Buckingham: Open University Press, 1994), 98.

[7] Quoted in V. Sogrin, *Politicheskaya istoriya sovremennoy Rossii 1985–1994. Ot Gorbacheva do Yel`tsina* (Moscow: Progress-Akademiya, 1994), 118.

It may be peculiar to listen to this hymn to private property from a born-again former Communist ideologist[8] turned propagandist of 'democratic' reforms, but his ideas about the 'normal' path of world development, which should be taken not only by Russia but by all other countries that lag behind world progress, and about the direct connection between this path and private property, sound very familiar to a student of Russian 'democratic' political culture. The representatives of this trend of 'democratic' ideas believed that the introduction of private property in itself was a sufficient guarantee not only of rapid economic growth and prosperity, but also of political freedom. According to Chubays, for example,

A market economy is an economy based on private property. . . . If property is divided between many owners, no one of them enjoys an exclusive right and physical opportunity to give orders to others, to determine the amount of their personal income or the level of their social status. . . . Nobody's views are dominant and all the more obligatory for the others. This is just impossible: the only power of a private owner over other people is that he can (or cannot) offer them better conditions than his competitor. In this sense a market economy is a guarantee not only of the more effective use of means, resources, basic funds, etc., but also a guarantee of the freedom of society and of the independence of citizens.[9]

The radical-market group, in full accordance with 'democratic' beliefs, wanted to subject Russia's foreign policy to the aims of rapid implementation of economic reform and Russia's inclusion in the 'civilized' Western world. This caused its one-sided pro-Western orientation, a 180-degree turn from classic Soviet ideology (though not from the foreign policy of the Gorbachev period, which, to a great extent, it contained).[10] In August 1991, at a rally in Moscow on the occasion of the defeat of the putsch, Kozyrev had already announced Russia's new official stand: for democratic Russia the USA and other Western democracies were natural friends and allies, just as they had been natural enemies of the totalitarian USSR.[11] The practical policy determined by this belief was defined by the Russian foreign minister as establishing 'friendly and eventually allied relations with the civilized world, including NATO, the UN, and other structures'.[12]

Like many ordinary 'democrats', 'democratic' leaders believed that the achievement of the goals of 'democratic' policy justified the breaking of

---

[8] Burbulis taught scientific Communism in Sverdlovsk for 15 years.

[9] Quoted in Sogrin, *Politicheskaya istoriya sovremennoy Rossii 1985–1994*, 118.

[10] See Margot Light, 'Foreign Policy Making', in Neil Malcolm, Alex Pravda, Roy Allison, and Margot Light (eds.), *Internal Factors in Russian Foreign Policy* (Oxford: Oxford University Press, 1996), 44–5.

[11] Andrey Kozyrev, *Preobrazhenie* (Moscow: Mezhdunarodnye otnosheniya, 1995), 211.

[12] Andrey Kozyrev, 'A Transformed Russia in a New World', *International Affairs* (Moscow), 4–5 (1992), 86. Light, 'Foreign Policy Making', gives a more detailed account of the theoretical background of Russian foreign policy.

outdated 'Communist' laws. For example, one of the co-chairs of the Democratic Russia Movement, Lev Ponomarev, called upon the new Russian leadership 'with revolutionary speed to distribute land, to privatize industry, trade . . . To act in the way Yel`tsin acted during the days of the coup. Yes, a number of his decrees, signed in a critical situation, were unconstitutional. But I would call them genius. They perfectly met political necessity. That is to say we should be pragmatists.'[13]

This Marxism turned inside out might be applauded by some right-wing Western economists and politicians, but it could hardly expect support from the majority of the population of Russia. Moreover, this kind of policy was not supported by all 'democrats'. The opposition of many 'democrats' to the Burbulis–Gaydar approach was only natural. Most of them stood for only limited privatization and for maintaining a significant role for the state, while the anarchists and socialists opposed privatization as such. Many 'democrats' did not see the disintegration of the USSR as a necessary condition for democratization, but supported only partial decentralization. The criticism from opposition-minded 'democrats' of a government controlled by libertarian 'democrats' became even sharper with a dramatic decline in the living standards of the majority of the population and growing inequalities. Since President Yel`tsin, who had been the leader of all of the 'democrats', originally gave his full support to this policy the criticism eventually turned into attacks on the president.

The evolution of the views of Yel`tsin himself cannot be explained without understanding the influence of 'democratic' beliefs. His own political views can be described as fully 'democratic' at least from mid-1988. In fact one can easily pinpoint the time when this former leading Communist accepted 'democratic' views. His letter of resignation to Gorbachev in September 1987 and his speech to the plenary meeting of the CPSU the following month, though unusually critical, did not contain any 'democratic' terminology or ideas, but were worded in the usual Communist way. However, his speech at the Nineteenth Party Conference of the CPSU in summer 1988 and several interviews at the same time more strongly reflect 'democratism'.[14] It can be seen that his conversion to 'democracy' occurred after he resigned from the powerful position of First Secretary of the Moscow organization of the CPSU. At that time 'democrats' were the only group ready to support him. It can surely be argued, as indeed it was later argued by some disillusioned 'democrats', that his acceptance of 'democratic' goals was only a tactical step to get the support of the 'democratic' movement in his struggle for power with Gorbachev, which he waged out of a pure ambition first to return to politics

---

[13] Quoted in Sogrin, *Politicheskaya istoriya sovremennoy Rossii 1985–1994*, 113.
[14] For texts of all these speeches see Boris Yel`tsin, *Ispoved` na zadannuyu temu* (Leningrad: Sovetskiy pisatel`, 1990).

and then to seize the leadership of the country. However, such an explanation seems to oversimplify the situation. The fact that the aims of the 'democratic' movement corresponded closely to Yel`tsin's personal quest for power surely played an important role in his intellectual development and in his choosing 'democrats' as his allies. But there were numerous examples of individuals with a similar background who converted to 'democracy'. Many 'democrats' were dissatisfied Party *apparatchiki* who believed in the letter of Party promises and social justice, fought for them, were defeated and sometimes sacked, and then grew dissatisfied with Communism. Yel`tsin was only the most high-ranking of them, but his path to 'democracy' was typical.

At the same time, as can be seen from the highly emotional pages of his first autobiography, Yel`tsin's acceptance of 'democracy' was a very personal act which occurred at a time of deep emotional crisis and closely resembled a conversion to a new faith, the mystical truth of which suddenly became clear to the future Russian president.[15] An indirect proof that Yel`tsin shared 'democratic' beliefs is the fact that some of his practical policies can only be explained from the point of view of his beliefs. For example, Yel`tsin's willingness to grant broad autonomy to some republics and even regions of Russia, which stimulated separatism, can be explained by his efforts to win the backing of the regional leaders in his battle with Gorbachev. But this cannot explain his insistence on the continuation of such a policy even after the splitting up of the USSR; that can appear logical only if one assumes that he sincerely accepted Russian 'democratic' beliefs about the necessity of decentralization and of the construction of the federation from below on the basis of voluntary agreement.

While from 1988–91 Yel`tsin's beliefs were 'democratic' they were closer to the communitarian-social justice type than to radical-market libertarianism. In his speeches at the time he laid much greater stress on the problems of justice and called for abolishing privileges, raising living standards, and giving more money to medicine, science, and education at the expense of military spending and foreign aid. He never mentioned anything like shock therapy or the privatization of heavy industry. Naturally, this programme was supported by all 'democrats' (though not all were equally enthusiastic): some liked the social justice part of it, others the stress on freedom and the determination to and the Communist monopoly on power; even for the most radical supporters of the market he was the only credible and realistic leader.

However, after August 1991 Yel`tsin's views radically changed and he totally supported the radical marketeers and Westernizers. The reason for this change probably lay in the fact that one of the essential proposals of this kind of 'democrat' was the division of the USSR: they argued, first, that the

---

[15] See ibid. 39–146. About the events at this time see also Lev Sukhanov, *Tri goda s Yel`tsinym: Zapiski pervogo pomoshchnika* (Riga: Vaga, 1992).

division of the empire would deal the deathblow to world totalitarianism, and, secondly, that when separated from the other republics Russia would be free of a heavy financial burden. This policy, aimed at the break-up of the USSR, dovetailed with Yel`tsin's personal plans for ousting Gorbachev. With no USSR there would be no Soviet presidency. Since the elimination of the USSR and the institution of market reforms and a pro-Western foreign policy, which was supposed to secure Western aid, were constituent parts of the Burbulis–Gaydar programme, it was easier for its leaders to persuade the president that their way of reforming the economy was more effective than more moderate alternatives and would not lead to a fall in living standards. That they succeeded in gaining the president's support could be seen already in November 1991, when Yel`tsin claimed: 'For about six months it will be worse for everyone, and then—lower prices, the consumer market filling up with products, and by autumn 1992, stabilization of the economy and gradual improvement in people's lives.'[16] When it became clear that these promises were unrealistic and that, on the contrary, the reforms would result in grow-ing inequalities, corruption, lawlessness, and lower living standards for the majority of the population, those 'democrats' who had regarded the struggle against all these social ills as their primary task under the Soviet regime natu-rally began criticizing the president and the government, which was run by their former allies. While from the point of view of the libertarian marketeers their critics were traitors to 'democracy' who sided with the 'red and brown' forces of totalitarianism, in the view of opposition-minded 'democrats' those in power were bogus democrats continuing to tolerate Communist-style injus-tice and disregard for the law.

For example, Mikhail Chelnokov, a former activist in Democratic Russia and the 'Radical Democrats' faction in the Russian Congress of People's Deputies, and later one of the leaders of the radically anti-Yel`tsin National Salvation Front, claimed that under Yel`tsin former *nomenklatura* Communists who had joined the 'democratic' movement for career reasons had returned to power.[17] Chelnokov and those who shared his views accused Gaydar's group of blind adherence to the principles of marketization and privatization and of disregarding the hardships of real people. As a result, they argued, what was going on in Russia was 'destruction without any creation'.[18] Chelnokov pointed to the Chinese reforms, where more gradual privatization was accompanied by the growth of production, as an alternative model.[19]

The foreign policy of the 'democratic' leadership was also criticized by the

[16] Quoted in Sogrin, *Politicheskaya istoriya sovremennoy Rossii 1985–1994*, 115.
[17] Mikhail Chelnokov, *Rossiya bez Soyuza, Rossiya bez Rossii* (Moscow: Novaya Sloboda, 1994), 5. Unlike Burbulis, Gaydar, Chubays, and other members of the 'market' group, Chelnokov himself was never a member of the CPSU.   [18] Ibid. 232.
[19] Ibid.

opposition-minded 'democrats', who regarded it as humiliating to Russia's interests. As Chelnokov put it: 'I am an opponent of nationalism and stand for equal, businesslike cooperation among all countries. But at the same time I am an opponent of the betrayal of the interests of my Motherland that is going on today in Russia.'[20] Many prominent 'democrats' who had earlier strongly supported Yel`tsin joined those opposing the government of radical marketeers. Apart from Chelnokov, they included Viktor Aksyuchits, Mikhail Astaf`ev, Yl`ya Konstantinov, and Viktor Rebrikov. They were later followed by the chairman of the Russian Supreme Soviet, Ruslan Khasbulatov (who was elected to this position as a 'democratic' leader with strong support from Yel`tsin), and by Aleksandr Rutskoy (who was elected vice-president on the same ticket with Yel`tsin).

In this argument between the two types of 'democrats' both sides were exaggerating. Surely, neither of them was either Communist or Nazi (though the logic of political struggle brought some bitter critics of the regime to form an alliance with the Communists and radical nationalists). Both sides shared beliefs typical of the political subculture of Russian 'democrats', but stressed different elements of it. Both wanted to destroy the Soviet system and create a Western-style 'civilized' society, but their visions of this society were different, and so they disagreed on the means of achieving it. Those who can be called 'capitalist marketeers' believed that civilized society should be based on a limitless market and the absolute domination of private property and free competition, and to achieve this aim as fast as possible they were ready to sacrifice equality and legality. Their critics, 'communitarians/legalists', though not totally against privatization, believed that it should not be accompanied by lower living standards and saw the interests of the majority, defined by welfare and relative equality, as higher goals. After the fall of the CPSU and the USSR it turned out that these very different people were no longer united by the common goal of fighting totalitarianism and they naturally became political opponents.

The victory of the radical-market supporters was, however, short-lived. Paradoxically, the Russian 'democrats' were deprived of power by democracy itself. As shown above, the views of the group of 'democrats' which found itself in power at the end of 1991 were those most remote from the beliefs of the majority of the population and even of the 'democrats'. Therefore practical democracy, in the form of the right of the masses to elect their leaders, could not serve their interests. The introduction of competitive elections in Russia was not at all an achievement of the 'democrats'; these were introduced by Gorbachev. This led to a situation in which for the first time in Russian history mass political culture began to be more and more the determinant of the country's political future. If earlier in history, both under the

---

[20] Ibid. 5.

tsars and under the Politburo, the country's leaders could enjoy a high level of political and cultural autonomy vis-à-vis the population and could afford to pay little attention to the political ideals of the people, from 1989 the population gained the right to express their ideals by choosing leaders which most reflected them. 'Democrats' were perhaps the last idealistic politicians in Russia who thought that it was not they who should change their policy according to the wishes of the electorate but that the masses, freed from unnatural totalitarianism, would naturally support their own 'right' course. These illusions soon disappeared, giving way to the growth in popularity of authoritarian developmental models among the Russian 'democratic' leadership.[21]

The first indirect indication of rising discontent in the population was the growing opposition in representative bodies to Yel`tsin's leadership. While in some cases this could be explained by Communist domination in the soviets, such explanations do not work in the case of the Moscow or St Petersburg city soviets, which were two-thirds 'democratic', or in the case of the Russian Congress of Peoples' Deputies, which originally supported all of Yel`tsin's policies, but one year later had turned into his bitter opponent. To be sure, in this conflict between different branches of power there was an element of power struggle which was caused by the unclear definition of the powers of each branch, by the incessantly changing constitution, and by the quest of each bureaucratic institution to gain as much power as it could. However, the fact that the deputies were closer than the executive to the electorate and that they brought the mood of the people to their meeting halls also played its role.[22] An indication of this mood was the striking fall recorded by opinion polls of the popularity of the president and especially of the government.

'Democratic' groups which believed the reason for the conflict with the parliament to lie in the intrigues of the 'red and brown' hoped to raise the popularity of presidential power and 'democratic' reforms by dissolving the parliament and all of the local soviets. However, since there was no longer any absolute confidence in the support of the population, the suggestion to suspend elections or to make them less free came from the very top. As a result, the presidential decree on the elections of 1993 provided significantly less opportunity for observing election results and there were reports of massive fraud, especially during the vote on the constitution. However, the leadership could not afford the total abolition of elections, since the very idea of elections was at the centre of the 'democratic' programme, to which it still claimed to adhere.

[21] Burbulis, for example, praised the Chilean experience and General Pinochet's policy on many occasions. After leaving the government, Burbulis maintained his positive opinion of the general.

[22] I have written in greater detail on the conflict between the branches of power in my 'The New Russia: Parliamentary Democracy or Authoritarian Regime?', *Oxford International Review*, 3:1 (1991), 42–3.

The results of the December 1993 elections nevertheless were very unexpected for the leadership. It is arguable just what Russians did vote for at that time, but surely they voted against the policy of the government and against the Russia's Choice bloc, headed by Gaydar, which was associated with it.[23] Though President Yel`tsin claimed victory over the parliament in autumn 1993 and in the referendum on the constitution in December of that year, the choice of the Russian people had consequences for his policy. Gradually becoming aware of the unpopularity of the policy of the radical-capitalist group of 'democrats', Yel`tsin fired many leading 'democratic' figures, including Burbulis, Gaydar and much of his team, deputy foreign minister Fedor Shelov-Kovedyaev, and others. In its pure form radical 'democratic' policy was pursued until the resignation of Gaydar in December 1992 but many of his policies survived until much later. After 1993 the government tried to change some of its policies: unlimited monetarism was called into question, periodic attempts were made to support industry and former collective farms and to raise state pensions and salaries in line with inflation. At the same time the central Gaydar strategy, which aimed at maintaining the exchange rate of the rouble and achieving a balanced budget in order to create the conditions for a natural growth of the economy, survived various cabinets headed by Viktor Chernomyrdin and Sergey Kirienko, up until the economic collapse of 17 August 1998. It was decisively rejected only by prime minister Yevgeniy Primakov, appointed under pressure from the State Duma in autumn 1998. In foreign policy minister Kozyrev had already been flexible and changed his policy, making it less pro-Western in accordance with the new wishes of the president, and helping Kozyrev to survive until 1996. In general, since the end of 1992 the Russian leadership had constantly felt under pressure from the public and had had to change first what is rhetoric and then its policies. In 1998 it had to make serious concessions and turn from its still in many ways a 'democratic', pro-Western, and radically pro-market policy to one which are more acceptable to the country's mass political culture.

It was only after this change that the majority of outside observers began to argue that Russia's democratization was in deep trouble (though some more attentive observers had warned about this much earlier). The overblown media coverage in 1999 of alleged corruption and money-laundering, implicating high-level government officials (including prominent former 'democrats'), was a tardy and excessive reaction not only to Russia's real and profound problems but also to the failure of most Western observers to disguise them in a timely and accurate fashion. However, most explanations

---

[23] On the 1993 elections, see: Stephen White, Richard Rose, and Ian McAllister, *How Russia Votes* (Chatham, NJ Chatham House, 1997), 107–29; Institut Politicheskogo i Voennogo Analiza, *Vybory v shestuyu Gosudarstvennuyu Dumu: itogi i vyvody* (Moscow: Chetvertyy filial Voenizdata, 1996).

were still traditionally occido-centrist and chose elements of Russian politics which were recognizable to a Westerner, once again drawing a black-and-white picture of the situation. The difficulties of Russian democratization were attributed to the allegedly ongoing struggle between democrats and Communists, or between reformers and conservatives, or between 'genuine democrats' and chameleons from the old *nomenklatura*. They were also seen as the result of deliberate betrayal or of inadequate Western assistance. But the problem went much deeper. Gorbachev's Russia lacked the necessary cultural preconditions for successful democratization, and instead of trying to create such conditions, Gorbachev, and later Yel`tsin, with the approval of their short-sighted Western advisers, pushed the country towards democratization 'here and now'.

This study of the political culture of the members of Russia's 'democratic' movement shows that the political views even of those 'democratic' activists who decisively rejected official Soviet ideology were nevertheless greatly influenced by it. Many ideas borrowed from the West were reinterpreted within the framework of a belief system that saw democracy as an ideal society which could solve all of mankind's material and spiritual problems. The noble goal of achieving such a society made it acceptable to disregard 'formalities', including the laws of the existing 'totalitarian' society. The state was seen as the main obstacle to an ideal democracy, and the maximal weakening of the state was believed to be the most important condition for its creation. Finally, 'democratic' activists viewed democracy not as a system of compromises among various groups and interests, or as the separation of powers, but as the unlimited power of the 'democrats' replacing the unlimited power of the Communists. Naturally, people who shared these beliefs could hardly create a liberal democracy based on the rule of law, the separation of powers, an independent judiciary, and respect for individual initiative and human rights. Moreover, being suspicious of state power as such, they could hardly create a workable state system. What emerged from the ruins of so-called totalitarianism was not a 'normal' democratic country, but a society of clans and cliques fighting for power. In full accordance with its political beliefs a ruthless (though hopeless) group of fanatical pro-Western and pro-market 'democratic' ideologues, who understood little of the beliefs and aspirations of the Russian people attempted to impose their abstract ideal on the nation. This ideal was not achieved, and the real loser has been the Russian people. Russia has not become a Western-style democracy with an effective market economy. Instead, it has turned into a disintegrating state where property and power have been seized by various clans and organized criminal groups. Although 'democratic' doctrinaires and fanatics must bear the blame, this does not mean that they wanted or foresaw the result.

Some elements of the 'democratic' political subculture will surely play an important role in the future of Russian politics, and Russia's future liberalization if that should come to pass, while as a united whole it ceased to exist with the elimination of the CPSU and the USSR at the very time when the most radical pro-market and pro-Western group of 'democrats' came to power, this happened because the central project which unified all 'democrats', namely the destruction of the 'totalitarian' regime, was achieved. The radical-market belief system survived for about another year and during this last year even became the dominant ideology of the leadership. However, it had to retreat under pressure from the dominant political culture of the population.

This does not mean that the 'democratic' political subculture disappeared without a trace. 'Democratic' beliefs of a radical pro-Western and pro-market type persisted in the ideology of some political groups, the most important of which, weakened but not completely dead, is Russia's Choice, headed by Gaydar. More moderate and legalistic 'democratic' beliefs were represented in the programmes of Yabloko, the strongest ofl the 'democratic' parties, which was joined by many 'democrats' disillusioned with the government's policy. The country's leadership, while distancing itself from purely 'democratic' groups and their policies, continued to claim democratic credentials and to use much of the 'democratic' rhetoric.

In a broader sense it can be said that the notions of the 'democratic' subculture greatly influenced the whole language of Russian politics and to a considerable extent became an integral part of it. In post-Communist Russia these notions, which earlier could be found only in the discourse of 'democratic' activists, became the basis of the language of much of the press, political speeches, party documents (including those of the Russian Communist Party, which accepted and actively developed some 'democratic' themes), and works on political science. While ceasing to exist as a discrete belief system, the 'democratic' political subculture of Soviet Russia profoundly influenced the broader political culture of the new Russia.

BIBLIOGRAPHY

BOOKS AND ARTICLES

ABERLE, DAVID F., 'A Note on Relative Deprivation Theory', in Sylvia L. Thrupp (ed.), *Millennian Dreams in Action: Essays in Comparative Studies* (The Hague: Mouton, 1962).

AFANAS`EV, YURIY, 'Otvety istorika', *Pravda*, 26 July 1988, p. 3.

ALEKSEEVA, LYUDMILA, *Istoriya inakomysliya v SSSR* (Vilnius and Moscow: Vest`, 1992).

ALEXEYEVA, LYUDMILA, *Soviet Dissent: Contemporary Movements for National, Religious and Human Rights* (Middletown, Conn.: Wesleyan University Press, 1987; English edn. of Alekseeva, *Istoriya inakomysliya v SSSR*).

ALMOND, GABRIEL, 'Comparative Political Systems', *Journal of Politics*, 18 (1956), 391–409.

—— and Verba, Sidney, *The Civic Culture: Political Attitudes and Democracy in Five Nations* (Princeton, NJ: Princeton University Press, 1963).

AMALRIK, ANDREI, *Will the Soviet Union Survive until 1984?*, ed. Hillary Stemberg (New York: Penguin, 1970; originally written in 1969 and distributed illegally).

ANDERSON, THORNTON, *Russian Political Thought: An Introduction* (Ithaca, NY: Cornell University Press, 1967).

ANDREEV, SERGEY, 'Prichiny i sledstviya', *Ural*, 1 (1988), 104–39.

—— 'Struktura vlasti i zadachi obshchestva', *Neva*, 1 (1989), 144–73.

ARBLASTER, ANTHONY, *Democracy*, 2nd edn. (Buckingham: Open University Press, 1994).

ARISTOTEL`, *Sochineniya*, 4 vols. (Moscow: Mysl`, 1983).

ARON, RAYMOND, *Democracy and Totalitarianism* (London: Weidenfeld and Nicolson, 1968; 1st publ. 1965 in French).

AVIS, GEORGE (ed.), *The Making of the Soviet Citizen* (London: Croom Helm, 1987).

BABKINA, M. A., *New Parties and Movements in the Soviet Union* (Commack, NY: Nova Science Publishers, 1991).

BABOSOV, E. M. (ed.), *Dve kul`tury—dva obraza mysli* (Minsk: Nauka i tekhnika, 1985).

BADIE, BERTRAND, *Culture et politique*, 3rd edn. (Paris: Economica, 1993).

BARBER, BENJAMIN R., 'Totalitarianism', in David Miller, Janet Coleman, William Connolly, and Alan Ryan (eds.), *The Blackwell Encyclopaedia of Political Thought* (Oxford: Basil Blackwell, 1987).

BARGHOORN, FREDERICK C., and REMINGTON, THOMAS F., *Politics in the USSR*, 3rd edn. (Boston: Little, Brown and Co., 1986).

BEK, ALEKSANDR, *Novoe naznacheniye. Roman* (Moscow: Sovetskiy pisatel`, 1988).

BELANOVSKIY, S. A., *Metodika i tekhnika fokusirovannogo interv`yu* (Moscow: Nauka, 1993).

302 *Bibliography*

BERDYAEV, NICOLAS, *The Origin of Russian Communism* (London: Geoffrey Bles, 1955; 1st edn. 1937).
—— *The Russian Idea* (London: Geoffrey Bles, 1947; 1st publ. 1946 in Russian.
BERDYAEV, NIKOLAY, 'Dukhi russkoi revolyutsii', in Nikolay Berdyaev,*Vekhi. Iz Glubiny* (Moscow: Pravda, 1991; 1st publ. 1918).
BERELOWITCH, ALEXIS, and WIEVIORKA, MICHEL, *Les Russes d'en bas: enquête sur la Russie post-communiste* (Paris: editions du Seuil, 1996).
BEREZOVSKIY, V. N. and KROTOV, N. I. (eds.), *Neformalnaya Rossiya. O neformal`nykh politizirivannykh dvizheniyakh i gruppakh v RSFSR (opyt sprav-ochnika)* (Moscow: Molodaya gvardiya, 1990).
BERLIN, ISAIAH, *Russian Thinkers* (London: Hogarth Press, 1978).
—— 'Two Concepts of Liberty', in Isaiah Berlin, *Four Essays on Liberty* (Oxford: Oxford University Press, 1969).
BIRCH, ANTHONY H., *The Concepts and Theories of Modern Democracy* (London: Routledge, 1993).
BLOCH, SIDNEY, and REDDAWAY, PETER, *Russia's Political Hospitals: The Abuse of Psychiatry in the Soviet Union* (London: Victor Gollancz, 1977).
—— *Soviet Psychiatric Abuse: The Shadow over World Psychiatry* (Boulder, Colo.: Westview Press, 1984).
BOGUCHARSKIY, V., *Aktivnoe narodnichestvo semidesyatykh godov* (Moscow: Izdatel`stvo M. i S. Sabashnikovikh, 1912).
BRINE, JENNY, 'Reading as a Leisure Pursuit in the USSR', in Jenny Brine, Maureen Perrie, and Andrew Sutton (eds.), *Home, School and Leisure in the Soviet Union* (London: George Allen and Unwin, 1980).
BROWN, ARCHIE, *The Gorbachev Factor* (Oxford: Oxford University Press, 1996).
—— 'Ideology and Political Culture', in Seweryn Bialer (ed.), *Politics, Society, and Nationality inside Gorbachev's Russia* (Boulder, Colo. and London: Westview, 1989).
—— 'Pluralism, Power and the Soviet Political System: A Comparative Perspective', in Susan Gross Solomon (ed.), *Pluralism in the Soviet Union* (London: Macmillan, 1983).
—— 'Political Culture', in Adam Kuper and Jessica Kuper (eds.), *The Social Science Encyclopaedia*, 2nd edn. (London: Routledge, 1996), 625–6.
—— review of Nicolai N. Petro, *The Rebirth of Russian Democracy: An Interpretation of Political Culture, American Political Science Review*, 90 (1996), 680–1.
—— *Soviet Politics and Political Science* (London: Macmillan, 1974).
—— (ed.), *New Thinking in Soviet Politics* (London: Macmillan, 1992).
—— (ed.), *Political Culture and Communist Studies* (London: Macmillan, 1984).
—— and Gray, Jack (eds.), *Political Culture and Political Change in Communist States* (London: Macmillan Press, 1977).
BRZEZINSKI, ZBIGNIEW, 'Soviet Politics: From the Future to the Past', in Paul Cocks, Robert V. Daniels, and Nancy Whittier Heer (eds.), *The Dynamics of Soviet Politics* (Cambridge, Mass.: Harvard University Press, 1976).
BUKOVSKY, VLADIMIR, 'Totalitarianism in Crisis', in Ellen Frankel Paul (ed.), *Totalitarianism at the Crossroads* (New Brunswick, NJ: Transaction, 1990).
BUNCE, V., and ECHOLS, J. M., III, 'Soviet Politics in the Brezhnev Era: "Pluralism"

or "Corporatism"?', in Donald R. Kelly (ed.), *Soviet Politics in the Brezhnev Era* (New York: Praeger, 1980).

BUTENKO, A. P. (ed.), *Sotsializm: sotsial`naya spravedlivost` i ravenstvo* (Moscow: Nauka, 1988).

BUTTERFIELD, JIM and WEIGLE, MARCIA, 'Unofficial Social Groups and Regime Response in the Soviet Union', in Judith B. Sedaitis and Jim Butterfield (eds.), *Perestroyka from Below: Social Movements in the Soviet Union* (Boulder, Colo.: Westview, 1991).

CHELNOKOV, MIKHAIL, *Rossiya bez Soyuza, Rossiya bez Rossii. . . . Zapiski deputata Rasstrelyannogo parlamenta* (Moscow: Novaya sloboda, 1994).

CHESHKO, S. V., *Ideologiya raspada* (Moscow: Koordinatsionno-metodologicheskiy tsentr prikladnoy etnografii Instituta etnologii i antropologii RAN, 1993).

CLARK, BRUCE, *An Empire's New Clothes: The End of Russia's Liberal Dream* (London: Vintage, 1995).

COLLINGWOOD, R. G., *The Idea of History* (Oxford: Oxford University Press, 1989; 1st publ. in 1946).

COX, TERRY, 'Democratization and the Growth of Pressure Groups in Soviet and Post-Soviet Politics', in Jeremy J. Richardson (ed.), *Pressure Groups* (Oxford: Oxford University Press, 1993).

DAHL, ROBERT A., *Democracy and its Critics* (New Haven, Conn.: Yale University Press, 1989).

—— *Dilemmas of Pluralist Democracy: Autonomy vs. Control* (New Haven, Conn.: Yale University Press, 1982).

—— *A Preface to Democratic Theory* (Chicago: University of Chicago Press, 1956).

DAVIDOVICH, V. I., *Sotsial`naya spravedlivost`: ideal i printsip deyatel`nosti* (Moscow: Izdatel`stvo politicheskoy literatury, 1989).

DAWSON, RICHARD E., and PREWITT, KENNETH, *Political Socialization* (Boston: Little, Brown and Co., 1969).

' "Delo" molodykh istorikov', *Voprosy istorii*, 4 (1994), 106–35.

'Demokratiya ne terpit demagogii', *Pravda*, 10 Feb. 1989, 3.

DEVLIN, JUDITH, *The Rise of the Russian Democrats: The Causes and Consequences of the Elite Revolution* (Aldershot: Edward Elgar, 1995).

DIFRANCEISCO, WAYNE, and GITELMAN, ZVI, 'Soviet Political Culture and "Covert Participation" in Policy Implementation', *American Political Science Review*, 78 (1984), 603–21.

DJILAS, MILOVAN, *The New Class: An Analysis of the Communist System* (New York: Praeger, 1958).

Dunlop, John B., *The Rise of Russia and the Fall of the Soviet Empire* (Princeton, NJ: Princeton University Press, 1993).

'Dvizhenie "Demokraticheskaya Rossiya": politicheskiy avtoportret', *Rossiyskaya gazeta*, 29 Nov. 1991.

DZARASOV, S. S., *Rossiyskiy put`: liberalizm ili sotsial-demokratism* (Moscow: Rossiyskiy gosudarstvennyy gumanitarnyy universitet, 1994).

FADEEV, VALERIY, *Pokhozhdeniya neformala: Ocherk 1988*, 2 vols. (Moscow: Russkoe slovo, 1992).

FAINSOD, MERLE, *Smolensk under Soviet Rule* (Cambridge, Mass.: Harvard University Press, 1958).

FEDOROV, V., 'Put` iz krizisa', *Grazhdanskiy Referendum*, 6 (1990), 3.

FIELDING, NIGEL (ed.), *Researching Social Life* (London: SAGE, 1993).

FIGNER, VERA, *Polnoye sobraniye sochineniy*, v (Moscow: Izdatel`stvo politka-torzhan, 1919).

FISCHER, GEORGE, *Russian Liberalism: From Gentry to Intelligentsia* (Cambridge, Mass.: Harvard University Press, 1958).

FISH, M. STEVEN, *Democracy from Scratch: Opposition and Regime in the New Russian Revolution* (Princeton, NJ: Princeton University Press, 1995).

FLERON, FREDERIC J., Jr., 'Political Culture in Russia', *Europe-Asia Studies*, 48 (1996), 225–60.

—— and HOFFMAN, ERIC (eds.), *Post-Communist Studies and Political Science: Methodology and Empirical Theory in Sovietology* (Boulder, Colo.: Westview, 1993).

FRIEDRICH, CARL J., 'The Unique Character of Totalitarian Society', in Carl J. Friedrich (ed.), *Totalitarianism* (New York: Grosset & Dunlap, 1964; 1st publ. 1954).

—— and BRZEZINSKI, ZBIGNIEW, *Totalitarian Dictatorship and Autocracy*, 2nd edn. (New York: Praeger, 1966; 1st publ. 1956).

GALBRAITH, JOHN K. *The New Industrial State* (New York: Penguin, 1968).

GAYDAR, YEGOR, *Gosudarstvo i evolyutsiya* (Moscow: Yevraziya, 1995).

GEERTZ, CLIFFORD, *The Interpretations of Cultures* (London: Fontana Press, 1993; 1st publ. 1973).

GELLNER, ERNEST, *State and Society in Soviet Thought* (Oxford: Basil Blackwell, 1988).

GIBSON, JAMES L., and DUCH, RAYMOND M., 'Emerging Democratic Values in Soviet Political Culture', in Arthur H. Miller, William M. Reisinger, and Vicki L. Hesli (eds.), *Public Opinion and Regime Change: The New Politics of Post-Soviet Societies* (Boulder, Colo.: Westview, 1993).

—— and Tedin, Kent L., 'Democratic Values and the Transformation of the Soviet Union', *Journal of Politics*, 54 (1992), 329–71.

GILBERT, G. NIGEL, and MULKAY, MICHAEL, *Opening Pandora's Box: A Sociological Analysis of Scientists' Discourse* (Cambridge: Cambridge University Press, 1984).

GLINSKI, DMITRY, and REDDAWAY, PETER, 'The Ravages of "Market Bolshevism"', *Journal of Democracy*, 10:2 (1999), 19–34.

GORBACHEV, M. S., 'Sotsialism i perestroyka', *Pravda*, 26 Nov. 1989, 1–3.

GORDON, LEONID, and KLOPOV, EDUARD (eds.), *Novye social`nye dvizheniya v Rossii. Po materialam rossiysko-frantsuzskogo issledovaniya* (Moscow: Progress-Kompleks, 1993).

GROMOV, A. V., and KUZIN, O. S., *Neformaly: kto est ` kto?* (Moscow: Mysl`, 1990).

GRUSHIN, BORIS, *Svobodnoye vremya: aktual`nye problemy* (Moscow: Mysl`, 1967).

GURR, TED ROBERT, *Why Men Rebel* (Princeton, NJ: Princeton University Press, 1971).

HAHN, JEFFREY W., 'Continuity and Change in Russian Political Culture', *British Journal of Political Science*, 21 (1991), 393–421.

HARASYMIW, BOHDAN, *Political Elite Recruitment in the Soviet Union* (London: Allen and Unwin, 1984).

HASS, ROBERT D., and TORNEY, JUDITH V., *The Development of Political Attitudes in Children* (Chicago: Aldine Publishing Co., 1967).

HAYEK, F. A., *The Constitution of Liberty* (London: Routledge & Kegan Paul, 1960).
—— *The Road to Serfdom* (London: Routledge, 1944).
HOLDEN, BARRY, *The Nature of Democracy* (New York: Harper & Row, 1974).
HOSKING, GEOFFREY, *Russia: People and Empire (1552–1917)* (London: HarperCollins, 1997).
HOSKING, G., AVES, J., and DUNCAN, P. (eds.), *The Road to Post-Communism: Independent Political Movements in the Soviet Union, 1985–1991* (London: Pinter, 1992).
HOUGH, JERRY, *The Soviet Union and Social Science Theory* (Cambridge, Mass.: Harvard University Press, 1977).
HYLAND, JAMES L., *Democratic Theory: The Philosophical Foundations* (Manchester: Manchester University Press, 1995).
INGLEHART, RONALD, *Culture Shift in Advanced Industrial Society* (Princeton, NJ: Princeton University Press, 1990).
INKELES, ALEX, and BAUER, RAYMOND A., *The Soviet Citizen: Daily Life in a Totalitarian Society* (Cambridge, Mass.: Harvard University Press, 1959).
—— and Levinson, Daniel J., 'National Character: The Study of Modal Personality and Sociocultural Systems,' in Gardner Lindzey and Elliot Aronson (eds.), *The Handbook of Social Psychology*, 2nd edn., iv (Reading, Mass.: Addison-Wesley, 1969).
Institut Politicheskogo i Voennogo Analiza, *Vybory v shestuyu Gosudarstvennuyu Dumu: itogi i vyvody* (Moscow: Chetvertyy filial Voenizdata, 1996).
ITENBERG, B. S., *Dvizhenie revolutsionnogo narodnichestva* (Moscow: Nauka, 1965).
KAINZ, HOWARD P., *Democracy East and West: A Philosophical Overview* (London: Macmillan, 1984).
KARA-MURZA, A. A., and VOSKRESENSKIY, A. K. (eds.), *Totalitarizm kak istoricheskiy fenomen* (Moscow: Filosofskoe obshchestvo SSSR, 1989).
KEENAN, EDWARD, 'Muscovite Political Folkways', *Russian Review*, 45:2 (1986), 115–81.
KOVAL`, B. I. (ed.), *Rossiya segodnya. Politicheskiy portret, 1985–1990* (Moscow: Mezhdunarodnye otnosheniya, 1991).
KOZYREV, ANDREY, *Preobrazhenie* (Moscow: Mezhdunarodnye otnosheniya, 1995).
KPSS. Spravochnik, 5th edn. (Moscow: Izdatel`stvo politicheskoy literatury, 1983), 438–40.
KRASULYA, VASILIY, *Dissident iz nomenklatury* (Stavropol`: Severo-kavkazskoye informatsionno-reklamnoye agenstvo, 1992).
KRYSKIN, YEVGENIY, Demokratiya i antidemokratiya v Penze: Nachalo protivostoyaniya (1989–91gg.), Penza, 1992 [no publisher mentioned].
—— 'Strashnaya godovshchina', *Penzenskiy grazhdanin*, 10 (Dec. 1989), 12–14.
—— 'Na Kipre pravit Kassio?', *Penzenskiy grazhdanin*, 5 (July 1989), 2–10.
K uchreditel`nomu s`yezdu Sotsial-democraticheskoy partii Rossiskoy Federatsii. Sbornik materiyalov No. 1 (Tipografiya Minuralsibstroya, 1990).
LANE, DAVID, *Soviet Society under Perestroika* (Boston: Unwin Hyman, 1990).
LAPIDUS, GAIL W. (ed.), *The New Russia: Troubled Transformation* (Boulder, Colo.: Westview, 1995).
LEITES, NATHAN, *A Study of Bolshevism* (Glencoe, Ill.: Free Press, 1953).
LENIN, V. I., *Collected Works* (London: Lawrence & Wishart; and Moscow: Progress Publishers, 1966).

LEONTOVICH, V. V., *Istoriya liberalizma v Rossii* (Paris: YMCA Press, 1980; 1st publ. 1957 in German).

LEPESHKIN, YU. V., 'Chto glavnoe v politicheskoy kul`ture?', in P. I. Simush (ed.), *Politologiya na rossiyskom fone* (Moscow: Luch, 1993).

LEVADA, YU. A. (ed.), *Sovetskiy prostoy chelovek* (Moscow: Mirovoy okean, 1993).

LEWIS, OSCAR, 'Further Observations on the Folk-urban Continuum and Urbanization', in P. M. Hauser and L. F. Schnore (eds.), *The Study of Urbanization* (New York: Wiley, 1965).

LOFLAND, JOHN, and STARK, RODNEY, 'Becoming a World-saver: A Theory of Conversion to a Deviant Perspective', *American Sociological Review*, 30 (1965), 862–75.

LOTMAN, JU. M., USPENSKIJ, B. A., *The Semiotics of Russian Culture*, ed. A. Shukman (Ann Arbor, Mich.: Michigan Slavic Publications, 1984).

LUKIN, A., 'Angloyazychnaya sovetologiya i obshchestvennye nauki v Rossii', *SSHA: economika, politika, ideologiya*, 9 (1995), 38–50.

LUKIN, ALEXANDER, 'Interpretations of Soviet State and Social Structure: Perceptions of Members of the First Russian Democratic Political Groups, 1985–1991', *Demokratizatsiya*, 3 (1995), 365–91.

—— 'The Initial Soviet Reaction to the Events in China in 1989 and the Prospects for Sino-Soviet Relations', *The China Quarterly*, 125 (1991), 119–36.

—— 'The New Russia: Parliamentary Democracy or Authoritarian Regime?', in *International Review*, 3:1 (1991), 42–3.

—— 'Predstavleniya "democraticheskikh" grupp o vneshnem mire', *Mirovaya ekonomika i mezhdunarodnye otnosheniya*, 8 (1995), 104–13.

McCLOSKY, HERBERT, and DAHLGREN, HAROLD E., 'Primary Group Influence on Party Loyalties', *American Political Science Review*, 53 (1959), 757–76.

McFAUL, MICHAEL, 'The Perils of a Protracted Transition,' *Journal of Democracy*, 10:2 (1999), 4–18.

—— MARKOV, SERGEI, *The Troubled Birth of Russian Democracy: Parties, Personalities, Programs* (Stanford, Calif.: Hoover Institution Press, 1993).

MALCOLM, NEIL, PRAVDA, ALEX, ALLISON, ROY, and LIGHT, MARGOT (eds.), *Internal Factors in Russian Foreign Policy* (Oxford: Oxford University Press, 1996).

MANDEL, ERNEST, *On Bureaucracy: A Marxist Analysis* (London: IMG Publications, [1973]).

—— *Power and Money: A Marxist Theory of Bureaucracy* (London: Verso, 1992).

MARX, KARL, letter to Engels, 2 July 1953, in K. Marx and F. Engels, *Polnoe sobranie sochineniy*, 2nd edn., xxviii, (Moscow: Gosudarstvennoe politicheskoe izdatel`stvo, 1962).

—— and ENGELS, FREDERICK, 'Manifesto of the Communist Party', in Karl Marx and Frederick Engels, *Selected Works* (Moscow: Progress Publishers, 1969), i.

Materialy XXVII s`ezda Kommunisticheskoy Partii Sovetskogo Soyuza (Moscow: Izdatel'stvo Politicheskoy Literatury, 1986).

MAY, TIM, *Social Research* (Buckingham: Open University Press, 1993).

MELIKSETOV, A.V., *Sotsial`no-economicheskaya politika Gomin`dana v Kitaye (1927–1949)* (Moscow: Nauka, 1977).

MERTON, ROBERT K., FISKE, MARJORIE, and KENDAL, PATRICIA L., *The Focused Interview* (London: Collier Macmillan, 1990).

MILLAR, JAMES R. (ed.), *Politics, Work and Daily Life in the USSR: A Survey of Former Soviet Citizens* (Cambridge: Cambridge University Press, 1987).

MILLER, ARTHUR H., HESLI, VICKI L., and REISINGER, WILLIAM M., 'Comparing Citizen and Elite Belief Systems in Post-Soviet Russia and Ukraine', *Public Opinion Quarterly*, 59 (1995), 1–40.

—— —— —— (eds.), *Public Opinion and Regime Change: The New Politics of Post-Soviet Societies* (Boulder, Col.: Westview, 1993).

—— —— —— 'Reassessing Mass Support for Political and Economic Change in the Former USSR', *American Political Science Review*, 88 (1994), 399–411.

MITROKHIN, S. S., 'Aksiologicheskie korni obshchestvennykh dvizheniy v SSSR', in A. N. Alekseev, E. A. Zdravomyslova, and V. V. Kostyushev (eds.), *Sotsiologiya obshchestvennykh dvizheniy: kontseptual`nye modeli issledovaniya 1989–1990* (Moscow: Institut sotsiologii RAN, 1992).

—— and Urban, Michael, 'Social Groups, Party Elites and Russia's New Democrats', in David Lane (ed.), *Russia in Flux: The Political and Social Consequences of Reform* (Aldershot: Edward Elgar, 1992).

MOZHAEV, BORIS, 'Poltora kvadratnykh metra', in Boris Mozhaev, *Sobranie sochineniy*, (Moscow: Khudozhestvennaya literatura, 1990; written in 1970), iii. 204–86.

Narodnoe khozyaystvo SSSR v 1987 g. (Moscow: Finansy i statistika 1988).

Neformaly: kto oni? Kuda zovut? (Moscow: Politicheskaya literatura, 1990).

NICHOLLS, DAVID, *Three Varieties of Pluralism* (London: Macmillan, 1974).

NIKIFOROV, V. N., *Vostok i vsemirnaya istoriya* (Moscow: Nauka, 1975).

NOVODVORSKAYA, VALERIYA, *Po tu storonu otchayaniya* (Moscow: Novosti, 1993).

NOZICK, ROBERT, *Anarchy, State and Utopia* (New York: Basic Books, 1974).

OBERSHALL, ANTHONY, *Social Movements: Ideologies, Interests, and Identities* (New Brunswick, NJ: Transaction, 1993).

PETER, L., 'Pochemu dela idut vkriv` i vkos` ili Yeshche raz o Printsipe Pitera', *Inostrannaya Literatura*, 1 (1 Jan., 2 Feb., 1987), 195–209 and 2 (1987), 175–89.

PETER, LAURENCE J., *Why Things Go Wrong or The Peter Principle Revisited* (London: George Allen and Unwin, 1985).

PETRO, NICOLAI N., *The Rebirth of Russian Democracy: An Interpretation of Political Culture* (Cambridge, Mass.: Harvard University Press, 1995).

PIPES, RICHARD, *Russia under the Old Regime* (New York: Scribner, 1974).

PIVOVAROV, YU. S., *Politicheskaya kul`tura poreformennoy Rossii* (Moscow: Rossiyskaya Akademiya Nauk, Institut nauchnoy informatsii po obshchestvennym naukam, 1994).

Platforma kluba 'Demokrat' (Vladivostok: 1989).

PLEKHANOV, G. V., *Sochineniya*, 24 vols. (St Petersburg/Leningrad: Gosudarstvennoe izdatel`stvo, 1923–7).

POPOV, GAVRIIL, *Snova v oppozitsii* (Moscow, Galaktika, 1994).

—— 'S tochki zreniya economista: O romane Aleksandra Beka "Novoe Naznacheniye" ', *Nauka i Zhizn`*, 4 (1987), 54–66.

POPPER, KARL R., *The Open Society and its Enemies* (London: Routledge & Kegan Paul, 1945).

PRIBYLOVSKII, VLADIMIR, *Dictionary of Political Parties and Organizations in Russia* (Moscow: PostFactum/Integral; Washington, DC: Center for Strategic and International Studies, 1992).

PRIBYLOVSKIY, VLADIMIR, *Slovar` oppositsii: novye politicheskie partii i organizatsii Rossii*, PostFactum Analytical Review, No. 4–5 (Moscow: Post Factum, 1991).

Programme of the Communist Party of the Soviet Union (Draft) (Moscow: Foreign Languages Publishing House, 1961).

Put` progressa i sotsial`noi democratii. Osnova programmy SDPR (Moscow and Sverdlovsk: 1990).

PYE, LUCIAN W., 'Political Culture', in David Sills (ed.), *International Encyclopedia of Social Sciences* (New York: Macmillan and Free Press, 1968), xii. 218–25.

RAEFF, MARC, 'The People, the Intelligentsia and Political Culture', *Political Studies*, 41 (1993), 93–106.

—— *Russian Intellectual History: An Anthology* (Brighton: Harvester Press, 1978).

RAWLS, JOHN, *A Theory of Justice* (Cambridge, Mass.: Harvard University Press, 1971).

'Redaktsionnaya', *Penzenskiy grazhdanin*, 1 (Mar. 1989), 3.

REDDAWAY, PETER (ed.), *Uncensored Russia: The Human Rights Movement in the Soviet Union* (London: Jonathan Cape, 1972).

REISINGER, WILLIAM M., MILLER, ARTHUR H., HESLI, VICKI L., and MAHER, KRISTEN HILL, 'Political Values in Russia, Ukraine and Lithuania: Sources and Implications for Democracy', *British Journal of Political Science*, 24 (1994), 183–223.

RIASANOVSKY, NICHOLAS V., 'The Norman Theory of the Origin of the Russian State', in Nicholas V. Riasanovsky, *Collected Writings: 1947–1994* (Los Angeles: Charles Schlacks, 1993).

RIAZANOVSKIY, V. A., 'Vopros o vliyanii normanov na russkuyu kul`turu', in V. A. Riazahovskiy, *Historical Survey of Russian Culture* (New York: L. Rausen, 1947).

'Rossiya: nedelimaya ili "delimaya" ', *Demokraticheskaya gazeta*, 7:13 (10 May 1991), 9.

Rossiya: partii, assotsiatsii, soyuzy, kluby. Spravochnik, Rossiysko-amerikanskiy universitet, Institut massovykh politicheskikh dvizheniy, 10 vols. (Moscow: RAU-Press, 1991–2).

ROZHDESTVENSKIY, S. R., *Materialy k istoriy samodeyatel`nykh politicheskikh ob`yedineniy v SSSR posle 1945 goda* (Moscow and Paris: Pamyat`, 1981–2).

RUMYANTSEV, O. G., *O samodeyatel`nom dvizhenii obshchestvennykh initsiativ (neformal`nye ob`edineniya i ikh rol` v perestroyke obshchestvennoy zhizni v SSSR)* (Moscow: Academiya nauk SSSR, Institut economiki mirovoy sotsialistich-eskoy sistemy, 1988).

RYBAKOV, B. A., *Yazychestvo drevney Rusi* (Moscow: Nauka, 1987).

SAKHAROV, ANDREI, *Progress, Coexistence and Intellectual Freedom* (London: Deutsch, 1968).

SAKWA, RICHARD, 'Christian Democracy in Russia', *Religion, State and Society*, 20:2 (1992), 135–200.

—— 'Khristianskaya demokratiya v Rossii', *Sotsiologicheskie issledivaniya*, 4 (1993), 126–34 and 7 (4 Apr., 7 Jul., 1993), 122–31.

—— *Russian Politics and Society* (London: Routledge, 1993).

SARTORI, GIOVANNI, *Parties and Party Systems: A Framework for Analysis* (Cambridge: Cambridge University Press, 1976).

—— *The Theory of Democracy Revisited* (Chatham, NJ: Chatham House Publishers, 1987).

SAVEL`EV, V. (ed.), *Malaya entsiklopediya rossiyskoy politiki. Osnovnye partii i dvizheniya, zaregistrirovannye ministerstvom yustitsii* (Moscow: Verkhovnyy Sovet Rossiyskoy Federatsii, Parlamentskiy Tsentr, 1992).

SCHAPIRO, LEONARD, *Totalitarianism* (London: Macmillan, 1978).

SCHMITTER, PHILIPPE, 'Still the Century of Corporatism?', *Review of Politics*, 36 (Jan. 1974), 93–4.

SCHUMPETER, JOSEPH A., *Capitalism, Socialism, and Democracy* (New York: Harper, 1942).

SEMENOVSKIY, V. I., *Politicheskie i obshchestvennye idei dekabristov* (St Petersburg: Tipogrphiya Pervoy spt. trudovoy arteli, 1909).

SHAKHNAZAROV, G. Kh., BOBORYKIN, A. D., KRASIN, YU. A., SUKHODEEV, V. V., and PISARZHEVSKIY, O. N., *Obshchestvovedenie. Uchebnik dlya vypusknogo klassa sredney shkoly i srednikh spetsial`nykh uchebnykh zavedeniy* (Moscow: Politizdat, 1971).

SHENIN, OLEG, 'Za steklyannoy stenoy chasto ostayutsya "neformaly" v pylu spora', *Pravda*, 5 Feb. 1988, 1.

SIMON, GERHARD, 'Political Culture in Russia', *Aussenpolitik*, 3 (1995), 242–53.

SKILLING, H. G., 'Interest Groups and Communist Politics', *World Politics*, 18:3 (Apr. 1966), 435–51.

—— and GRIFFITHS, F. (eds.), *Interest Groups in Soviet Politics* (Princeton, NJ: Pronceton University Press, 1971).

SMELYAKOV, N. N., *Delovaya Amerika. Zapiski inzheneva* (Moscow: Izdatel`stvo politicheskoy literatury, 1967).

SOGRIN, V., *Politicheskaya istoriya sovremennoy Rossii 1985–1994. Ot Gorbacheva do Yel`tsina* (Moscow: Progress-Akademiya, 1994).

SOLZHENITSYN, ALEXANDER, 'As Breathing and Consciousness Return' in Alexander Solzhenitsyn (ed.), *From Under the Rubble* (London: Fontana/Collins, 1975; 1st publ. in Russian as *Iz pod glyb* (Paris: YMCA Press, 1974)).

—— 'The Mortal Danger', in Erik P. Hoffman and Robbin F. Laird (eds.), *The Soviet Polity in the Modern Era* (New York: Aldine, 1984).

Sotsiologicheskaya sluzhba fonda, 'Demokraticheskaya Rossiya', *DR-Socio*, 4 (9 Nov. 1991).

*Spravochnik po 'neformal`nym' obshchestvennym organizatsiyam i presse*, Informatsionnyy byulleten` SMOT, 5 (Moscow: 1988) and 16 (Moscow: IAS (informatsionnoye agentstvo SMOT), 1989).

STARK, RODNEY, and BAINBRIDGE, WILLIAM SIMS, *The Future of Religion: Secularization, Revival and Cult Formation* (Berkeley, Calif.: University of California Press, 1985).

—— 'Networks of Faith: Interpersonal Bonds and Recruitment to Cults and Sects', *American Journal of Sociology*, 6 (1980), 1376–95.

STAVSKAYA, N., 'Ustav dlya sporyashchikh', *Slovo lektora*, 10 (1989), 49.

SUKHANOV, LEV, *Tri goda s Yel`tsinym: Zapiski pervogo pomoshchnika* (Riga: Vaga, 1992).

SZAMUELY, TIBOR, *The Russian Tradition* (London: Secker & Warburg, 1974).

TOKES, RUDOLF L. (ed.), *Dissent in the USSR: Politics, Ideology, and People* (Baltimore, Md.: Johns Hopkins University Press, 1975).

TOURAINE, ALAIN, *La Méthode de l'intervention sociologique* (Paris: Textes, 1993).

TOURAINE, ALAIN, *Solidarity. The Analysis of a Social Movement: Poland 1980–1981* (Cambridge: Cambridge University Press, 1983).

TOURAINE, ALAIN, *The Voice and the Eye: An Analysis of Social Movements* (Cambridge: Cambridge University Press, 1981).

TROTSKY, LEON, *In Defence of Marxism: Against the Petty-Bourgeois Opposition* (New York: Merit, 1965).

TSIMBAEV, N. I., *Slavyanofil`stvo* (Moscow: Izdatel`stvo Moskovskogo universiteta, 1986).

TUCKER, ROBERT, 'Sovietology and Russian History', *Post-Soviet Affairs*, 8:3 (1992), 175–96.

UL`YANOV, NIKOLAY, 'Kompleks Filofeya', *Voprosy istorii*, 4 (1994), 150–63.

URBAN, MICHAEL E., and MCCLURE, JOHN, 'Discourse, Ideology and Party Formation on the Democratic Left in the USSR', in Michael E. Urban (ed.), *Ideology and System Change in the USSR and East Europe* (New York: St. Martin's Press, 1992).

USEEM, BERT, 'Solidarity Model, Breakdown Model and the Boston Anti-busing Movement', *American Sociological Review*, 45 (1980), 357–69.

USPENSKIJ, B. A., 'Historia sub specie semioticae', in D. P. Lucid (ed.), *Soviet Semiotics: An Anthology* (Baltimore, Md.: Johns Hopkins University Press, 1977).

VAL`DENBERG, VLADIMIR, *Drevnerusskie ucheniya o predelakh tsarskoy vlasti. Ocherki russkoy politicheskoy literatury on Vladimira Svyatogo do kontsa XVII veka* (Petrograd: Tipografiya A. Benke, 1916).

VASILYEV, LEONID, 'After Bankruptcy: What is Happening to the CPSU', *New Times*, 49 (4–10 Dec. 1990), 7–11.

VENTURI, FRANCO, *Roots of Revolution: A History of the Populist and Socialist Movements in Nineteenth Century Russia* (London: Weidenfeld and Nicolson, 1960; 1st publ. 1952 in Italian).

VINOGRADOV, PAVEL, 'Pokhozhdeniya atomarnykh lichnostey na zakate', *Krasnoyarskiy komsomolets*, 6 and 8 Apr. 1993, p. 2.

VOSLENSKIY, MIKHAIL, *Nomenklatura: gospodstvuyushchiy klass sovetskogo obshchestva* (Moscow: MP 'Oktyabr`, 'Sovetskaya Rossiya', 1991).

VOSLENSKY, MIKHAIL, *Nomenklatura: Anatomy of the Soviet Ruling Class*, trans. Eric Mosbacher (London: Bodley Head, 1984).

WALKER, ROBERT (ed.), *Applied Qualitative Research* (Aldershot: Gower, 1985).

WELCH, STEPHEN, *The Concept of Political Culture* (London: Macmillan, 1993).

WHITE, ANNE, 'The Memorial Society in the Russian Provinces', *Europe-Asia Studies*, 47 (1995), 1343–66.

WHITE, STEPHEN, *Political Culture and Soviet Politics* (London: Macmillan, 1979).

—— GILL, GRAEME, and SLIDER, DARRELL (eds.), *The Politics of Transition: Shaping a Post-Soviet Future* (Cambridge: Cambridge University Press, 1993).

—— ROSE, RICHARD, and MCALLISTER, IAN, *How Russia Votes* (Chatham, NJ: Chatham House, 1997).

WHYTE, WILLIAM FOOTE, *Street Corner Society* (Chicago, Ill.: University of Chicago Press, 1943).

WITTFOGEL, K.-A., *Oriental Despotism: A Comparative Study of Total Power* (New Haven, Conn: Yale University Press, 1957).

YADOV, V. A. (with the cooperation of V. V. Semenova), *Strategiya sotsialogicheskogo* *issledovaniya. Opisanie, ob`yasnenie, ponimanie sotsial`noy real`nosti* (Moscow: Dobrosvet, 1998).

——, (ed.) *Sotsiologiya v Rossii* (Moscow: Izdatel`stvo Instituta Sotsiologii RAN, 1998).

YAKOVLEV, ALEKSANDR NIKOLAEVICH, *Gor`kaya chasha: Bol`shevizm i Reformatsiya Rossii* (Yaroslavl: Verkhne-Volzhskoe knizhnoye izdatel`stvo, 1994).

YEL`TSIN, BORIS, *Ispoved` na zadannuyu temu* (Leningrad: Sovetskiy pisatel`, 1990).

YOUNG, MICHAEL, and WILLMOTT, PETER, *Family and Kinship in East London* (Baltimore, Md.: Penguin, 1957).

ZEN`KOVSKIY, VASILIY, *Istoriya russkoy filosofii* (Leningrad: 1991; 1st publ. 1948).

ZENKOVSKY, SERGE A., *Russkoe staroobriadchestvo: dukhovyne dvizheniia semnadt-satogo veka* (Munich: Wilhelm Fink Verlag, 1970).

ZHIGULIN, ANATOLIY, 'Chernye kamni', *Znamya*, 7 (1988), 10–75 and 8 (1988), 48–119.

UNPUBLISHED MANUSCRIPTS

'Deklaratsiya ob obrazovanii Penzenskogo fronta v podderzhku perestroyki. Proekt' [Penza, Dec. 1989].

'Deklaratsiya uchreditel`nogo sobraniya Rossiyskogo christiansko-demokratich-eskogo dvizheniya (RKhDD)' [Moscow, 1990] .

Dvizhenie za svobodu i demokratiyu, 'Obrashcheniye k demokraticheskim silam strany' [Moscow, 1989].

Krasnoyarskiy komitet sodeystviya perestroyki, 'Otkrytoe pis'mo Krasnoyartsam' [Krasnoyarsk, 1989].

KUDRYAVTSEV, I., 'Oppositsiya i totalitarizm v SSSR' [Moscow, 1992].

'Nekotorye resul`taty oprosa uchastnikov diskussii v klube "Perestroyka" 25 aprelya 1988 g.' [Moscow, 1988].

'Obrashcheniye kluba izbirateley Taganskogo i Proletarskogo rayonov k narodnym deputatam SSSR' (Moscow, 7 June 1989).

Penzenskiy front v podderzhku perestroyki, 'Programma. Proekt' [Penza, 1989].

POLUYAN, PAVEL, 'Ob`yasneniye P.V. Poluyana prokuroru tsentral`nogo rayona goroda Krasnoyarska A. I.Grishinu' ([Krasnoyarsk], 13 Mar. 1989).

—— 'Ot byurokratii k demokratii' [Krasnoyarsk, 1989].

Records of meetings of the Oktyabrskiy District Union of Voters' [Moscow, 1990–91].

SHCHERKIN, ANDREY, 'Protsessy zarozhdeniya, razvitiya i stanovleniya politicheskikh partiy i massovikh obshchestvennykh dvizheniy v Pskovskoy oblasti v 1988–1994' [Pskov, 1994].

Sotsial-demokraticheskaya partiya Rossiyskoy Federatsii, 'Put` progressa i sotsial`noy demokratii. Osnova programmy SDPR. Vremennaya redaktsiya' [Moscow, 1990].

[Sotsialisticheskaya Partiya], 'Put` k svobode. Programma Sotsialisticheskoy partii. Proekt' [Moscow, 1990].

—— 'Revolyutsionnaya reforma. Proekt' [Moscow, 1990].

'Sovmestnoe zayavlenie o neprimenenii nasiliya v reshenii politicheskikh problem. Proekt' [Moscow, 1989].

YELISTRATOV, V. I., diary and notes, [Belinskiy, 1989–90].
ZAMYATIN, ANATOLIY, 'O sotsial-democratii i Sotsial-demokraticheskoi partii Rossii' [Penza, 1990].

PERIODICALS

Moscow

Official:

Izvestiya
Komsomol`skaya pravda
Moscow News
Nauka i Zhizn`
Ogonek
Pravda
Znamya

'Democratic':

Byulleten` obshchestvennoy organizatsii Grazhdanskoye Dostoinstvo (Civic Dignity)
Byulleten` soveta partii (Democratic Union)
Demokraticheskaya gazeta (DPR)
Demokraticheskaya Rossiya (DPR, later independent)
Den` za dnem (Doverie)
ESDEK (SDPR)
Express-Khronika (independent)
Glasnost` (Independent)
Grazhdanskiy referendum (Moscow Popular Front)
Informatsionnyy byulleten` Sotsial-demokraticheskoy Assotsiatsii (SDA)
Novosti sotsial-demokratii (SDPR),
Obshchina (konfederation of Anarcho-syndicalists)
Otkrytaya zona (Demokraticheskaya Perestroyka)
Svobodnoye slovo (Democratic Union)
Vpolgolosa (Democratic Union)

Kaliningrad:

Vestnik 'Solidarnosti' Society (Kaliningtad)

Krasnoyarsk:

Official:
Krasnoyarskiy komsomolets

'Democratic':
Pravo Golosa (Krasnoyarsk Committee for Assistance to Perestroyka)

Magnitogorsk:

Kaplya (SDPR)

Nevinnomyssk:

Demokrat (DPR)

Orenburg:

Golos (voter's union of the industrial association Strela)

Penza:

Democraticheskoe obozrenie (independent)
Listok 'Grazhdanskoy initsiativy' (Civic Initiative)
Penzenskiy Grazhdanin (Civic Initiative)

Pskov:

Official:

Molodoy Leninets
Profsoyuznaya gazeta
Spektr (later *Rossiyskiye vedomosti*)

'Democratic':
Veche (Pskov Popular Front)

Stavropol`:

Official:
Stavropol`skaya pravda

'Democratic':
Demokraticheskiy vestnik (Stavropol` Popular Front)
Grazhdanin (Stavropol` Popular Front)
*Khronika bor`by za demokratiyu* (Stavropol` Popular Front)

Vladivostok:
Demokraticheskiy vestnik (DPR)

LIST OF INTERVIEWS

Name	Occupation at time of 'democratic' activities	Group(s)	Date of interview

PENZA, APRIL AND SEPTEMBER 1994

Name	Occupation at time of 'democratic' activities	Group(s)	Date of interview
Didichenko, Georgiy Ivanovich	lawyer	Human Rights Group	4 Apr.
Kislov, Aleksandr Ivanovich	journalist	Democratic Russia	29 Sept.
Kryskin, Yevgeniy Ivanovich	engineer	Civic Initiative	3 Apr.
Manuylov, Valentin Igorevich	philosophy lecturer	Politclub	4 Apr.
Shlykov, Vladimir Pavlovich	physicist	Popular Front	4 Apr.
Yerasov, Aleksandr Yevgenievich	businessman	Popular Front	3 Apr.
Zamyatin, Anatoliy	construction worker	SDPR	29 Sept.

BELINSKIY, PENZA *OBLAST*`

Name	Occupation	Group	Date
Grachev, Yevgeniy Aleksandrovich	museum researcher	Discussion Club	5 Apr.
Vorobyev, Fedor Fedorovich	arts teacher	Discussion Club	5 Apr.
Yelistratov, Vladimir Ivanovich	CPSU regional committee instructor	Discussion Club	5 Apr.

KRASNOYARSK

Name	Occupation	Group	Date
Klepachev, Nikolay Aleksandrovich	construction engineer	Popular Front	19 Apr.
Kutakov, Yevgeniy Viktorovich	student	Popular Front	20 Apr.
Loskutov, Sergey Nikolayevich	worker	Popular Front	21 Apr.
Novikov, Vyacheslav Aleksandrovich	physicist	Democratic Russia	20 Apr.
Obryadin, Oleg Yevgenievich	law student	Democratic Union	21 Apr.
Poluyan, Pavel Vadimovich	philosophy lecturer	Popular Front	19 Apr.
Sirotinin, Vladimir Georgievich	engineer	Memorial	20 Apr.

VLADIVOSTOK

Name	Occupation	Group	Date
Borovik, Pavel Ivanovich	accountant	Democratic Union	25 Apr.
Brodyanskiy, David Izrailevich	professor of archaeology	Democratic Russia	24 Apr.

Name	Occupation at time of 'democratic' activities	Group(s)	Date of interview
Cherepkov, Viktor Ivanovich	navy officer	Democratic Russia	25 Apr.
Chernetskiy, Grigoriy Aleksandrovich	scientist	Vladivostok Voter's Union	22 Apr.
Fel`dman, Teodey Izrailevich	engineer	Democratic Russia	23 Apr.
Grinchenko, Il`ya Konstantinovich	telegraphist	Club Demokrat, SDPR	24 Apr.
Korovin, Yevgeniy Mikhaylovich	secondary school student	Democrat Club, SDPR	24 Apr.
Krylov, Vladimir Semenovich	teacher, later worker	Democrat Club, SDPR	24 Apr.
Makhora, Vladimir Filippovich	student	Popular Front	23 Apr.
Rybalko, Viktor Ivanovich	worker	Democratic Union	23 Apr.
Shokolenko, Sergey	journalist	Democratic Union	23 Apr.

STAVROPOL`

Name	Occupation	Group(s)	Date
Borodin, Yevgeniy Konstantinovich	land surveyor	Popular Front	3 Sept.
Chesnokov, Konstantin Grigorievich	army officer (retired)	Popular Front	4 Sept.
Dubovik, Gennadiy Petrovich	engineer	Popular Front	3 Sept.
Kaznacheeva, Taisiya Petrovna	philosophy lecturer	Popular Front	2 Sept.
Krasulya, Vasiliy Aleksandrovich	journalist	Popular Front	2 Sept.
Lipchanskaya, Alla Vasilyevna	philosophy lecturer	Popular Front	2 Sept.
Lushnikov, Oleg Removich	worker	Popular Front	4 Sept.
Popov, Sergey Ivanovich	medical researcher	Popular Front	3 Sept.
Solodskikh, Vyacheslav Andreevich	youth organizer	Popular Front	4 Sept.
Suslova, Elena Sergeevna	archivist	Popular Front	4 Sept.

NEVINNOMYSSK, STAVROPOL` *KRAY*

Name	Occupation	Group(s)	Date
Vansovich, Olga	nurse (retired)	*DPR*	5 Sept.
Knyazeva, Valentina Ilyinichna	accountant	*DPR*	5 Sept.

PSKOV

Name	Occupation	Group(s)	Date
Father Pavel (Adel`geym)	Orthodox priest	Memorial	25 Sept.
Ivlev, Aleksandr	student	Memorial, Democratic Union	25 Sept.

Name	Occupation at time of 'democratic' activities	Group(s)	Date of interview
Nikol`skiy, Valeriy	student	Memorial, Popular Front	24 Sept.
Pavlov, Aleksandr	worker	Pskov Voter's Union	25 Sept.
Skcherkin, Andrey	worker, later journalist	Memorial, Democratic Russia	25 Sept.

ORENBURG

Antoshkina, Lyudmila Ilyinichna	engineer	Democratic Russia	21 Dec.
Gayazov, Ravil` Gayanovich	student	Politclub	23 Dec.
Golovin, Sergey Ivanovich	oblast` Komsomol committee instructor	Politclub	23 Dec.
Nikiforenko, Yuriy Vasil`evich	city Communist Party committee official	Voter's Union	23 Dec.
Popov, Petr Pavlovich	engineer	Voter's Union	22 Dec.
Rayzman, Grigoriy Froimovich	researcher	Democratic Russia	21 Dec.
Romanov, Aleksandr Ivanovich	civil aviation pilot	Democratic Russia	22 Dec.
Shapovalenko, Vladislav Aleksandrovich	gas engineer	Democratic Russia	21 Dec.
Shul`cheva, Ol`ga Borisovna	philosophy lecturer	Memorial, Democratic Russia	22 Dec.
Stetsenko, Vladimir Georgievich	worker	Orenburg Discussion Club	22 Dec.
Yeykin, Vitaliy Ivanovich	engineer	Democratic Russia	22 Dec.
Zlotnikova, Tamara Vladimirovna	ecologish	Democratic Russia	21 Dec.

MOSCOW

Belkin, Yuriy Vladimirovich	journalist	Oktyabr`skiy District Union of Voters	15 Sept. 1993
Eliovich, Aleksandr	schoolteacher	Democratic Union	25 Aug. 1995
Fadeev, Valeriy Valerievich	schoolteacher	Perestroyka Club, Memorial	13 Aug. 1993
Gezentsvey, Il`ya Borisovich	engineer	Oktyabr`skiy District Union of Voters	27 Aug. 1993
Krivov, Andrey	schoolteacher	Doverie	22 July 1994 (interviewed in Paris).

Name	Occupation at time of 'democratic' activities	Group(s)	Date of interview
Lyuboshits, Yefim Yakovlevich	retired army officer	Oktyabr`skiy District Union of Voters	18 Sept. 1993
Rumyantsev, Oleg Germanovich	researcher	Perestroyka Club	1994 (interviewed in Oxford).
Shakhnovskiy, Vasiliy Savel`evich	engineer	Demokraticheskaya Platforma	5 Jan. 1997
Shubin, Aleksandr Vladlenovich	student, subsequently researcher	Obshchina	26 Jan. 1995 (interviewed in Oxford).
Sublina, Mariya Mikhaylovna	economist (retired)	Oktyabr`skiy District Union of Voters	28 Aug. 1993

Vladimir Shlykov and Father Pavel (Adel`geym) refused to be recorded; written notes of their answers were taken.

INDEX